SHADOWS OF POWER

AN ALLEGORY OF PRUDENCE IN LAND-USE PLANNING

The RTPI Library Series

**Editors: Cliff Hague, Heriot Watt University, Edinburgh, Scotland
Robin Boyle, Wayne State University, Michigan, USA
Robert Upton, RTPI, London, UK**

Published in conjunction with The Royal Town Planning Institute, this series of leading-edge texts looks at all aspects of spatial planning theory and practice from a comparative and international perspective.

Planning in Postmodern Times
Philip Allmendinger

The Making of the European Spatial Development Perspective
Andreas Faludi and Bas Waterhout

Planning for Crime Prevention
Richard Schneider and Ted Kitchen

The Planning Polity
Mark Tewdwr-Jones

Shadows of Power: an Allegory of Prudence in Land-use Planning
Jean Hillier

Forthcoming:

Sustainability, Development and Spatial Planning in Europe
Vincent Nadin, Caroline Brown and Stefanie Dühr

Planning and Place Identity
Cliff Hague and Paul Jenkins

Public Values and Private Interests
Heather Campbell and Robert Marshall

Urban Planning and Cultural Identity
William J.V. Neill

SHADOWS OF POWER

AN ALLEGORY OF PRUDENCE IN LAND-USE PLANNING

JEAN HILLIER

Routledge
Taylor & Francis Group

LONDON AND NEW YORK

First published 2002
by Routledge, 11 New Fetter Lane, London EC4P 4EE

Simultaneously published in the USA and Canada by Routledge, 29 West 35th Street, New York, NY 10001

Routledge is an imprint of the Taylor and Francis Group

© 2002 Jean Hillier

Typeset in Akzidenz Grotesk by GreenGate Publishing Services, Tonbridge, Kent
Printed and bound in Great Britain by Biddles Ltd, Guildford and King's Lynn

British Library Cataloguing in Publication Data
A catalogue record for this book is available from the British Library

Library of Congress Cataloging in Publication Data
A catalog record for this book has been requested

ISBN 0-415-25631-3 (PB)
ISBN 0-415-25630-5 (HB)

For Tejo

An Allegory of Prudence, Titian © The National Gallery, London

CONTENTS

PREFACE

'*Il me regarde en me donnant à voir le tableau.*' This phrase encapsulates my feel-ings about land-use planning decision-making practice, and about this volume in particular. Literally translated the phrase means 'it looks at me by offering the picture for my view'. Yet the French verb, '*regarder*' can be translated as either 'to look at' or 'to concern'. In this book I both am concerned with, and by, the picture of local plan-ning decision-making practice and I also offer a picture of planning theory and practice for the view of readers.

Some ten years ago, a recent arrival in Australia, I found myself in a position of having reached an agreement with someone regarding action on a particular issue. Some weeks later, the 'boss' took me severely to task for a lack of action. Referring to my notes of the action agreement, I pointed out to the 'boss' the agreed roles of each person. I was more than taken aback, therefore, when the other individual (senior to myself) was then brought into the conversation only to deny all knowledge of any such agreement and rationalise our original meeting in an entirely different way. The 'boss' sided with my senior.

I relate this incident because it started me thinking about what is 'truth', its contingency, the ability to persuade others of something, and the role of power and status in influencing decision outcomes. I was still pondering these issues when I attended the 1991 AESOP/ACSP conference in Oxford and heard John Forester present a paper on planning as communication and on Habermasian systematic dis-tortion of communication. I was inspired.

As a result, I began to listen to planning practice rather than simply look at it. One of my particular concerns is that planning theory should be grounded in prac-tice and vice versa. Talking with practitioners leads me to believe that much of what takes place in everyday practice is as yet untheorised: the power-plays of elected members on planning committees who overturn officer recommendations in front of a packed public gallery just before a local election, the tactics which officers may use to achieve policy decisions in the cause of social justice or market facilitation and so on. Talking with practitioners also suggests that consensus is rarely reached over the messy issues in planning where deep-rooted values and emotions are involved.

Taking these together, I have explored theories of consensus-building and attempted to relate them to the actually existing worlds of planning practice. I have uncovered what seem to be perfectly 'normal' tactics of lobbying influential people,

of civil disobedience, media 'stunts' and symbolic gestures, as relatively marginalised and voiceless groups attempt to get their messages across to
decision-makers. Such tactics seem to be so generally accepted that they often do
not 'make' the Western Australian state-wide newspaper, appearing only on an
inside page of the free local suburban weeklies. Whilst planning officers may disap-
prove of such strategies as being outside of their formal public participation
processes, 'going round the back', they nevertheless accept their reality.

In the midst of my writing about such ideas, the 11 September attack on the
World Trade Center (WTC) occurred. This attack has deeply disturbed me, not least
because of its unacceptable barbarity in targeting civilians, but also because, it too,
seems to me to be an act of 'going round the back'. I began to worry about a question of the difference between protesters shouting slogans outside Parliament,
residents staging a media spectacle of chaining themselves to bulldozers and dis-
rupting processes of property development, construction workers refusing to work
on a nuclear power station and people attacking the WTC. Are they parts of the
same spectrum of activist 'lobbying' in effect? As Iris Marion Young (2001: 673)
writes, sometimes activists are 'convinced that an institution produces or perpe-
trates such wrong that the most morally appropriate thing for them to do is to try to
stop its business'. Young (2001: 676) also indicates another reason for public
protest as 'to make a wider public aware of institutional wrongs and persuade that
public to join … in pressurising for change'.

The difference for me lies in the level of violence and the appalling loss of life
which resulted. For me, it is organised violence which transforms lobbying and
activism into terrorism – 'the continuation of politics by other means' (Kaldor, 1998:
95).

I happened to be reading Jacques Lacan at the time of the attack. I could not
help but to also read events through a Lacanian lens. Is the WTC attack the catastrophe which Lacan talks about as giving body to the Real of our time, a
symbolisation of the lack of the logic of capital? Is it a Lacanian Truth-Event which
can 'operate only against the background of the traumatic encounter with the
undead/monstrous Thing'[1] where 'the void of the death drive, of radical negativity, a
gap that momentarily suspends the Order of Being' (Zizek, 1999: 162–3) will continue to resonate for some time?

In attempting to understand the raw Real of the WTC catastrophe, I tried to
think through what Zizek (2001: 2) terms 'the ideological and fantasmatic coordi-
nates which determine its perception'. The symbolisation of an attack on the WTC is
an attack on the centre of financial capitalism. Attacks on capitalism have long been
part of activist tactics. From the time of Robin Hood onwards, to a much-acclaimed
French farmer attacking a McDonald's hamburger store, through to the mass mobilisation of a wide cross-section of groups in what has become known as the 'Battle

in Seattle', activists have targeted symbols of capitalist ideology in attempts to 'make the intangible actual, the vastness somehow human-scale' (Klein, 2001: 23).

Could Osama bin Laden then be considered as one in a long line of bandits, but on an international scale? Eric Hobsbawm defines social banditry as follows: 'banditry simultaneously challenges the economic, social and political order by challenging those who hold or lay claim to power, law and the control of resources' (2001a: 7). The WTC attack certainly did that.

Hobsbawm continues that bandits today are 'apt to be described ... as "terrorists"' (2001a: 19). He makes the point that social bandits have traditionally tended to be 'peasant outlaws' who the 'state' or 'lord' regard as criminals, but who remain within peasant society and who are 'considered by their people as heroes, as champions, avengers, fighters for justice, perhaps even leaders of liberation, and in any case, as men to be admired, helped and supported' (2001a: 20). Witness the rallying of fundamentalist Muslims internationally in support of bin Laden.

Moreover, Hobsbawm suggests that social banditry involves forms of 'resistance to the rich, to foreign conquerors or oppressors, or to other forces destroying the traditional order of things – all of which may be linked in the minds of bandits' (2001a: 21–2). It is a strategy of restoration of the traditional order of things 'as they should be' (i.e. as they are believed to have been in some real or mythical past) (Hobsbawm, 2001a: 29–30).

Yet in no way would I categorise bin Laden in the same manner as Robin Hood, the 'noble robber' (Hobsbawm, 2001a) who has become the international paradigm of social banditry, or even as Ned Kelly, the Australian bush-ranger outlaw who raided banks, sometimes killing police officers in the process, but whose legend has become the mythologised epitome of Australian 'underdog' resistance to authority. Bin Laden would appear to fall into Hobsbawm's category of 'avenger', having become not only an extremist Islamic hero, but also a hero in several South American nation-states where citizens hold negative opinions of 'Yankee imperialism',[2] not in spite of the fear and horror that terrorist action has inspired, but in some ways because of it. Making some mark on impersonal, globalised Western capitalism and on US imperialiam is regarded as a triumph.

The 11 September attack transgressed the Western 'fantasy' of civilised 'natural order', both as the inevitability and legitimacy of capitalism and as a code of accepted non-violence. It represents a radical break from this natural order: 'the pure Evil of a violence', or Freudian death-drive (Zizek, 1991: 206).

I emphasise that I am *not* an apologist for bin Laden. As a pacifist I cannot condone violent loss of life. Yet teaching communicative action and reciprocity to students of planning theory just two days after the WTC attack has caused me to try to think through George W. Bush's question 'why do they hate us?' (*New York Times*, 21 September 2001). I will never know, but the answer may lie in the WTC as symbol of virtual capitalism, of financial speculations and decisions taken which enormously affect, but remain disconnected from the actual worlds which marginalised peoples inhabit. The WTC and the USA may signify such issues as the GATT, the WTO and the IMF/World Bank Structural Adjustment Programs which have differentially and disproportionally affected the powerful 'Northern' states and the less economically powerful 'South'.

We all know how even at a local scale initial grievances can get worked up emotionally in people's minds until they become acts of deliberate oppression and humiliation which demand retribution and/or revenge, whether on a noisy or inconsiderate neighbour or a local authority planning department. Such antagonistic forces become a major source of dislocation in which reason and emotion come to be mutually exclusive. Faced with the perceived power and (perhaps misunderstood) authority of a local government department, we can begin to understand why actors might 'go round the back' and take informal, even illegal, action to make their voices heard.

I cannot but think that if only there were some means by which the voices of the marginalised might be listened to with respect when they have differing opinions to those of the powerful, or when they begin to feel threatened and oppressed – some forms of public spheres where agonistic confrontation can take place – then people might not feel the need to take such drastic, unpardonable, tragic action. I am drawn towards the words of Subcomandante Insurgente Marcos, spokesperson for the Mexican Zapatistas, representing the voice of a people struggling for democracy by using their word as their weapon. Using the metaphor of an echo, 'a reflected image of the possible and forgotten' (2001: 121), Marcos evokes the potential of

> an echo of our smallness, of the local and particular, which reverberates in an echo of our own greatness. ...
>
> An echo that recognises the existence of the other and does not overpower or attempt to silence it.
>
> An echo that takes its place and speaks its own voice, yet speaks the voice of the other.
>
> An echo that reproduces its own sound, yet opens itself to the sound of the other ...
>
> An echo that turns itself into many voices, into a network of voices that, before Power's deafness, opts to speak to itself, knowing itself to be one and many, acknowledging itself to be equal in its desire to listen and be listened to, recognising itself as diverse in the tones and levels of voices forming it. ...
>
> Humanity, recognising itself to be plural, different, inclusive, tolerant of itself, full of hope, continues (Marcos, 2001: 122–3).

How may we at a local scale achieve Marcos' (2001: 130) dream of 'peace every-where for everyone, with dialogue as a way that makes its own way and from which springs hope, with reason and heart as its driving force'?

The question for me, which applies to planning practice as to democratic polit-ical practice, is not that of how to arrive at a rational consensus, but to mobilise feelings and emotions towards some forms of 'democratic designs' which can chal-lenge what actors feel to be imperialism, whilst simultaneously embracing plurality/difference and democracy. The answers will not lie in this book, however, but I do hope that the content will stimulate readers to think and to seek their own answers.

Jean Hillier
Perth, March 2002

ACKNOWLEDGEMENTS

Writing a book in less than six months in my 'spare time' whilst carrying a full teaching load and several research projects was never going to be easy. Evenings and weekends ceased to exist.

I am grateful to Cliff Hague who wrote to me one Christmas inviting me to consider producing a book for the RTPI Library series. It took me a year to think about the idea and eventually to say yes, after several emails with Cliff and exchanges of cricket- and football-related correspondence, and yes, one day the English cricket team *will* beat Australia in a Test, but not just yet!

The book represents the development of my initial thoughts on Habermas, stimulated in particular by John Forester's paper at the 1991 ACSP/AESOP conference, through reading Foucault, and later Bourdieu, Lacan and Zizek. The empirical content of case studies and practice stories has been derived from various sources.

Research in the North East Corridor was conducted through ARC Large Grant A79602576. My thanks go to all those who gave their time to be interviewed for my project; to Karen Rooksby, Phillida Rooksby and Anne Wilson for interviewing; and also to Nola Kunnen, Patsy Healey and Theo van Looij for their various forms of support, encouragement and insightful comment.

The Regional Forest Agreement material was collected under the auspices of an ARC Small Grant. I thank the many people who gave time to be part of this research and to Rod Owens for conducting several of the interviews with such passion for the subject matter.

I also thank all the planners and elected representatives with whom I talked and without whose stories Chapters 9 and 10 would not have been possible.

Ideas in other chapters have sometimes been significantly reworked from a range of conference papers, journal articles and book chapters which I have written and presented over the last few years and for which I have received valuable feedback. I should like to acknowledge in particular, in alphabetical order: Pierre Bourdieu, Jason Byrne, John Forester, Patsy Healey, Charles Hoch, Margo Huxley, Nola Kunnen, Phil McManus, Seymour Mandelbaum, Chantal Mouffe, Oren Yiftachel and Iris Marion Young for enabling me to 'bounce' ideas off them and for enriching my thinking.

Previously published work which has been significantly revised, deconstructed and restructured as a jigsaw throughout various chapters includes: 'Beyond confused noise: ideas towards communicative procedural justice', J. Hillier, *Journal of Planning Education & Research* (1998) 18: 14–24 © 1998 by Jean Hillier. Reprinted by permission of Sage Publications (Chapter 4); 'Representation, identity and the communicative shaping of place', in A. Light & J. Smith (eds) *Philosophy and Geography III* (1998) Maryland: Rowman & Littlefield, 207–32 (Chapter 5); 'Imagined value: the poetics and politics of place,' in A. Madanipour, A. Hull and P. Healey (eds) *The Governance of Place* (2001), Aldershot: Ashgate (© 'Imagined value: the poetics and politics of place', Jean Hillier, 2001, Ashgate) (Chapter 5); 'Going round the back? Complex networks, informal action in local planning processes', *Environment & Planning A* (2000), Pion Ltd. 34: 33–54 (Chapter 6); 'Can't see the trees for the wood', *Planning Theory & Practice* (2000) 1, 1: 59–79 (www.tandf.co.uk) (Chapter 7); 'Mind the gap' in J. Hillier and E. Rooksby (eds) *Habitus: A Sense of Place* (2002), Aldershot: Ashgate (© 'Mind the gap', Jean Hillier, 2002, Ashgate) (Chapter 9); 'Direct action and agonism in democratic planning practice', in P. Allmendinger & M. Tewdwr-Jones (eds) *Planning Futures: New Directions in Planning Theory* (2002), London: Routledge (Chapters 11 and 12); Jean Hillier, 'Paradise proclaimed? Towards a theoretical understanding of representations of nature in land-use planning and decision-making', was published in *Ethics, Place and Environment* 1 (1), 1999, pp 77–9 (http://www.tandf.co.uk); 'To boldly go where no planners have ever ...', *Environment and Planning D, Society & Space*, Pion Ltd. 11: 89–113, for all of which copyright permission has been received, and the following conference papers: 'Practical action, political vision: planners as missionaries or chameleons?', (2001) presented at WPSC Congress, Shanghai (Chapter 10); 'More than reason: interstitial politics, informal action and the potential of associative democracy' (1998) presented at ACSP conference, Pasadena (Chapters 11 and 12).

I would also like to acknowledge the following figures: Figure 2.1 The Group Engagement Model, © (2000) From Cooperation in Groups by Tom R. Tyler & Steven Blader. Reproduced by permission of Taylor & Francis, Inc., http://www.routledge-ny.com; Figure 7.1 The South West Forest Region: Towards a regional forest agreement, CALM, 1998a: 57; Figure 12.1 Social Decision Processes, From Comparative Studies in Administration, James D. Thompson *et al.*, Eds, © 1959 by University of Pittsburgh Press. Adapted and reprinted by permission of the University of Pittsburgh Press; Figure 12.4 courtesy of the International Journal of Environment and Pollution, www.indersceince.com.

I should like to thank Nola Kunnen and Diana MacCallum, two of my PhD students, who have offered me much mental stimulation with their respective research into participation and community development and discursive analysis of community panels respectively. My thanks for the new perspectives they have given me and for the insights I have gained into my own work.

I am also grateful to David Amborski and the School of Urban and Regional Planning at Ryerson Polytechnic University, Toronto, who leaped into the breach to provide me with more than generous facilities in 1998 whilst I was on study leave and to Joe Springer, who occupied the adjacent office at Ryerson, and who sustained me with talk of Caribbean cricket and public participation. Closer to home, my thanks to Malcolm Traill and Heather Marr for support and the wherewithal to write in undisturbed quiet on the occasions when I needed it most.

The Planning Theory students at Curtin University of Technology have borne the brunt of my latest theoretical musings and ideas for the last few years, as I have attempted to find out whether my thoughts make sense in the world of actually lived planning practice. In the same vein, I thank Glen Searle of the University of Technology, Sydney, for allowing me similarly to test ideas on his Masters students.

I give special thanks to all the friends I have neglected during the last six months in my pursuit of 'The Book'. I thank, in particular, Judith Allen and Nola Kunnen for their patience and understanding when their emails remained unanswered.

My warmest thanks to Patsy Healey, who has been far more than a mentor to me: a good friend over the past fifteen years or so. And more than anyone else, to Theo van Looij who, as a reflexive planning practitioner, has been an invaluable source of information about the realities of planning practice and has served to restrain some of my less practicable theoretical notions, who has helped with computerising my scribbled diagrams and prevented me from kicking the computer in my frustration with its whims, but especially as a partner who has supported me with such generosity and patience, toiling up mountains both literal and metaphorical. I promise, weekends *will* exist.

FIGURES

TABLES

PART 1

INTO THE SHADOWS

CHAPTER 1

SHADOWS OF POWER: an allegory of prudence in land-use planning

PREAMBLE

More years ago than I readily admit, I came fresh out of university to my first job serving as a planning officer with a county council planning authority in a then de-industrialising South Wales in the UK. The person who would now be known as the executive manager (planning), then simply the deputy chief planner, amused the department with his constant use of the terms 'political will' and 'prudence'.

Political will and prudence were always together, so much so that the departmental cartoonist depicted them as an old, somewhat argumentative couple. This pair was the departmental joke, regularly signing memos and being responsible for all the mistakes or oversights we made. Yet I have to admit that I never really understood the meaning of this old couple until I embarked on this current research and realised just how important is planners' use of prudence[1] in dealing with the vagaries of political will.

I hereby dedicate this book to political will and prudence.

INTRODUCTION

The reality of planning often disappoints. In its operation and its outcomes, planning practice fails to live up to its promise. Into an ideal thought-world of planning policy and decision-making come political realities. This book is concerned with public policy, and in particular, the communicative processes of policy- and decision-making. My background in the area of urban and regional planning has led me to develop an interest in the important who, how and why issues of policy decisions. Who really takes the decisions? How are they arrived at and why are such processes used? What relations of power may be revealed between the various participants?

'In the shadow of power' is a Mexican proverbial expression implying the subtlety of power, rather than overt power. John Forester's seminal work talks about planning in the *face* of power (1989). I believe that the power and power-plays which planning practitioners both 'face' and engage in are subtle. Instances of power include power games between elected representatives, from which planners are excluded; power struggles within the authority's bureaucracy; pressure from ratepayers, developers, etc.; power struggles between practitioners and elected representatives. I explore all of these shades and shadows of power using actual stories from planning practice, i.e. practical public action or the micropolitics of practice.

A basic tenet of my work is my belief that local planning decisions, particularly those which involve consideration of issues of 'public space' cannot be understood separately from the socially constructed, subjective territorial identities, meanings and values of the local people and the planners concerned. Planning cannot achieve empirical reality through the work of planners alone. It is essentially intertwined with a whole range of other participants and their networks, each bringing to the process a variety of discourse types, lifeworlds, values, images, identities and emotions. I therefore explore ways in which different values and mind-sets may affect planning outcomes and relate to systemic power structures. By unpacking these and bringing them together as influences on participants' communication, we may come to see influences at work in decision-making processes that were previously invisible.

As an educator of planning students I hear far too many complaints from ex-students that what they learned in the classroom bears little relation to the reality of practice. They tell of frustration and anger that elected representatives or their boss can simply change their mind or make a decision and undo what may be months of a planner's hard work. Classical educational approaches to planning narrate an essentially linear planning process. However, a concentration on traditional planning policy-making and decision-making ideas of survey–analysis–plan or officer recom-mendation–council decision–implementation obscures the complexity of the process. Such notions assume that policy- and decision-making proceed in a rela-tively technocratic and value-neutral, unidirectional, step-wise process towards a finite end point. There the line stops – until students enter the world of practice and recognise the gaps in their knowledge, the gaps in planning theory and the shadows which fill those gaps.

If planning theory is to be of real use to practitioners, it needs to address prac-tice as it is actually encountered in the worlds of planning officers and also of elected representatives. In this book I aim to shed light on the shadows so that prac-titioners may be able to better understand the circumstances in which they find themselves, to anticipate reactions and conflict and to act more prudentially or effectively in what is in reality a messy, highly politicised planning decision-making practice. I aim to link, in John Forester's words, 'practical action' with 'political vision'.

I unashamedly admit that I have been inspired by the work of Patsy Healey, Judith Innes and John Forester in particular, and like Forester, I hope in this book to show how insights from practice can lead to stronger and deeper theory. I hope to open a window onto practical decision-making, public participation and governance.

Bagnasco and LeGales (2000: 26) refer to governance as the capacity to organise collective action towards specific goals. This capacity involves the mobilisation of a range of networks of actors with varying understandings and representations of the issue/s under consideration. The actors will sometimes engage each other positively in a search for an outcome in which differences are minimised and 'injustice, oppression and exploitation are muffled' (Body-Gendrot and Beauregard, 1999: 15). On other occasions, conflicts will be too deep-rooted and 'togetherness' becomes extremely narrow, if not impossible.

Citizens are becoming increasingly active, not simply through consumerist power, or as relatively passive electors at periodical representative democratic elections, but as agents who challenge the activities of the institutions and organisations which shape their lives. The ideals and practices of planning come increasingly under local scrutiny.

I agree with Forester (1999: 3) on the importance of planners dealing with 'far more than "the facts" at hand'. If planning is to be taken seriously in the future, Albrechts and Denayer (2001: 371) suggest that planners must adjust their 'toolkits' or mindsets to the changing needs and challenges of democratic society. As Young (2000: 4) points out, however, 'we have arrived at a paradoxical historical moment when nearly everyone favours democracy, but apparently few believe that democratic governance can *do* anything. Democratic processes seem to paralyse policy-making' (emphasis in original).

That some practitioners will resist is inevitable. Making decisions inclusively is difficult. 'Working with others that we disagree with, that we do not understand, that we do not have much respect for, or that we might even dislike is just plain hard.' In addition, elected representatives want results and they want results immediately. Time is of the essence. Added to this, for many professional planners, the 'solution' to the 'problem' is obvious. 'We think we know what should be done, and we do not want to listen to other people's views.' Alternatively, some planners may be happy to talk and spin out information seeking so that they seem to be doing something without actually risking anything. Performance-measurement is important and mistakes must be avoided. 'Or perhaps we don't want to take responsibility' (all quotations from Briand, 1999: 8).

The above presents an appealing case for a habit or disposition based theory of planning agency which I explore through the chapters of this book and which I aim to develop into a theory of discursive democratic planning praxis in a society characterised by power structures. I use the term 'discursive' rather than 'deliberative' or 'communicative' for my theory for several reasons, summarised as follows. Discursive processes are social and intersubjective. They involve communication which may be rhetorical or irrational rather than necessarily being calm and reasoned. Finally, discussion allows unresolved contestation across discourses (Dryzek, 2000).

Towards consensus? from Habermas to Healey

Early public policy in the field of urban and regional planning was related to municipal reform. In the later nineteenth century in Western Europe urban areas were
suffering problems of over-rapid development. High incidences of disease were
related to air and water pollution, poverty and overcrowding. Solutions were sought
through physical manipulation of the environment. Surveyors, architects and engi-
neers thus founded the discipline of planning, emphasising virtues of technical
expertise, certainty, large-scale 'God's-eye' vision. By the same logic, the complex
machine (Simon, 1982) of society could also be reconstructed through 'social engi-
neering'. Such a view of planning and public policy is rooted in the enlightenment
traditions of scientific knowledge and reason.

In the twentieth century, Mannheim (1940) advocated a form of planning
based on the notion of 'rational mastery of the irrational'. Through the use of scientific knowledge (linked to the increasing availability of computers in the 1960s and
1970s), professional planners could supervise economic and social development.

Planning policy-making was an essentially modernist project bringing reason
and technical rationality to bear on capitalist urbanisation. Planners produced and
implemented blueprint master planning schemes physically arranging land uses to
achieve functional objectives. Acting in the belief that reality could be controlled and
perfected once its internal logic was discovered, planners believed they could 'liberate through enlightenment' (Beauregard, 1989: 385).

Corresponding to their belief in the liberating potential of knowledge, planners
maintained an allegedly critical neutrality. They thus disengaged themselves from
the interest of any particular group, taking decisions on behalf of the 'public' in the
'public interest' as a reductionist whole: 'the public interest would be revealed
through a scientific understanding of the organic logic of society' (Beauregard,
1989: 386). Public participation was extremely limited, largely comprising information as to decisions already taken, or choices offered between alternative options
structured in order to produce the 'correct' result, further legitimating the role of the
planners. Technical rationality was regarded as a superior means of making public
decisions to asking the uninformed public themselves.

Such models of 'rational decision-making' dominated public policy in
Western Europe in the 1960s and 1970s. Their influence is still felt due to inertia of
the 'system' both in Europe and to a greater extent in countries such as Australia
which developed their practices from a British foundation. However, the last twenty
years have witnessed the 'dissolution of the landmarks of certainty' (Lefort, 1986:
29). Fordism has given way to new flexible structures of capital and labour; nation
states have broken apart and restructured; there is an increasing globalisation of
capital. Philosophically, French and German authors in particular have challenged

the dominance of the modernist values of science and reason. In their stead authors have turned to historical allusion and spatial understandings and multiple discourses embracing difference.

The concepts of active citizenship and public participation have been reborn, together with new interpretations of democracy as being inclusive rather than representative. Language has become a central concern. Since social actions are more satisfactorily explained in terms of the motives and beliefs of the participants, and since valid knowledge is derived not from mere facts but from a situated understanding of information, language is of key importance in helping us understand our lives and surroundings.

In the public policy sphere there has been increasing disillusionment with planning (Goodchild, 1990), both in its process of reaching decisions and in the outcomes of those decisions. Planners have found themselves the targets of protest against residential demolition for freeway and redevelopment programmes, and against loss of green areas. People want to be more than political spectators, to be a part of the decision-making process rather than discover what is happening to them and their areas when it is too late. People were 'taught that planning is technical and methodological, but [have learned] that it is political and manipulative' (Throgmorton, 1991: 2).

Planning practice increasingly comprises notions of mediating between participants in a policy decision-making process, talking, explaining and listening to a multiplicity of different stories and options. Yet decision-making involves far more than weighing the merits of respective arguments. As Forester (1989) asks, what about the place of value judgement, accountability, the power of information, political, social and economic power relations between participants? Who participates? Does the form of participation oppress or exclude some groups and allow others, more articulate, to dominate?

Democratic decision-making practice, however, cannot stand alone, It must be informed and guided by appropriate theory if it is not to become 'visceral, opportunistic and reactive' (Friedmann, 1987: 389). Such theory cannot be arbitrarily invented. It must evolve from critical analysis of experience and social vision whilst being dynamic enough to continuously absorb new learning.

Political theorists have thus launched what Fischer (1993: 166) terms 'a frontal attack' on the dominant conceptions of liberal democratic theory. Such theorists maintain that the top-down structures of liberal democracy have turned away large numbers of people from political processes (especially voting at local elections) and have led to the development and implementation of policies which benefit only the elite few.

In this regard, Jürgen Habermas has demonstrated how technocratic decision strategies confer scientific legitimation on decisions which would not generate consent in open public deliberation. His counter to such scientistic practices is for revitalisation of the public sphere to include communicative discussion and opinion formation leading to consensual agreement on decisions.

Michel Foucault has also examined the relationships between power and knowledge to demonstrate the control functions of professional expertise. Foucault shows how, far from being value-neutral, disciplines such as planning serve particular power interests. Planning discourse does not simply distort communication: its discursive practices constitute the very objects of communication themselves.

In this book I develop a new discursive theory of local land-use planning decision-making. In Chapter 2 I attempt to reconcile the ideas of Jürgen Habermas' theory of communicative action with Michel Foucault's attention to the power relations underlying decision-making and to issues of asymmetry, non-reciprocity and hierarchy. I identify points of contact between the work of Foucault and Habermas and the gaps between them. There are important areas of congruence and complementarity which, in combination, serve to strengthen a new critical model. Habermas, for example, provides the normative dimension lacking in Foucault's work, and in turn, the universalistic theories of Habermas lack the particularistic analyses of power provided by Foucault. Neither scheme alone provides an adequate framework for critical social inquiry. However, I believe that the strengths of both theories are complementary and it is possible to 'reconcile' them in the construction of a theoretically informed model of discursive democracy relevant to planning practice.

The adaptation of Habermasian ideas for planning practice owes much to the work[2] of John Forester (1989, 1999), Patsy Healey (1992a, 1992b, 1997a, 2000), Judith Innes (1995, 1996, 1998, 2000) and Leonie Sandercock (1998).

Forester's critical pragmatist approach recognises how the communication of planning officers serves to shape actors' attention, hopes and expectations through speaking and listening, asking and answering, acting practically and communicatively in claiming, counterclaiming, promising and predicting (1989: 20–21). Forester not only recognises planners' efficacy and influence as above, but also their 'possible political functions' (1989: 11) when working in the face of power. His later book, *The Deliberative Practitioner* (1999), highlights the influence of power on planning practice and the importance of planners anticipating and responding to relationships of power and domination. As Forester pointedly remarks, 'let us stop rediscovering that power corrupts, and let's start figuring out what to do about the corruption' (1999: 9).

Forester is in agreement with Patsy Healey in believing that 'carefully crafted deliberative discussions are realistically possible in adversarial contexts' (1999: 84) and that they can lead to mediated multiparty agreements (1999: 249). Healey's (1997) emphasis lies in the development of inclusionary, collaborative processes through paying attention to the hard and soft infrastructures of institutional design. In addition to the hard infrastructure of planning systems, Healey argues that planners

Lacan was fascinated by aspects of language and decisions. His notions of the impossibility of the Real and the ineradicable constitutive gap between the Real and its representation in reality are applicable to discourse and to consensus. Real information, Real meaning and Real consensus are but unrecoverable presences, fantasies of our desire. We function through believing and acting as if they are grounded, but traumatic realisation of the lack (*l'objet petit a*) eventuates. 'Satisfaction is kept in a permanent state of postponement' (Strohmeyer, 1997: 172) due to the undecidability of decisions. Real meaning is an inarticulate and traumatic exteriority that cannot be fitted into the symbolic universe (Gregory, 1997). Truth or consensus cannot be achieved through either language or communication. There is always the constitutive Other of conflict.

Democratic planning decision-making is inevitably messy, time-consuming, turbulent, frustrating and exasperating. As Briand (1999: 199) tells us: 'expect chaos'. Planners should perhaps expect at best to domesticate antagonism to agonism. We need to accept that in many circumstances consensus will not be possible, and that the best we can do is to make disagreements between stakeholders less intense, less divisive and less harmful. Compromise or 'settlement' can be attractive alternatives to consensus as Habermas himself now recognises.

I also recognise the role of informal and direct action as well as formal ways of working, especially when formal structures for deliberation overly limit the alternatives that may be considered.

> When such hegemonic discourse operates, parties to deliberation may agree on premises, they may accept a theory of their situation and give reasons for proposals that others accept, but yet the premises and terms of the account mask the reproduction of power and injustice (Young, 2001: 685).

Young therefore argues a need for 'reasonable citizens' not to consent to such structures, but to agitate for change. Much lobbying and other persuasive activity takes place on an informal basis. People engage in multiplex relational activities, some formal, others informal. As I indicate in Chapter 13, the informality of Diana MacCallum's community committee case permits committee members' voices, experiences and representations to intertwine and policy suggestions to develop innovatively in comparison to the tightly controlled, executive-dominated hierarchical structure of the other community committee which she examines. In this latter committee, people and ideas are forced into a straightjacket of an executive habitus which limits relations and hinders innovation.

In similar vein, authors such as Engwicht (1992), Blanc (1995) and Kunnen (2000) suggest an intermediary role for an informal advocate to ensure that Sandercock's (1998) insurgent as well as 'surgent' or more submissive voices are heard by planning decision-makers.

ON THEORISING, POSITIONING AND METAPHORICS

I believe in practical planning theory, theory which is both grounded in practice and which helps to explain and understand practice. Theory should have a strong feeling for social reality. I concur with Alvesson and Sköldberg's (2000: 275) view that 'empirical material can inspire ideas and theories, endowing them with credibility, clarifying them and, in the case of theories, making them more stringent'.

It was listening to practitioners' stories of the reality of planning decision-making which inspired me to attempt to modify Habermasian-based theoretical ideas; to go beyond theories of consensus to theorise agonistic planning practice. There is no end point to theorisation. By the time that this book is (hopefully) on library shelves, my and other authors' thinking will have evolved, based on reading and listening to texts and stories. In this way the empirical material I have drawn from practice should be seen as an argument in my efforts to make a case for a particular way of understanding the social reality of planning in the context of a never-ending debate.

Practice-centred theorising is important for Forester (1989, 1999) whose aim is 'to show how insightful practice can lead to stronger and deeper theory' (1999: xi). It is also advocated by Flyvbjerg as phronetic research, which takes its point of departure in local micropractices and seeks 'the Great from the Small' (2001: 134).

I offer a critical interpretive understanding of local planning decision-making practice and its affective, rational and irrational components. As will be discovered, behind some actions there is a long story; behind others there is little to tell. The picture of planning practice is painted from colours of varying textures and shades, some 'thick' and some 'thin' (Geertz, 1973), some dark and some light. I pay attention to the many rich layers of meaning and symbolism which constitute my practice pictures.

Such thick description (Thompson, 2001) is more than mere facts. I take pains to paint 'the voices, feelings, actions and meanings of interacting individuals' (Denzin, 1989: 83) and networks/groups. My work is both descriptive and interpretive. I employ a critical ethnographic approach (Thomas, 1993) to ascertain the values, images and representations which underpin actors' behaviours. My narrative enquiry then develops the descriptions and interpretations of planning decision-making from the perspectives of participants from various backgrounds and incorporates them into a new picture of planning theory.

Even without the theorising, I hope that planning practitioners will be able to relate to the stories and perspectives; to recognise similar situations to their own experiences; to understand more about actors' behaviours and motives, and to 'learn in practice about the fluid and conflictual, deeply political and always surprising world they are in' (Forester, 1999: 26). Theorisation of experiences thus enables those experiences to be shared amongst a wide range of practitioners attentive to the complexities of planning practice.

My practice research could be described as a kind of triple hermeneutics. As Alvesson and Sköldberg (2000: 144) explain, simple hermeneutics concerns individuals' interpretations of themselves and their own (inter)subjective cultural reality. Double hermeneutics involves the interpretive research of interpretive beings. Triple hermeneutics not only encompasses the double hermeneutics of research but also includes the critical interpretation of unconscious processes (habitus), ideologies, power relations and other expressions of dominance which entail the privileging of some interests over others.

I employ a metaphor of chiaroscuro as a linking mechanism which runs through the work. Metaphor elucidates similarity in difference – similarities between the artistic techniques of chiaroscuro painting and the application of highlights and shadows to the overt and covert, formal and informal, open and hidden transcripts of planning decision-making practice. The selection of chiaroscuro as metaphor reflects my view of the nuances and shades of everyday planning which, unpacked, help us to understand what is happening in the picture as a whole.

I recognise that there is no such thing as an unmediated picture; that any portrait or reading is always the result of interpretation on the part of both the author and the viewer/reader. I thus recognise three important characteristics of practice-related theory: theory can only explain portions of practice in contexts of reality; theoretical perspectives inform the way in which practical situations are problematised; and theoretical approaches are e(n)valuated through interpretation. Theorising, then, is a blend of individualistic interpretation, paradigm and a practical context. My theorising is a triangulation of a broad range of theoretical perspectives woven through the interpretive/e(n)valuated personal experiences of myself and planning 'practitioners' (especially officers of planning and elected representatives) within the context of application. My theorising thus inevitably includes my presence, my personal values and reflexivity in the process.

I bring my own habitus to my interpretations of practice stories and to my theorising. My habitus stems from my working-class origins and my opportunity to 'get on in the world' as a baby boomer woman, which was significantly enhanced by benefiting from a welfare state in the UK of the 1960s with strong commitments to free education, health care and provision of housing. I have developed a practical concern for social justice and justice to the environment and would like to see planning practice working far more effectively to counter the systematic marginalisation, if not exclusion, of the multiple voices of the poor and especially of people of colour/indigenous peoples.

I still cling to a Marxist-based understanding of the dominance of capital. I still seek to change the world. The revolutionary spirit has faded somewhat, however, and my current theorising sits predominantly within the democratic and planning systems. I believe in the promise of planning to make the lives of those 'at the

bottom of the heap' more comfortable; that without some form of planning intervention, civil society would be reduced to a marketplace 'in which the vulnerable would
fare extremely poorly' (Fischler, 2000: 365). I do not, therefore, unlike Yiftachel and
Huxley (2000), question the institution of planning and its founding intentions as
such. I do, however, question the *practices* of planning as often found in Western
societies such as Western Australia. I also believe that disruption of established
power structures and the creation of new forms and expressions of power which
advantage the disadvantaged frequently involve commencing from footholds within
the existing system (Wainwright, 1994).

Although my practice stories are drawn from Western Australia (WA), I trust
that my theorising does not subsume the particular at the expense of wider useful-
ness. Alternately, I do not intend by any means to portray 'planning' as an
unproblematic global activity, adhering to a similar rationale and logic wherever
readers may be located. My relational approach seeks to disavow any fixed,
absolute conception of space. In accepting that space and time are relations
derived from processes and events (Harvey, 1996: 256), rather than specific areas
with delineated boundaries, I leave it to readers to relate the WA practice stories to
stories of their own and trust that sufficient areas of cognisance exist for the stories
to make some sense.

Where I believe that local context is important to the comprehension of a story,
I include a brief overview of Western Australian statutory and other material. Since
my concentration is on planning theory and principles, however, I attempt to keep
contextualisation to a minimum. The praxes of planning will inevitably vary over time
and space. I hope that the questions I raise in this book and the reflections, analyses
and theoretical argumentation I offer in response, may provide a stimulus to planning
scholars and practitioners concerned with democratising local planning decision-
making practice wherever they may be.

AIMS

I have four main aims which I seek to achieve:

1.   To clarify the potential contributions of Michel Foucault and Jürgen Habermas
     to planning theory and practice.
     Debate between Foucauldian and Habermasian-based explanations and
     understandings of planning processes is not an either/or, as Bent Flyvbjerg's
     (1998a, 1998b) work perhaps would suggest. It can be a both/and. I briefly
     and simply trace the development of both Habermasian and Foucauldian con-
     cepts and indicate how, with regard to planning, the Habermasian school (e.g.

Innes, Healey *et al.*) has emphasised a more normative approach to communicatively building consensus, and the Foucauldian school (e.g. Flyvbjerg,
Murdoch and Marsden) has concentrated on the explanatory role of power,
language and representation in affecting decisions and outcomes.

2.   To integrate a theoretical understanding of communication, representation and
     habitus with practical planning.

     I use detailed stories from planning practice to illustrate the ways in which the
     various actors (planners, local residents, elected representatives, developers,
     etc.) in participatory planning strategies not only make 'meaning', but enact
     complex relations of power. Analyses of examples of participatory strategies
     which were consciously based on Habermasian communicative consensus-
     building processes clearly indicate some of the shortcomings of the theory,
     the shades of participation, of power and power games.

     It is in these shadows that Foucauldian analysis may offer some illumination.
     Unpacking the various selective narratives, representations and stories of dif-
     ferent actors, their tactics and logics, can help us better to understand what is
     happening.

     I also turn to the Bourdieuian concept of habitus in enhancing understanding
     of the behaviours of elected representatives and planning officers in decision-
     making.

3.   To develop new discursive planning theory from insightful practice.

     I offer a new take on planning theory, grounded in practice, which appreciates
     that most decisions will not be consensual and that there are still considerable
     gaps in our understanding and theorising. Nevertheless, I aim to fill at least
     one of these gaps: that between officer recommendation and elected repre-
     sentative decision, between the authority of professional planners and the
     politics of public authorities. I introduce not only the habitus but also Mouffe's
     development of agonistic democracy from its roots in the impossibility of the
     Lacanian Real into the simple Habermasian/Foucauldian ideas outlined earlier.
     The book thus encompasses what Zizek (1999: 5) refers to as the 'geo-
     graphic triad' of German idealism, French political philosophy and
     Anglo-American cultural studies.

4.   To provide a foundation for planning officers to act more effectively in the
     shadow of inequalities of power.

     The book offers student and practitioner readers an opportunity to inquire and
     learn together by reading insightful stories of success and failure, by coming
     to see issues, relationships, power games in new ways and bringing the power
     out of the shadows.

STRUCTURE OF THE BOOK

The chapters which follow include reflections on the aims listed above. I consider local land-use planning decision-making practice in relation to Habermasian communicative action theory and Foucauldian notions of power; the conflicts of values, images, identities and their representation by different stakeholders in planning practice; the meaning and role of participatory discussion in planning decision-making and the ways in which various actors 'subvert' formal practices; the nature of participation in planning decisions through both formal and informal strategies; the impediments to consensus-formation and the likelihood of ineliminable conflict and the possibilities for compromise.

In this introductory chapter I explain the purpose of the book, its aims and structure. I explain the importance of praxis – of the mutually reinforcing interrelationships of theory grounded in practice and practice grounded in theory.

Part 2, Shadow Talk: Conversations with Habermas and Foucault, examines the debate between powerful communication and communicating power; between Habermasian and Foucauldian schools of thought as related to planning practice. I trace the development of Habermasian and Foucauldian concepts (Chapters 2 and 3 respectively) and indicate how planning scholars have used theories derived from these ideas as a basis for explanation of decision outcomes and normative recommendations for consensual decision-making. I identify the common thread between the two theoretical traditions to be language and communication.

I propose a simple theoretical model in Chapter 4 which becomes the basis for critique and development throughout the remainder of the book. Recent work on consensus-building emphasises the role of communication in attempting to find common ground between participants. Actors need to speak with rather than past each other if reciprocity is to be achieved. The notion of procedural justice is fundamental to consensus-building strategies. Actors respect just treatment in a just process.

Part 3, Chiaroscuro Practice: the Shades and Lights of Planning, is grounded in practice stories. Chapter 5 outlines that language is the basis of articulation of actors' values and the ways in which those values are communicated/represented in decision processes through discourses, stories and story-lines. An understanding of actor-network theory indicates how some actors persuade others towards their points of view.

In the spirit of chiaroscuro as revealed halves, Part 3 comprises two main stories. I tell and analyse these stories from the world of planning practice. I utilise empirical material from a path-breaking Habermasian-inspired public participation strategy for strategic planning policy-making (Chapter 6) and from the resources-planning strategy of the Regional Forest Agreement in south west Western Australia

(Chapter 7). The stories indicate clearly the advantages of inclusive planning but also the unforeseen problems and pitfalls which may occur (such as unresolvable differences of opinion, tactics of lobbying, etc.) and which may result in unjust outcomes for some groups in society.

I tell stories which unpack the representations which actors use. I engage in reflective consideration on the role of cultural perceptions, images, values and mindsets in local planning policy-making. I discuss ways in which different planners and community groups perceive themselves, their own or others' geographical places and other groups, revealing cultural differences of self- and place-identity, of discourses and values. I explore ways in which different values and mindsets affect planning outcomes and relate to systemic power structures. I analyse the narratives, images and story-lines and reveal the underlying values which lie beneath in the shadows.

In Part 4, Shadow Negotiations, I attempt to fill the gap between officer recommendation and elected representatives' decisions by opening up the hidden transcripts of the politics of decision-making, the very logic of democratic practice. These communicative behaviours which precede and are construed in the ritualised formal process of political decision-making form a shadow of power in which practitioners and theorists work. I attempt to throw light on such shadows by introducing the concept of habitus in Chapter 8, before exploring the sense of place and feel for the game of planning both of elected representatives (Chapter 9) and of planning officers (Chapter 10).

Part 5, Out from the Shadows, comprises an integration of a power-full understanding of narrative, representation and discourse with ideas of consensus-building. I debate the 'goodness of fit' of the two chiaroscuro halves, drawing on work of Tewdwr-Jones and Allmendinger, Flyvbjerg et al. and identifying dovetails, gaps and remaining shadows. I lay the foundations for building my new theory in Chapter 11 by examining issues of identity and interest representation, from new social movements and lobbying networks to proposals for associative democratic frameworks. I also explore the paradox of liberal democracy itself and ask whether, given this paradox, consensus is actually achievable.

In Chapter 12 I ground my work in the empirical stories told earlier and push forward to work through possibilities for moving beyond antagonism to agonism, accepting that some differences may be irreconcilably entrenched and that conflict is not necessarily a bad thing. I recall Arendt's agonistic conception of the public sphere and explore the Lacanian foundations of Mouffe's agonistic democracy.

In the concluding Part 6, Shadow Play, I briefly summarise the point reached so far before identifying some of the remaining shadows hanging over planning practice.

PART 2

SHADOW TALK: CONVERSATIONS WITH HABERMAS AND FOUCAULT

CHAPTER 2

A CONVERSATION WITH JÜRGEN HABERMAS

INTRODUCTION

This book is about theories of non-coercive public debate and discursive decision-making. I take Deleuze's view of theory as a 'toolbox' (Deleuze, 1986: 208) and Foucault's (1991) suggestion that books be regarded as 'experience books' rather than 'truth books'. As such, I seek out theories as tools which are grounded in everyday life and practice. I examine issues of communicative persuasion from theories of convincing argumentation to those of power-full coercion and manipulation and investigate the debate between powerful communication and communicating power.

'Policy making should be more than and different from the discovery of what people want; it should entail the creation of contexts in which people can critically evaluate and revise what they believe' (Reich, 1988: 6). Traditional forms of policy-making in the arena of urban and regional planning are particularly threatened by such statements. Planners' modernist commitments to professional expertise, political neutrality and the efficacy of rationalism are undermined by demands for the inclusion of difference and participatory decision-making. Beauregard (1989) finds the chasm ever widening. Will planning fall, or is there a future for public policy-making?

I believe there is a future. Healey (1992b) offers five directions which policy-making might take. Not mutually exclusive, they range from a retreat to rigid scientific rationalism, through moral and aesthetic idealism, to democratic socialism inclusive of difference, to a communicative conception of rationality which enables purposes to be communicatively discovered. I favour the last direction. I believe in difference and that when different views are expressed, informed and open negotiation is the most democratic way to search for an acceptable solution.

Democracy should be participatory. In relation to public policy-making it should include a great deal of local experimentation, a maximum of social mobilisation and a non-dogmatic view of the problem (Friedmann, 1987). Issues of truth, trust and power become key. Without truth can one have trust? Must power be equally shared? What are the links between truth and power? And between knowledge and power?

In this chapter I trace the development of Habermasian and Foucauldian concepts and outline key aspects of the so-called Habermas–Foucault debate. In so doing, I recognise their common concerns as well as their distinctive ideas. That said, I take pains to relate the concepts to planning and steer away from 'descent' into the heavier philosophical underpinnings of the debate. There exists a plethora of material to which readers interested in the philosophical fundamentals are referred. (See, for example, volumes by Hoy (1986); Honneth (1991); Gutting (1994); Kelly (1994); White (1995); Ashenden and Owen (1999); and Dews (1999)).

I also indicate how scholars have used theories derived from the ideas of Habermas and Foucault as a basis for explanation of decision outcomes and normative recommendations for consensual decision-making. I identify the common thread between the two theoretical traditions to be language and communication.

Communication is central to all forms of decision and policy-making. Establishment of facts, appeals to norms of legitimacy, inner dispositions expressed by a speaker and the framing of attention are involved (Forester, 1992). Through communicative action, formerly oppressed people may be capacitated as meaning may be clarified, ambiguity and contradictions reduced and an acceptable outcome negotiated. Opening up debate also encourages awareness of conflicts and asymmetrical relations of power. An understanding of the who, how and why issues of such power relations, together with communicative negotiation may help to challenge the domination of elites and professionals in determining the discourses and practices that comprise the reality of public policy-making.

In the development of methodologies for change, issues of communication and of power must both be handled critically and constructively. We can then begin to give meaning to 'good' and 'bad' ways of decision- and policy-making (Healey, 1992b), to 'progress' and to democracy. I believe that Habermas and Foucault offer important theoretical and methodological tools in attempting this task. In Part 2 of this volume, I 'converse' with these authors in turn in order to elucidate the key issues and 'tools' before beginning to build a new theoretical model in Chapter 4.

In examining the role of communication in participants' attempts to collaboratively make decisions, I also highlight the importance of actors speaking with rather than past each other. The notion of procedural justice (examined in Chapter 4) is fundamental to consensus-building strategies. Actors respect just treatment in a just process.

In this chapter, I outline briefly some aspects of liberal and participatory democracy before moving on to explore the work of Jürgen Habermas in detail.

POWERFUL COMMUNICATION

THE LIBERAL REVIVAL OF DEMOCRACY

Jürgen Habermas' work represents a continuation of the liberal tradition of democracy which began with Thomas Hobbes and John Locke and underwent a more (albeit limited) participatory turn in Rousseau's conception, to be later refined by Hannah

Arendt. Arendt (1963) emphasised the idea of political freedom based on the universal human right of participation. She argued the basic need for human speech and action in order to maintain citizens' freedom. Her emphasis on diversity and the rights of individual action and expression of opinions without coercion provides links forward to Habermas' theory of communicative action.

Through Arendt's 'participatory' conception of citizenship (Passerin d'Entreves, 1992) the active engagement of citizens in the determination of affairs of their community provides them with a sense of political agency and efficacy, of being participators in government. Arendt disliked political representation as being a substitute for direct citizen involvement and proposed instead a federated system of councils enabling citizens to be actively engaged in determining their affairs. 'It is only by means of direct political participation, by engaging in common action and in public deliberation, that citizenship can be reaffirmed and political agency effectively exercised' (Passerin d'Entreves, 1992: 61). In addition, Arendt's participatory conception of democracy is based on the principle of plurality: it recognises difference of people and of values.

Arendt (1963, 1968a) further claimed that the possibility of reactivating the political capacity for impartial and responsible judgement depended on the creation of public spaces for collective deliberation and democratic debate in order for citizens to test and enlarge their opinions. 'Judgement cannot function in strict isolation or solitude; it needs the presence of others "in whose place" it must think, whose perspectives it must take into consideration' (1968: 220–1).

The validity of judgement thus depends on the ability to look at the situation from a variety of different perspectives. This ability, in turn, can only be achieved in a public setting where individuals have the opportunity to exchange opinions and to articulate their differences through democratic discourse (Passerin d'Entreves, 1992).

Arendt's thinking about the public sphere evolved over time. In *The Origins of Totalitarianism* (1951/1995a), she emphasised a procedural approach to associational space where 'men act together in concert' (cited in Benhabib, 1992a: 78). Public space is the space where 'freedom' can appear through common action coordinated through speech, persuasion and reciprocity: 'the more people's standpoints I have present in my mind while I am pondering a given issue, and the better I can imagine how I would feel and think if I were in their place, the stronger will be my capacity for representative thinking and the more valid my final conclusions, my opinion' (1968: 241). It is this form of the public sphere upon which Habermas builds his discourse model of moral communicative action.

By the time *The Human Condition* (1958) was published, however, Arendt's conception of the public sphere had shifted from regarding it as associational space to agonistic space. Agonistic space is political, conflictual and competitive. As will be demonstrated later in this book, Arendt's agonal ideas provide links from

Nietzsche to Foucault, Mouffe and even Lacan. They appear far from what Habermas presents in his consensus reading. Arendt's version of agonistic politics not only places her at a distance from Habermas, but also those (such as Foucault) who regard discourse without agon as limited.

Arendt broadens a Nietzschean focus on an agonistic quality of action, which masks the 'true world' of coercions and violence in an 'apparent' world of centred subjectivity, by reasserting the deliberative element present in both action and judgement (Villa, 1996). She does this, however, by making an appeal not to reason or dialogue but to aesthetic taste (reflected in the later work of Pierre Bourdieu, *Distinction*, 1984). Since agonistic political action would threaten to fragment the polis, however, Arendt cultivates an ethos whereby actors are more committed to playing the game than winning it (1968a: 210).

PARTICIPATORY DEMOCRACY

Hannah Arendt has offered us a valuable perspective on opening up public spaces for capacitating, all-embracing debate and learning through collective action. It is to develop these ideas and to the concept of participatory democracy which I now turn.

Immanuel Kant's influence in the field of philosophy has been immense. For the purposes of this chapter, I mention extremely briefly only his ideas relating to the social contract (as a basis for communicative ethics) and to the notion of active citizenship (as a basis for participatory democracy). The underlying premise of communicative ethics is that reason is a natural disposition of the human mind and that intersubjective agreement on issues can be obtained between rational minds. Each participant or individual moral agent would will, without self-contradiction, a universal maxim for all. Such ideas have been developed by Habermas who substitutes argumentative conversation for Kant's thought experiment ('to think from the standpoint of everyone else') to achieve consensus or a general will. The Kantian principle of universalisability thus generates morally binding maxims of action which all participants can recognise. 'The ends of a subject who is an end in himself must, if this conception is to have its full effect on me, be also, as far as possible, my ends' (Kant, 1964: 98).

Turning to the principle of active citizenship, Kant suggested that any system of basic institutions must provide for the greatest degree of autonomy possible. One specific area of autonomy must be that of active citizenship (citizens able to exercise their will freely). The system of basic institutions must be structured so as to lead to social choices approximating the general will, and there must be reason to think that empirical decisions approximating the normative general will result from the institutional framework rather than from duty (Smith, 1991). In this manner, policy decisions will maximise the freedom of each participant consistent with the freedom of all others.

Theories of participatory democracy are constructed round the assertion that individuals, groups and institutions cannot be considered in isolation from each other. Decisions should be arrived at through an open and uncoerced discussion of the issue at stake with the aim of arriving at an agreed judgement (Miller, 1993). Moreover, the process of reaching a decision will also be one in which initial preferences may be transformed to take account of the views of other participants. The final decision should thus be that outcome which either best meets the various participants' claims or represents the fairest compromise between the expressed points of view.

The concept of participatory democracy is very different from that of traditional liberal democracy. Mansbridge (1980) contrasts traditional liberal notions of democracy (electoral representation, majority rule, one citizen–one vote) or adversary democracy, with what she terms 'unitary democracy' (consensual, based on common interest and equal respect). Whereas liberal democracy gives equal weight to individual preferences, participatory democracy relies on individuals possibly laying aside their individual preferences in deference to notions of overall fairness and common interest. One of the key features of participatory democracy is that rather than seeking the 'correct answer' (Miller, 1993), it is a process of open discussion in which all points of view may be heard and which thus legitimates the outcome which is seen to reflect the discussion leading to it.

Barber proposes such a process of 'strong democracy' as a challenge to 'the politics of elites and masses that masquerades as democracy' (1984: 117). He believes citizens to be extremely capable of 'reasonable public deliberation and decision' (1984: 133) and of creating a community characterised by 'self-government by citizens rather than representative government in the name of citizens' (1984: 151).

THE WORK OF JÜRGEN HABERMAS

Back in 1980, John Forester suggested that critical theory has an important role to play in the praxis of urban and regional planning and public policy-making as it offers a new way of understanding action (what a planner does) as attention-shaping (communicative action) rather than more narrowly as a means to some end (instrumental action).

Habermas (1985a: 12) summarised his ideas of communicative action in a single phrase: 'the conviction that a humane collective life depends on the vulnerable forms of innovation-bearing, reciprocal and unforcedly egalitarian everyday communication'. It is these forms of reciprocal and egalitarian communication with which I am concerned at present.

As such, I concentrate on simplifying those elements of Habermas' 'forbiddingly dense' (Dews, 1986: 4) theory of communicative action which I consider have relevance to public policy decision-making. I do not, therefore, cover Habermas' 'unfinished project of modernity' as a whole. Nor do I take on the modernity/postmodernity debate with which Habermas has engaged.

In what follows I take a brief look at the Frankfurt School and the main influences on Habermas' ideas before turning to notions of system, lifeworld and the public sphere as a basis for Habermasian critical theory. I then discuss the development of Habermas' thought from reason to communication (what has been termed the linguistic turn) and move on to his universal pragmatics of communicative action. Discussion of the potential relevance and application of a theory of communicative action to planning policy-making follows, while final sections present a critique of the theory and its implications.

ORIGINS

Early Frankfurt School theorists, such as Marcuse, Adorno and Horkheimer, attempted to reconstruct the logic of Marxism in order to make it relevant to a situation of twentieth-century capitalism. The Frankfurt theorists believed that Marx underestimated the extent to which the workers' (in particular) false consciousness could be exploited in order to maintain the existing economic and social systems. False consciousness leads to domination, obedience and discipline as workers believe that they can achieve modest personal improvements through compliance with expected norms, but that larger-scale changes would be impossible (Agger, 1991). Frankfurt theorists were thus influenced not only by Marx but also by classical non-Marxists such as Durkheim, Weber and Parsons. They were drawn into debate with positivists who limited rationality to technical rationality and knowledge to scientific knowledge. Gradually, the Frankfurt theorists regarded even Marxism as too positivist and lacking the dialectical ability to go beyond given 'facts'. Such debates and criticisms were carried out largely in isolation from developments in the philosophy of language, which was itself regarded as positivist and technological.

Jürgen Habermas, however, replaced the problem of (false) consciousness with that of language. He regarded developments in the philosophy of language as a new point of departure for social theory. For Habermas, an expanded conception of reason which includes normative and critical dimensions requires a theory of language in order to justify that the truth of statements is linked to the intention of the good and true life. The linguistic turn developed by Habermas thus began as an attempt to show how a society free from unnecessary domination is anticipated in acts of communication. (For detailed consideration of the relationship between Habermas and Marxism see Bohman, 1999.)

While arguing this point, Habermas was careful, however, to distance himself from the view that interpretive, linguistic understanding was the only basis of social theory. He suggested that social theory should integrate interpretive understanding with a critique of ideology and the empirical conditions under which traditions historically change. (There are certain similarities here, I believe, with the development of Foucault's ideas too.) Habermas turned to Freudian psychoanalysis (see Chapter 12) offering a 'depth hermeneutics' for understanding distortions of communication: 'we cannot "understand" the "what" ... without at the same time "explaining" the "why"' (McCarthy, 1976: xiii).

Habermas is occupied with exploring the institutionalisation of emancipatory learning processes through the notion of rational practical discourse – the public and non-coerced strength of the better argument. Democracy is formulated as 'a rationally motivated and discursively redeemable consensus formation' (Rundell, 1991: 133). Obviously, such a formulation implies a very particular reading of the philosophical powers and capacities of language, and not surprisingly, Habermas has fallen for much criticism.

As with many philosophical thinkers, Habermas' ideas have evolved over time, often in response to debates with his critics and to his reading of, and attempts to incorporate ideas from, an increasingly wide range of material.[1]

LIFEWORLD AND SYSTEM

Habermas distinguishes between the two concepts of lifeworld and system. According to Habermas (1990: 137), the lifeworld is a product of both historical traditions surrounding people and the processes of socialisation in which they are reared; their perspectives of the acting subject. It has three structural components: culture, society and personality (1987a: 137). As Cohen and Arato (1992) explain, to the extent that actors mutually understand and agree on their situation, they share a cultural tradition. As they coordinate their actions through intersubjectively recognised norms, they act as members of a social group. As they do both of these, they internalise values and develop individual and social identities. Lifeworlds are both situation and background, both conscious and unconscious (Love, 1995). Reproduction of both the cultural–linguistic background as well as the sociological components of the lifeworld occurs through communication and through the emergence of institutions specialised in the reproduction of culture, society and identity. The lifeworld is thus the realm of personal relationships.

Actors' values, representations and identities thus reflect and are reflected in their lifeworlds. Habermas accepts the plurality of actors' lifeworlds and of their voices and discourses, but retains the notion of a universal subject. In so doing, Habermas appears unable to translate such lifeworld plurality into his consideration of the other as I will elaborate below (see also Hillier, 2000a).

In contrast, systems, such as the capitalist economy and bureaucratic administration (such as urban and regional planning) operate via the steering media of
money and power. There is no common orientation of actors in the 'system', but
rather society is impersonally integrated through 'functional or cybernetic feedback'
(Calhoun, 1992: 30–31). The system forms the context within which lifeworld operates. It has developed from the rationalisation and colonisation of the lifeworld,
exemplified by the establishment of legal protection or property, of institutionalised
government and so on.

The expansion of market and administrative systems has led to what
Habermas terms the colonisation of the lifeworld by the system. Such colonisation
suppresses the expression of generalisable interests, hinders and distorts communication and subordinates consensus-oriented/communicative action, expressed as
'public opinion' or 'the will of the people', to system goals.

Habermas regards this situation as a 'tug-of-war' (Pusey, 1987: 107) between
the lifeworld and the system. Through communicative action, actors can express
defensive reactions (see also Foucault's concept of resistance) to colonisation of
the lifeworld, for example through local protests against state taxes or bureaucrati-
sation of government activities, to the ecology, women's and anti-nuclear
movements, etc. The clash between lifeworld and system takes place in the public
sphere, at the seam of civil society and the state.

COMMUNICATIVE ACTION

The centre of Habermas' theorising is a theory of communicative action based in linguistic communication. Habermas (1976) stresses the role of actors engaging in
mutual understanding. Language functions as the means and context for social
intercourse, and of understanding one another. Mutual understanding leads to
rational (reasoned) consensus. Habermas' use of the word rational/ity is linked to
reasoning: 'how speaking and acting subjects acquire and use knowledge' (1984:
11). Communicative rationality thus represents the activity of actors reflecting about
their background assumptions about the world, questioning them and collectively
negotiating new norms.

In the concept of communicative action, Habermas integrates language and
practice. Language as communicative action is also emancipatory. By taking the role
of participant in a situation, actors discover the meanings implicit in that situation.
Through self-reflection and intersubjective discussion, participants may deepen
their understanding and change their positions en route to negotiating a consensual
outcome. As such a speech-community can be built only on the basis of trust, not on
power, communicative action serves to emancipate participants from domination

and oppression. Habermas often equates technology with ideological domination. For Habermas, then, emancipation through self-reflection can deconstruct the predominance of such technical interests which tend to fetishise scientific method and obscure the self-reflective move in knowledge formation. In communication, individuals appear actively as unique beings and every interaction they make unifies their multiple perspectives of perception. Individual lifeworlds thus contribute to the formation of an intersubjectively shared lifeworld (Habermas, 1986).

The theory of communicative action thus represents a 'theory of society conceived with a practical intent' (Habermas, 1974: 3) in which 'truth' is negotiated through the discursive generation of a rational consensus between communicatively competent participants.

Habermas' theory owes much to Arendt's (1951, 1968a) ideas about human capacity for disinterested, independent judgement through reciprocal imagination. However, he rejects Arendt's conception of an agonistic public realm in favour of reducing her public sphere to its formally deliberative dimensions.

Habermas' is thus a selective reading of Arendt, rerationalising the public sphere to aim at consensus rather than success or control: 'the basic phenomenon [for Arendt] is ... the formation of a common will aimed at agreement' (Habermas, 1983: 172). Through emphasising and reducing Arendt's 'sharing of words and deeds' to the idea of communication and agreement, Habermas turns the consensus-building force of communication into an end in itself.

The theory of communicative action is normative. It methodologically frames enquiry round the idea of the unconstrained, unifying, consensus-bringing force of argumentative speech, in which everyday norms and values are discussed and renegotiated according to the 'unforced force of the better argument' (Habermas, 1973b: 240). Through communicative action interests and needs can be collectively interpreted and solutions to problems agreed. Individual values are not treated as arbitrary or idiosyncratic and discussion is free from domination through the exercise of power, strategising or manipulation and (self) deception.

IDEAL SPEECH AND DISTORTED COMMUNICATION
Habermas distinguishes two main cases of rationality: one in which knowledge (often scientific) is used instrumentally as a means of successfully gaining strategic ends and a second in which knowledge is used communicatively for purposes of understanding and discussion of issues. The goal of the first case is instrumental control, compared to communicative understanding and consensus in the latter. Instrumental or strategic action follows technical rules and can be evaluated in terms of efficiency in dealing with the physical world. The knowing, self-reflective active subject is thereby refined out of existence and replaced by an apolitical, non-participatory functionary whose job it is to perform the tasks necessary for the reproduction of a

socio-economic system that serves the interests of a small minority of the population (Mumby, 1988). Communicative action or action oriented to reaching understanding, alternatively, can only take place in a social context and when social intercourse is co-ordinated not through the 'egocentric calculations of the success of the actor as an individual, but through the mutual and co-operative achievement of understanding among participants' (Roderick, 1986: 109).

Forester (1988) suggests that the above distinction represents the contradic-tion between the disabling (or parasitic (Habermas, 1984)) communicative power of bureaucratic or capitalistic, undemocratic institutions and the collective, enabling power of democratic political criticism. I would argue that the praxis of urban and regional planning predominantly falls into the instrumental and strategic action cate-gories although as Forester (1989, 1993a, 1999a) points out, planning is also communicative by nature, explaining, announcing, recommending etc. as it does.

Bohman (2000) indicates a considerable problem with Habermas' ideas on rationality. Bohman asks what happens if communication becomes so restricted or 'distorted' that actors cannot reflect on their rational capacities. Habermas is faced with a paradox: if communication is the medium of both self-reflection and political distortion, it would appear that there is nothing outside of communication that can administer a corrective. The theory thus lacks consideration of the ways in which actual relations of power and social asymmetries cause conflict, undermining the conditions of successful communication and creating distortion.

Habermas does not adequately describe 'the paradoxical condition of dis-torted communication as communication that violates its own conditions of success' (Bohman, 2000: 5). Instead, he explains distortion as 'latent strategic action'. As I shall demonstrate in Chapter 5, Habermas' development of a non-circular solution to the paradox of distortion is 'lacking'.

It must also be recognised that while agreement in terms of outcome tends to presuppose understanding on the part of participants, the reverse is not the case. Understanding does not presuppose agreement although it may represent a stage in reaching agreement. Habermas rather obscures this essential difference.

Much depends on the rationality of communication. Habermas approaches rationality through a series of universal pragmatics or assumptions or 'rules' of argu-mentation (e.g. all actors are allowed to participate, to introduce ideas into discussion and to question others) and assumptions that all participants are com-mitted equally to reaching agreement and that they are committed to accepting only valid claims (Campbell, 2001). The commitment to accepting only valid claims breaks down into the mutual assumptions that participants are speaking truthfully, comprehensibly, sincerely and legitimately. Such an 'ideal speech situation', how-ever, is inevitably idealised and counterfactual: 'we are quite unable to realise the ideal speech situation; we can only anticipate it' (Habermas, 1970: 372).

The fact that the conditions of actual speech are rarely, if ever, those of the ideal speech situation, does not render the ideal illegitimate. The ideal speech situation can serve normatively as a guide for the process of communication and as a critical standard against which actually achieved agreements and (policy) decisions can be measured. Moving from the counterfactual to the factual, we can identify instances of seduction, mistrust, selfishness, abuse of power and so on, which contribute to systematically distorted communication and the production of a false consensus.

What, then, is systematically distorted communication (SDC)? A concept developed by Habermas (1970) from Marx's notion of false consciousness, systematically distorted communication involves assumed rather than real understanding between participants. A false consensus may subsequently be reached. The consensus is false rather than genuine because something, often not apparent to all concerned, has prevented the participants from communicating fully and effectively. Habermas (1970) terms this 'pseudo-communication'. He identifies that pseudo-communication may be the result of cultural, temporal or social distance, a problem of hermeneutics, or it may be the result of manipulation and power-play (Hillier, 1996).

However, just as the ideal speech situation is counterfactual, systematic distortion of communication is unlikely to disappear. Nevertheless, by examining not only the 'what' of communicative distortion but also the 'why', we can identify the power-plays of particular interests and attempt to counter them.

Consideration of power-plays and the systematic distortion of communication raises the issues of ethics and morality. Habermas' ideal speech situation embodies universal principles (communicative competence, etc.) in order that a rational consensus may be achieved in the context of a variety of possibly conflicting opinions. These universal principles rely on the inner logic of moral argument for their validity. In addition, the rules that all participants should be given the right to make claims and to criticise others and that contested norms are accepted without coercion once their consequences are understood by everyone are ethical rules, although they offer no substantive ethical orientation. There is no basis or need, therefore, for adjudicating between Habermas' 'plurality of values' providing that agreement is required on normative principles only. The aim is to seek a moral 'consensus on what is to be done while differing about why' (Dryzek, 1990: 43).

Habermas' theory of communicative action thus postulates that actors are able to distance themselves from their lifeworlds, bracket their own particular interests and rationally question their beliefs and assumptions through open discussion. Subjective questions (such as, what is the best thing for me to do?) are replaced by a hypothetically generalised question (what is the best thing for us to do?) (see Clare, 2000). For Habermas, such a generalised question provides the context for participants to achieve mutual understanding. Mutual understanding hinges not only on participants engaging the ideal speech situation when speaking, but also affording each other mutual respect and engaging in reciprocity (putting oneself in the other participants' metaphorical 'shoes').

CRITIQUES

Bearing in mind a planning-oriented audience, I gloss over the philosophical critiques of communicative action to concentrate on three areas of most potent criticism: Habermas' omission of considerations of power, his non-acknowledgement of the limitations of human action and his bracketing of difference. I leave consideration of consensus formation to Chapter 5.

A lack of explicit methodology for dealing with power, especially in situations of policy-making, has been identified as a major shortcoming of Habermasian theory. Policy agreement is regarded by Habermas as basically a matter of changing people's understanding and attitudes. The main problem he identifies in achieving this is systematically distorted communication although there is no discussion of inherent power-plays in distorting communication or how to overcome them.

For a useful normative theory of communicative action, what is important is not a theoretical analysis of power, nor a corrective treatment added to the theory, but rather a conception of power which can both enhance our understanding of why events occurred and suggest methods of dealing with the implications of that understanding. The work of Michel Foucault, I believe, has much to offer in this regard as I will discuss below. Here I concentrate on Habermas, his treatment of power and his power-less shortcomings.

Deetz (1992) suggests that Habermas equates power with domination and regards power negatively as being in opposition to reason. However, I would argue that Habermas regards a reasoned consensus as being a very positive form of power, although I would concur that *en route* to achieving such a consensus, it is power-play which may violate and destroy the conditions necessary for that consensus. Habermas (1991: 246) defines power as 'the ability to prevent other individuals or groups from realising their interests'. Power, influence and domination operate through structures of distorted communication. Habermas regards technical rationality as the main instrument of systematically distorted communication. The role of technology is that of prediction and control rather than that of understanding. As Flyvbjerg (1998a) demonstrates so clearly, the use of complex technicalities and techniques, bureaucratic language and jargon, either intentionally or otherwise, thus inhibits understanding and contributes to the power of one or some people over others. In the realm of urban and regional planning, professionals with expert knowledges and skills (planning, legal, environmental, etc.) have an immediate potential to dominate and influence outcomes over lay persons who are without such 'understanding'. No matter how much experts might disclaim it, professional 'mystique' is perceived as a clear source of domination and tension. The tension, though, is not directly between democracy and technology/science but between democracy and expertise, the *use* of technology.

Bohman (2000) demonstrates, moreover, that power and distortion of communication may not be strategic acts, but rather, inevitable aspects of communication due to asymmetries in communication produced by unequal social relations of power between speakers and their audience/s. Distorted communication may thus not be purpose-full but symptomatic of a lack, or what Marx (1970: 33) termed as representational failure, representing 'something without representing something real': a lack of manifest relation between meaning and validity; a lack of manifest relation between meaning and intention; and/or a lack of relation between meaning and action for actors other than the speaker.

A different reading of Habermas (e.g. by Fraser, 1989; Honneth, 1991 and Buechler, 2000) makes a penetrating criticism of Habermas' notion of power in his distinction between system and lifeworld. The authors argue that it is this distinction which functions as a kind of dualism that enables communication to be separated from power. They suggest that the distinction is based on two theoretical fictions, however: that an action system can occur independently of the normative building of consensus, and that a communicatively integrated action sphere (the lifeworld) can occur independently of domination by relations of power. This latter, in particular, is a myth as there are inevitable relations of domination and exploitation within the family and wider society which will have been internalised within people's personalities so that it becomes implausible to suppose their eradication without those people becoming different people (Lukes, 1982; Bourdieu's concept of habitus (see Part 4)).

'Powerful forces do, then, stand ready to frustrate incipient discursive designs' (Dryzek, 1990: 82). Powerful actors behind participants or participants themselves may manipulate others by cloaking private interests in a rhetoric of public concern, by making superficial concessions to opponents and securing acquiescence, by offering symbolic participation in name only. Secrecy, pretence and falsehood become normal functional practices because participants believe that by being completely transparent, open and honest they are rendered vulnerable to manipulation by others who are less so.

There is an inevitable tension between power, ethics and justice. It is this tension which power-brokers do not respect but try to resolve one-sidedly. Habermas, alternatively, suggested that the tension should be respected through the principle of universalisability built into an ideal speech situation. This gives us a standard against which to determine power-play and the level of justice (the extent to which the generaliseable interests of participants are not met). Habermas (1970) argues

that if the conditions for communicative action are met, justice is the underlying principle on which policy decisions will be made. Yet Habermas and we all know that the
conditions for successful communicative action are counterfactual.

> Insofar as we master the means for the construction of an ideal speech situa-
> tion, we can conceive the ideas of truth, freedom, and justice, which interpret
> each other — although of course only as ideas. On the strength of communica-
> tive competence alone, however, and independent of the empirical structures of
> the social system to which we belong, we are quite unable to realise the ideal
> speech situation; we can only anticipate it (Habermas, 1970: 372).

Habermas' ideal speech situation replaces one form of power with another.
Decision-making autocracy gives way to a supposedly democratic situation in which
decisions are reached discursively and agreed upon by all participants. Power is
theoretically transferred from the hands of the few to those of the many. However,
power of 'expertise' may simply be replaced by power of articulation and rhetoric.
Habermas overlooks the social lifeworld constituents and constraints on communication (lack of common language, reticence and other inhibitions) with the result
that consensus may be forged by the stronger imposing their will on the weaker,
perhaps even unknowingly. As Kohn (2000: 409) tellingly writes: 'reasonableness is
itself a social construction which usually benefits those already in power'.

Habermas also fails to consider the asymmetrical distribution of power to
implement resource allocation decisions even if they have been based on consensus. How do participants know that, once they leave the negotiating table, the
planners will implement the policy decision exactly as formulated? Although round
the table everyone may be equal, power structures, both actual and perceived, lurk
outside.

As Young (1990, 2000) and Huxley (1998) have pointed out, the possibility of
complete self-knowledge, reflexivity, clarity and transparency to oneself and to others is problematic. This would suggest the improbability of achieving some form of
collective autonomy. Huxley (1998: 10) states that the situatedness of human lives
in their unique lifeworlds, of history, custom and tradition, creates conditions which
are beyond complete comprehension. Complete reciprocity is impossible: 'a dream'
(Young, 1990: 232).

Walzer (1994: 33) also suggests that justice requires the defence of difference: 'different goods distributed for different reasons among different groups of
people'. Justice thus becomes a 'thick' moral idea 'reflecting the actual thickness of
particular cultures and societies' within a 'thin' set of universal principles.

Many other authors (see, for instance, Benhabib, 1990a, 1992a; Young, 1990;
Fraser, 1992) have similarly criticised Habermas' early work for its abstraction away
from the concrete individual identity of participants so that everyone is able to treat all

others as equal rational beings entitled to the same rights and duties as they would wish for themselves (the generalised other). In so doing, Habermas annuls differences between people. Participants become equal by bracketing difference. Difference is turned into exclusion.

In addition, Flax (1992) questions the grounds for claiming that reason is privileged. She argues that its claim to be independent of contingencies is untenable and that feminism undermines the belief that reason is, can, or should be independent of the contingencies of embodiment, language, the unconscious or intersubjectivity. By holding onto the concept of reason to arrive at consensus, Habermas ignores the deep cleavages of gender, class, race, culture, etc. which some authors argue can only be resolved through power struggles (Moore Milroy, 1990). More seriously, Young (1990: 102) argues that Habermas' commitment to impartiality, which is in fact illusory, simply 'expels particularity and desire and sets feeling in opposition to reason'. I believe that Habermas was asking for people to try and achieve as impartial a consensus as possible whilst recognising and accepting differences. Yet Habermas' response is unconvincing. He suggests that 'the individual appeals to the projected universal community not for agreement about norms but for *recognition* of her claim to authenticity and of herself as a unique and irreplaceable individual' (Hohengarten, 1992: xix). The unity engendered by communication does not eliminate the difference between individuals, but rather confirms it. As such, 'linguistically attained consensus does not eradicate from the accord the differences in speaker perspectives, but rather presupposes them as ineliminable' (Habermas, 1992: 48).

RECENT DEVELOPMENTS

In his recent theoretical developments, Habermas (1996, 1998, 2001c) reinforces his commitment to the achievement of common desirable social goals (e.g. justice and manageability (Albrechts and Denayer, 2001)) through deliberative communication. He still seeks to restore a lost unity of technical reason and moral responsibility in a manner which emancipates society. Although he endorses difference, in a form similar to Benhabib's invocation of the 'concrete other', he recognises the oppressive potential of a politics of recognition and suggests recourse in the field of legal structures in his 1996 work, *Between Facts and Norms*. Habermas here develops the implications of communicative action into a theory of law and the democratic state.

In *Between Facts and Norms* Habermas engages what Scheuerman (1999: 154) terms 'a sophisticated neo-Kantian brand of contract theory' in a detailed discursive conception of the normative and institutional specifics of a rejuvenated public sphere. Based in his experiences of post-unification Germany, he finally leaves his Marxist roots behind, recognising the 'system imperatives' of the market system. He also recognises actors' social complexity (rather than simply bracketing difference) and talks of a diversity of public spheres. Habermas even indicates (1996: 159–61) that processes of bargaining and compromise have a legitimate role to play in decision-making if consensus is unachievable; that we need to go beyond traditional knowledges and values, facts and norms, to develop a praxis of social decision-making able to incorporate difference and oppositional representations and ways of knowing, and which is informed by principles of equality and justice (Hillier, 1998a).

Habermas retains the central idea that even diverse actors should be 'convinced by reason' (Chambers, 1995: 236) that the institutions and norms of their community are in the general interest. He turns to law as the primary institutional complex responsible for social integration in pluralist societies: 'a will-formation institutionalised according to the rule of law' (1996: 486). Communicative action now becomes a discourse theory of law in Habermas' model of procedural democracy.

Baynes (1995: 205) summarises Habermas' thesis as follows:

> in highly differentiated and pluralist societies the task of social coordination and integration falls to institutionalised procedures of legitimate lawmaking that transform into binding decisions the more diffuse public opinions initially produced via the anonymous communication network of a loosely organised and largely autonomous public sphere.

Habermas' recognition of the contingent, often unpredictability, of the public sphere has led him to distinguish this realm from that of democratic law-making institutions. Such institutions and procedures represent the mechanisms by which public 'opinions' are transformed into universalisable reasons (Rattila, 2000).

Habermas thus advances a notion of politics that operates simultaneously on two levels: (i) the proceduralised deliberations of legislative and decision-making institutions, and (ii) informal deliberations of public spheres. The informal public spheres provide the legislative institutions with material which is moulded[2] and enacted into law (1996: 182). Legislative institutions (such as parliaments and local authorities) are 'merely a technical device' (Scheuerman, 2000: 159) to 'focus' the process of political debate and avoid the 'anarchy of unchecked communication' (Kavoulakos, 1999: 37). They must remain 'porous' to civil society, however, if they are to ascertain, recognise and deal with issues successfully (Habermas, 1996: 307–8). At both levels, communicative power predominates.

Does Habermas' revised model answer his critics? The notion of the 'concrete other' as developed by Benhabib and adopted by Habermas is a move forwards. The concrete other does not seek to abstract away from or even to tolerate difference, but instead celebrates difference as being the essence of identity. It is a 'pluralism that valorises diversity and dissensus, recognising in them the very condition of possibility, of a striving democratic life' (Mouffe, 1995: 265), a sentiment echoing Young's (1990) call for democratic publics to give voice to the differences within them.

Recognition of concrete otherness means abandoning the reductionism and essentialism of the generalised other and acknowledging the contingent social construction of identity. It also entails accepting that a participatory decision-making process itself is part of the dynamic; that identities may be reconstructed as representations are made and debated. The process 'is not simply the projection of group "interests" onto the screen of state policy, but indeed precedes this in the intricate processes of articulation through which such identities, representations, and rights claims are themselves contingently constructed' (Mouffe, 1992: 121).

Mouffe (1988, 1992, 1993), however, has suggested that acceptance of the idea of a concrete other threatens the very possibility of Habermasian communicative action where identity must be grounded in an unencumbered self, and where antagonism, division and conflict related to difference disappear in an all-inclusive consensus. Acceptance of the concrete other accepts that some people's existing rights and identities are constituted on the exclusion or subordination of the rights of others. It therefore perpetuates a situation of marginalisation and oppression.

Benhabib disagrees that this need be. She states that the standpoint of the concrete other enables participants

> to view each and every rational being as an individual with a concrete history, identity and affective–emotional constitution. Our relation to the other is governed by the norm of complementary reciprocity: each is entitled to expect and to assume from the other forms of behaviour through which the other feels recognised and confirmed as a concrete, individual being with specific needs, talents and capacities (1990a: 341).

Benhabib later clarifies this idea further by adding that 'in assuming this standpoint, we abstract from what constitutes our commonality, and focus on individuality. We seek to comprehend the needs of the other, his or her motivations, what s/he searches for, and what s/he desires' (1992a: 159).

It is evident that Benhabib does not regard concrete otherness as compromising universalisability of needs recognition and interpretation. In what she terms 'interactive universalism' participants are able to take up the perspective of the other and develop an 'enlarged mentality', a sensitivity to, and appreciation of, the wide range of moral considerations which are relevant in particular circumstances (1992a: 165).

It is through communication, through dialogue with others, that people can understand their differences and reach 'a contested but negotiable practical understanding' (Shotter, 1993: 116) of different non-assimilable ways of being and ways of knowing. Young's (1990) doubts about mutual understanding and reciprocity remain nevertheless.

In addition, Rättilä (2000) criticises Habermas' discussion of weak and strong publics with its distinction between informal participation and formal decision-making. She suggests that such separation may result in 'a built-in tendency to keep "high politics" away from the direct influence of citizens' (2000: 51). It may well enhance rather than challenge asymmetries of social power and further colonisation of the lifeworld by the system.

The distinction is blurred further as the system colonises the lifeworld, for example, through the increasing juridification of social life. In such a process, the state might impose increased rules and regulations on citizens or increase its collection of data on them, thus redefining citizens and their everyday life situations. An individual citizen's public existence, in this manner, becomes defined in terms of strategic–rational relationships to bureaucracies. There is an incessant process of abstraction of people from everyday life situations and the creation of an 'insidiously expanding domain of dependency' (White, 1988: 113). Lifeworld colonisation by this process of defining, categorising and organising people is reminiscent of Foucault's ideas concerning how discipline operates through surveillance and normalisation. The implications of power are similar.

In addition, if communicative power is to rely on the medium of law to determine administrative power, is the significance of communicative power thereby substantially reduced? Scheuerman (1999: 163) points out that it is 'utopian' to hope that communicative power can often gain the upper hand in relation to either market and/or bureaucratic mechanisms. In what may be regarded by some as a 'watering down' of communicative action, Habermas retreats into the realm of the legislative, administratively dominated 'normal' politics of liberal democratic systems or into what Zizek (1999: 190) terms 'para-politics', the attempted depoliticisation of politics. Political conflict is reformulated into a 'competition … between acknowledged parties/agents, for the (temporary) occupation of the place of executive power'. Is this retreat a 'watering down', however, or rather a realistic appreciation of democratic society?

RELEVANCE FOR PLANNING

What is the relevance for planning that can be taken from the above discussion of communicative action? Detailed discussion will continue throughout this book. What follows here serves as an introduction to some key issues only. I believe that planning practice is concerned with public policy-making which has traditionally involved planners, as professional experts taking the lead in shaping people's attention and understanding of situations. Such planning practice, although communicative, has not comprised communicative action in the Habermasian sense, but would be regarded rather as strategic or instrumental.

The theory of communicative action teaches us, however, that outcomes negotiated consensually, through a process of uncoerced reasoned debate with all participants working collaboratively, are more readily owned and accepted by participants than those imposed by the bureaucratic system. Communicative debate should incorporate the multiplicity of people's experience or lifeworlds in a regained public sphere in which mutual understanding is reached through everyone being able to speak and doing so as truthfully, comprehensibly, sincerely and legitimately as possible. All participants should treat each other and each opinion with respect, attempting reciprocally to understand why they say what they do, and thinking reflexively about their own opinions in the light of new knowledges.

> In a situation of profound disagreement, it is not only necessary for 'them' to try to understand things from 'our' perspective, 'we' have to try in the same manner to grasp things from 'their' perspective. They would never seriously get a chance to learn from us if we did not have the chance to learn from them, and we only become aware of the limits of 'our' knowledge through the faltering of 'their' learning processes. The merging of interpretive horizons, ... the goal of every process of reaching understanding does not signify an assimilation to 'us', rather, it must mean a convergence, steered through learning, of 'our' perspective *and* 'their' perspective − no matter whether 'they' or 'we' or both sides have to reformulate established practices of justification to a greater or lesser extent (Habermas, 1992: 138, emphasis in original).

A Habermasian account of planning would recognise the communicative potential in the planners' role and work from there. It would see how planners' actions shape others' expectations and understandings.

> Just as information is processed, collected or spread, so involvements are developed and participation is shaped, relationships and networks are built and altered, affected and interested persons are selectively included or excluded, expectations and hopes are set, raised and lowered differently among different actors, and political engagement is likewise encouraged for some and thwarted for others (Forester, 1982: 64).

A Habermasian approach would seek to alter the strategic or instrumental elements of the above 'job description' to practical−communicative elements, changing:

processing information	to	*shaping attention*
problem solving		*problem reformulating*
seeking detachment to further objectivity		*seeking criticism to check bias and misrepresentation*

gathering facts	*addressing significance: gathering facts that matter and interacting*
treating participation as a source of destruction	*treating participation as an opportunity to improve analysis*
informing decisions	*organising attention to formulate and clarify possibilities*
supplying a single product, a document with 'answers'	*developing a process of questioning possibilities, shaping response and engagement*
reinforcing political dependency of affected persons	*fostering meaningful political participation and autonomy*
passing on 'solutions'	*fostering policy and design criticism, argument and political discourse*
abstracting from social relations	*reproducing social and political relations*

(Forester, 1982: 65)

Planners should then recognise that the 'results' would be no more than 'recommendations relevant to the pursuit of contingent purposes in the light of given preferences' (McCarthy, 1990: vii).

Planning is and should be relational, interpretative and interactive. Interaction involves networks of different individuals and organisations being engaged with each other in debate and negotiation; each group having its own discourse, knowledge and meaning systems and telling its own stories. The role of planning should be to engage in 'respectful discussion within and between discursive communities, respect implying recognising, valuing, listening and searching for translative possibilities between different discourse communities' (Healey, 1993: 242).

However, as Oelschlaeger (2000) indicates, Habermasian theory is placeless; it disconnects place and citizenship. By its very nature, planning practice is not placeless. Whilst 'placeless theorising' may be 'consonant with the Western intellectual tradition' (Oelschlaeger, 2000: 393), as far as planning theory is concerned, place must count. Habermasian theory thus requires contextualising. Since what constitutes 'place' is inevitably contingent, however, I leave it to readers to ground Habermasian theory in place/s appropriate to themselves, noting also Marsh's (2000: 564) criticism of Habermasian communicative action as being inherently Eurocentric.

I reiterate the questions I asked previously elsewhere (Hillier, 1993: 109).

Is such a scheme realisable? Will groups and individuals hear and respect different voices and stories? What is to prevent the pursuit of private interest, paralysis and chaos? Will powerful groups systematically distort information? Will communicative action or discursive democracy simply add to the complexity of the planning process, resulting in more delays in decision-making? Will compromises achieved simply reflect existing power structures and thus both tacitly endorse and reinforce the structures of inequality in a given society and solidify initially unequal bargaining positions? Such arrangements, whilst appearing consensual, would actually be functions of power relationships.

Notions of the state and its power, and especially the work of Michel Foucault, are relevant to these questions and it is to them which I now turn.

CHAPTER 3

DISCUSSING MICHEL FOUCAULT

INTRODUCTION

In this chapter I offer a very brief set of definitions of the notion of power as an introduction to the power-full work of Michel Foucault. Given my intention to explore the possibilities for reconciliation of Foucauldian and Habermasian ideas relating to discursive democracy, I conclude the chapter by highlighting what both authors in turn have perceived as their differences and convergences.

COMMUNICATING POWER

With relation to the particular field of urban and regional planning, the traditional immersion of planners in power relations has often undermined an opportunity to build upon and improve the framework for rational democratic discussion and decision. 'As decisions are made, relations of power are reproduced too' (Forester, 1992: 46). A greater understanding of power is thus important in both the comprehension and taking of planning decisions.

There has been much theorising about power but relatively little agreement on its definition. Davis (1988: 71) presents a summary of definitions (after Lukes, 1974) as follows:

- Power is something which is possessed; it can only be exercised; it is a matter of authority.
- Power belongs to the individual; it belongs only to collectives; power does not belong to anyone, but is a feature of social systems.
- Power involves conflict; power does not necessarily involve conflict; power usually involves conflict, but does not have to.
- Power presupposes resistance; power is primarily involved in compliance (to norms); power is both.
- Power is tied to repression and domination; power is productive and enabling.
- Power is bad, good, demonic or routine.

It is small wonder that even the same authors (including Foucault) occasionally change their opinions. I feel that it is slightly unfair, however, to simply leave this crude tabulation of definitions without stressing two key points of understanding.

Any interpretation of power is inextricably tied to background assumptions which are methodological and epistemological and also to moral and political assumptions. The identification of power is thus inevitably both theory-relative and value-dependent. In fact it is impossible to conceive of non-value-dependent theoretical perspectives.

Max Weber, for instance, stressed the asymmetrical capacity to realise power as being important rather than its actual realisation. He defined power as 'the probability that an actor in a social relationship will be in a position to carry out his own will despite resistance, regardless of the basis on which this probability rests' (Weber, 1978: 53).

For Robert Dahl, power amounts to the control of behaviour in that 'A has power over B to the extent that he can get B to do something that B would not otherwise do' (1957: 201). Both Weber and Dahl focus on ideas of power *over* someone.

Giddens defines power as 'the capability of an actor to intervene in a series of events so as to alter their course' (1976: 11). Power is not therefore seen as having necessarily predetermined intent or control over something or someone. Every person (agent) has a range of causal powers and is, at any given time, able to 'make a difference'. Even when their activities are severely restricted there is always a sense of 'could have done otherwise' (Giddens, 1984). The exercise of power always involves a two-way relationship, expressing autonomy and dependence in both directions. This means that even when people display outward signs of compliance with even the most oppressive situations, one cannot conclude that they had no alternative. Compliance may well have been the result of a rational assessment of the situation and of possible alternatives.

Focus thus shifts from the question of 'who' has the power as posed in traditional theories, to that of 'how' participants attempt to exercise power and the skills and resources they employ in so doing. Power is a process in which members of society ongoingly and routinely construct, maintain, but also change and transform their power relations. Structures involving those of domination are thereby reproduced as power practices both at the micro- and macro-levels. Yet the exercise of power is not simply top-down or repressive, it is also productive, enabling and positive. Studies of power relations should therefore involve taking both dimensions into account and showing how power is connected to constraint *and* enablement (Davis, 1988).

THE WORK OF MICHEL FOUCAULT

Michel Foucault's work on power demonstrates such negative and positive aspects of power described above *par excellence*. His concern is with the 'how' of power and relating that 'how' back to its root causes: 'a critical investigation into the thematics of power' (1982a: 217).

An examination of Foucault's work enables us to begin to understand power both very broadly and yet very finely, in the multiplicity of micropractices which comprise everyday life; to appreciate that power reactions are 'non-egalitarian and mobile' and that power is a relational process rather than a commodity operating both from the top down and from the bottom up.

Power to Foucault is a general matrix of force relations at a given time, in a given society. Power relations are 'intentional and non-subjective', 'imbued, through and through, with calculation' (1978: 95). While at the local level there may be a high degree of conscious decision-making and politicking, individuals basically make decisions for their own advantage. This means that the overall actions of power relations in a society do not imply a conscious subject. 'People know what they do; they frequently know why they do what they do; but what they don't know is what what they do does' (Foucault in Dreyfus and Rabinow, 1982c: 187).

In talking about power, Foucault often uses the terminology of war; 'should we not analyse it primarily in terms of struggle, conflict and war?' (in Gordon, 1980: 90). Foucault examined the validity of what Gordon (2000: xxi) terms the 'hypothesis of war'; the idea that the analogy of war could serve as a tool for political analysis; '*la guerre peut-elle valoir comme analyseur des rapports de pouvoir?*'[3] (1989: 86), '*l'ordre civil est fondamentalement un ordre de bataille*'[4] (1989: 87); '*il est dans la bataille, il a des adversaires, il se bat pour une victoire*'[5] (1989: 89). Power is competitive, using truth selectively; '*une vérité qui fonctionne comme une arme*'[6] (1989: 89). Foucault regards power as simply a form of warlike domination and conceives problems of power in terms of relations of war. He utilises concepts of battle tactics and strategy for analysing power structures and political processes. I view Foucault's notion of power as expressed above, as a reprise of Nietzsche's (1901) will-to-power. This power manifests itself in a discourse through which it engages, perhaps arbitrarily and for its own purposes, in the invention of 'truth'. 'Power produces; it produces reality; it produces domains of objects and rituals of truth' (Foucault, 1975: 194).

Power is both positive and negative in struggle. It is also omnipresent, producing itself at every moment, everywhere. Power and knowledge are intrinsically related (a concept developed from Nietzsche) as expressed in the now-famous sentence

> power produces knowledge … power and knowledge directly imply one another … there is no power relation without the correlative constitution of a field of knowledge, nor any knowledge that does not presuppose and constitute at the same time power relations (Foucault, 1975: 27–8).

Unsurprisingly, therefore, Foucault is highly critical of the liberal view (represented by authors such as Dahl), that one can analyse power in terms of A's ability to make B do something s/he would otherwise not do, as being 'utter sterility' (Taylor, 1986: 89). Because acts of power are by their very nature heterogeneous, they cannot be described in such a culturally neutral and homogeneous way. Foucault's conception of power without a subject inevitably sets aside the liberal model where power is a matter of one person/actor exercising control over and imposing their will on others. Similarly, despite drawing heavily in *Discipline and Punish* (1977a) on a Marxist account of capitalist power, Foucault's later work on power moves away from Marxist roots to an explicit counterposition of power as a positive enabling force.

POWER-FULL THEMES
I turn now to brief discussion of some of the major themes recurring in Foucault's work in relation to power, upon which I will build below. The first of these themes is *discipline*.

Discipline for Foucault is a technique or mechanism which proceeds by the organisation of individuals in space. It requires and has developed a number of conditions for its implementation. As Sheridan (1980) indicates, Foucault listed four main conditions for discipline. First, discipline is cellular: the space in which individuals are subjected to discipline is divided into more or less self-contained units (local planning authorities for example).

Second, the disciplines have initiated a control of activity (planning regulations, development control?). Third, persons undergo a process of training for the development of greater skills (planning and local government education?) and finally, discipline carefully arranges combinations of forces within a precise system (zoning schemes?). In addition, within a discipline, each individual (planning applicant?) becomes a 'case', which is at once an object for knowledge and a site for the exercise of power. While Foucault's empirical research centred on prisons, asylums and hospitals, I suggest that town planning fits the above conditions fairly well and thus qualifies as a discipline, particularly as Foucault himself commented that 'space is fundamental in any exercise of power' (in Rabinow, 1984: 252). The aim of disciplinary technology is thus to forge 'a docile body that may be subjected, used, transformed and improved' (Foucault, 1975: 136) through the control of space.

Disciplinary power operates through the surveillance and observation and *normalisation* of its subjects. Every individual must conform to a certain idea of 'normality', to become manageable for the purposes of power. Normalisation is everywhere, in schools, prisons, hospitals and in society at large where the normalised idea of 'the general public' oppressively objectifies and homogenises human beings, falsifying their real essence, and thus often reduces gender, ethnic and other characteristics to the phallocentric anglo, middle-class male.

Normalisation is also associated with an increasing appeal to statistical measures and techniques (also a symbol of power for the trained professionals over the non-comprehending lay population) and the claim of impartiality for such techniques.

Discipline operates primarily on the body; both the body public (people as a whole) and the individual body. The body is an object to be analysed, normalised and manipulated: a 'docile body'. Foucault terms his interpretation of the management of the relations of power, the body, the individual, sex and truth, '*biopower*'.

Foucault stated that there are no relations of power without *resistances* (Gordon, 1980). Since power exists everywhere, resistance is possible everywhere. It is the very form of power that subjugates that also produces the possibility of refusal (Game, 1991). Resistance incorporates macro-level strategies of class struggle and micro-level local criticisms and insurrections ('the insurrection of subjugated knowledges') – 'opposition to the power of men over women, of parents over children, of psychiatry over the mentally ill, of medicine over the population, of administration over the ways people live' (Foucault, 1982a: 780). Thus, resistance opposes the ways in which 'the effects of power … are linked with knowledge, competence and qualifications: struggles against the privileges of knowledge. But they are also an opposition against secrecy, deformation and mystifying representations imposed on people' (Foucault, 1982a: 781).

However, Foucault does not propose a normative theory offering guidance for strategies of resistance. He remains bound up in Nietzsche, suggesting the unmasking of power and truth (Foucault, 1984a: 351), but because of this Nietzschean idea of truth imposed by a regime of power, Foucault cannot envisage liberating revolutionary transformations coming from within that regime. Unmasking can only destabilise the regime, it cannot overthrow it.

Foucault, then, does not offer us a new form of society, or of decision-making, but rather a kind of resistance movement, local-specific (a 'plurality of resistances') within the existing form. Foucault's theory is thus a 'tool-kit' not for revolution but for local resistance (Walzer, 1986), a resistance perhaps manifest in local demands for new, increased participation in policy- and decision-making processes.

POWER AND KNOWLEDGE

How, then may resistance become empowerment? If we start from Foucault's ideas that power can be productive as well as negating and that power and knowledge are integrated, then if knowledge engenders power, strategies of resistance should encompass the acquisition of knowledge. Resistance should 'entertain the claims to attention of local, discontinuous, disqualified, illegitimate knowledges', a 'union of erudite knowledges and local memories' (Foucault in Gordon, 1980: 83).

Using lessons from women's social mobilisation in Latin America, Friedmann (1992) demonstrates the potential of empowerment through local acquisition of knowledges, through networking and organisation, acting collectively rather than in isolation. Boulding (1989) terms such power 'integrative power'. It relies on knowledge and communication of knowledge. As Boulding writes (1989: 110), 'it may well be that the ultimate dominance of integrative power rests on the fact that integrative behaviour creates communications and builds up communication networks that extend far and wide over time and space'.

Power, for Foucault, belongs to a 'productive network' in which language is important. He believed that the relations of power which constitute the social body cannot be established or implemented without the production and functioning of a discourse. Discourse is thus related to knowledge (the will to knowledge) and to power (power/knowledge). Does such a conception preclude deliberation across discourses? Dryzek (2001: 658) suggests not, recognising that a 'loose' Foucauldian conception of discourses makes possible reflective choice and deliberation across them. Here, Bourdieu's (1993) notion of a discursive field, as outlined in Part 4, will be useful.

In particular, power invites people to speak, to assess and articulate themselves. In one of his final interviews in January 1984, Foucault linked the ideas of communication and transparency of speech with those of truth and emancipation, inviting comparison with the ideas of communicative action and discursive democracy. 'Who says the truth? Individuals who are free, who arrive at a certain agreement' (Foucault in Bernauer and Rasmussen, 1988: 17).

Foucault not only offers us a theory of knowledge, but one which attempts to incorporate the relations between knowledge, truth and power. As Habermas is concerned with truth for communicative rationality, Foucault, too, admits that 'my own problem has always been the question of truth, of telling the truth, the *wahrsagen* – what it is to tell the truth – and the relation between "telling the truth" and forms of reflexivity, of self upon self' (Foucault, in Kritzmann, 1988: 33). In particular, Foucault (1977b) indicates discourse to be a translation of domination into language through prohibitions and exclusions on what we can speak about, who may speak, when and how and the opposition between the true and the false (reminiscent of Habermas' systematic distortion of communication).

Foucault's version of knowledge is, however, far more tempered than that of Habermas. Foucault warns about inherent bias in 'facts' and 'knowledge' and the problem of taking them at face value. He shows how disguises, masks and illusions foist falsehood upon us in the guise of truth, how 'truth' manufactured by power turns out to be untruth. (Taylor, 1986: 94). However, because of his Nietzschean idea of truth imposed by a regime of power, Foucault cannot envisage liberation through a transformation of power relations within the regime. It may be that it is at this point that consideration of communicative action may be of value as it appears to offer what Foucault seeks when he wants to rehabilitate subjugated and local knowledges against an established dominant 'truth', particularly as he positively embraces the idea of language and communication as a means for moving people to concerted action. Dreyfus and Rabinow (1986: 115) comment that an all-embracing theory

> has yet to be worked out, but it has to do with articulating common concerns and finding a language which becomes accepted as a way of talking about social situations, while leaving open the possibility of 'dialogue', or better, a con-flict of interpretations, with other shared discursive practices used to articulate different concerns.

Foucault is also concerned with the issue of subjectivity. One of the keys to Foucault's work is his respect for differences and the notion that individuals create their own identities through ethics and forms of self-constitution. The body is thus an object, both the subject of manipulation (the docile body) and of power. By working with other bodies, in coalition, to form social networks, power may be reinforced. It is in such a manner that women's groups, gay and lesbian groups, civil rights, environmental, etc. groups have found the power to lobby and advance their causes.

RELEVANCE FOR PLANNING

Community action or residents' action groups could also be included in the above list. Examination of power at the 'capillaries', at the local level, leads to consideration of a spatial interpretation of Foucault's work.

Foucault himself (in Gordon, 1980: 69) admits having an obsession with space, because it is through space that he recognises the relations between power and knowledge: 'space is fundamental in any exercise of power' (quoted in Rabinow, 1984: 252). He also suggests that 'a whole history remains to be written of spaces – which would at the same time be the history of powers' and that power 'becomes a question of using the disposition of space for economio-political ends' (both quotes from Gordon, 1980: 148–9).

Urban and regional planning is an inherently normative discipline. As such it mobilises space and architecture. As Ewald (1992) indicates, for Foucault planning/architecture are no longer the expression of power but they are power itself. Power is often rather *ad hoc* and incrementally applied, however. Often 'the tactics take shape in piecemeal fashion without anyone's wittingly knowing what they add up to' (Hacking, 1986: 35). Individual technocrats or committees may have limited goals in their own minds, but put together they form complex and often self-contradictory mechanisms of power. Through surveillance, examination and normalisation planning becomes the instrument, the technique and the apparatus not only of control of the subject, but also of the possibility of objectivity in the subject's self-reference and self-judgement. In other words it spatially, economically, socially etc., locates people, reminds people of their place and gives everyone their identity. As I shall demonstrate below, this function is both oppressive and capacitating, as people identifying common cause may find the power to resist.

Foucault also offers insight-facilitating analysis of the power and legitimacy of government officials and elected representatives; 'power makes men mad and those who govern are blind' (quoted in Gordon, 1980: 51). In his later lectures at the Collège de France, Foucault defined and explored the concept of governmental rationality or 'governmentality', being the government both of others and of one's self. His thinking evolved from ideas of negative oppression as expressed in the quotation above, to ways of involving the governed to work with the government, without any assumption of compliance, on actual problems: 'working with a government does not imply either subjection or total acceptance. One can simultaneously work and stubbornly resist. I even think that the two go together' (1981: 21). Perhaps the ideas of Foucault and Habermas are not really so far apart after all.

Foucault (in Gordon, 1980: 99) tells us that social networks should be studied from the bottom up,

> starting that is from its infinitesimal mechanisms, which each have their own history, their own trajectory, their own techniques and tactics, and then see how these mechanisms of power have been — and continue to be — invested, *colonised*, involuted, transformed, displaced, extended, etc. by ever more general mechanisms and by forms of global domination (emphasis added).

This is a statement reminiscent of Habermas' notions of colonisation of the lifeworld.

Foucault thus proposes that power is best understood through the micropolitical terms of the networks of power relations subsisting at every point in a society. He shows how power may be exercised from the bottom up to capacitate and give pleasure as well as to coerce: 'the word "how" is the key to Foucault's concept of power' (Barrett, 1991: 136). He argues that the 'little question' of what happens or how does not eliminate consideration of the what, who and why of power, but rather acts with them to allow a critical investigation of the thematics of power.

By examining 'the strategies, networks, the mechanisms, all those techniques by which a decision is accepted and by which the decision could not but be taken in the way it was' (Foucault in Kritzman, 1988: 104–5), Foucault shows how power relations can be heterogeneous, working in different directions, for different ends.

The possibility of change is seen as part of the very play of power. In order to move towards progressive change, Foucault suggests that people have to explore and build upon the open qualities of human discourse (see also Habermas) and thereby intervene in the way knowledge is produced and constituted at the particular sites where a localised power-discourse prevails. Local and particular forms of narrative (counter- or reverse-discourses) and struggle thus provide an opportunity not only for examination of power relations in planning (see Hillier, 1993) but also for getting power-full messages across, as statements are valuable political resources (Foucault, in Shapiro, 1989).

Foucault is concerned that people should cultivate and enhance decision-making at the local level, resisting the institutions, techniques and discourses which attempt to oppress them. He instructs people to 'develop action, thought and desires by proliferation, juxtaposition, and disjunction – to prefer what is positive and multiple, difference over uniformity, flows over unities, mobile arrangements over systems' (in Rabinow, 1984: xiii). Such statements accord strongly with movements away from the all-encompassing narratives and decisions of politics and of planning to a countervailing stress on the local and particular forms of difference, resistance, participation and empowerment.

Since power is exercised at innumerable points, it has to be challenged, locally, point by point in a plurality of resistances. Foucault's political theory, in fact, has been likened to a 'tool kit' for local resistance (Walzer, 1986), whether this be resistance to the power of men over women or of administration over the ways people live (Foucault, 1982a). Resistance is a struggle against the powerful privileges of knowledge as compared to a local lack of knowledge due to the mystique and secrecy imposed upon people. Resistance revolves around the question 'who are we?' – not only to discover who we are but that we may refuse to be what the system has made us, a reversal of totalising normalisation.

It is therefore the very form of power which subjugates that also produces the possibility of refusal and reversal: 'there is no power without potential refusal or revolt' (Foucault, 1981: 253). Because power is a network, there exists the potential for each local insurrection of subjugated knowledges to have a marked impact on wider institutions and their practices and discourses.

CRITIQUE

Foucault has been subject to the criticism that he opens up a space for rethinking power and political strategies, but provides very little normative content to fill that space. He concentrates on resistance to rather than transformation of power, leaving an 'unresolved problem' (Honneth, 1991: 162).

Fraser (1981) accuses Foucault of giving a 'value-neutral' account of power which has disposed with the need for a normative framework for distinguishing between acceptable or just and unacceptable or unjust forms of power and for overcoming those deemed unacceptable. Marris (1982) also criticises Foucault for not following his project through, because unless understanding leads to actions, nothing is learned from it. In addition, Marris finds that Foucault does not explain how local resistances and actions are to be integrated in any larger system, or how intractable conflicts of interest are to be reconciled.

This omission indicates a 'typical ignoring of democracy' (Best and Kellner, 1991: 68), a word Foucault rarely employs, which in turn leads to a problem with his decentred politics since democracy is inevitably a socially constituted project. Foucault thus theoretically excludes a practically effective social and politico-theoretical dimension of reaching normative agreement. This is the position at which communicative action may be of relevance.

RELATIONS AND GAMES OF POWER

One word of caution. I have identified above that Habermas' recent work on communicative action has taken a legal turn. Foucault's analyses of power, however, are opposed to what he calls the 'juridico-discursive' model in which power is seen as possessed by the state, especially the law. Foucault regarded juridical power as 'a renunciation of freedom, a transference of rights, the power of each and all delegated to a few' (1982: 220). He considered such power as being essentially negative and restrictive (1980) even though Habermas would emphasise that the intention behind his own construction of such a model is enabling and constitutive.

Foucault would deny that any rules of public debate could be fair in that all rules allow some actors to dominate others; they allow some to win the argument and force others to concede. Foucault denies a difference between reason and power, between discussing an issue and manipulating actors' viewpoints unreasonably. Both, to Foucault, are forms of overpowering. Any new format for discourse is simply another new mode of power (White, 1991: 17) and as Tewdwr-Jones and Allmendinger (1998: 1979) point out, there is a danger that seeking consensus may actually serve to silence rather than give voice to the already marginalised. It would thus appear to be somewhat naive for planners to operate with a concept of reason/rationality without understanding the role of power.

One of Foucault's central contributions is his insight that people always act in relations of power. The two guiding ideas behind much of Foucault's work are the productivity of power and the constitution of subjectivity through power relations. As Gordon (2000: xix) points out, to Foucault, productive power relations are 'integral to the modern social productive apparatus and linked to active programs for the fabricated part of the collective substance of society itself', while the impact of power relations is not limited to repressive forces, but also 'comprises the intention to teach, to mould conduct, to instil forms of self-awareness and identities'.

The exercise of power is 'a mode of action upon the actions of others'; the 'way in which certain actions modify others' (Foucault, 1982a: 219–21). In other words, the exercise of power consists of guiding the conduct of others in various ways. Foucault termed this conduct 'governmentality'. Governmentality refers to more than the means by which the conduct of subjects is governed in political relationships but in *any* relationship, such as parents of children, schools, hospitals, etc. Governmentality includes all 'modes of action, more or less considered and calculated, which were destined to act upon the possibilities of action of other people' (Foucault, 1982a: 221).

Space here precludes a detailed examination of Foucault's concept of governmentality, which in itself has formed the subject of several major works (see, for instance, Dean, 1999). Suffice it to highlight the applicability of governmentality to planning practice. For planning, structuring the possible field of action of others involves more than simply intervening to prevent an action, and includes restructuring the types of action open to a person by restricting what they can do. Planning's relationship of power is therefore on people's *options* for action. Planning governs conduct by modifying people's understanding of the alternatives from which they must choose. It is 'designed to govern someone's conduct by modifying their subjective representation of the practically possible future' (Allen, 1998: 177). Governmentality is a 'right manner of disposing things so as to lead *not to the form of the common good* ... but to an end which is "convenient" for each of the things that are to be governed' (Foucault, 1991a: 95, emphasis added). Foucault here challenges the traditional conception of planning as acting in the common good.

The idea of governmentality develops Foucault's critique of the juridico-discursive model of power as sovereignty. Government through legal institutions becomes just one aspect of governmentality, ranging from states of domination to more open-ended power relations, which, like all aspects of power, are reversible (Foucault, 1984a: 19).

Foucault terms a range of different power-plays as *games*: 'strategic games between liberties' (1984a: 19), varying from games of persuasion and reasoned argument to those of manipulation and indoctrination. As identified above, he makes no distinction between the power relations underlying each of these behaviours, however, which for authors such as McNay (1994) glosses over issues of normative responsibility and moral considerations, which are crucial to planning practice. Yet as Huxley (2001) emphasises, Foucauldian analysis of power is essentially nonnormative. It is not in itself aimed at correcting the misuse of technical rationality or at creating better regulations, but at highlighting the unwitting effects of regimes of practices and opening up ways of thinking differently. 'Power is therefore compartmentalised ... into a process to be *recognised* by stakeholders' (Tewdwr-Jones and Allmendinger, 1998: 1980, emphasis in original).

FOUCAULT ON HABERMAS[7]

I agree with Hoy (1986: 131) that 'Foucault's own conception of the importance of his studies of power configurations is, then, that they show the inadequacy of and provide an alternative to the Frankfurt School's still too traditional conception of the relation of power and knowledge.' Foucault believes that since knowledge cannot be described as other than part of a power network, there cannot be such a thing as Habermas' conception of non-ideological knowledge freed from power struggles: 'there exists no general principle – including the "force of the better argument" – by which all differences can be resolved' (Flyvbjerg, 1998a: 201).

I return to the issue of power later, but look here at Foucault's concern with Habermas' *universalism*. Foucault calls it an 'illusion' (1989: 90) arguing for the particular over the general. However, as McCarthy (1990: 445–7) points out, the differences between Foucault's genealogy and Habermas' social theory are often misrepresented, not least by the authors themselves. McCarthy demonstrates that Foucault's Nietzschean legacy means that he too universalises. He often invokes an ontology of the social that treats exclusion, subjugation and homogenisation as inescapable. In addition, he generalises, and ontologises the concept of power, and distinctions between just and unjust, legitimate and illegitimate, coercive and consensual forms of power tend to disappear. 'Foucault calls too many different sorts of things power and simply leaves it at that' (Fraser, 1989: 32).

Despite this lapse into universalism, however, one of Foucault's strengths remains his demonstration of how the patterns of acculturation in societies have imposed constraints on their members. Foucault, unlike Habermas, allows us to examine, for example, the ways in which asymmetries of power and resources impinge upon the 'universal rights' of liberty and equality in terms of gender, class, ethnicity and so on.

Universality is replaced by the plurality of lifeworlds and the local character of truth, argument and validity. The *a priori* is replaced by the empirical, certainty by contingency, unity by heterogeneity, homogeneity by the fragmentary (McCarthy, 1990). Universality, and the rationality on which it is based in Habermas, thus disintegrate; they become '*de plus en plus fragile, de plus en plus méchante, de plus en plus liée à l'illusion, à la chimère, à la mystification*' (Foucault, 1989: 90).[8]

Foucault's 'genealogical critique', however, may not be a rationalist style of argument, but neither is it irrational. It is simply a style of critique which does not assume the form of a judgement by reference to incontestable principles or suppose a single procedure to settle all disagreements (Rajchman, 1988). As such, I believe that it has much to recommend it.

Foucault also differs with Habermas on the role of *consensus*. Foucault is reluctant to agree that consensus is fundamental to the establishment of democratic, ethical decision-making, although he is definitely against non-consensus, which rules people without their consent. Foucault's objection to the notion of consensus lies in his understanding of it as being a 'partial representation of the multiple and contingent relations between politics and ethics that arbitrate the arrangements of power in a given regime of truth … it contains artifice, blurs the contingency of its own truth, and participates in the defeat of otherness' (Dumm, 1988: 218).

Consensus, therefore, is 'dangerous', (Foucault, in Rabinow, 1984: 343) and one should always be aware of what trade-offs, compromises and omissions have gone into the making of any apparent consensus. Foucault proposes, instead, a transformation of states of domination into open and symmetrical strategic games. (McCarthy, 1990). How these games would operate in practice is not covered, however – a moot point, in particular, because of Foucault's criticism of Habermas' ideal of perfectly transparent communication as utopian.

Habermas blames ideology for preventing the realisation of society based on rational assent. Foucault, on the other hand, rejects the concept of ideology in favour of a detailed, historical analysis of particular forms of experience. There is far more to the prevention of free pursuit of interests than technical rationality or the systematic distortion of communication. Rather, it is the actual tangible procedures that determine the forms of our experiences, the historic effects of how 'truths' are produced.

I turn now to the important issue of *power* wherein lies what is probably the greatest weakness in Habermas' theory. 'The question of power remains a total enigma. Who exercises power? And in what sphere?' (Foucault, in Bouchard, 1977: 213). Habermas (1991: 247) has replied to such criticism by arguing that he has not excluded the phenomena of dissent and power, but that 'macrosociological power relations are mirrored in that microphysics of power which is built into the structures of distorted communication'. Despite his understanding of power as 'the ability to prevent other individuals or groups from realising their interests' (1991: 246), Habermas' ideal speech situation, by definition, assumes argumentation free of domination; freedom from power.

Habermas argues that communicative action is in itself empowering ('the fundamental phenomenon of power is not the instrumentalisation of another's will, but the formation of a common will in a communication directed to reaching agreement' (Habermas, 1986: 76)) in its internal freedom from power, as compared with the manipulative use of power characteristic of strategic action. Habermas thus pits the power of a rational consensus against the power of domination (Hoch, 1992).

Such an understanding of power contrasts with the arguments of Foucault who is interested in the relations of power which traverse and influence institutions, their contexts and practices. In contrast to Habermas' emphasis on symmetry, reciprocity and universality, Foucault directs attention to the relations of asymmetry, non-reciprocity and hierarchy and to the ways in which they include and exclude, make central and marginal, assimilate and differentiate (McCarthy, 1990).

Foucault thus discovers power operating in structures of thinking and behaviour which Habermas regards as devoid of power relations. He demonstrates how structures, such as negotiation and communicative action, which Habermas offers as enabling structures, are in fact simultaneously constraining. Habermas tends to assume that bracketing political and economic power is sufficient to make speakers equal in negotiation. He fails to observe that the social power which can prevent people from being equal speakers derives from both economic dependence and/or political domination and also from an internalised sense of the right one has to speak or not to speak, and from the devaluation of some people's style of speech as against others (Young, 1993). Habermas thus not only brackets political and economic power, but cultural and social power as well.

Incorporation of consideration of the socio-economic, political and cultural ways in which social reality is constructed into a theory of communicative action would not negate the importance of concepts such as systematically distorted communication but rather deepen their consequences. For example, we could understand the ways in which and the reasons why qualified experts and licensed professionals or 'panoptical scientific observers' (McCarthy, 1990: 443) exercise coercion over the public by the gentle force of administration and the imperceptible deployment of techniques based on detailed technical 'knowledge'. Moving on from this understanding, as Mumby (1988) suggests, instead of fixing the scope of emancipation in terms solely of an ideal speech situation, communicative action could then be tied more directly to the actual lived experiences of social practice.

It is the question 'why', above, which is the key to an understanding of power relations. Returning to the issue of systematically distorted communication, even Habermas (1970: 209) admitted that,

> the what, the semantic content of a systematically distorted manifestation, cannot be 'understood' if it is not possible at the same time to 'explain' the why, the origin of the symptomatic scene with reference to the initial circumstances which led to the systematic distortion itself.

Who seeks to persuade, seduce, manipulate whom? And why? We should remember, as we contemplate analysis, that 'the S and C are as important as the D in SDC;[9] the S gives us class and institutional location; the C gives us not symbol and meaning, but performance, action, speech acts' (Forester, 1992, pers. comm.). As communication is examined power-plays become apparent, as Flyvbjerg (1998a) clearly demonstrates. Flyvbjerg warns us to be aware of the thin divide between rationality and rationalisation. He illustrates how rationalisation masquerading as rationality can operate as a principal strategy in the exercise of power. 'Power *defines* what counts as knowledge and rationality, and ultimately, ... what counts as reality' (Flyvbjerg, 1998a: 27, emphasis in original).

I have indicated points of weakness in Habermas' overly philosophical position on universality, rationality, consensus and ideology. They are relatively minor, however, compared with his bracketing of socio-economic, cultural and political issues, the variety, particularism and mutual incompatibility of social expectations (Zolo, 1992) and their interrelationships with power. Habermas, then,

Habermas' lifeworld is not entirely dissimilar to Foucault's genealogy. The concept of lifeworld recognises the interdependence between an historically shaped understanding of the world and the experience and practice possible within its horizon. Practice (including speech/language) is informed by world structures and of individuals' understanding and experiencing of the world (McCarthy, 1987). Genealogy, too, is an historically based contextual concept for understanding 'local discursivities' and their interrelationships with actors in particular and the world in general.

Both authors thus accept that members of social groups' actions and speech are situated within a context of the historical and sociological conditions of the distribution of resources, advantages and status which make up their personal identities. Every identity and speech act is thus particularistic, contingent and highly variable (Zolo, 1992).

Habermas argues that achievement of communicative rationality (via the ideal speech situation) is hindered by the systematic distortion of communication, which I believe finds a parallel in Foucault's notion of discipline. Discipline is a mechanism of control. Through surveillance, examination and normalisation using scientific techniques/mathematics/statistics (Habermas' technical rationality) and language (through prohibitions, exclusions and blurring the opposition between the true and the false), qualified professionals and experts replace coercion of citizens by violence with the 'gentler force' of administration. Citizens are thus subjected to the colonisation of their lifeworld/s (Habermas) through Foucault's disciplinisation and normalisation processes.

Both systematically distorted communication and discipline, then, are concerned with asymmetrical power relationships, often with the state dominating and oppressing various groups in society. Through what both authors term strategic action the state (or other groups of individuals) seeks to further its own aims.

Habermas and Foucault both regard power as being a negative force, through domination and oppression, but also a positive force. Habermas suggests that through mutual understanding and reciprocal self-reflection, aiming towards a democratic, uncoerced consensus, participants may be empowered in the sphere of decision-making. Whilst Foucault might hesitate in agreeing with the need for consensus, he too, believes in the existence of ascending power, which may be exercised from the bottom up to capacitate and liberate. Both believe in the importance of language and communication in conferring power, with Foucault suggesting that citizens explore and build upon the open qualities of human discourse to intervene in the ways knowledge is produced and constituted locally.

There are points of convergence, even on the difficult issue of reciprocal recognition. Reciprocal recognition between actors underpins communicative action, but as Thompson (1999) demonstrates, while Foucault is traditionally viewed as being hostile towards such thinking (see, for instance his statement that 'nothing in man [*sic*] … is sufficiently stable to serve as the basis for self-recognition or for understanding other men' (1984a: 87–8)), he does employ notions of symmetry, egalitarianism and equality as terms of critical evaluation in his examination of social practices, and he is committed to the ideal of reciprocity between subjects in relationships in which there is potential reversibility of power. As Thompson indicates, therefore, Foucault and Habermas both produce an account of reciprocal recognition of others as 'related yet separate, and equal yet different' (1999: 197).

Foucault urges localised resistance to domination and the power-full privileges of knowledge. His insurrections of subjugated knowledges are similar to Habermas' sub-institutional, extra-parliamentary resistances by new social movements. Both can be understood as forms of resistance to tendencies to colonise the lifeworld and as also having an emancipatory potential, furthering the search for personal and collective identity and promoting the revitalisation of buried possibilities for expression and communication. Habermas thus recognises that the practical struggle of social groups may be an important complement to linguistic understanding. Whilst Foucault goes no further than advocating resistance, Habermas, however, describes resistance as an intersubjective process that 'begins with the destruction of reciprocal conditions of communication, continues through the practical resistance of morally injured subjects, and finally comes to rest in the communicative renewal of a situation of mutual recognition' (Honneth, 1991: 271). The 'institutional organisation of society' is thus locally renegotiated between all actors to achieve a compromise moral consensus formation. Should this newly negotiated system again prescribe normatively an unequal distribution of burdens and advantages, the struggle is set in motion again (Honneth, 1991)

Habermas therefore provides us with a normative theory (albeit a fairly utopian one), in contrast with Foucault's analytical approach. Fraser (1981: 286) comments: 'clearly what Foucault needs and needs desperately are normative criteria'. Alternatively, Habermas would benefit from greater analytical consideration of power relations rather than confining power to the status of an 'interloper' (Hoch, 1992: 207) which destroys and violates the conditions for successful communicative action. In addition, Habermas needs to embrace the scope for plural constructed heritages, for different voices and experiences, which Foucault offers.

I would agree with White (1988: 204) that Habermas' model of communicative action possesses a dialogical responsibility that draws 'attention to the model's own limits and the necessity of its being supplemented'. I believe that aspects of Foucault's work can provide that supplementation, giving the model of communicative action greater conceptual power through linking it to social and material practices, by introducing a critique of power relations and directing attention away from all-encompassing narratives to a countervailing stress on local and particular forms of difference and participation. In the developments of both authors points of contact are recognisable, although several gaps remain. On the whole though, I tend to agree with Hoch (1992: 208) that there is 'room for coexistence' between the two, and with McCarthy that 'Foucault and the Frankfurt School should be located rather close to one another on the map of contemporary theoretical opinions' (1990: 441); that 'the point is not to choose between them but to unite them' (1990: 464); that by interpreting 'Foucault's work in such a way that it turns into a supplement of Habermas' work ... we might actually manage to achieve consensus and harmony between the two, winding up with Habermas' work "corrected" by Foucault's and *vice versa*' (Richters, 1988: 636–7), whilst doing justice to both the difference and commensurability between them.

I regard it as beyond my project here to finely detail all the points of difference, similarity and complementarity between Habermas and Foucault as the debates are wide-ranging and sometimes overly complicated and misunderstood. I refer interested readers to material by Bernstein (1992), Best and Kellner (1991), Hoch (1992), Honneth (1991), McCarthy (1990), Poster (1992) and Richters (1988), together with Kelly (1994) and the recent volume by Ashenden and Owen (1999), both specifically on the subject of the Habermas–Foucault debate.

STARTING TO BUILD A NEW THEORY OF DISCURSIVE DEMOCRACY

I reiterate pleas by Best and Kellner (1991: 298), Agger (1991), Lara (1998), Thompson (1999) and Dreyfus and Rabinow (1986: 115) for a new interpretive theory which 'has to do with articulating common concerns and finding a language which becomes accepted as a way of talking about social situations, while leaving open the possibility of ... a conflict of interpretations, with other shared discursive practices used to articulate different concerns'. In response I offer the following ideas for a simple theoretical model of discursive democracy which will be critiqued and developed in later chapters.

Such a theory should be a model of alleviation of social conflict grounded in a theory of communication. It assumes the form of a struggle among actors for the recognition, acceptance with respect, and valuation of their identities until all actors possess equal chances to participate in the organisation and policy decision-making of their common life (Honneth, 1991). It should enable us to analyse intelligently, discuss and intervene in public policy decisions (Best and Kellner, 1991). It should recognise both actual and perceived structures and relationships of power affecting the actors, and while advocating a process based on communication, it should realise that some people and groups are in far more authoritative positions, politically, economically and psychologically, to speak than others.

What would be the key elements of such a model? I run through them briefly here before adding elaboration below. For practical purposes I relate the model to a local level of decision-making, such as neighbourhood or local authority. The sheer volume of possible participants would probably render the model inoperable at a more macro scale. I therefore attempt to reclaim the notion of public spheres as arenas for debate at the local level, enabling decisions to ascend from the bottom upwards via public participation. For the present, I hold the assumption that the political arena is basically neutral and that diverse groups can meet on essentially level terms in the discursive arena. This assumption will be challenged and removed in following chapters (Parts 3 and 4).

I am interested in the 'how' questions of Foucault and the 'why' of Habermas, in addition to the obvious issues of 'what' and 'who'. Who entails everyone. Nobody should be excluded who is/will be/could be affected by the policy decision. Why involves the reduction of conflict, the sharing of ownership of and the legitimation and accountability of the resulting decision. How concerns a process of what I term discursive democracy, or communicative interaction with power.

The role of communication/language is vital. Each participant should be able to express their views freely. The model also includes an appreciation of the socio-economic, cultural and historical contexts of the speakers. It recognises, celebrates and works through difference as expressed through a plurality of voices, relating to gender, class, ethnicity, age, sexual preference, etc., and establishes a chain of equivalence among their demands so as to articulate them through the principle of democratic equivalence (Mouffe, 1991).

In the model in its current simplistic form, policy decision-making becomes transparent through the sharing of knowledges, the reaching of mutual understanding through respectful listening to all opinions, however different, the reciprocity of thinking oneself in other participants' positions and self-critical reflexivity which recognises the value of other arguments and changes one's own accordingly. The structure of the process forces participants to claim their power, recount their skills and resources, and focus on what is possible rather than what is oppressive.

The current simple model proposes that policy decisions are agreed on the basis of negotiated discussion between all participants. I raise here the issue of consensus and suggest, for the moment, that some form of consensual agreement is a desirable outcome (see Innes, 1995, 1996; Innes and Booher, 1997, 1998a; Healey, 1997a, 1998a). I take the issue of the possibility of consensus further in Chapter 5.

Even so, I warn here against seeking thin consensus, simply a working consensus covering up unequal relations of dominance, compromise and trade-offs between participants, in which some actors rely on reason and others use rationalisation rather than reason to create the reality they want.

If empowerment means improving people's ability to participate in and exercise influence over decisions affecting their survival (in its broad sense, embracing issues such as control of resources, freedom from oppression, etc.), then empowerment should be based on negotiated win–win agreements – with direct involvement of all groups – rather than on delegation and representation where 'majority groups, or perhaps more often powerful vested interests claiming to represent the interests of fortuitously silent majorities, are able to directly control many social decisions to the direct cost of minorities and local community groups' (Howitt, 1992: 4).

However, win–win outcomes are not always possible, and full consensus cannot often be expected, as people from different lifeworlds, speaking from different discourses, are unlikely to reach total agreement. Decisions are often 'tragic' in that some group/s may be disadvantaged, but a negotiated agreement does offer the theoretical advantages over an elite decision of including diversity, of recognising and admitting the power differences, tensions and conflicts, not merely between specific interests, but between conceptions, forms of knowledge, and ways of valuing and discussing things (Majone, 1989; Healey, 1992b; Wolf, 1993). To reach such a situation which procedurally does justice to the values and identities of participants, understanding of, and respect for, the motivations (including the power games) of those holding to a different 'why' are crucial. It is to issues of procedural justice that I now turn.

CONSIDERATIONS OF PROCEDURAL JUSTICE

'There is one overriding moral principle that every citizen has good reasons to accept and to honour in practice: that is the principle of institutionalised fairness in procedures for the resolution … of conflicts' (Hampshire, 2000: 79).

In this section I argue that a model of discursive democratic planning decision-making should entail a process of justice. Justice is an ongoing process which leaves space for the consideration of differences. It works through difference, using concepts of reciprocity and self-reflexivity (Flax, 1992) to focus on what is possible. Justice does not necessarily imply the reaching of consensus, but entails mutual understandings and negotiated agreements which are respectful and honour conflicts of opinion if they cannot be completely resolved.

Justice thus involves a sense of connectedness and obligation to others. It demands an active form of participatory citizenship in which participants see themselves as part of a local community which can act collectively to make decisions and to take responsibility for those decisions.

I consider two separate notions of justice: procedural justice and relativised justice (see Hillier, 1998b, for more detail). The intuitive idea behind procedural justice is very simple: do unto others as you would have others do to you. As Lind and Tyler (1988) indicate, the political arena (including town planning policy decisions) is an important site for implementing procedural justice. It is important to determine not only that the outcome is fair, but also the extent to which the procedure resulting in the outcome is fair to all those affected.

One of the key philosophers whose ideas have formed the foundation for the concept of procedural justice, John Rawls (1971), argued that justice results from fairness in the basic structure and procedures of society. Rawls defined fair procedures as those that would be agreed to or endorsed by an individual who was informed of the procedure in question and who knew that they would occupy some position in society, but who did not know what that position would be (a 'veil of ignorance', 1971: 12).

Relativised justice (O'Neill, 1993) provides a step forward from the idealised justice of the early Rawls and Habermas' concept of the generalised both of which abstract from the particularities of participants. Relativised justice acknowledges the differences among participants and grounds justice in the discourses, identities and values of actual communities. However, since principles of relativised justice are in this manner based in tradition, local context, etc. they will probably endorse problems of inequalities of power, sexism, racism, etc. 'Any relativism tends to prejudice the position of the weak' (O'Neill, 1993: 304).

O'Neill suggests that we can overcome these obstacles by taking account of the context and particularities of participants' lives and cultures, but must not endorse established inequalities of power. As such, we need to embrace certain abstract principles of justice to guide the process of just decision-making.

Habermas (1996) turns to this operational issue in *Between Facts and Norms* in which he seeks ways in which to implement communicative decision-making at the scale of the German state. He suggests a need for procedural democracy based on deliberative politics but says little about any procedures for actualising this beyond that

> there be a warranted presumption that public opinion be formed on the basis of adequate information and relevant reasons and that those whose interests are involved have an equal and effective opportunity to make their own interests (and the reasons for them) known (Baynes, 1995: 216).

Habermas tends to assume that the process will be just, since all participants are theoretically treated as equal, and since decision-makers somehow will communicate with citizens' groups etc.

Research by Lind and Tyler (1988), Earley and Lind (1987), Thibout and Walker (1975), Leventhal (1980) and Leventhal, Karuza and Fry (1980) has found that decisions are more likely to be accepted by those affected when the procedure used to generate the decision allows their perceived fair participation. More recent research has also indicated that procedurally just judgements often have more influence on people's attitudes and behaviours than do their assessments of their personal self-interest (Tyler, Boeckmann, Smith and Huo, 1997); that perceptions of fair procedures discourage retaliation in the face of poor outcomes (Skarlicki and Folger, 1997) or exit from the group (Donovan *et al.*, 1998). Fair participation comprises having the ability to express one's opinions and tell one's stories (voice),[11] being listened to with respect, having access to adequate information, being able to question others, having some degree of control over the decision-making procedure and resultant outcome, demonstrating that decisions are made impartially and receiving good feedback. More recently, Deutsch (1994) has identified moral traits such as perceived trustworthiness and honesty, and Fisher (1994) has shown clear and honest communication and mutual respect to be important in generating fair, cooperative decisions.

Results from work by Moore (1986) and Syme *et al.* (1991) suggest that people actually make judgements about the fairness of government policies and actions that are distinct from their assessments of whether they benefit from those policies and actions. In other words, people whose interests may be adversely affected will nonetheless accept the decision because they have been dealt with fairly, they understand the other participants' positions, and they have had the opportunity to contribute to the debate. Mansbridge (1995a: 343) also adds people's belief that they will find themselves among the gainers on other issues and that losses may not be perceived as complete losses if the winners are regarded as part of the community. 'It may be just as important from the point of view of the public to feel that the decision was arrived at "fairly" as for them to approve all aspects of the final plan' (Syme *et al.*, 1991: 1793).

Table 4.1 presents a list of principles which may be useful in guiding planning officers seeking to work through procedurally just communicative processes.

Even with procedural justice, it is almost certain that some participants will lose out by the final decision. However, if the participation strategy has been procedurally just, these 'losers' should nevertheless feel satisfied with the fairness of the process, if not entirely with that of the outcome.

A second problem relates to inequalities of power, both actual and perceived, and the bias or manipulation of the process in favour of the powerful. As Hampshire (1989: 164) writes, 'can the duties and obligations of fairness and justice, of a minimum level of decency in dealing with persons who have incompatible conceptions of the good, survive the challenges of political expediency?' Public participation programmes normally take place in a 'common' language (English, often replete with planning terms), and use participation rituals (written submissions, public meetings, etc.) with which some participants (particularly planners) may feel more comfortable

Table 4.1 Some principles for a procedurally just communicative planning practice

Components of procedural justice	
Procedural components:	
fairness:	availability and accuracy of information:
• confidence in the process	• availability
• clarity of/confusion about the	• accuracy
process	• language
• flexibility/rigidity of the process	• completeness
voice:	• comprehensibility
• amount	• relevance
• timing	• facts versus values
• inclusiveness	• different forms acceptable
• equity/equality	consistency and impartiality:
• affirmative action	• across participants
• free expression/emotions given value	• across time
• possible methods of communication	• affirmative action across participants
• opportunity to question others	process control:
feedback:	• institutional constraints
• comprehensiveness	• facilitation/mediation
• justification	• opportunity to initiate new topics
• perception	• power in/balance
• timeliness	• safeguards against bias
• sincerity	• appeal
	• ability to generate alternative options
Interactional components:	
respect and dignity:	
• consideration of differences of beliefs and culture	
• equity	
• active listening	
• trust	
• concern for well-being of others	
• seeking of mutual understanding	
• recognition and valuing of difference	
Components of communicative justice	
Procedural components:	
comprehensibility:	legitimacy:
• process	• credibility
• information	• justification
• language	
• openness/transparency	
Interactional components:	
• respect/sincerity	
• honesty/truthfulness	decision-maker impartiality:
• legitimacy	• impartially taken decision
	• decision based on information in debate
	• proper enactment of procedure

Source: Hillier, 1998b: 20–1

than others (Hillier, 1995; Bernstein's notion of communication as a suffocating straightjacket (1991: 51)).

Similarly, some well-organised, well-connected and well-resourced interest groups are often able, through their networks, to influence decision-making more than other groups, while those people unable to be present at meetings, etc. who have few resources and weakly developed networks (including future residents) go unheard.

A move towards more discursive forms of decision-making could well exacerbate such inequalities. Planners could attempt to implement some forms of positive action (such as employing translators, providing transport to meetings, etc.) in order to redress traditional socio-cultural imbalances and to equally privilege many different forms of discourse and communication (see, for example, Young, 1990, 1995). Incorporation of principles of positive action is necessary in my view to avoid domination of discussion by the already-advantaged, the articulate and the pushy. As planners are rarely seen by other participants as having a disinterested voice, there may also be a need for a strong and trusted external facilitator or mediator to withstand pressure from organised articulate groups (including the planners) both within and outside of the formal participation process.

It will also not be possible to avoid excluding some points of view or representations, such as those of future generations (see, for example, Eckersley (1999), O'Neill (2001)). It is therefore very important to recognise those exclusions, what they are, what they imply and for whom, instead of ignoring or concealing them.

There still remains potential for manipulation of the procedure, however, particularly if agencies are aware that if participants perceive they are being treated fairly, they will be more acquiescent. Planners should endeavour to be honest and transparent in their dealings with other participants so as not to give rise to a situation of false consciousness whereby people believe a given procedure to be structured and conducted fairly when in fact it is not.[12]

Because discursive processes rely on the powers of persuasion it may be relatively easy for more articulate participants to sway decisions. In such circumstances, agreements reached may be spurious. 'Weaker' participants may have been 'duped by offers they did not understand or overwhelmed by "offers" they dared not refuse' (O'Neill, 1993: 319). Facilitators may be necessary to ensure that all participants fully comprehend all arguments and proposals. There may also be a case for a 'cooling off' period (perhaps a week?) for people to be able to think through the implications of arguments and proposals.

Tyler and Blader (2000) have incorporated several of the above aspects of procedural justice into their new group engagement model (Figure 4.1).

The meaning of procedural justice	Procedural justice and co-operation	Connections to the group	Motivations for co-operation	Types of co-operative behaviour

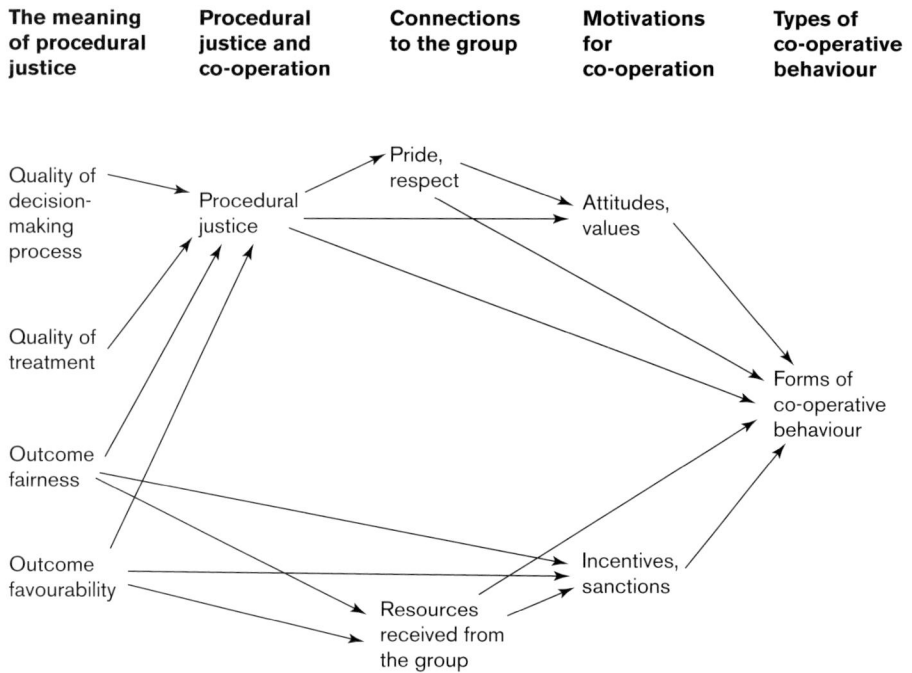

Figure 4.1 The group engagement model (Source: Tyler and Blader, 2000: 16)

In such a model procedures are evaluated not, or less, by the outcomes to which they lead but by relational criteria, including assessments of neutrality and trustworthiness of the authorities (judged by both formal rules and informal actions)[13] and the degree to which people are treated with dignity and to which respect is accorded their rights. Tyler and Blader emphasise that participants' assessment of the quality of their treatment during the process is as important as the quality of the decision-making process itself.

Also important are an image of the favourability or fairness of the outcome/s which participants receive and the resources (including tangible resources such as status, pride and respect) gained and/or lost through participation. As Tyler and Blader state:

> the fairness of group processes and procedures is an important determinant of how people relate to groups and a key antecedent of their group-oriented co-operative behaviour. Both co-operative behaviour itself, and the social attitudes and values that encourage such behaviour, are strongly affected by procedural fairness judgements (2000: 79).

Does a participatory decision-making system which is procedurally just meet the preferences of different members of society? It cannot satisfy everyone in terms of outcomes, but it may go some way towards satisfying participants that they have been treated as fairly as possible. Planners should bear in mind Eide's assertion that the 'task as planners is not to define people's problems for them and calculate the "right" solution' (in Wildavsky, 1979: 261), but to increase people's capacities of defining their own problems and working through avenues of response together with them. Public policy-makers have an ethical responsibility to serve the varying needs of all different constituencies rather than simply acting as arbiters of the particularistic interests of those with the loudest voices (Jennings, 1987). All those individuals toward whom the policy is directed or who will be affected by the policy decision could be actively brought into a procedurally just deliberative process in which the goals and values of the policy are discussed and formulated. How people are treated in the participation process is often as important as what they get as a result of it. The participation process could thus represent a genuine and sincere effort by planners to incorporate people's views and experience, rather than a cosmetic exercise to quieten criticism.

There can be no one single procedure that maximises procedural justice applicable in all situations. Aspects of Lind and Tyler's (1988) two models of procedural justice, however, offer us some valuable insight. Lind and Tyler (1988: 222–30) outline a model of *informed self-interest* which suggests that people are fundamentally concerned with maximising their own outcomes, but are prepared to curb their egoistic preferences in order to obtain outcomes that are available only through cooperation with others. A fundamental compromise is 'the acceptance of outcomes and procedures on the basis of their fairness, rather than on the basis of their favourability to one's own interests' (1988: 223). People begin to take wider and longer-term perspectives of the issues involved. They begin to balance short-term personal gain and long-term benefits. Tolerance for negative outcomes is increased.

The *group value* model (Lind and Tyler, 1988: 230–40) suggests that individuals working in groups are more likely to put aside their own self-interest and act in a way that helps all group members. Such behaviour should hold for individuals acting as representatives of groups/organisations as well as those negotiating in a group round-table situation. The main strength of the group value model, according to the authors, is 'in accounting for such effects as the value-expressive function of voice and the importance of politeness and dignity as factors in procedural justice' (1988: 239).

It is apparent from procedural justice literature that people react to procedures in ways explicable by both self-interest and group value models. The two sets of psychological processes seem to be functioning at the same time, with each set affecting the participants' beliefs, attitudes and behaviours.

Taking these two models into consideration suggests that we could benefit from establishing procedures of participatory planning decision-making which observe universals of procedural justice such as fairness, respect, dignity, truthfulness, impartiality and so on, but which are contextual and have a sensitivity to the particularities of difference of participants.

The model of discursive democratic decision-making developed in this chapter offers a way forward. The communicative interaction component of the model offers a method of conflict resolution which encourages collaborative methods of decision-making. Incorporation of procedural justice into communicative interaction strengthens Habermas' ideas[14] and shifts the burden of communicative interaction from consensus achievement to that of a fair and just ongoing moral conversation. The core concept of procedurally just communicative action, then, is not that everyone could or would agree to exactly the same set of principles or policy outcomes, but that these principles or outcomes have been adopted as a result of a procedure that all are ready to deem reasonable and fair. 'It is not the *result* of the process of moral judgement alone that counts but the *process* for the attainment of such judgement which plays a role in its validity and, I would say, moral worth' (Benhabib, 1990c: 12).

Benhabib's comment raises the thorny issue of whether Habermasian based communicative practice becomes so bound up with procedures that it omits consideration of outcomes. Habermas would answer that his theorising provides consideration of both aspects in a social epistemology: 'a way in which political communities can arrive at justified agreement as to what is just' (Campbell, 2001: 245).

In an ideal world, justice and the outcome of communicatively democratic decision-making procedures would coincide. Coincidence would occur because the discursive process would be transparent, maximising the socio-economic and cultural knowledge available to all participants. Everyone would thus be able to understand each other's experiences and value their priorities based on such mutual understanding. According to Young (1993), this form of comprehensive social understanding would contribute to the transformation of participants from being motivated by self-interest to being motivated by justice. It would also develop some of the 'social wisdom' necessary to arrive at just decisions. Justice would thus be 'discovered or invented by all those affected by a problem or policy coming together and discussing it under circumstances free from domination; the most just solution is the one they all can agree to under those circumstances of free speech' (Young, 1993: 17).

CONCLUSIONS

My view of discursive democracy in the model developed in this chapter is of a process of open discussion in which all points of view can be heard and that the policy outcome/s which result/s is/are legitimate when they reflect the mutual understandings (through reciprocity, reflexivity, respect, cooperation, etc.) that preceded them. I do not regard there as being any 'correct answer' to be found. One of the key aspects of policy-making through power-full communicative interaction is its contingency. It is a flexible process, the scale of and participation in which can be adapted to the particular situation. Policy-making through discursive democracy is directed towards the evolution of society to meet the needs of its constituents rather than adjusting and normalising individuals to fit the needs of the state and the discipline of urban and regional planning.

I have developed my current model of local discursive democracy from a critique of the work of Jürgen Habermas and Michel Foucault, centred on the theme of discursive argument. I regard key aspects of the work of Habermas and Foucault to be complementary rather than oppositional, as neither scheme alone provides an adequate framework (see also Alexander, 2001). I have attempted, therefore, not to choose between them but to reconcile them in constructing a theoretically informed yet practical model of decision-making. It recognises that, in land-use planning decisions, actors will behave both communicatively and strategically at different times. It is a model which incorporates working through instead of with differences and pooling power in attempting to negotiate emancipatory and capacitating, procedurally just policy decisions at the local level.

As Habermas (1990) admitted, his framework does not aim to set up substantive orientations and ends, but rather it establishes a *procedure* by which consensual ends or decisions can be reached. Together with the recognition of power structures brought from Foucault, the model of discursive democracy or planning through debate offers a way forward in the development of a creative, inventive form of planning rather than merely a power-broking form (Healey, 1993, 1997a).

In subsequent chapters I examine potential shortcomings of this model as revealed by stories from practice, and begin to build a new theory which aims to account for the realities of practice and communicative power-plays.

PART 3

CHIAROSCURO PRACTICE: THE SHADES AND LIGHTS OF PLANNING

CHAPTER 5

SHADOW MAGICS

Through assembling (choice) bits …
one may bring alive,
open the text to multiple ways of knowing
  and multiple sets of meaning,
allow multiple voices to be heard,
  to speak to (or past) each other
    as well as to the contexts from which they emerge
      and to which they contribute.
(Pred, 1997: 135)

INTRODUCTION

A feature of planning practice in the Western world in the late twentieth and early twenty-first centuries has been an insistence that 'room must be made for progress; the essential facilities of a growing … society must go somewhere' (Plotkin, 1987: 2). The empirical patterns of land use which represent such 'progress', however, are often the results of the complex interplay of actors' diverse cultural perceptions, images and values underlying the activity of local planning policy-making. To divorce analysis of the output from the process amounts to divorcing analysis of action from discourse. Such a divorce misconstrues the nature of planning decision-making. As a result, we fail to understand the choices through which people become participants in processes and contribute to decisions.

In this part, I tell and analyse stories from the real world of planning practice. I engage in reflective consideration of the role of cultural perceptions, images, values and mind-sets in local planning policy-making. I tell stories which unpack and discuss the ways in which different planners and community groups perceive themselves, their or others' geographical places and other groups respectively, revealing cultural differences of self- and place-identity, of discourses and values – in other words, situated knowledges and representations of such. I explore, with relation to actor-networks, ways in which these different values and mind-sets affect planning outcomes and relate to systemic power structures.

I utilise empirical material from a path-breaking Habermasian-inspired public participation strategy for strategic planning policy-making (Chapter 6) and from an extensive consultative resource-management exercise (Chapter 7). The stories illustrate the advantages of inclusive planning, but also the unforeseen problems and pitfalls which may occur, such as exclusion of certain values, unresolvable differences of opinion, tactics of lobbying, etc. and which may result in unjust outcomes for some groups in society and for the environment. In analysing these stories, I reveal the underlying values and power-plays which lie beneath the shadows and which a Habermasian model of practice omits.

I am motivated (as is Forester, 1999) to integrate a power-full understanding of practice with the importance of representation, of how practical performances not only make meaning, but enact complex relations of power. The stories thus 'organis[e] attention, practically and politically, not only to the facts at hand, but to why the facts at hand matter' (Forester, 1999: 29).

It is my hope that, on reading such stories, planning practitioners will find moments and themes which resonate with their own practice lives, and that these moments and themes will broaden their understanding of the 'fluid and conflictual, deeply political and always surprising world they are in' (Forester, 1999: 26), and will stimulate reflection on how they could possibly work differently and more effectively. Practical 'rationality' depends far less on regulations and formulae than on a practical understanding of the specifics of a situation, the ability to unpack its complex messiness and to react appropriately.

In telling the stories I emphasise not only the politics of, but also the multiple relationships which constitute local policy- and place-making: the networking, negotiations and bargaining activities which take place within and between groups of actors. These are often the real 'powered-up' sites in which options and decisions are generated (McGuirk, 2000). Like Forester, I aim to demonstrate how insight into planning practice can lead to stronger and deeper planning theory.

I introduce three particular frameworks in this chapter: those of representation, actor-network theory and of lobbying. I outline these frameworks below before introducing the context for my practice stories.

REPRESENTATION

As Harvey (1993: 17) writes: 'the material practices and experiences entailed in the construction and experiential qualities of place must be ... interrelated with the way places are both represented and imagined'. An understanding of the subject in practice is fundamental for planners. Subjectivity is always present in the framing of representations (Schon and Rein, 1994). 'We do frame representations: we explicitly formulate what our world is like, what we aim at, what we are doing' (Taylor, 1993: 49–50).

Actors form representations of themselves, of others and of 'objects', such as nature. Representations are 'uttered' verbally through texts; oral, written (in hard copy or electronically) and/or graphic (cartoons, photographic or video images) (see, for example, Lynch and Woolgar, 1990). The representations on which decisions and actions are taken are thus virtual representations narrated through texts and interpreted through practices of reading.

Actors contend with each other over the definition of a problematic policy situation. As Schon and Rein (1994: 29) write: 'their struggles over the naming and framing of a policy situation are symbolic contests over the social meaning of an issue domain, where meaning implies not only what is at issue but what is to be done'.

Framing refers to a particular way of representing knowledge (Goffman, 1974; Rein, 1989; Tannen, 1993), interpreting problems and providing an evaluative framework for judging how to act. Frames therefore make sense of complex realities for different people and often form the basis for action.

Harvey (1973: 31) suggests if that we are to 'evaluate the spatial form of the city, we must, somehow or other, understand its creative meaning as well as its mere physical dimensions'. We need to go beyond identification of conflicts of interest to unpack the cultural differences in participants' lifeworlds which influence their ways of giving meaning, value and expression to tangibles and intangibles and the different aspects of meaning which are formulated through such interpretations: the poetics of place. We need to understand how the same sets of signs are read differently by different people and how people make connections between their interpretations of things and the overall ordering process of the planning system.

It should not be surprising, then, that people react to proposals for urban change in a variety of ways, not all of which are comprehensible to others involved, yet which may well be patterns of action guided by deeply entrenched beliefs, norms and values from their lifeworlds. 'Social space, therefore, is made up of a complex of individual feelings and images about and reactions towards the spatial symbolism which surrounds that individual' (Harvey, 1973: 34). It should also not be surprising that many of these different images and values conflict with and counteract each other.

Planners' traditional 'external' and powerful location has important implications for the understanding and discussion of claims, values and identities. It has tended to obviate a truly participatory approach in which participants have the opportunity to enter into relationships of reciprocal respect. Instead, it has hegemonically validated particular, specific forms of evidence, stressed the importance of a separation between the knower and the known, and treated personal characteristics of the knower as irrelevant. Observations are regarded as objective intellectual positions rather than as social constructs, thereby denying local contextuality and difference. Stories are irrelevant.

Professional planners have thus tended to practise a framework which preserves a rupture between the actual, local, historically situated experiential
representations of local people and a systematically developed 'expert' consciousness of society. They pursue a Cartesian vision from nowhere (Nagel, 1986; Hillier
and van Looij, 1997), engaging Haraway's (1991) 'god-trick' in which they stand
outside the world they inhabit as a layperson outside work hours, divorcing themselves from the reality of their 'lay' experiences. Planning practice transposes the
represented 'reality' of people into the conceptual currency by which it is governed.
In this way, planning practice legislates reality rather than discovers it.

Planners fail to recognise that their own rational technical discourse and its
professional terms and definitions are themselves social constructs. Moreover, they
deny themselves, as well as other participants, the opportunity to ensure that their
stories are respectfully understood. Stories provide a link between private and public realms, they provide insights into meanings, behaviours, values, representations,
images and identities.

Places become earmarked for development or redevelopment, alternatively
writing off the people who live in them as private or public tenants as worthless
whilst simultaneously boosting the land values for those who own it. The
political–economic possibilities of place re/construction become coloured
(metaphorically and physically) by the evaluative practices of place representation.

Through recognition that 'norms, beliefs, identity and practices are intersubjectively constituted and historically and contextually contingent' (Leonard, 1990:
261) we can explore different values, images and identities and how they relate in
the planning process. It offers the opportunity to examine the 'knowing from within'
(Shotter, 1993) of various participants and how such knowing is relationally placed
within social, moral and political systems.

In addressing influences on the formation and expression of participants' values,
representations, images and identities, Habermas' concept of the lifeworld provides
us with a helpful starting point. In brief, participants' lifeworlds comprise their perspectives of the acting subject. The lifeworld is a product of both historical traditions
surrounding people and the processes of socialisation in which they are reared
(Habermas, 1990: 137). Lifeworlds are both situation and background, both conscious and unconscious (Love, 1995: 57).

Actors (and therefore their lifeworlds) come together at nodal points, or temporary fixations, around which identities and politics are sutured in dialogic
contestation of identities. A communicative participation programme can act in this
manner as the nodal point or temporary fixation for the meaning and discussion of
identities and values.

In the stories narrated in this part I move from a focus on the representation and
the 'object' thus constituted to focus on the relations through which that object arises.

Networks and actor-network theory

Mulgan (1997: 20) comments that the 'defining feature of this world is connexity'. The potential decision influence of interrelated networks of actors is receiving a resurgence of attention (although without the closed-system limitations of its heyday in the early 1970s), drawing particularly on research from disciplines such as anthropology, sociology and social work (see, for example, Willmott, 1986; Mulgan and Landry, 1995; Burns and Taylor, 1997) and recognition of the importance of the networks which people call upon as part of their coping strategies in 'everyday life' (Gilroy and Speak, 1998; Healey, 1998b). Networks may be understood as complex sets of social relations along which energy flows. The planning system directs, prevents and stimulates such flows in various directions, based on some, often unarticulated, concept of the 'public good' or 'public interest'.

Plan-making is located within a series of alliances and networks of governance activity. The process of planning reflects the quality of such relationships, or their 'interrelational capacity', as actors affect and are affected by, negotiate and re-negotiate rules and procedures, discourses and power relations (Healey, 1997b, 1997c).

Society comprises 'a web of interlocking networks of affiliation and interaction which are structured around a multiplicity of institutions, formal and informal' (Amin and Hausner, 1997: 10). Networks are relational links through which people can obtain access to material resources, knowledge and power. The role of networks as a form of mutual community support has a well-documented history (e.g. Young and Wilmott, 1957; Gans, 1962; Stack, 1975; Burns and Taylor, 1997), especially with regard to the urban poor and inhabitants of remoter rural communities. In addition, authors including Amin and Hausner (1997) and Jessop (1990, 1997) among others, are increasingly recognising that economic actors operate similarly through associational networks. Although some networks will be formally incorporated, others will be informal and *ad hoc*, mobilising various actors on a perceived 'as needs' basis. Actors may draw upon several of their individual multiple relational networks (such as a lawyer golfing partner, a planning officer from the Parent Teacher Association, in addition to more formal ties with others through business and/or political contact) in selecting interaction on a particular issue.

The institutional capital and capacity (Amin and Thrift, 1995a; Healey, 1997b) generated by such networks thus embraces the collective abilities of the actors' relationships, alliances and coalitions tempered by the contexts and arenas in which they come together. A major factor leading to inequality between actors and their ability to influence policy outcomes may therefore lie in the socio-economic and political richness of the networks to which they have access.

It is apparent that different types of actors, rationalities and networks often coexist. As Hunter and Staggenborg (1988) and Amin and Hausner (1997) indicate, however, it becomes important not simply to recognise the existence of such links, but also to consider the form, type and qualities (including strength of ties, form of power relations, etc.) of the networks involved if we are to understand the complexities of policy-making activity.

Recognition of the existence and importance of interpersonal contacts or networks in decision-making has led to the development of policy network theory as part of the wider conceptual literature on subgovernments, policy coalitions and issue networks. As Jordan (1990) explains, the idea of subgovernments, as outlined in the USA by Griffith (1939), Freeman (1955), Lowi (1964) and Cater (1964), argued that governmental policy decisions are made through informal 'whirlpools' or centres of activity in which actors interested in that area of policy participate within the system of government. 'A subgovernment consists primarily of a limited number of interest group advocates, legislators and their aides, and key agency administrators who interact on a stable, ongoing basis and dominate policy-making in a particular area' (Berry, 1989: 239). Lowi (1964) further identified a regularised or 'iron' triangular relationship between such actors and pointed out that the private interests involved in the subgovernments could actually become dominant.

Gradually, this image of a narrow, stable, tightly controlled subgovernment became anachronistic and the restricted notion of subgovernment was replaced in the USA in the 1960s by the more flexible, more conflictual concept of a policy network (Atkinson and Coleman, 1992; Rhodes and March, 1992). Policy networks or communities are predominantly, but not essentially, based on an interpersonal basis of contacts rather than the formalised structure of subgovernments. They are 'sets of developed linkages between groups through which communication occurs, information and other resources are transferred and alliances continue to shift' (Dalton, 1996: 199). Rhodes and Marsh (1992) identify five types of networks by degree of openness ranging from tightly knit policy communities to loosely integrated issue networks. (See Table 5.1.)

As indicated by Table 5.1, policy communities have restricted memberships and arrangements are characterised by a shared understanding of policy problems with limited disagreement over the possible range of solutions (Dalton, 1996: 201). In contrast, issue networks are open to the entry of any groups able to claim an interest in an issue. They are often temporary and *ad hoc*, existing whilst the issue remains important, and bringing together a wide range of actors often with little in common other than the issue at hand. Conflict between actors is rife. These concepts would appear to embrace the activities of professional officers, perhaps in conjunction with an elite of societal actors, often economic agents (a policy community), and of the various groups and individuals involved in participating in a local planning decision (an issue network).

Table 5.1 Types of policy networks: characteristics of policy communities and issue networks

Dimension	Policy community	Issue network
Membership number of participants	Very limited number, some groups consciously excluded	Large
Type of interest	Economic and/or professional interests dominate	Encompasses range of affected interests
Integration frequency of interaction	Frequent, high-quality interaction of all groups on all matters related to policy issue	Contacts fluctuate in frequency and intensity
Continuity	Membership, values and outcomes persistent over time	Access fluctuates significantly
Consensus	All participants share basic values and accept the legitimacy of the outcome	A measure of agreement exists, but conflict is ever present
Resources distribution of resources (within network)	All participants have resources; basic relationship is an exchange relationship	Some participants may have resources, but they are limited, and basic relationship is consultative
distribution of resources (within participating organisations)	Hierarchical; leaders can deliver members	Varied and variable distribution and capacity to regulate members
Power	There is a balance of power among members, although one group may dominate	Unequal powers, reflecting unequal resources and unequal access. It is a zero-sum game

Source: Rhodes & Marsh (1992: 251)

Rhodes and Marsh's (1992) typology may be criticised for relegating the issue of power to being only one of a number of dimensions in their analysis. In contrast, Howlett and Ramesh's (1995) adaptation of van Waarden's (1992) and Lindquist's (1992) work provides an interesting taxonomy of various forms of policy network categorised according to the role and relative power of state/societal relations within the network (Table 5.2).

Another recent addition to the policy network literature is the concept of an Advocacy Coalition Framework developed by Sabatier (1987, 1993, 1999). The distinctive feature of the Advocacy Coalition Framework is its emphasis on the role of ideas and values in the policy process. Sabatier (1993: 27) argues that shared beliefs are the principal 'glue' of politics. He suggests (1987) that coalitions form around 'deep core' beliefs of shared fundamental normative and ontological axioms.

Table 5.2 Taxonomy of policy networks

		Number/Type of network participants			
		State agencies	*One major societal group*	*Two major societal groups*	*Three or more groups*
State/societal relations within network	*State directed*	bureaucratic network	clientelistic network	triadic network	pluralistic network
	Society directed	participatory statist network	captured network	corporatist network	issue network

Source: Howlett & Ramesh (1995: 130)

There is consensus between actors within the coalition on a 'policy core' of basic choices with regard to the issue at hand, while 'secondary aspects' are open to negotiation and compromise. This structure would also seem to apply at the inter-coalition scale in instances of conflict between two or more belief systems. Whereas coalitions are unlikely to shift ground on their core beliefs, they may be prepared to make compromises on the secondary aspects. These concepts may facilitate our understanding of the differences which certain patterns of relations may make to policy outcomes.

If we regard the various networks of participants involved in decision-making processes as complex sets of energy flows, by unpacking and deciphering these networks and their representations we may be able to begin to understand more clearly the values, issues and interests at stake and how social agency (pressure/interest groups, etc.) is constructed in the process itself.

Although owing allegiance to (and therefore limited by) systems theory, popular in the 1970s, Friend, Power and Yewlett's (1974: 348) exploration of energy flows in planning decision networks retains much of its relevance today. In particular, the propositions that 'planning necessarily involves explorations through inter-agency networks' and 'complexity in problem structure leads to bargaining over adjustments to shared opportunity space' and their empirical investigations into decision-networks in Britain provide an interesting forerunner to Flyvbjerg's (1998) recent analysis in Denmark and my analysis in Australia (Hillier, 2000a).

Local planning and policy decision-making processes involve the complex interplay of a range of actors (planning officers, elected members, members of local communities, technical and other experts and professionals, etc.). Each actor brings their own (or their group's) representations of issues, places and nature to the process.

The question of which representation/s will prevail is the result of the negotiations and conflicts of formal public participation processes, informal lobbying manoeuvres and so on. No representations are neutral. No decision is neutral. The concept of actor-networks, explained briefly below, offers a methodology to unpack the various strands of negotiation and help our understanding of the ways in which different values and representations influence planning outcomes.

land-use planning decision-making processes act as points of temporary fixation for the meaning of place as networks of actors with different representations come together. Conflicting representations are temporally and temporarily linked in discursive or dialogic contestation.

In an actor-network, actors in discrete situations become bound into wider sets of relations which alter the nature of their existing worlds (Murdoch and Marsden, 1995: 378n3). Commitment to such networks provides forms of identity and the basis for action. In activities such as public participation, several different actor-networks (including those of non-human 'actors', such as aspects of nature (especially Callon's (1986) example of scallops in St Brieuc Bay; and Latour, 1992), and non-human intermediaries between actors and networks, such as texts or money) will overlap and align with each other.

Constructing a new network/s by drawing upon actors and intermediaries already in established networks (e.g. the local authority planning system, residents' associations, etc.), the actor-network approach thus combines aspects of economics (it is things which draw actors into relationships), sociology (actors come to define themselves, and others, through interaction), and politics (Murdoch, 1995: 752). It allows us to begin to understand how certain actors/networks are able to impose their views over those of others.

Actor-network theory is based on the idea that as actors struggle with each other, they determine their existence, define their characteristics and attempt to exert themselves upon others through various human and non-human intermediaries. Callon (1986, 1991) terms the act of an actor exerting itself upon others as 'translation'. This process involves the four, but not necessarily sequential or mutually separate, stages of

- incorporation – actors join and are woven into networks;
- interessement – actors exert influence over others via persuasion that their position is the best one. Competing alliances are undermined;
- enrolment – actors lock others into their definitions and network so that their behaviour is channelled in the direction desired by the enrolling actor/s;
- mobilisation – the actor now speaks for/acts as ventriloquist for (Haraway, 1992)/represents the others who have become 'redefined' and passive. The representations of interest made by the lead actors are accepted as legitimate by those ostensibly being represented. The represented are reduced to being recipients of action.

Translation is therefore the mechanism by which society and nature or 'social nature' (Whatmore and Boucher, 1993) takes form. Unpacking these mechanisms enables us to begin to understand some of the power relationships in the decision process, explaining 'how a few obtain the right to express and to represent the many silent actors of the social and natural worlds they have mobilised' (Callon, 1986: 224).

The notion of power is central to the actor-network approach, developing, as it does, Foucauldian ideas of power/knowledge. Action is power-full. 'Those who are powerful are not those who "hold" power but those who are able to enrol, convince and enlist others into associations on terms which allow these initial actors to "represent" all the others' (Murdoch and Marsden, 1995: 372). In so doing, they displace or speak for the others whom they have deprived of a voice by imposing their definitions, images and perceptions upon them.[1] A network is thus composed of representations of beliefs, values, images and identities, of self, others and place, including nature and the environment. Debate and conflict occur if new representations challenge ('betray') the legitimacy of the old.

Actors will utilise whatever resources/intermediaries (including scientific documents, surveys, petitions, etc.) are available to them in order to persuade other actors to their representation or view in the pursuit of their goals.[2] Inevitably, some actors will be able to mobilise greater resources than others. In addition, although representers claim to speak for those represented, 'a representation cannot capture all there is to be represented' (Marsden et al., 1993: 31). The represented, or non-present (e.g. nature, people of lower socio-economic status who tend not to participate, those not yet moved into the area, the unborn, etc.) could always 'say' more and differently. 'Translation' if left to its own devices is seldom equitable or just.

Place and the environment are therefore 'shaped' by the representations of actor-networks. They are dynamic—constructed representations by actors at a particular point in time, building upon the remains of previous rounds of representation and struggle.[3]

Actor-network theory deflects the focus of policy-making analysis away from the idea of self-contained propositional utterances 'spoken from nowhere' by planners as though in a neutral space, towards 'textured locations where it matters who is speaking and where and why, and where such mattering bears directly upon the possibility of knowledge claims, moral pronouncements, descriptions of "reality" achieving acknowledgment, going through' (Code, 1995: x). Translation becomes a struggle for discursive hegemony and a means of representing the reality of nature and society (whatever it may be), remaking it and altering it in the process.

It is also important to note that the struggle over translation does not take place in a vacuum, but in the context of the existing institutional praxis and actor-spaces (Law, 1992) of planning. This gives planners and those participants who are comfortable with the discourse of planning a distinct advantage over those who are not. The abilities to 'persuade, impress and inspire … are distributed unevenly' (Turner, 1994: 111), and as a result, 'any representation tends to take sides, even as it comforts itself with the illusion that it does not' (Clegg and Hardy, 1996: 698).

Power in a Latourian sense is the ability to get others to perform actions. It is a performative collective action enacted in interactions between actors rather than held by a singular actor (Callon and Law, 1995). Networked interaction is thus not something that takes place within a power structure, but is rather the process through which that power structure is actually created, reproduced and altered. The processes through which power is enacted are unstable and dynamic and as McGuirk (2000: 653) describes, power is 'a fluid effect, mobilised through the performance of interactions, composed and reproduced in the myriad networks and associations of governance'.

LOBBYING AS DIRECT ACTION

Following Melucci's (1996) understanding of direct action as intervention in the political system, breaking the 'rules of the game', we can distinguish between formal and informal (Lukes, 1974; Ostrom, 1990; Harvey N., 1996; Healey, 1997d), insider and outsider (Jordan and Maloney, 1997; Cracknell, 1993) or institutional and non-institutional (Offe, 1985) activities. As bargaining, decision-making and influencing activities increasingly take place outside of the formal structures and processes of governance, informal, outsider or non-institutional activities are playing a more important role.

Insider strategies may be summarised as attempts to influence decisions from within the institutions of the planning system, thereby implying a willingness on behalf of actors to abide by the formal rules set down. Outsider strategies, in contrast, tend to rely either on generating sufficient public concern through the media to force decision-makers' hands on vote-sensitive issues, and/or lobbying decision-makers directly.[4]

Forms of direct action, such as lobbying,[5] have probably been a part of governance as long as governments have existed. Groups and individuals have lobbied for purposes of receiving information and for stating their cases for or against something. Lobbying is intrinsically related to power. People lobby those with greater power in order for they themselves in turn to achieve more power. Pal (1997: 213) provides a succinct description of the essential differences between lobbying, representation and consultation activity (Table 5.3).

Table 5.3 Differences between lobbying, representation and consultation

	Lobbying	Representation	Consultation
Direction of communication	primarily one-way, from interest groups to government	primarily one-way, from interest groups, associations, elected politicians and experts to government	primarily two-way, from government to groups or clients, and from those groups and clients to government
Objective	to change legislation or policy to suit the interests being represented	to convey views, information, perspectives and interests of a broader community into the policy process	to improve service as well as support for services and policies through communication with clients and stakeholders
Government	viewed primarily as key decision-makers, politicians and senior officials	viewed primarily as the political executive	viewed primarily as the department or agency delivering services
Non-government	viewed primarily as interest groups and associations representing relatively narrow or specific interests	viewed primarily as citizens with fairly general interests and values that need to be reflected in the policy process	viewed primarily as clients and stakeholders with respect to a specific policy or programme
Examples	industry association meets with minister, resident action groups petition to elected representatives, senior officials telephone minister	elections, polling, task forces and royal commissions	round-tables, extended workshops that involve discussion and analysis of policy issues and programme design and delivery

Source: adapted from Pal (1997: 213)

The traditional 'model' of planning policy-making, directed by government, supplemented by representation from the public, holds decreasing validity at the beginning of the twenty-first century as analysts and practitioners realise the importance of complex networks and associational systems and the strategic value and power of information. Policy outcomes depend on the actors in communities and the nature of their networks.

The operating reality of local decision-making for many planning issues in the 2000s is of a 'churning collection of the "involved" variously competing and co-operating with one another to influence the multiple levers and vast activities of government' (Heclo, 1989: 312). The question to which I now turn is that of *why* the various factions join an issue network and become 'involved'.

Theoretical explanations of lobbying developed in the USA vary markedly from those developed in Britain and Europe, reflecting the different practices experienced in each system, as demonstrated well by Eyerman and Jamison (1991). What is evident across virtually all Western systems, however, is that a traditional association between political unrest and the lower classes has been inverted. Protests and demands for participation are now more likely to be expressed by the well-educated and articulate, professionally oriented middle classes concerned by perceived threats and risks to their quality of life. The important issue is that these groups of people already have political and economic standing and through their position in issue networks serve to further their advantage over those on the political and economic margins.

I term as 'reactive' a set of theories which locate lobbying activity as a result of some disturbance to or deprivation for a group or individual. Disturbance theories (e.g. Truman, 1951) suggest that people are stimulated to organise and lobby other actors because they are affected by a disturbance (such as a planning proposal) which changes their 'equilibrium' (social, economic, environmental, etc.) with society. Deprivation theories are similar in that they suggest that protest and lobbying are primarily based on feelings of frustration and political alienation (Dalton, 1988). There thus exists an identifiable cause-and-effect relationship between some event/s and lobbying activity in reactive theories.

'Proactive' theories, alternatively, are those which regard direct action as an important resource to gain certain ends. Ostrom's (1992) account of opportunistic rent-seeking activity falls into this category. Rent-seeking involves making active efforts to obtain disproportionate advantage from activities by attempting to manipulate the people who make decisions. As theorised in the USA by Olson (1965) and Tilly (1975), the resource-mobilisation model regards protest and lobbying activity as a valid and normal political resource to be used by groups in pursuit of their objectives.

Essential differences between the two approaches include resource-mobilisation theories as being proactive, offensive, teleological, strategic and predominantly US-based, focusing on a group level of organisations and treating individuals as depersonalised units, thereby silencing the subject. In contrast, disturbance theories are reactive, defensive, and predominantly European-based, focused on individual motivation and socialisation, concerned at an 'actor' level where interest is centred on individual and personalised group actions.

As we shall see below, pressure group activity (lobbying, etc.) may include aspects of both approaches. Lobbying is not simply an outlet for feelings of frustration and alienation. Policy or process dissatisfaction may provide the motivation to lobby, but the activity of lobbying itself may be more appropriately explained by the resource-mobilisation model.

What are the implications of these theories for local planning decision-making? As identified above, key components of direct action or lobbying activity are communication and interpersonal networks with access to people in positions of power. These aspects often privilege the already privileged.[6] Marginalised groups in society become further excluded from decision-making processes as privileged oligarchies form which result in decisions further favouring established interests and perpetuating social injustice.

In addition, Flyvbjerg's (1998a: 141) analysis of planning decisions in Denmark reveals that actions are often dictated by whatever works best to achieve one's aims: 'the raw exercise of power tends to be more effective than appeals to objectivity, facts, knowledge, rationality, or the "better argument", even though rationalisation may be used to legitimate the exercise of raw power'. Flyvbjerg lists such strategies as including pulling strings, overt politicisation, making undocumented assertions, manipulation of facts, outright lying, use of the media and letter writing to key actors as being 'part of the arsenal' (1998: 193) of informal action. Compared with such activity, Habermasian formal rational argument tends to hold a much weaker position.

CHIAROSCURO AS REVEALED HALVES: DISCOURSES, STORY-LINES AND STORIES

In the practice stories which follow I present examples of discursive debates over representations of the meanings and values of land and nature. I define discourse as 'a specific ensemble of ideas, concepts and categorisations that are produced, reproduced, and transformed in a particular set of practices and through which meaning is given to physical and social realities' (Hajer, 1995: 44). Whilst these case studies do not delve into the different levels at which discourse operates (see Healey, 1999), attention is paid not only to the content of what is uttered, but also to its contextual frame. I demonstrate how certain networks of groups or actors attempt to transform the dominant discourse of government to undermine the accepted discourse and to deploy a new discourse, with new frames and story-lines.

A story-line is 'a generative sort of narrative that allows actors to draw upon various discursive categories to give meaning to specific physical or social phenomena' (Hajer, 1995: 56). Hajer suggests that people do not draw on comprehensive discourse systems in their arguments, but that they use selected story-lines to evoke, perhaps subconsciously, a wider discourse. Story-lines, rhetoric and symbolism play important roles in ordering people's understanding of issues and of positioning them in debate. Story-lines are reductionist. They simplify the complexity of an issue and allow other (lay) actors to relate the debate to themselves.

The two stories I relate in the following chapters demonstrate the chiaroscuro of planning; its shades and lights. Chiaroscuro is a generic term which does not describe a particular manner of operating. To illuminate my arguments, therefore, I refer to the terms tenebrism (sharply contrasted lights and darks as depicted in much of Caravaggio's work) and sfumato (a soft, delicate atmospheric haze or smoky effect produced by subtle transitions between areas of lighter and darker colour, as in the work of Leonardo da Vinci).

My tenebrist stories are taken from the Swan Valley in the North East Corridor of Perth, Western Australia. I tell stories from various groups of people involved in attempting to influence a planning decision concerned with urbanisation of a semi-rural area on the metropolitan fringe. My analysis is based on a contextualised reading of the discursive and symbolic terrain generated by the urbanisation proposal. I demonstrate how individuals and groups can reinterpret and reimagine place, symbols and practices, and how they can mobilise different values and logics to serve their purposes. As individuals, groups and organisations struggle to transform the social relations between them, they produce new 'truths' by which to explain and understand themselves, their practices and their societies.

I identify the use of strength, organisation, strategy, political contacts and influence outside of the formal participation process to influence decision-making in ways which may never formally enter the public domain, and may never be formally expressed, visible or recorded. They are unlikely to be normalised into a rational communicative, consensus-seeking debate.

As Phelps and Tewdwr-Jones (2000) point out, it is these realities of distortions, politics and power-plays which Habermasian theorists tend to overlook. These realities are the 'sub-surface interactions' which appear if one 'scratches the surface' of seemingly democratic, open and inclusionary planning processes. Such actions introduce the reality of politics into what was essentially a moral theory of Habermasian communicative action (see Flyvbjerg's (1998a) discussion of *Realpolitik* and *Realrationalität*). Power is integral to planning decisions. Knowledge and power are intrinsically related. The forms of power at work in society are embedded with knowledge – both of substance (what) and process (how) and equally those forms of knowledge are embedded with power relations.

My sfumato stories concern representations of nature, and especially those of old-growth forests in Western Australia. 'Planning represents an important institutional terrain for the contestation of the meaning and relations of the natural environment' (Whatmore and Boucher, 1993: 168). The contestation of environ-mental issues reflects both the complexity of the interrelationships between the various biotic and physical components of ecosystems which, due to their complex-ity, are open to competing interpretations and the varying socio-economic values which people attribute to ecosystems (Hayward, 1996). The justification for envi-ronmental policy planning rests ultimately on some conception of 'balancing' different values and representations in the determination of a desirable public good.

For environmental policy to be effective, however, it must deal with the incom-patibility of, and tensions between, the differing frames of the actors involved: e.g. the relatively short-term aspirations and economic values of some actors, the longer-term aspirations of conservation of other actors, and the capacity of institutions of governance. Examination of policy-making for forests as a strategic environmental resource offers an opportunity to analyse the tensions between an institutional need to respond to the multifunctional requirements of the international and local eco-nomics of the forestry industry and to pressures to retain a biologically diverse forested landscape of culturally intrinsic and instrumental value.

I examine the case study of the Regional Forest Agreement (RFA) process in south west Western Australia (WA) as an arena of political conflict over environ-mental resources. I show how different discourses and frames are used to interpret, contest and remould the policy agendas of environmental planning and natural resource management. An environment is therefore 'a certain kind of produced, lived and reproduced space constructed out of the struggles, compromises and temporarily settled relations of complexity and cooperating social actors: it is both a thing and a process' (Cline-Cole, 1998: 311).

I investigate the 'struggles, compromises and temporarily settled relations' of forest policy-making, identifying the strong political, economic and cultural dimen-sions which underlie conflicts and alliances. The forests of south western WA are situated at the nexus between global networks (of capital and trade) and national, regional and local socio-economic–political networks (of governance, labour unions, environmental interests, etc.). Tensions between the conflicting demands and values of these networks may be extreme. These tensions are concerned with power and the way groups of people dominate each other, as well as they way they seek to dominate nature.

I examine the socio-spatial narratives of the RFA process as strategic repre-sentations of the social relations both between groups of actors and between actors and the forests. In reality the trees cannot exist as a named entity outside the social relations of production. They are socially as well as physically, spatially and temporally embedded. They have no fixed meaning, but a variety of meanings attrib-uted through representation − representation necessarily by others, as trees themselves have no accepted individuality to participate in policy-making (Hillier,

2000b). Representation is politically organised subjection. To some actors, trees may signify part of an historic forest ecosystem; other actors may attribute them with spiritual significance, whilst others may see only the economic commodity of wood. The RFA process becomes a contest of packaging and promoting these plural rationalities of trees and forests, a contest in which some actors, it seems, can't see the trees for the wood.

Conclusion

I offer the two practice stories in the following chapters as they contain important underlying themes which are common internationally and with which practitioners from around the world should identify, although the specific legislative contexts may differ.

My ongoing relationships with these two stories over the past decade or so has enabled the collection of longitudinal narrative data which facilitates deeper understanding of processes and power-plays than would analysing a snapshot of frozen time from within the stories.

The stories also enable a practice-grounded critical reflection on the Habermasian and Foucauldian ideas discussed in Part 2. They illustrate omissions and shortcomings of the simple discursive model presented and point the way towards its refinement in order that it may more accurately reflect real-world practice.

CHAPTER 6

TENEBRISM IN THE NORTH EAST CORRIDOR⁷

CONTEXT

Perth is located in the south west of Western Australia (WA) on the Indian Ocean coast. Urban and regional planning began in WA with white settlement of an Aboriginal-occupied country in 1829. Since that time, the Perth metropolitan region has grown from a small, isolated colonial outpost into a modern metropolis with a population forecast of some two million people by 2021. Several local authorities, in particular those at the urban fringe, such as the Shire of Swan, are experiencing increases of up to six per cent a year, while population densities remain notoriously low. In 1990 Perth's overall urban density was just 10.8 persons per hectare, a figure comparable with that for rural Europe. Perth thus represents a sprawling mass whose tentacles are reaching out to devour the green fringes of the built-up area. The Swan Valley represents one of these fringes in the north east of the metropolitan area. Located in a region of overall water shortage, relying on ground water reserves, the valley is a delicate, low-lying environment with a high water table, prone to flooding. White residents enjoying semi-rural lifestyles, engaging in viticulture, smallholding farming and so on, live close to Aboriginal communities in an area of considerable Aboriginal and white settler heritage. The practice of settler communities living *on* the land, exploiting it for its natural resources and using it to grow crops and for building upon, contrasts starkly with the Aboriginal concept of living *with* the land, in sustainable harmony, a land alive with spirituality, rich with human sharing in the past and present. Yet what represents some 50,000 or so years of history and culture is in danger of disappearing under Western-influenced 'civilisation' and bureaucracy.

The strategic planning policy system in WA attempts to achieve broad policy objectives through the specification of private rights in land and property development through a regulatory approach to the zoning of land. Strategic plan-making is undertaken by shire/local authority planning officers in the context, in the Perth region, of the Metropolitan Region Scheme, a blueprint master zoning plan. Although public consultation is mandatory in some form, the Minister for Planning remains the final decision-maker. Local authority and state department strategies require Ministerial approval, which is by no means a fait accompli. The Minister can, and does, override local considerations in a 'wider interest'.

The North East Corridor (NEC) story effectively begins in 1985 when the Parliament of the State of Western Australia gave approval to the Swan Valley

Policy, designating the area as a green lung for the city of Perth (see Table 6.1). In 1987, however, the State Planning Commission (now Department of Planning and Urban Development (DPUD) and later the Ministry for Planning (MfP)), released its document *Planning for the Future of the Perth Metropolitan Region*, which proposed a corridor of urban development running through the area. Although never

Table 6.1 Timetable of events relating to proposed urban development in the Swan Valley and North East Corridor

1985	Swan Valley Policy approved by WA Parliament
1987	SPC *Planning for the Future of the Perth Metropolitan Region*
Dec 1990	DPUD release of *Metroplan*
	DPUD release of the *Urban Expansion Policy*
Jan 1991	Appointment of Swan Valley Development Officer
1991	Swan Valley Development Committee appointed
Mar–Aug 1991	Swan Valley Policy Review first draft
Oct 1991	Release of *North East Corridor Planning Issues and Growth Options*
Dec 1991	Swan Shire stance on key issues
	SVRRA form community involvement sub-committee
Jan 1992	Swan Valley Policy Review process completed
	Draft policy sent to Minister of Planning
Feb 1992	Shire proposes 'advisory committees'
	SVRRA lobbies for more participatory approach
Mar 1992	Round-table meeting
May 1992	Locality groups commence meetings
	Shire launches consultation process
	DPUD announces 21-week consultation period
Jul 1992	Advisory Group meeting – beginning of mistrust
Sep 1992	First draft Structure Plan presented by Shire
Oct 1992	Final Advisory Group meeting
	Environmental Audit presented on final day of submissions to DPUD
Nov 1992	Second draft Structure Plan presented by Shire and sent to DPUD
1993	Friends of the Valley formed
Mar 1994	*North East Corridor Structure Plan Final Version*. DPUD
May 1994	Perth–Darwin Highway proposals. DPUD
May 1994	Metropolitan Region Scheme (MRS) Major Amendment – North East Corridor. DPUD
1994	Voices of the Valley formed
Nov 1994	MRS Amendment presented in Parliament
	March on Parliament
	Swan Valley Planning Bill (1994) presented to Parliament
	MRS Amendment passed through Parliament
Jun 1995	Swan Valley Planning Bill passed
from 1995	Residential development of the North East Corridor

statutorily legislated, the strategy was released for public comment and residents began to realise that their area and lifestyle were under potential threat.

The land at Ellenbrook (see Figure 6.1) had been speculatively purchased at the end of the 1980s/early 1990s by a small number of private actors (dominated by one Japanese-owned and one Perth-owned development company) consolidating holdings around land transferred to Homeswest (the state housing authority) from other government departments, and implicitly rezonable as 'residential'. Once word spread of Homeswest's interest in a parcel of non-urban land, other speculative purchases were also made in the locality. Given the location of Ellenbrook in relation to the then urban fringe of Perth, and its requirements for infrastructure, pressure for urbanisation fell inevitably on the North East Corridor.

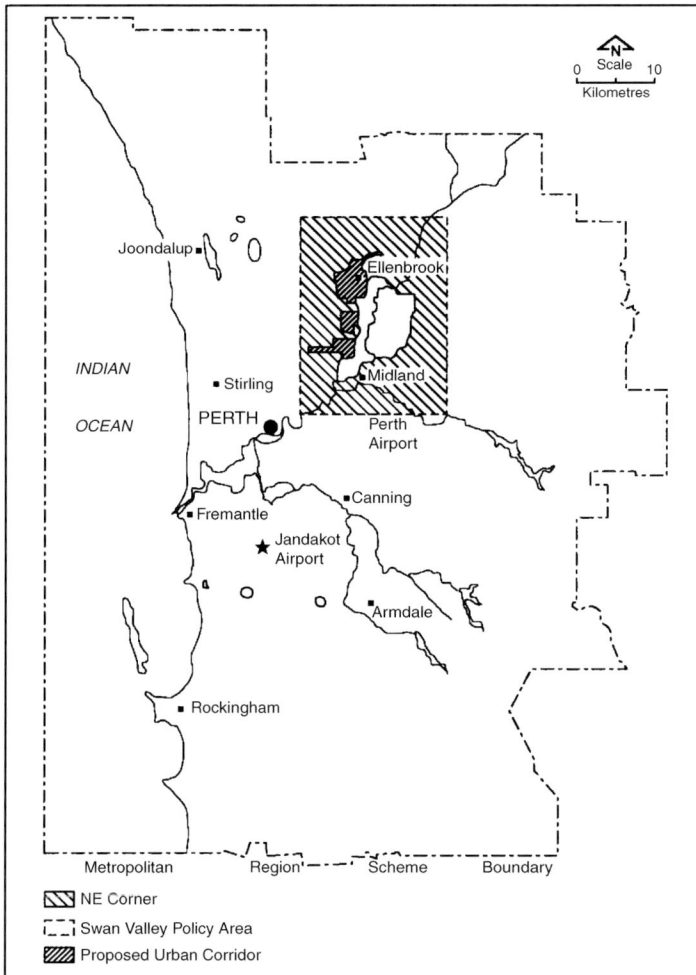

Figure 6.1 Location of the Swan Valley and the North East Corridor (Source: Hillier, 2000a: 41)

In 1990 DPUD released *Metroplan* and the *Urban Expansion Policy* which identified a potential population by 2021 of 225,000 people for the Swan Valley, an increase of some 220,000 over the existing total. The existing Swan Valley Residents' and Ratepayers' Association (SVRRA) began to gather information and to meet with local council officers and councillors and to lobby DPUD for a greater level of community input into the planning process.

In October 1991, however, DPUD released a further paper *Planning Issues and Growth Options* for the North East Corridor, being the first stage in the preparation of a detailed structure plan for urban development in the area. The public were asked for comment only on the two offered options of linear versus cellular growth in the valley to house an extra 140,000 people, but the SVRRA felt that residents should be entitled to greater participation. They therefore approached the planning department of the local authority, the Shire of Swan, to request a higher level of community consultation on the Shire's input to the North East Corridor issue. At the same time the SVRRA engaged in community consultation. It organised mail-drops, street meetings, public meetings and petitions to raise public awareness of the issue. SVRRA wanted to establish how residents felt about the issues and what they wanted the eventual outcome to be. They recognised the diversity of interests within the area and the potential for intra-community conflict. They wanted, if possible, to establish a consensus amongst the residents themselves, which had been negotiated fairly on the basis of as much information as possible. It seemed only a small step further to involve the Shire, DPUD, Homeswest (the WA public housing agency), the developers and so on, in the negotiation process. The SVRRA suggested this overtly Habermasian-inspired idea to the local authority who accepted it.

In March 1992, a round-table meeting was organised, fully funded by the Shire, with twenty-five participants (including twelve community representatives, four councillors and people from DPUD, Swan, the developers, infrastructural authorities and so on). A neutral facilitator, familiar with Habermasian communicative action, and a recorder managed the meeting with an objective to build an agreement and negotiate compromises between groups with different interests.

The meeting was regarded as a great success. The community felt that at last they were able to relate to public servants in a general sharing of knowledge and power. Locality Groups were established for seven geographic areas in the Swan Valley, at which all respective residents, property owners and people who worked in the area could participate. People elected from each Locality Group represented the range of views from their groups at the Issues Group level which officers and councillors from the Shire of Swan also attended. Local residents thought that they were engaged in a negotiative process of participatory planning policy-making with the Shire and state authorities. They believed that they would have a considered input into the decision-making process. However, planners at both levels appeared to have regarded this same process as one of consultation rather than of communicative negotiation and consensus-building with the public.

The essential difference between the two viewpoints was not clear at the outset. Although planners agreed to the local community having far more voice than ever before, the basic agenda of urbanisation of the North East Corridor had been set. It was non-negotiable. Planners at both state and shire levels had had a pro-development mind-set with regard to the area since the 1980s and were not about to change their view that local residents should only be allowed to influence minor details of government proposals. The local residents did not recognise this for some time.

As time passed, however, and the local authority began to feel pressurised into producing a draft structure plan for DPUD, officers realised that more participatory forms of planning are often lengthy, and that the local community understood and knew far more than the planners originally thought. A mixture of time pressures to produce a strategy, feelings of vulnerability to both DPUD and community pressure backed by local knowledge, together with a resistance to considering alternative options for development, all resulted in an escalation of tension. The Shire of Swan was in a difficult position sandwiched between statutory obligations and a persistent community with strong arguments.

Whatever the reasons, trust broke down irrevocably between the Shire and DPUD on the one hand and local residents on the other. Both sides then began to manipulate the 'truth' in attempts to further their own agendas: Shire and DPUD planners to plan for urbanisation of the North East Corridor and residents to minimise the extent of urbanisation in their areas and to argue for 'sympathetic' development of any new urban growth.

To cut a long story short, the Shire of Swan presented the second draft of its proposed *Structure Plan for the North East Corridor* to DPUD in November 1992. Urban development was still to take place in the area, with provision for some 110,000 new residents by 2021. No public comment was requested on this document, which was essentially reproduced as DPUD's *North East Corridor Structure Plan Final* version released in March 1994 (a delay of sixteen months). The DPUD Structure Plan broke with tradition by refusing public comment on it but directed comment instead to the seven-page Metropolitan Region Scheme amendment for the area, released at the same time as the Perth–Darwin Highway proposals and supporting documents.

In summary, in the North East Corridor a Habermasian-inspired democratic participatory approach to planning aimed at achieving consensus among community groups and government staff. Over time, though, the staff in the formal planning agencies in state and shire government, together with several residents in the North East Corridor, lost respect for the process. They used their authority, contacts and discourses to set agendas and to lobby key actors. As will be demonstrated below, the Friends of the Valley became the most powerful actor in determining the final planning outcome in the North East Corridor. The Friends of the Valley informally and strategically lobbied for their representation of the area to be accepted rather than that of the shire and state planners, the SVRRA or the Nyungah Aboriginal people.

Fifty-five actors in the North East Corridor public participation process were interviewed regarding their images of the Swan Valley area and their perceptions of the North East Corridor planning decision process. Actors included officers of governance at state level(DPUD/Ministry for Planning, Main Roads Department, Water Corporation, Department of Environmental Protection) and at local authority level, elected members, developers and local residents. Local resident respondents included vignerons, 'horsiculturalists' (owners of horse-properties), poultry farmers, artists, teachers, architects, craftspeople and others. An interview was also conducted with Mr Robert Bropho of the Aboriginal Nyungah Circle of Elders.

The stories below are those of multiple subjectivities, of actors with a variety of identities, images and values. The Swan Valley is a place which many actors call home, but it has become a place of power-plays, conflict and struggle, full of difference and touched by the power brought to bear on it by the identities and networks which strove to ground themselves in its place (Honig, 1996).

REPRESENTATIONS

Most of Swan Valley folk
Don't want the urban cells
We thought we'd made it very clear
We think the draft plan smells.

We folks who love this valley
Won't stand back any more
And watch the city planners
Add another to their score.

We speak a different language
To the planners at DPUD
Who baffle us with bulldust
As they plan the urban flood.

We ask for a rural strategy
Take a look at what we got
Whopping great big suburbs
With tiny suburban lots.

We always thought a village
Was a country little place
But the Planners draw a suburb
Taking all the rural space.

Please help us save our valley
Let's give it our best shot
Stand up and fight for what is right
It's the only chance we've got.

For we love the open spaces
Where our kids are safe to roam
You see this is our heritage
It's the place that we call home.

So come to our Swan Valley
Enjoy it while you can
Then tell the Shire and DPUD
To shove their urban plan.

(from Jujnovich, 1992)

In order to lend some comprehensible structure to the analysis, I have chosen to explore actors' representations under broad categories of officers of governance (predominantly planning officers) and local residents,[8] using headings of several themes which were mentioned regularly in the interviews: the environment, home, rural lifestyle, a working area and heritage. There also appeared to be distinct differences between the actors themselves in terms of their perceptions of their and others' self- and place-identities and representations. For instance, there were marked differences, sometimes overlapping, sometimes conflicting, between those who were pro-urbanisation and anti-urbanisation, between long- and short-term residents (excluding Aboriginal peoples), between Euro-Australians and Aboriginal people and between what were perceived as being legitimate or illegitimate uses of land.

I am aware of the hegemonic dangers of classification and the potential trap of regarding categorised identities as fixed. I offer the classifications as temporary aids to cognition rather than cognition itself (Horkheimer and Adorno, 1991: 219) and hold them open to scrutiny and reformulation. The categories are diverse composite identities, full of differences of opinion, values and images, offered as a temporary determination only: 'a provisional nodal point subverted, asserted, and reconstituted through [the] contingent social relations' (Natter and Jones, 1997: 149) of the North East Corridor/Swan Valley public participation process to illuminate the contrast between shades of light and dark.

OFFICERS OF GOVERNANCE — FORM AND FUNCTION

Officers of governance tended to use functional and professional representations of the Swan Valley area, centred on issues related to their work. An officer from the Department of Environmental Protection, for example, described the Swan Valley in terms of its

> key issues: a source of groundwater, uncleared bush. (101)

Planning officers' imagery was dominated by location and topography:

> a large area divided by the river into two distinct parts. (004)

and land use:

> a mix of urban/rural residential and rural (001)
> a scenic route on the western side. The eastern rural area is a working area with wayside stalls. (021)

Space is assumed to be neutral, 'complacently understood to be fully defined by dimensional measurements … and by trigonometric descriptions of the geometrical relationships between objects, which are thought to sit in a kind of vacuum' (Shields, 1997: 187). Space is a 'container' of activity of living, farming and tourism.

There is little explicit recognition of the value judgements in any of these representations. Where officers did give some overt impression of value, it was often negative:

> it's really not core, but grazing with weeds. (004)

The area is not seen as an entity in itself with intrinsic value, but rather for what it can produce – its extrinsic economic value. As such, from the above planners' images, it would appear to be of little value other than for subdivision for residential development. Land is regarded as a resource, to be given value through human exploitation and 'productivity'. This use value is economically measured.

Only one planning officer, despite stating planning to be a 'technical job', saw beyond functional imagery to:

> a very special place, of high landscape value to the community and of high her-
> itage value. (072)

His was to be a voice, however, literally in the wilderness.

A planning officer's view of the Swan Valley and the North East Corridor tends to be Euclidean and instrumental. It regards the area in two-dimensional form on a map, geometrically divisible into discrete lots for the provision of housing and urban infrastructure, and as having no value in itself, 'but rather its only value lies in its being "put to work" as an instrument in the restless process of production: the "being of things" is eclipsed by the "doing of things"'. (Hoggett, 1992: 107). This is a view of 'physical space' which, Bauman (1993: 145) suggests, is arrived at through the 'phenomenological reduction of daily experience to pure quantity, during which distance is "depopulated" and "extemporalised" – that is, systematically cleansed of all contingent and transitory traits', which may include Aboriginal history and sacred sites.

Planners' visual geography is presented as being objective, a verifiable truth. Aesthetic and cultural values are ignored or transformed into quantities in equations of spatial residential demand and supply. The rational technical corporate narrative of planning focuses on 'growth' and 'progress', marginalising alternative stories about the meaning and value of place (Trigger, 1997). To question this narrative of space is to question planners' reality (Shields, 1997).

LOCAL RESIDENTS – 'STRONG, CAPABLE AND CREATIVE INDIVIDUALS'
A 'peaceful, restful and beautiful' environment
Despite the Shire's tourism advertising of the Swan Valley being dominated by envi-
ronmental images and permeated by the colour green (Shire of Swan, 1996), few local residents mentioned the natural environment as an important theme. Of those who did so, most were impressed by:

> a peaceful, restful and beautiful area (047)
> an impression of space and open areas. (106)

The founders of the Ellenbrook Environmental Group specifically mentioned the 'flora and fauna' (112) and the importance of nature:

> natural resources can't be replaced (112)

but only one resident took a more holistic view:

> this is all an environmental system which is part of the health of the river. It all
> contributes in an intrinsic way to the health, … an intrinsic link between what
> happens on the land and the health of the area and the river. (045)

Others held a less favourable image of the environment:

> a bit scrappy; urban blight (107)
> lots of renters and vacant lots (107)
> full of noxious weeds (Patterson's Curse) (049)
> a dust bowl — waste land (041)

and supported plans for urbanisation to produce what they regarded as 'a more aesthetical [*sic*] environment'. (049)

Home — 'the place of milk and honey'
For most residents, the Swan Valley as home is an integral component of their imagery and identity of the area and its value to them. Whether as a working area or affording a rural lifestyle as explored below, the notion of home was frequently mentioned, with respondents often emphasising their lineage in the valley as a badge of pride and legitimacy (of both residence and opinion):

> I've lived here all my life. My parents and grandparents lived here. It's a fifth generation business. (109)
> One's childhood and having been brought up here and your father and father's fathers having worked on the land. (056)
> I've lived here for 23 years. I've brought up my kids here. (107)

A colonial pedigree was regarded as a matter of some honour. The 50,000 years or so of Aboriginal presence in the area, however, was invisible. The Swan Valley identity is of a white settler area, the descendants of whom still live there and call the valley 'home'.

Several residents clearly regarded their home as property, an economic investment *in lieu* of/in addition to their superannuation, or as an asset to leave to their children:

> I saw my own land as superannuation. (107)

while others perceived it as a haven, emphasising the aesthetic value of the area:

> my image of this place is 'paradise'. It's the place of milk and honey, because one person sells milk and someone else sells honey. (043)

Home, therefore, is imagined as a site of security (financial/lifestyle) and identity. It is portrayed as a place of nurturing (raising families and crops) and respect. However, as is well known, home is often in reality a site of insecurity and threat. It is these anxieties, translocated to the external environment of the Swan Valley, which spurred residents to become involved in the participation programme in order to 'protect' their romanticised image of home.

A rural lifestyle of 'spacious comfort'

The location of the Swan Valley on the fringes of the Perth metropolitan area offers residents a semi-rural environment, with vistas over a green landscape, combined with reasonably good access (thirty minutes by car) to the CBD:

> the best of both worlds (063)
>
> there is close proximity to the city and race tracks and there is the country-type lifestyle (048)
>
> rural but close to the city. (105)

The image of a rural lifestyle is clearly important to residents, who spoke emotively and emotionally about the area. Residents valued:

> the peace and quiet of the place (051)
>
> space away from noise and people (051)
>
> an alternative place to live. It's affordable and is spacious (044)
>
> freedom and space … spacious comfort. (064)

Spaciousness is a key aspect of the above. The residents value space and low density living as a good environment for both raising children and for retiring:

> animals and space. A good place to bring up a family (070)
>
> an ideal spot for retirement and relaxing. (068)

One person even suggested that:

> neighbours get on because of the distance. (070)

contrasting with planners' oft-heard claims that high residential densities are necessary for 'building community'.

Aesthetic values are important, based in subjectivity and in intangibles such as 'freedom', 'peace and quiet' and 'space'.

'IDENTITY TO THE VALLEY' — A WORKING AREA

For other residents, the image of the Swan Valley is as a working area. This is an economic image, based in affording residents an income. It also gives them an identity, either from viticulture:

> this area's primary industry is viticulture and dried fruit production. It also gives identity to the Valley. (056)

from poultry farming:

> viticulture, winery and poultry farming in a heavy way – a classical rural area (073)

or craft and tourism:

> I work from home as an artist and we make furniture. We're strong, capable and
> creative individuals of the land. (042)

The notion of a 'Right to Farm' was mentioned on several occasions:

> I come from the Right to Farm point of view (056)
> you need things like the Right to Farm policy (104)
> we're heavily involved in the Right to Farm. (073)

These statements raise ethical questions of who and what has rights – humans?
nature? – whether property rights include rights over types of use, and whether that
use may impact upon others (such as wind-borne pesticides, salinity, etc.). Should
farmers have a Right to Farm if they thereby degrade and salinate their land?

TOURISM — AN OPPORTUNITY FOR 'GROWTH'
Economic values also underlie the identity of the Swan Valley as a tourist area:

> an opportunity for tourist growth as a green area so close to the city. (108)

There is disagreement, however, between those people who envisage tourists as
being attracted to open space and green landscapes and who oppose plans for
urbanisation:

> if we don't protect it we're mad (041)

and those who earn their living from tourist-related industries (crafts, restaurants,
etc.), some of whom regard urbanisation (providing it is not in their back yards) as
offering the potential for increased custom:

> because we have to make money (042)
> you legislate so people will invest money and develop agricultural tourism and a
> style of living that will make money and give employment to quite a lot of
> younger people. Not just a park. Some people think with tourism, everything has
> to be beautiful, look nice, not smell. We are a working area. (042)

Parks, which do not 'make money', are thus implied to be of little, if any, value.
Aesthetic values are seen as of secondary importance to economic values (and
associated odours) even though it may be the aesthetic qualities which actually
attract tourists to the valley.

Several of the vignerons were themselves ambivalent, recognising potential
problems linked with an increased population in proximity to vineyards (restrictions
on pesticide spraying, hours of wine-making, etc.), yet relishing the prospect of an
increased market for their produce. They resolved their dilemma by lobbying:

to save as much of the Swan Valley as possible, especially the most vital parts (especially the fertile soils for vines) and were prepared to give up areas like West Swan and Henley Brook which aren't really part of the Valley anyway (109)

– except to those who live there perhaps?

I also question the extent to which incoming residents to the North East Corridor would be likely to purchase local handmade furniture, paintings and boutique wines from the cellar door.

HERITAGE — A PIECE OF WHITE HISTORY

As indicated in the section on imagery/identity as 'home', many residents were proud of the perceived heritage of the Swan Valley area. This heritage was almost exclusively seen as white colonial settler heritage:

> I'm from a family of first settlers. I have a sense of admiration for those early immigrant settlers like the Yugoslavs and the Italians (071)
> born in the Valley into a pioneering family. Full of heritage (062)
> the Slav and Italian people who made the Swan Valley and showed us how to grow grapes. (047)

The 50,000 years of Aboriginal heritage in the area remained invisible, unvalued.

Some people felt 'insulted' that officers of governance appeared to ignore their views:

> I feel very insulted that they take so little notice of those who have looked after the land for so many years … I don't think they realise what it means to work a piece of land and own it for part of your lifetime, and then they come in and say 'we are going to take a portion of it'. It's not fair. The bureaucracy come and take what land they say they need away. It leaves you hurt and annoyed by having something that is yours taken away. They don't understand the central importance of the pieces of land. (047)

A resident of English colonial descent, whose ancestors may have engaged in 'cleansing' the land of Aboriginal people, here passionately expresses anger and loss at land being 'taken away'. She ironically has no thought for the Aboriginal peoples who themselves 'looked after the land for so many years' only to have it 'taken away' from them. She cannot recognise the 'hurt' and 'annoyance' which Aboriginal people must have felt and still feel.

Only one resident recognised the heritage of Aboriginal people in the Swan Valley:

> Aboriginals were never given special interest as the original owners of the land. (112)

contrasting with the *terra nullius* assumptions of other residents, developers and officers of governance.

DIFFERENCES OF OPINION

As illustrated by the above, residents' self- and place-identities, representations of the area and values often varied widely with respect to the same issue. I now turn to offer some understanding of these variations, according to crude distinctions between those who were pro-urbanisation or anti-urbanisation, Euro-Australian or Aboriginal, long-term or short-term residents, and between what was regarded as 'legitimate' or 'illegitimate' use of land.

'Our own interests at heart' – pro-urbanisation and anti-urbanisation
There were residents who

> were arguing that the land was their superannuation and they'd be unable to sell it if it wasn't zoned urban (109)

and others who

> will naturally sacrifice other people's back yards for their own. (109)

Several residents who supported the urbanisation proposals believed their land was bound to increase in economic value:

> We wanted a subdivision of our land to 1 to 5 acre blocks, but this proposal was knocked back … We've lost in finances by thousands of dollars. (049)

Others, such as the craftspeople, largely supported urbanisation as they regarded an increased population as a source of potential custom and income:

> because we have to make money we understand that we couldn't let the development of Perth by-pass the Valley because Joe Blow and such and such didn't want it. (042)

On the other hand, residents who opposed urbanisation tended to do so from a more aesthetic and lifestyle perspective. Their image of the Swan Valley was, as indicated earlier, that of 'spacious comfort' (064) and for keeping 'a horse [in] the peace and quiet of the place'. (051)

In the North East Corridor, however, predominantly due to effective lobbying and mobilisation of others by the Friends of the Valley, a network comprising a number of valley businesspeople (restaurateurs, artists, vignerons, etc.), the image of the eastern side of the valley as a working area of small businesses with tourism-generating potential, became accepted and influenced the Minister for Planning's decision to relocate new residential development in the west. For 'lifestylers' such as the above, 'the horse had already bolted' (108)!

'About our values' – Euro-Australian and Aboriginal residents
As indicated above, the image of the Swan Valley held by most residents was of an area of white settler heritage, people who 'improved' the land through industrious and courageous settlement. Aboriginal people did not 'figure' (047) in such an image.

Aboriginal people were often represented in the negative, with claims of sacred sites being in the way of white people and progress:

> Aboriginals got involved claiming the land was the home of the golden swamp tortoise or some such thing (043)
> the Aboriginal Bennett Brook campaign was a 'no go' area. This area was declared a special place and preserved. As far as the people who have been living in the area for generations, their values were not considered whatsoever. (055)

Residents' revisionist representations of local history ignored the length of Aboriginal presence in the Swan Valley and the important spiritual value of sacred sites:

> sacred sites were claimed to be in the area. If you bring in minority groups (i.e. Aboriginal people), they focus on their own need, have their own agenda, alienate the institutions and the majority of the community and take over (067)

– as if Euro-Australian interest groups act differently!
This local councillor continued:

> there is a time to bring them in, when a broad set of parameters have been set. Bropho is not indigenous to the area. Involving them reduces our credibility as a group with the departments and instrumentalities. (067)

Omission of Mr Bropho's honorific as a Nyungah Elder may be due to cultural ignorance. However, the speaker cannot comprehend that his claim that only indigeneity affords legitimacy of opinion would equally silence the voices of everyone else.
A suggestion that Aboriginal people were

> the original owners of the land (112)

was not echoed by any other Euro-Australian residents.

Aboriginal representations and place-identity of the Swan Valley are very different from those of the Euro-Australians. Aboriginal people value the land for its spiritual and mythological significance. They come from and are part of the land. Their everyday existence, their past and their future are intrinsically interrelated with the land, as Mr Robert Bropho, of the Nyungah Circle of Elders, indicates:

we're the last of the river people in this area … All the dreaming stories are still
within our minds.

We've stood here hard and long. My mum stood here – she's dead – my sisters
and brothers, my granddaughter, we sit for a cause and a purpose. The land is
important.

Us people, me and my friends, my sisters and brothers, my mother and father
that's dead, we stood in those vineyards when they was in full bloom …, but all
that's gone, that's gone … The top of the vineyards with the Reid Highway cut-
ting across and smashing out the areas where we trod once; all the springs up
along Bennett Brook have stopped flowing, the natural springs where we drunk
water.

**The loss of family and of the land is heartfelt. It threatens Aboriginal people's very
existence:**

you're building your white society, your concrete jungles, your suburbias, …. but
where's ours, what was once ours? We can be forced out, dragged out of the
land, our roots out, pushed out, moved here, moved there, assimilated, become
nothing, become part of a movement that'll die out.

These trees here won't be on the land any more. They'll be gone: sheoak, jarrah,
woolly bush. They'll all be gone. … All the natural plants will be flattened and
under the concrete highways and byways and cities.

**Yet the Aboriginal people have a vision. It is based in their past and in nature, the
land:**

we're looking up the track, to what white man calls the future, – we call it the
'hopes of tomorrow'. We look that way with the experience of what we came
through; things we've encountered while passing through, back there in the
past, to where we are now, and we have got a vision.

The plans we've got in our minds, we need space too.

But these visions are threatened:

all our dreaming stories could be in and round those hills and these valleys and
all of a sudden developers come and they want to start building. … Gradually all
that tree line and the dreamings and things disappear. In the place of that
there'll be a concrete jungle. Our visions don't look good against the concrete
jungle.

Essentially, as Mr Bropho says:

it's about our values.

These stories highlight the entirely different world in which Aboriginal people live as compared to the concerns of the Euro-Australian residents and the planning system. We see the importance of spiritual values and cultural argument against economic values and technical argument, the perception as alien of paper, reports, maps and charts, and of the planning system and what it represents. Memory and tradition are keys to beginning to understand Aboriginal attachment to the land. Memory is embodied in identity. There is little objective distinction between space and time.

In the tone, as well as the content of the stories, we recognise 'issues, details, relationships and even people' (Forester, 1993b: 31) who have been ignored and unappreciated in the past. We recognise not only claims that Aboriginal people have over the land, but the importance of their self- and place-identity and 'a history of betrayal and resulting fear, suspicion, distrust – which must be acknowledged, respected and addressed if working relationships are to be built' (Forester, 1993b: 31).

'Johnny-come-latelies' – long-term and short-term residents
Excluding Aboriginal people, evidence of long-term residence and connections to the Swan Valley tended to be represented as a badge affording legitimacy of identity, image of the area and its land use:

> age or length of time people had been in the district did affect people's viewpoints. (048)

Opinions from long-term residents were vaunted as being of greater value than those of 'transient' (062) newcomers or 'Johnny-come-latelies' (073):

> our area was familial or historically based. The other groups were less tolerant. (056)

Long-term inhabitants identified themselves as 'stable' and loyal to the area. 'Stable residents who called Swan Valley "home"' were perceived as being more likely to oppose urbanisation than

> other, more transient people [who] would be happy to stay until development and then take the money and run (062)
> newcomers wanted to sell (063)
> there was obviously an element of the new people on the block opposing the traditionalists. There was some resentment ... by the traditionalists. New people were more prominent and interested and involved. ... They were probably more articulate and also knew how to work the process. (106)

Shorter-term residents, who wanted to protect their spacious lifestyle, were made to feel decidedly non-valued:

we have no history here (102) (residents for ten years)
we feel very vulnerable (051) (residents for eight years).

These opinions may well be 'sour grapes' on the part of those who resented the Minister for Planning's urbanisation decision, influenced by the actor-network of relative 'newcomers' and

people who don't even live in the area (049).

'Grazing with Weeds'? — 'legitimate' and 'illegitimate' uses of land
Some uses of land were definitely regarded as being more valuable, even more legitimate, by longer-term Euro-Australian residents. Vignerons, and several other residents, perceived viticulture as the highest valued use of land. Other land uses were worthless by comparison:

areas for vineyards, and other areas — non-viable land (055)
not suitable for living or to make a living because it's full of noxious weeds
(Patterson's Curse) and it's not a viable productive option. (049)

Even preservation of the environment was valued as second-rate:

a fertile area which should be left to agriculture, ... however, DPUD wanted to
protect bits that are good agricultural land. (047)

Horsiculture, or hobby farming, was not regarded as a legitimate use of land by traditionalist residents:

the area is steeped in tradition and importance. Lots of the good soil is wasted
there (e.g. by hobby farming)... You should have to buy a licence with the land
to ensure appropriate land use. Lifestylers are often silly. (115)

This vigneron resident comments that the Swan Valley is 'steeped in tradition'. He does not mean Aboriginal tradition, however, but rather white colonial tradition, especially of 'serious' farming. He clearly regards hobby farming/horsiculture as a 'waste', an 'inappropriate' use of the land, presumably as compared with vine growing, and goes as far as to suggest that land purchasers should be licensed for appropriate uses. Leaving land 'fallow' is not envisaged as an appropriate use: it is not productive.

Others would even prefer to see residential development:

it's full of noxious weeds (Patterson's Curse) ... more suitable for village zoning.
... More manageable, an ideal area for increasing rating lots; opportunity for
more people to enjoy valley life, and the size of properties that could be established would help to eradicate weed, animal studs, etc. The result would be a
more aesthetical environment. (049)

(I question whether roofs of new suburbs would be more 'aesthetical' than open vistas of grazing lands, and whether it is these vistas which people 'enjoy' as an essential part of 'valley life'.)

Neither did planning officers regard horsiculture as a legitimate activity in the area:

> it's really not core but grazing with weeds (004)
> the shire came and observed the area, said it wasn't being viably used and thus would be suitable to be repossessed. (057)

Such sentiments were expressed vociferously and made horsiculturalists feel marginalised and unvalued:

> the feeling that came out of the whole process was the pressure that we had to do something with our property; we couldn't just sit out here with our one horse and have acres of land …
> you had to justify the land being left almost idle, otherwise we were warned that people will come in and build houses on it. The shire basically gave us that impression. … They'd imply you would be better off if you had something going for the land so that you could justify the property (051)
> the shire didn't consider us much of a priority. … They used the Patterson's Curse covered land as an excuse, saying, 'well, this land is useless. We may as well build here'. (051)

Land, according to the enrolling colonial narrative, is a resource which must be brought into productive use for economic gain. Land is seen as a marketable commodity with commercial value. Amenity, aesthetic and spiritual values do not count. Non-productive uses are unjustifiable, illegitimate.

These stories indicate the range of representations residents have of the Swan Valley and highlight the often sharp contrasts between representations, the tenebrism of chiaroscuro. Representations include those of the Swan Valley as an area of colonial history, of spacious environment, and offering a rural lifestyle, all of which need to be preserved as accessible to them. The identities of many are as property owners with a concern for the value of their investments. Local residents view their properties as much more than units of shelter. They are financial investments, lifestyle symbols, social settings and bases for business and leisure activities (Healey, 1997d). Residents recognise the diversity of their identities, values and aspirations, and within the overall network of non-indigenous residents in the Swan Valley there nested several smaller, often overlapping actor-networks. Even within the smaller networks there were often different representations of the valley and a lack of complete agreement as to desired outcomes. Some networks, such as the Friends of the Valley, were more successful than others in enrolling the ultimate decision-maker, the Minister for Planning, and persuading him of their values and points of view:

> general quality values (quality of life) were dismissed as irrelevant or incidental.
> Dollar values were given much higher value (103)
> aesthetic values don't seem to count any more. (057)

Overall, actors' representations and values jostled together as each actor attempted to

> define what we think the valley should be. (056)

As this respondent continued:

> in a way we were forming a valley identity and exploring who we are. (056)

Self- and place-identities are inextricably intertwined. They are complex and dynamic. Whichever representation/identity and concomitant values enrolled and mobilised others at any point in time in the Swan Valley story depended, as one planning officer recognised,

> on the ongoing politics. (022)

ACTOR-NETWORKS

I have attempted to depict the Swan Valley in the North East Corridor of Perth, Western Australia, as a nodal point where sets of social relations and identities, representations and images of place, meanings and values temporally and temporarily intersect. State government proposals to urbanise the North East Corridor and the public participation process which followed, led to the construction of agency as actors formed into temporary networks and jostled for influence over the planning decision. Complex chains of actor-spaces aligned around alternative representations of the Swan Valley and the North East Corridor: pro-urbanisation, anti-urbanisation and so on.

I call upon actor-network theory to help unpack the processes of translation of representations. Actors' stories of images of themselves and of other groups, and of their and others' geographical places reveal complex and dynamic alliances and differences. There are many networks at play. Overlapping, contrasting and conflicting representations, images, identities and values are evoked for substantive and political purposes.

Such representations are intrinsically related to actors' beliefs, social relations, institution structures, material practices and power relations (Harvey, 1996). Actors bring conceptions from their lifeworlds and previous and ongoing interrelationships with other actors into a process constrained by the institutional structure and practices of the Western Australian planning system, in which power relations are inherently unequal.

Planners are experts. The difference between experts and laypersons is essentially that laypersons' knowledge, as we have seen, embodies tradition and cultural values; it is local and de-centred. Planners' expertise, on the other hand, is disembedded, 'evacuating' (Giddens, 1994: 85) the traditional content of local contexts, and based on impersonal principles which can be set out without regard to context – a coded knowledge which professionals are at pains to protect.

> Expert systems decontextualise as an intrinsic consequence of the impersonal
> and contingent character of the rules of their knowledge-acquisition. Place is
> not in any sense a quality relevant to their validity; and places themselves …
> take on a different significance from traditional locales (Giddens, 1994: 85).

Planners traditionally believe themselves to be neutral, rational experts (see Hoch, 1994), offering objective and balanced appraisals rather than making value judgements. Yet planners must inevitably bring their own values into their work, making judgements as to the good versus the right – what is important, which interests should carry how much weight, what is possible to be achieved and so on. Planners and governance reserve the ultimate power to define, redefine, organise and reorganise space into a place of their choosing.

Planners, therefore, often seek to enrol other actors into their representations. Their goal is mobilisation: acceptance of their plans as legitimate by local residents. Public participation programmes are often utilised as the means of persuasion, but as Hoch (1994: 110–11) warns, 'when planners treat plans solely as weapons of political warfare, they lose faith in the power of ideas and images'. Planning should be regarded as more than a process of competitive bargaining. Such an attitude blinds planners to the legitimacy of multiple subject positions and values and robs them of opportunities to think critically and to engage in truly deliberative decision-making.

In the Swan Valley/North East Corridor story, actors attempted to enrol other participants, and especially the decision-makers, into their representations, some far more successfully than others. As one would expect, given the statutory powers of planning officers, their rational technical images and values of the area had an important, but, in this instance, not a determining influence on the Minister for Planning's decision to urbanise the western side of the Swan Valley rather than the technically more suitable eastern side.

Even less successful were the indigenous Aboriginal actors. Memory and mythology are intrinsically bound up with the construction of Aboriginal representations. In the stories told above, memory and traditional knowledge are being used politically, yet the actor-network of Aboriginal actors was totally unable to 'enrol' the planners. Despite a meeting of the two networks, Callon's stage of 'interessement' was not reached. Aboriginal people failed to persuade the planners of the importance of their representation of the area. The two sets of actors failed to recognise and understand each others' intermediaries: Aboriginal sacred sites and stories and the texts, maps and plans of the planners.

The decision was influenced by the astute channelling of energies by actors (the Friends of the Valley) on the eastern side of the Swan Valley into the representation of their area as a working area, vital to the livelihoods of vignerons, etc., and as an area with substantial economic potential for generation of tourism dollars, through marketing its white colonial heritage, local crafts and produce. The representational poetics of place are strong and appealing – as are the politics. As Callon and Latour (1981: 292) comment: 'strength is *inter*vention, *inter*ruption, *inter*pretation and *inter*est' (emphasis in original).

It is to such political lobbying activity which I now turn.

LOBBYING – COMPLEX NETWORKS AND ENERGY FLOWS

Energy flows through complex networks in the form of communication. Forms of communication are therefore the intermediaries which actors utilise in order to persuade or enrol others to their particular points of view. Intermediaries may be texts, such as planning documents, consultants' reports, letters, surveys, petitions, newspaper articles, TV coverage, photographs, etc.

In examining the networks and intermediaries of the North East Corridor participatory planning process I am interested in

> identifying those social relations, power structures and socio-cultural grids of communication and interpretation ... which limit the identity of the parties to the dialogue, which set the agenda for what is considered appropriate or inappropriate matter for institutional debate, and which sanctify the speech of some over others (Benhabib, 1990b: 353–4).

Communication may take place face to face, by telephone or by written and/or graphic text, between individual people or in larger numbers. It may take place as part of the formal public participation process or informally.

Figure 6.2 represents a stakeholder map (see Bryson and Crosby, 1992) of actors involved in the North East Corridor (NEC) planning decision-making process. There is a distinct division between formal and informal communication networks. The stakeholder map indicates that in the North East Corridor process the formal channels of communication were essentially hierarchical and representative, with local residents, individually or as members of broader interest groups, having representation on a series of spatially bounded Locality Groups, which in turn nominated representatives onto an Advisory Group reporting to the local authority planning department. The Shire of Swan planning department advised the state-level Ministry for Planning, which then advised the Minister for Planning who was responsible for the plan decision.

Although other actors took part in this 'official' process, as depicted in Figure 6.2, the core network of actors is illustrated in Figure 6.3 as the main formal hierarchical network. If we refer back to the network typologies outlined earlier, the network pertaining to the formal North East Corridor participatory process typifies Howlett and Ramesh's (1995) pluralistic network or Rhodes and Marsh's (1992) issue network. It is essentially state-directed.

As can be seen from Figure 6.2, much energy was expended along informal channels of communication between actors. I ask who engages in informal networking, why, what triggers informal networking, when it takes place and how, and what intermediaries are invoked in order to enrol others to an actor's particular viewpoint.

WHO NETWORKS INFORMALLY?

The *speculative landowners/developers* networked informally for some time, from the late 1980s, with the Ministers for Housing and Planning to persuade them of the need to rezone the land to urban for residential development and to amend/establish zoning schemes accordingly. The relational resource was extremely strong with government agencies either owning or having a vested interest in a high proportion of the land under consideration. The capacity to achieve the desired outcome was so strong that once the network had been formed and the Minister enrolled to their viewpoint, the Minister was effectively mobilised to represent the other actors who became passive in the process.

Once the planning process was under way, the *Minister for Planning* became involved in several networks. He (and his Liberal government successor) were key actors in the process. The Minister engaged in interessement with public sector infrastructure providers who were faced with making major revisions to their investment programmes in order to service a previously unplanned-for corridor to the north east of Perth. He also separately engaged in interessement with planners from the Ministry for Planning to ensure that their formal recommendations were in line with his expectations. The Minister was also one of the prime recipients of communications from the other various networks of actors, in his position of power as ultimate decision-maker on the future of the North East Corridor.

The *local authority planners from the Shire of Swan* predominantly acted through the formal procedure, but also contacted Ministry for Planning staff, other agencies of governance and private sector 'experts' for information on certain issues. The local authority planners also received communications from local resident networks, as did

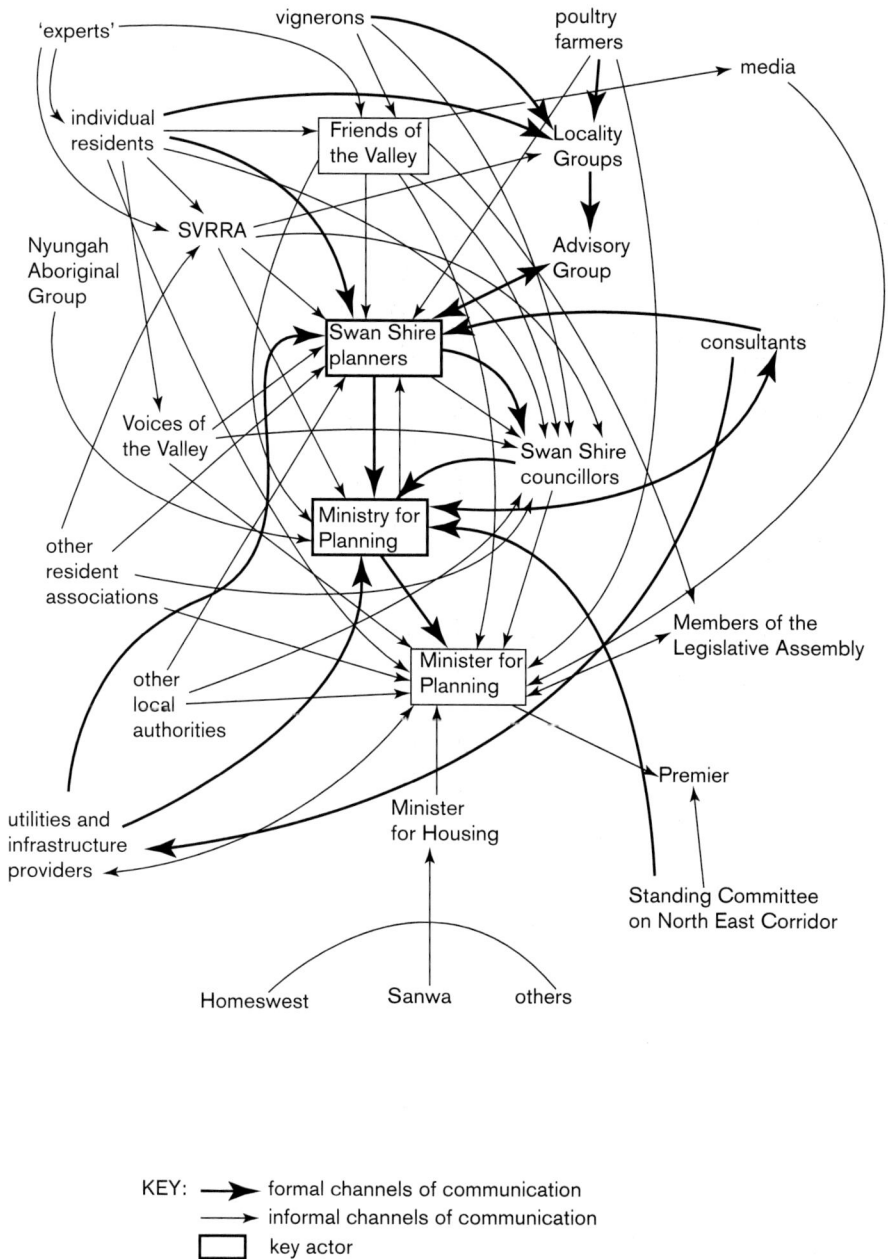

Figure 6.2 Flows of communicative energy and networks (Source: Hillier, 2000a: 44)

The following labels appear in the figure:

'experts'
vignerons
poultry farmers
media
individual residents
Friends of the Valley
Locality Groups
SVRRA
Advisory Group
Nyungah Aboriginal Group
Swan Shire planners
consultants
Voices of the Valley
Swan Shire councillors
Ministry for Planning
other resident associations
Minister for Planning
Members of the Legislative Assembly
other local authorities
Premier
utilities and infrastructure providers
Minister for Housing
Standing Committee on North East Corridor
Homeswest
Sanwa
others

KEY: → formal channels of communication
→ informal channels of communication
☐ key actor

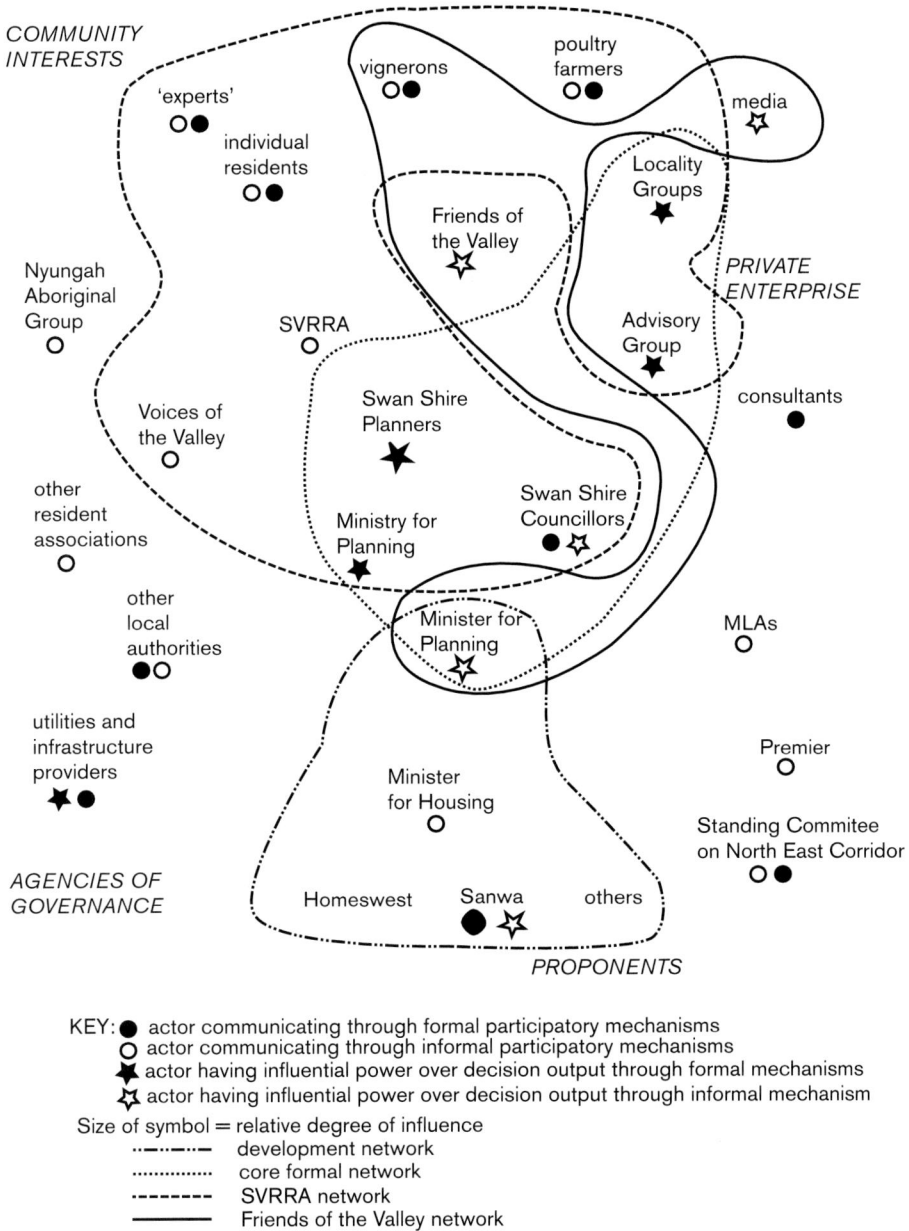

COMMUNITY
INTERESTS

vignerons
poultry
farmers
media

'experts'
individual
residents

Locality
Groups

Friends of
the Valley

PRIVATE
ENTERPRISE

Nyungah
Aboriginal
Group

SVRRA

Advisory
Group

consultants

Swan Shire
Planners

Voices of
the Valley

Swan Shire
Councillors

other
resident
associations

Ministry for
Planning

other
local
authorities

Minister for
Planning

MLAs

utilities and
infrastructure
providers

Minister
for Housing

Premier

AGENCIES OF
GOVERNANCE

Standing Commitee
on North East Corridor

Homeswest   Sanwa   others

PROPONENTS

KEY: ● actor communicating through formal participatory mechanisms
○ actor communicating through informal participatory mechanisms
★ actor having influential power over decision output through formal mechanisms
☆ actor having influential power over decision output through informal mechanism

Size of symbol = relative degree of influence
··—··—··—   development network
···············   core formal network
--------   SVRRA network
————   Friends of the Valley network

Figure 6.3 Formal and informal networks (after Friend, Power & Yewlett, 1974) (Source: Hillier, 2000a: 45)

those at the Ministry for Planning. These networks both requested information and attempted to influence the formal recommendations on the North East Corridor. Energy flows were widespread and of long duration, but the capacities formed were fairly weak, reflecting the planners' relative lack of power in the decision-making process.

Individual residents and the Voices of the Valley (a small group of residents from the western side of the Swan Valley) also engaged in lobbying activity with relatively little success overall. Residents and the 'Voices' lobbied planning staff and elected representatives at both local and state levels. Unfortunately, the relational resources were weak in that there were a low number of people involved, they had few influential contacts, and as far as the 'Voices' were concerned, they were formed far too late in the process, after the Friends of the Valley had already established a high profile and much influence in favour of their objective of protecting the eastern side of the valley (which implied diverting the bulk of urban development to the west). Their capacity to achieve their aim of protection of the western side of the Swan Valley was thus extremely low.

The *Friends of the Valley* was the most powerful actor in determining the final shape of urbanisation in the North East Corridor. Formed in 1993, a year into the formal planning process, the Friends of the Valley comprised only eight or nine members, each carefully selected by the two founders. The Friends of the Valley members were all educated, articulate, professional local residents, one with previous experience of lobbying activity, who had excellent contacts with powerful and high-profile actors in WA. The Friends of the Valley consciously decided to channel its energies only into informal networking, targeting key persons, such as the Minister for Planning and the editor of the state's only daily newspaper, *The West Australian*. Their aim was to keep the eastern side of the valley as it is, to make it 'a living, working, breathing valley' through getting the weight of Western Australian public opinion behind them through the media. In this way, the capacity of eight or nine people could be multiplied exponentially.

It is important to emphasise that networks are not static. They are contingent upon the issue under consideration. They are social creations of the issue. Some people were members of several networks, contemporaneously or otherwise. Membership of networks fluctuated according to interests, demands and interpersonal contacts. By the end of the process, three distinct networks of informal communication may be discerned, as depicted in Figure 6.3.

- A 'development' network comprising the landowner/developers and relevant state government ministers. This network provides a classic example of a Rhodes and Moore policy community.
- The Friends of the Valley network. The Friends of the Valley provided the most intense lobbying activity, largely through strategic use of the media, and

significantly influenced the planning outcome. The Friends of the Valley were not involved at all as an actor in the formal public participation process organised by the local authority and state planning departments. The Friends of the Valley is an issue network in both Rhodes and Moore's and Howlett and Ramesh's terms.

- The Swan Valley Residents' and Ratepayers' Association (SVRRA) network. The SVRRA network predated the Friends of the Valley. The group's energies mainly channelled individual residents towards supporting Locality Group representatives in the formal network and engaging in letter-writing and other similar exercises to the press, planning officers and elected councillors and members of State Parliament. This Rhodes and Marsh issue network would be classified by Howlett and Ramesh as pluralistic.

It is apparent that the more successful actors were (apart from the Minister for Planning and the developers) those of upper middle-class, educated socio-economic status, and were predominantly women. More marginalised people (those from non-English speaking backgrounds, Aboriginals, the poor) tended to be fairly passive members of the formal locality group networks only, or, in the case of the Aboriginal Nyungah community, left on the outside of both formal and informal processes.

These informal networks may also be analysed using Sabatier's (1993) Advocacy Coalition Framework. Members of the stable development network or policy community share common ground, ideas and values of a pro-development ethos and economic interest. The Friends of the Valley coalition shared a core policy desire to protect the eastern side of the Swan Valley from development. A secondary aspect was the non-urbanisation of the entire Swan Valley area, which the group compromised in favour of their core desires by accepting the inevitability of new residential development, but attempting to direct it to the less topographically suitable western side. The SVRRA network cannot be termed an advocacy coalition as its members were often divided with regard to their core ideas and values. Some members sought to protect their semi-rural lifestyle and rejected development proposals completely, whereas others regarded their properties as a potential source of income from residential subdivision. It is probably this lack of consensus in the SVRRA, as compared to the Friends of the Valley, which resulted in its relative lack of impact and of influence on the final planning outcome.

WHY NETWORK INFORMALLY?

Actors network informally in order to further their own ends, whether these are ideological (e.g. environmental, social justice), economic or other (facilitating one's statutory duty). Actors utilise their networks to obtain information (e.g. technical information from planning and other agencies of governance or indications of what policy advisers and decision-makers may be thinking) or to give information, in an attempt to engage in interessement with other actors, or to assist policy-makers to take a more informed decision.

Virtually all actors used their networks informally to obtain information, for reasons of speed in the course of their duties (a telephone call is far quicker than writing a formal letter) and/or to give them perceived knowledge advances which might be translatable into power (see material on power-knowledge). Similarly, all actors used their networks to give information, ranging from the developers and the Minister to the residents and other interest groups.

Actors not only generated energy flows along these networks, but also between networks (via actors with intersecting relationships) and within them. Interest groups, such as the Swan Valley Residents' and Ratepayers' Association, obtained valuable information from several of their members with direct or indirect connections to other actors and networks, including Main Roads Department, the Water Authority of WA (now the Water Corporation), etc. as well as giving feedback to local residents.

WHAT TRIGGERS INFORMAL NETWORKING ACTIVITY?

I concentrate here on the interessement/enrolment aspects of networking activity which aim to persuade others to a certain viewpoint. I propose four, not mutually exclusive, categories of trigger as follows:

A   Disturbance/entropy point in the formal process.
B   Previous experience of local public participation processes in which lobbying was undertaken.
C1   Wider parameters – an issue trigger – e.g. member of an environmental organisation with lobbying activity.
C2   Wider parameters – an activity trigger – e.g. member of trade union with lobbying activity.

Examples of all four were found in the North East Corridor study. All quotes, unless otherwise stated, are from actors interviewed in the course of the study.

A   Individual actors (e.g. individual residents, the Minister, etc.) engaged in informal lobbying activity at points in the formal process where they became frustrated with issues such as a lack of progress, a lack of available information, a lack of achieving their objectives. Lobbying took place predominantly of decision-makers or their advisers (planners) or of information providers (consultants, experts, infrastructure agencies) who were persuaded to certain courses of action.

The Friends of the Valley were formed one year into the formal process purely as a result of frustration: '[I] got the impression I was being brushed off'; 'the SVRRA wasn't listened to at all; so the Friends of the Valley was set up,

with lots of influential people involved, and all of a sudden, we got listened to';
'we took the arguments out of the valley'. One of the Friends of the Valley's
members had advocated use of direct action from 'day one', but had been persuaded by the other founder to 'give the [formal] process a try' first. It is of
interest that the woman who advocated direct action had previous experience
of such through chairing her local Parent–Teacher Association (an activity trigger), whilst the other woman had no previous experience of any participatory
activity.

B   Some of the Swan Valley residents with previous experience of local planning
     public participation engaged in lobbying tactics, as 'that's what you do' as part
     of the process. Methods used tended to be low key, however, such as writing
     letters to local and state elected representatives, conducting local surveys and
     presenting findings to the local authority.

     The developers, aware as they were of the planning system for rezoning
     land, and the delays and uncertainty which public participation processes
     might cause, decided to speak directly to the key decision-maker, the Minister
     for Planning.

C   At least one active resident was stimulated by the environmental issue trigger.
     ('You can point out the boost to the economy and multiplier effect, but it's the
     hidden costs to the environment.') A member of a wider organisational net-
     work, he formed the Ellenbrook Environmental Group. A dedicated and
     leading activist in the SVRRA and the formal Locality Group process, he
     engaged in limited and localised direct action, organising public meetings,
     talks from experts, local surveys, 'plotting wildlife, water courses, etc.' He
     believed in the formal process although he was aware of its limitations: 'with
     written submissions, the community often felt it was too hard'; 'if you do not
     attend the workshops, etc. then you have no input'.

As mentioned above, one of the founder members of Friends of the Valley was triggered to taking direct action by the activity trigger of her Parent–Teacher
Association. A staunch union member and activist was similarly motivated to join his
Locality Group where he played a prominent role in targeting Labour politicians as
'procedures are never fair when dealing with bureaucracy' and 'the decisions are
made not even by government, but by the powerbrokers, unapproachable by any of
the (formal) processes we have been through'. Unfortunately, his rhetoric appears to
have more energy than his activity: 'it's like wrestling in treacle with an octopus'!
These examples indicate that such groups tend not to go outside of tactics which
they have tried and found to work on previous occasions.

My expectation, as outlined earlier, was that those actors with no or little previous experience of direct action or lobbying activity, together with the local and state

planners involved, would tend to adhere to the formal participation process as established by the planners and regard informal lobbying as 'going round the back'. This expectation was largely born out. Quotations from residents include:

> 'was too a-political for the people I was representing. Others did lobby. Some dodgy stuff went on. It wasn't a very democratic process.
> Consultation makes decision-making more accountable.
> There was some political motives and certainly political lobbying and manipulation attempted. We tried to avoid it as much as possible. We tried to keep things as open as possible.
> That's cheating.
> Secret meetings etc. Various dirty tricks were wheeled out.'

Those local actors, however, with a background in more grassroots-based approaches, through union, interest group, etc. activity, tended to regard lobbying as a resource-mobilisation tactic, both valid and valuable, to be used as soon and as much as possible:

> This is about personality, not about issues.
> There's a lesson: don't spend your life saying it's not fair. You just have to get on and play the game.
> Just because you've participated, just because you've played by the rules, doesn't mean you're going to win, but you go away having learned something. Someone who thinks 'if I play by the rules I'm going to win', well, that person's got a huge lesson to learn. It's a lesson in life that you use.
> Doing a bit of 'in-your-face' stuff.
> A vehicle to snooker change.
> We investigated ... what you could get away with.

And for one elderly woman, fame was:

> 'I've nearly been on the front page of *The West Australian*'.

Perhaps two quotations which sum it all up are:

> At the end of the day it's how you use what you've got.
> In life you never get what you deserve but what you negotiate.

Local wisdom!

It should also be stated that formal participatory processes can be triggered as a result of pressure from informal processes. The North East Corridor participatory exercise was itself created after sustained pressure from the SVRRA on the local authority, backed up by 'experts' advocating the merits of negotiative communicative processes.

WHEN DOES INFORMAL NETWORKING TAKE PLACE?

In the North East Corridor the developers undertook a certain amount of informal networking with relevant government ministers before the formal process of rezoning began to take place. Given the power of this network to affect and take the final decision, many actors appear to have been correct in their assertions that the formal exercise was largely a fait accompli and that scope existed only for minor alterations to the pattern of urbanisation.

> It was cosmetic.
> The decision was made, but the shape of the decision wasn't complete.
> It was a shallow exercise.

My expectation that those actors with previous lobbying experience would be more likely to engage in informal activity early in the formal participation process rather than at some later point of disturbance was unfounded, however. Apart from the proposal of the Friends of the Valley member, most direct action, apart from minor acts of giving and obtaining information, was triggered by frustration at a lack of progress (Friends of the Valley), or a specific event (foundation of Voices of the Valley was stimulated by the apparent success of Friends of the Valley and its implications for the western side of the Swan Valley).

It is impossible to state whether direct action earlier or later is more effective. The most successful actors were the developers who mobilised the Minister for Planning before the formal process commenced and the Friends of the Valley who mobilised mass public opinion at a much later stage, just prior to the final recommendations and decision being made.

HOW DOES INFORMAL NETWORKING TAKE PLACE?

The key influence is personal contacts. The old adage of 'it's who you know, not what you know' appears to hold true in the North East Corridor. The Friends of the Valley's main relational resource was the friendship of one of its founder members with the chief editor of *The West Australian* newspaper. Once this actor had been enrolled into the Friends of the Valley viewpoint, he was able to use the media as intermediary to exert enormous pressure on the Minister as decision-maker: 'That's the power of the whole thing. We got the front page of *The West Australian*, the *7.30 Report*, people were writing articles every day at one stage.' The use of *The West Australian* effectively mobilised the public of WA (some 1.7 million people) into accepting the representation made by the Friends of the Valley. It would perhaps be a foolhardy politician who ignored such energies.

As stated earlier, the founder members of the Friends of the Valley specifically invited the other core members to join because of their personal networks. They also selectively lobbied only the most influential actors. Friends of the Valley represents an example of informal networking at its most powerful and successful.

Other aspects of informal activity include knowledge of the planning and political systems (knowing who to lobby and when), amount of finance available (for leafleting, hire of halls, etc.), time available and the number of people available (to increase the number of personal relational and other resources). Interestingly, the Friends of the Valley comprised a very small group of people who were all full-time professionals, who had no previous experience of participation in the planning system and who spent relatively little money on their activities. It does not follow, therefore, that actors need to be rich in factors other than key relational resources in order to generate high levels of energy flows and exert power over an outcome.

CONCLUSIONS

In the North East Corridor story, 'we are dealing with events chained together by the multiple expectations, imputations of interests, misread communications, fears, grudges, and finally by the concrete projects of the parties involved with or against each other' (Knorr-Cetina, 1981: 33). These chains are communicated along networks as energy flows of varying intensities and power. Actors may still communicate along with traditional forms and institutions (such as the formal planning approach to public participation), but they also communicate and generate energy flows along new areas of activity and identity (use of media, direct action, the community development approach, etc.). The 'political opportunity structure' (Gelb, 1989) in place at a particular point in time may act to determine the relative intensity of the various approaches utilised.

Networks are contingent and dynamic as actors form and disband associations and coalitions according to the issue under consideration and the strategic alliances they believe will assist their cause. Actors selectively choose communication partners from among their multiple networks. Power is established and 'truths' legitimated via the intermediaries employed – including consultants' reports, media coverage, telephone conversations and so on – rather than the 'rational' arguments voiced at the representative forums of the formal participation process.

Through astute channelling of energies, actors such as the Friends of the Valley managed to manipulate a new situation definition (substantial decrease of the extent of urbanisation of the eastern side of the North East Corridor) *despite* the area being technically far more suitable for urban development than the western side, the original planners' definition. As Flyvbjerg (1998a: 36) comments, 'power ... produces that knowledge and that rationality which is conducive to the reality it wants'. The use of the media as intermediary by the Friends of the Valley was critical.

The *West Australian* became more an arena for advertising their viewpoint than a setting for rational debate. It raises the questions of the role of the media in the public sphere, the extent to which it can provide a forum for the discussion of a range of different values and interests, and whether less well connected (or 'acceptable') actors would have such access to its energies and influence.

In the North East Corridor case, the process became not one of producing 'stronger' rational argument (communicative action) within the formal participation process, but rather of developing strategies and tactics (strategic action) outside of it. The Friends of the Valley strategy exemplifies Flyvbjerg's (1998a: 80) rhetorical 'why use the force of the better argument when force alone will suffice?'

Unknown to (or rather unaccepted by) most of the community interests, however, lay the government's predetermined agenda that residential development would take place. The not-always transparent involvement of public-sector institutions in owning and developing the land at Ellenbrook meant that 'institutions that were supposed to represent what they themselves call the "public interest" were revealed to be deeply embedded in the hidden exercise of power and the protection of special interests' (Flyvbjerg, 1998a: 225).

In this story I have shone a tenebrist spotlight on the North East Corridor to reveal the planning process in chiaroscuro halves – of the formal Habermasian-inspired participatory process and the behind the scenes, informal lobbying activities of the Friends of the Valley.

I have attempted to reveal the varying shades of the actors' representations and the power of their networks. I have demonstrated how the Nyungah Aboriginals were almost completely left 'in the shadows' whilst networks with more palatable representations of the area basked in the light. I have illuminated the role of the media as intermediary in transforming the voice of the Friends of the Valley from that of eight or nine actors to a significant proportion of the population of Perth and in so doing shifting the power from the hands of the state and local authority planners to those of the Friends of the Valley.

My next set of stories offers contrasting narratives of nature and a process in which smokescreens and smudged lines were drawn in the forests.

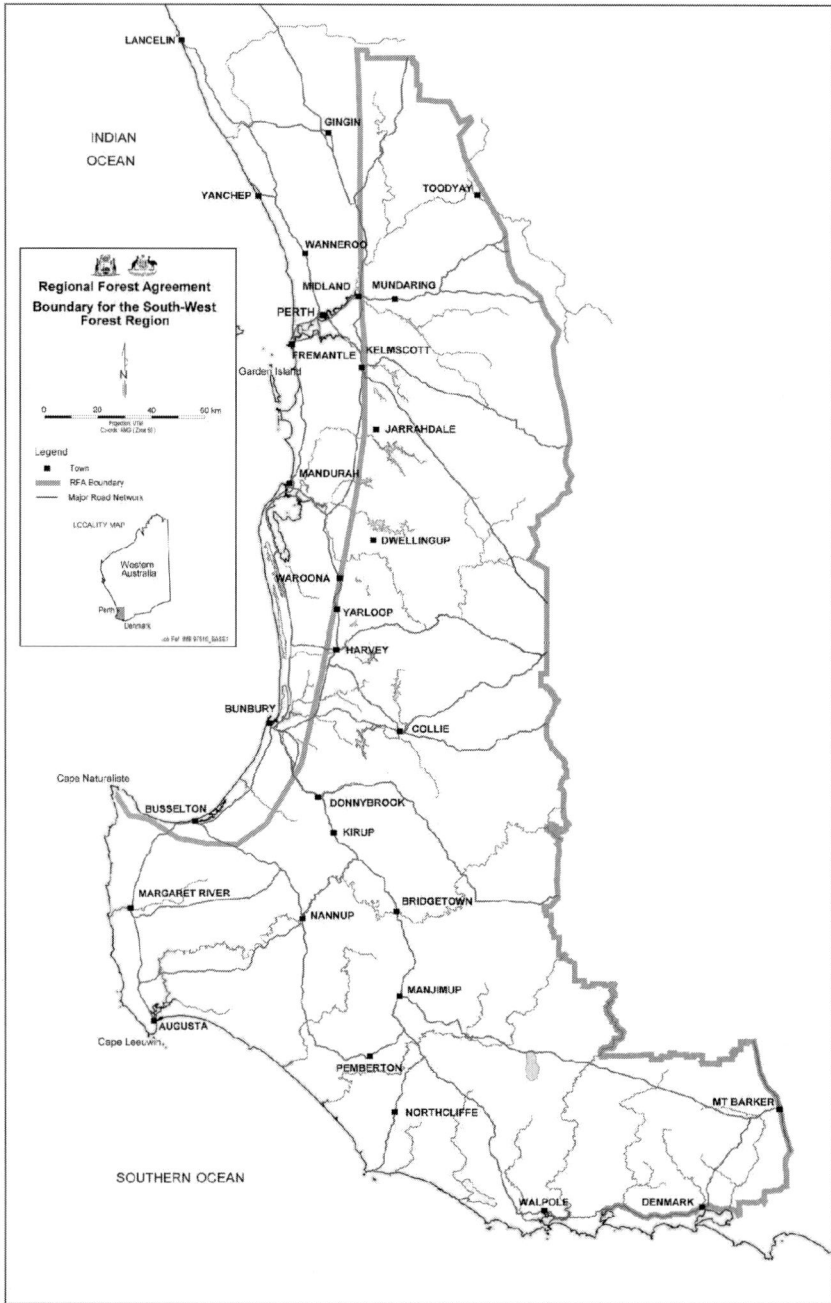

Figure 7.1   The South West Forest Region: towards a regional forest agreement (Source: CALM, 1998a: 57)

CHAPTER 7

SFUMATO IN THE FORESTS

CONTEXT: THE WESTERN AUSTRALIAN REGIONAL FOREST AGREEMENT[9]

> This unremitting forest, – it disturbs me. Far, far too many trees (Pynchon, 1998: 615).

In Western Australia native forests are confined mainly to the south west of the state (see Figure 7.1). Predominant native forest types are jarrah, marri and karri[10] forest. Of the 4.25 m ha in the South West Forest Region, about 1.87 m ha (44 per cent) are privately owned and mainly cleared for agriculture. The remaining 2.58 m ha (56 per cent) is in public ownership (Crown Land), predominantly under native forest and pine and eucalyptus plantations. Of the WA state government (CALM) managed land, some 745,000 ha (31 per cent) is formally protected in designated reserves, while 64 per cent is considered to be an economic resource. In 1994 1.2 m ha of Crown Land jarrah-marri and karri-marri forest was made available for logging or 'harvesting' under the 1994–2003 Forest Management Plan (CALM, 1998a).

Trees to be harvested are the '*mature and senescent*, damaged or under-stocked forest and other forest growing at well below potential growth rates: thinning overstocked stands …; and salvaging damaged or diseased trees that would otherwise be lost' (CALM, 1998a: 33) (emphasis added). Mature and senescent trees tend to be found in old-growth forests.

Table 7.1 illustrates the annual timber harvest rates as set out by the Forest Management Plan (1994–2003), the Regional Forest Agreement (RFA) of May 1999 and the revised RFA (July 1999), together with the volumes of timber harvested in 1996–7.

Data in Table 7.2 illustrate how little of the trees becomes value-added timber, contrasting with the high percentages which become woodchips, firewood and waste.

In 1992 Australia's National Forest Policy Statement (Commonwealth of Australia, 1992) presented a vision for ecologically sustainable management of Australian forests in which the role of citizens in the community was emphasised, together with the scientific and economic roles of forests: 'a holistic approach to managing forests for all their values and uses so as to optimise benefits for the

Table 7.1 Annual timber harvest rates (in cubic metres)

Forest Type	Forest management plan	Production 1996–7	RFA (May 1999)	RFA (July 1999)
Karri				
Grade 1 sawlogs	214,000	152,000	178,000	50,000
Other logs	203,000	190,000	*	*
Additional to gross bole	75,000	12,000	*	*
Total	**492,000**	**354,000**		
Jarrah				
Grade 1 & 2 sawlogs	490,000	453,000	286,000	286,000
Other logs	870,000	47,000	*	*
Additional to gross bole	300,000	109,000	*	*
Total	**1,660,000**	**609,000**		
Marri				
Sawlogs	69,000	7,000	80,000	80,000
Other logs	490,000	453,000	*	*
Total	**559,000**	**460,000**		

*Data not yet available
Source: CALM, 1998a: 42, 51; 1999a: 18

Table 7.2 The fate of native trees in south west Western Australia (1996–7)

354,000 m³ of karri logs were produced
57% became woodchips
18% became structural timber
2% became value-added timber
23% became firewood, sawdust and waste.
609,000 m³ of jarrah logs were produced
10% became structural timber, including railway sleepers
16% became value-added timber
22% became charcoal
52% became firewood, sawdust and waste.
460,000 m³ of marri logs were produced
99% became woodchips
0.4% became structural timber
0.04% became value-added timber.

The estimated annual gross value of timber and wood-based products in WA has been calculated at $400m, or approximately ten per cent of West Australian GSP.
Exports of wood and wood-based products were valued at $123.3m in 1996–7.
(Sources: CALM, 1998a; WAFA, 1998a)

community' so that 'a range of sustainable forest industries ... will be expanding' and that 'forests and their resources are used in an efficient, environmentally sensitive and sustainable manner' (Commonwealth of Australia, 1992: 1). Agencies of governance in Australia clearly believe that nature as forests should be strategically planned and managed using appropriate techniques to 'ensure harmony' (Macnaghten and Urry, 1998: 189) between the different, competing interests.

Negotiation of Regional Forest Agreements (RFAs) between the Commonwealth and state governments establishes the management and use of forests for the successive twenty years. The RFAs provide a 'blueprint for the future management' of an 'internationally competitive and ecologically sustainable forest products industry' and 'a world class forest system reserve' (Environment Forest Taskforce, 1997: 1) outside of which, trees 'will be available for wood production' (Environment Forest Taskforce, 1997: 1). Commonwealth targets for conservation include reservation of 60 per cent of old-growth forest identified at time of assessment: old-growth forest being defined as 'ecologically mature forest where the *effects of disturbances are now negligible*' (NFPSIS, 1997: S6.2.1, emphasis added)

As indicated in the Chronology (Table 7.3) the RFA Public Consultation Paper (PCP) was released on 25 May 1998. The RFA was finally signed on 4 May 1999.

The RFA outcome was claimed by the state government as 'a good balance between jobs and investment and protection of important forests' (CALM, 1999b: 1). It included a 12 per cent (150,885 ha) increase in formal conservation reserves; the creation of twelve national parks; reductions in levels of sawlog cut of jarrah to 286,000 m^3 and of karri to 171,000 m^3 from 2004 and an increase in sawlog cut of marri to 80,000 m^3 from 2004 (see Table 7.1). In addition, $41.5m was allocated for the timber industry to create up to 500 jobs through downstream processing and value adding and for Business Exit Assistance for mills and timber workers negatively affected by industrial restructuring. As government ministers stated, 'the overall emphasis was to provide certainty to the timber industry' (Tuckey and Edwardes, 1999: 1).

Reactions to the RFA varied from acceptance by the timber industry to anger and claims of deception from conservation groups. It appears that although 55,000 ha of 'new' old-growth forest reservation was announced, some 9,300 ha of previously approved old-growth reservation was revoked. Of this 45,700 ha net gain, some 26,300 ha is woodland or non-commercial old-growth forest which would anyway be unsuitable for logging. Furthermore, 70 per cent of the 150,885ha of new reserves was in regrowth rather than old-growth forest and over 350,000ha of the total land reserved in the RFA was not forested but rather coastal heath, scarplands, rocky outcrops, sand dunes, sedgelands, swamps, an exotic tree park, land cleared for agriculture, a prison farm and even gravel pits and rubbish tips. In contrast, the highest quality tall tree types, coincidentally the most depleted and least well represented in conservation reserves, had generally been retained for logging (WAFA, 1999).

Table 7.3 Chronology of RFA-related events in Western Australia

Date	Event
1992	National Forest Policy Statement
1995	RFAs: the Commonwealth Position
6 Feb 1998	Comprehensive regional assessments and RFA for WA published
Feb 1998	Intended date of signing WA RFA
25 May 1998	'Towards a RFA for the SW Forest Region of WA' – a paper to assist public consultation released
5 July 1998	Rally for old-growth forests, Perth
31 July 1998	Closure of submissions on public consultation
Sept/Oct 1998	Intended date for signing RFA
4 May 1999	RFA signed
11 May 1999	High Conservation Forest Bill passed in WA Legislative Council
May–Aug 1999	Rallies, demonstrations throughout SW WA for and against RFA. Destruction of 'forest rescue' camp
2 July 1999	Liberals for Forests established
27 July 1999	WA government revises RFA
23 Aug 1999	Federal government debates RFA powers. Senate votes to amend Act twice before it is withdrawn in Lower House
25 Nov 1999–2000	Fragmentation of CALM. New Department of Conservation and State Conservation Commission; new Forest Products Commission and Ministers
Feb 2000	Bunnings Forest Products renamed the Southern Timber Company (SoTiCo) and sold to Marubeni (Japan)
Feb 2001	New State Labour government (plus two Liberals for Forests in the Upper House) immediately halts logging of old-growth forests, revises logging targets and announces new National Parks
2004–13	Forest Management Plan: consultation begins 2001

Opposition to the RFA increased throughout May and June as such information became available. Such opposition, and demands for the protection of old-growth forest, were not confined to stereotypical environmental groups, but breached traditional divisions of class, age and race. In early July 1999 a new political party, Liberals for Forests, broke away from the ruling Liberal Party, claiming to have the support of 31 per cent of traditional Liberal and 47 per cent of Liberal/National Party coalition voters. To an administration whose continued majority depended on marginal seats in parliament, Liberals for Forests presented a considerable threat.

The WA government announced a revised RFA in July 1999. Revisions included the phasing out of logging in old-growth karri and tingle forests by the end of 2003 and a reduction in the karri sawlog cut to 50,000 m³ per annum from 2004. The original RFA cut levels remained for jarrah and marri (see Table 7.1). No new conservation reserves were announced, despite pressure from the National Party to protect up to twenty-one high-conservation blocks in line with the Bill passed through the Upper House of the WA Parliament in May. The government estimated that the revised RFA could cost 1,500 jobs in the south west timber industry and pledged that affected individuals would be well compensated. The timber industry reacted strongly. Often-violent demonstrations occurred, with 'forest rescue' camps being smashed and burned.

In February 2001, the Labour Party inflicted a surprise defeat on the WA Liberal administration. To the delight of the two new Liberals for Forests members of the Upper House of Parliament, the incoming Labour administration announced an immediate cessation of logging in 99 per cent of old-growth forests and directed that around 340,500 ha of old-growth forests be added to the existing reserve system.

Having learnt from the RFA which proved disastrous for the Liberal government, the new Labour administration is preparing its Forest Management Plan in an overtly communicative and participatory manner. A round-table of interest groups has been established together with a project Steering Committee inclusive of most interests. It is intended that several open forest forums will be held throughout Perth and the south west. It remains to be seen whether a theoretically more open and participatory Habermasian-style process will meet with more acceptance and success than its predecessor.

The story I narrate here is that of the Regional Forest Agreement (RFA) process. The main actors involved in WA included:

- WA state government: the Minister and Ministry for the Environment, the Department of Conservation and Land Management (CALM).
- Commonwealth government: Minister and Ministry for the Environment, Department of Primary Industry and Energy, Minister for Forestry and Conservation.
- Political parties.
- 'Environmental groups': The West Australian Forest Alliance (an umbrella group representing some twenty environmental organisations), the Conservation Council of WA, The Wilderness Society, etc.
- The timber industry: including Wesfarmers/Bunnings Forest Products (transnationally owned and since February 2000 renamed the Southern Timber Company, and subsequently sold to Marubeni of Japan), the Forest Industries Federation (WA).

- Pro-logging groups: e.g. the Forest Protection Society, since December 1999 renamed Timber Communities Australia.
- Citizen-workers of south west forest towns involved in the timber industry, tourism, etc., trade union groups.
- The WA population in general: including groups such as Men & Women in Suits, doctors, 'New Agers', as well as individuals.
- The trees: particularly old-growth forests.

Stakeholders may act individually, or in combination in temporary alliances of what may be otherwise antagonistic tendencies. Perth doctors and businesspeople have allied with more stereotypical, younger 'greenies' in a broad community of anti-old-growth logging interest, combining into a strategic assemblage (Deleuze and Guattari, 1987) temporarily uniting the disparate elements of its formation.

A different form of temporary alliance is exemplified by groups such as the Forest Protection Society (FPS), now Timber Communities Australia. The WA FPS represents the mobilisation of timber-industry employees, families, friends, shareholders, customers, suppliers and vendors for the retention of old-growth logging.

As we can see from this non-exhaustive list of stakeholders, 'threats to nature are no longer just threats to nature; instead, pointing them out threatens property, capital, jobs, trade-union power and the economic basis of entire sectors and regions' (Beck, 1995: 122).

REPRESENTATIONS

Representations of old-growth forests are often more subtly drawn than those in the North East Corridor story above. Whilst there are some stark contrasts in representation (between dark and light shades), there are many blurred, smoky effects of almost infinitesimal transitions between areas of colour, reflecting the ecology of the forests themselves. The old-growth forest story represents sfumato; a luminous modulation of light and shade where deep colour contrast is used relatively sparingly.

I offer a portrait of the double-edged role of science and technology regarding nature, serving as both a cause of its exploitation and degradation and a source of its identification and preservation. In drawing this picture, I examine the tensions between scientific, spiritual and other values, frames and story-lines and politics. Underlying these tensions lies the dominant governmental technocratic orientation in environmental resource management and policy-making and the environmental movement's ambivalent relationship to science. For many environmentalists a more satisfactory process would be based in a less technocratic, if not completely different, type of science linked to participatory citizen involvement – a form of environmental democracy.

Figure 7.2 Karri forest (Source: anon (nd.) postcard image, Hunter as in Hillier, 2000b: 85)

I read texts in the public domain as examples of the various narratives and frames invoked and the ways in which they inform and organise practice. These texts range from Commonwealth and state government reports and media releases (both from the Internet and newspapers), to other actors' reports, press releases, newsletters and brochures, photographs, and even cartoons, CDs and novels.

Representations of nature may become political issues mediated through the planning system. The human decision-making process involves the complex interplay of a range of actors (planning officers, elected members, members of local communities, technical and other experts and professionals, etc.). Each actor brings their own (or their group's) interpretations and representations of nature to the process. In conflicts where the 'common good' (i.e. of people) conflicts with the 'good' of nature, nature has no accepted individuality to participate in decision-making. It must rely on representation by other actors.

How are these representations constructed and circulated? No representation is neutral. How are representations connected to power relations? I ask which particular representations of nature determine and legitimate specific practices. How is deliverance enacted in practice?

As a framework for analysis I utilise a simple classification of evaluative frames and environmental narratives or story-lines developed in Australia (Hillier, 1998c), set in a crude temporal division of concern between short term (up to twenty years, the duration of the RFA, once signed) and long term.[11]

I follow Eder's (1996) discourse-frame methodology for analysis of the RFA policy process:

• identification of actors' cognitive framing devices and their attitudes towards relationships with the forests;
• analysis of constructions of symbolic packaging for reasons of communication.

FRAMES AND STORY-LINES

An illusion, a shadow, a story (Lines, 1998).
The contested character of the native forests in south west WA stems from the complexity, not only of the interrelationships between the scientific biotic and topological components of forest ecosystems, but also of the economic and socio-cultural frames through which actors regard them and the stories which they tell.

Referring to the framework in Table 7.4, I ask questions about what frames control the meaning of the old-growth forest story-lines. To what ends are the stories discursively used in the debate, and with what outcomes?

TREES AS A RESOURCE

'Money answereth all' (Lines, 1998: 116).
One of the most obvious frames to identify is that of regarding the forests as a resource. I distinguish here between individuals viewing forests as a source of personal income and the timber companies and state government which appear to regard the south west forests as a resource commodity from which the maximum amount of revenue should be obtained.

Many of the texts produced during the RFA process and subsequent comments from agencies of governance and the timber industry exemplify use of a commodity narrative within a short-term temporal resource frame:

> the need to recognise that Australia's wealth came from its primary resources: long-term resource security, sought by timber, mining and tourism industries; without harvesting forests will die of old age, revenue will be lost (CALM, 1998a: 110).
>
> The key issues are: the rights and, in fact, the demands of consumers for forest products... . Big investments have been made in the Australian forestry industry and more is needed. ... The economy needs such investment and our balance

Table 7.4 Frames and story-lines

	Short term		Long term		
Story-line	Resource	Personal income	Environmental preservation		
			scientific	aesthetic	spiritual
Scientific	Governance; timber industry	Citizen workers; Unions; FIF (WA); FPS	WAFA EPA		
Colonial	Governance; timber industry	Citizen-workers; unions; FIF (WA); FPS			
Romantic		Tourism operators		Rural lifestylers; WAFA; WA popn.	'New Age' popn. WA
National	Governance	Tourism operators			
Ecological			WAFA		
Conservation	CALM	Tourism operators	WAFA EPA	Rural lifestylers; WAFA; WA popn.	'New Age' popn. WA
Commodity	Governance; timber industry	Tourism operators; citizen-workers	WAFA	Tourism operators	
Aboriginal	Nyungah				Nyungah

of trade cannot afford importing more forest products. A regional forest agreement (RFA) is therefore based on assessing and addressing these problems. It is not purely an environmental exercise (Tuckey, Federal Minister for Forestry and Conservation, 1999: 14).

All we want is security of resource (John MacLeod, timber industry employee, cited in Armstrong, 1999: 24).

The old-growth forests are commodified in the utterances above as a resource for the timber industry. The importance of the industry to the WA state economy is stressed.

Of particular interest is the Federal Minister for Forests and Conservation Wilson Tuckey's statement that 'consumers' have 'rights' to forest products.[12] The 'consumers' implied appear to be purchasers of felled timber rather than tourists and fauna who may 'consume' the living forest.

Other texts employ story-lines of *scientific rationality* to justify their framing of forests as a resource. Agencies of governance, in fact, appear to place extra emphasis on the scientific credibility of their reports:

> The WA RFA will be based on extensive and wide ranging scientific research. ... More than 200 experts ... Rigorous scientific assessment of existing and newly collected environmental, heritage, social and economic data ... 38 research projects (CALM, 1997: 1).

> More than 153,000 flora records covering 3,244 plant species came from a range of sources both within and outside CALM. The RFA region was found to contain 462 plant species of conservation significance, 43 of which were declared rare (CALM, 1998c: 1).

In addition to the text quoted above, Appendices 6 to 9 of the Public Consultation Paper (CALM, 1998d) contain some forty-six pages of densely packed quantitative data which require considerable time and effort in cross-referencing to understand. Only a very low proportion of readers will be able or willing to do so.[13]

The government is keen to establish scientific credibility for the RFA. However, many questions may be asked even about the above texts. The weight of the scientific reports, their titles and the academic qualifications and organisational affiliation of the authors seem to carry more weight than either their scientific competence or the validity of their scientific investigations.

Governance attitudes have also been described as *colonial* story-lines:

> The corporate culture at CALM is the colonial mentality writ large: dogmatic in its belief in its rightness; authoritarian both in its top down approach and its heavy hand against any dissent; and paternalistic in its patronising attitude towards anyone outside its ranks who dares have an opinion (James, 1998: 14).

Nature is something to be exploited. In its original state it has no value. Value is only given by bringing what is socially (colonially) perceived as a 'natural resource', such as 'land', into 'productivity'. The introduction of 'civilisation' to Australia with white settlement in the nineteenth century was not surprisingly followed by the widespread 'domination' or destruction of plant and animal life in acts of geographical violence. As Dunphy (in Thompson, 1986: 27) has noted, 'tree destruction became a kind of national complexus ... For some settlers the very zenith of land "improvement" was a holding absolutely short of trees – a grassy desert'. Today, for some planners, the very zenith of land improvement may be urbanisation. Both types of improvement are similar, however, in that they are essentially driven by market forces. 'The prevailing practices dictate profit-driven transformation of environmental conditions and an approach to nature which treats it as a passive set of assets to be scientifically assessed, used and valued in commercial (money) terms' (Harvey, 1996: 131).

PERSONAL INCOME FRAME

Save jobs, save families (Forest Protection Society)
The Public Consultation Paper (CALM, 1998c) suggests that there are some 1,842 people directly and about 18,000 indirectly employed in timber production and timber using industries in WA, although not all those so employed will live in the south west. In addition approximately 5,000 people may be engaged in the tourism sector, whilst others are employed in apiculture, floriculture (wildflowers), mining and mineral processing.

The south west forests thus represent a source of income for a considerable number of people and their families, who realistically regard the forests as a commodity from which they draw revenue. Some feel that the conservation of old-growth forests would threaten their incomes and actively demonstrate in favour of the logging industry:

> Save our timber industry; save the little towns in the forests of the southwest; save jobs, save families ... 7,000 jobs would be lost if all the remaining old-growth forest were put in reserves, thus affecting the lives of 16,000 people (anon, 1998a).

This utterance is one of the few to make a distinction between old-growth and other native forest. Most of the timber industry texts refer to native forest in general as opposed to plantation forest. Use of the term 'native' forest, conflating both old-growth and regrowth trees, loses the distinction between them. This is an important issue because the environmental groups' opposition is not to felling of previously logged regrowth areas, but of 'virgin' old-growth forest.

City People Don't Kill our Communities (timber workers' banner)
The rural timber workers have set up a dichotomy between themselves and what they perceive as Perth-based urban conservationists and decision-makers. This dichotomy (albeit somewhat over-simplistic, ignoring, as it does, the dependence of the south west tourism industry on visits predominantly by residents from Perth) replicates the 'us–them' polarisation invoked in environmental disputes internationally. 'Them' – the city people – are implied as middle-class 'greenies', who have little thought for any but themselves and who are ignorant of the ramifications of their influence on political decisions and of the 'real' issues, such as jobs and incomes.

> How will we pay the mortgage, rates, phone and power bills? … heaven help my
> children if they need new shoes. My children did not ask to be born (Fornero,
> 1999: 12).

Other local residents are strongly against logging of the old-growth forests, however, as they derive their livelihoods from the aesthetic experiences and attractions
which the forests offer:

> Nature-based tourism … plenty of opportunities for a tourism bonanza – if only
> we keep our old-growth forest (McDonald, 1998: 10–11).
> The residents say they rely on the unique forest to bring tourists into the area,
> providing spin-offs for local tourist ventures, and logging the block would spell
> the end of tourist-related industries and the town (Rechichi, 1998: 43).

The actors engaged in tourism-related industries often employed romantic narratives when describing the RFA area:

> log fires, rain on the roof, walks in the forest, romance (Coppins, cited in
> Zekulich, 1998: 5).

ENVIRONMENTAL PRESERVATION FRAME

It's not harvesting; it's slaughter (WA Conservation Council)
Most of the actors demonstrating an environmental preservation frame do so
through a *scientific* story-line. The West Australian Forest Alliance (WAFA), in particular, claimed to have taken a rational scientific approach to refuting the
government's statistics in both the original and revised versions of the RFA and in
developing its alternative proposal (WAFA, 1999) for a conservation reserve system
and sustainable timber production in WA.

The WAFA (a coalition of some twenty environmental groups in WA) has relied
predominantly on assembling 'facts', developing arguments and justifying their statements and refuting others with scientific data in order for their arguments to become
accepted as legitimate and therefore empowered in the RFA process. The disciplinary force of the government's scientific discourse has lead to the conservationists
answering within a scientific framework.

The WAFA is faced with the dilemma of whether to argue on the terms set out
by the government, or to use other frames and story-lines. Although scientific narratives tend to carry considerable weight in enrolling the public and persuading
people to a certain point of view, the use of *aesthetic* frames is often also effective,
particularly with the lay public. Several actors, including timber community residents,
employed *romanticised* story-lines to persuade others of the aesthetic merits of the
forests.

Photographic images of beautiful forested landscapes contrast with images of the devastation wrought by clearfelling. CDs and videos, poetry, letters to the press, etc. engage the public's imaginations:

> The timber had been trucked out, and tractors and bulldozers had knocked over and ripped apart every remaining plant, treated the debris as rubbish and dragged and pushed it into heaps, ready for burning. Elsewhere, holocaust fires had left white ash, charred limbs and blackened stumps (Lines, 1998: 109–10).

Lines' evocation of the Holocaust invites consideration of old-growth forests as victims of calculated genocide and comparisons with TV images of human victims of terrorism with 'charred limbs and blackened stumps'.

Several actors question the use of the word 'harvest' with its romanticised connotations of abundance and good farm management:

> Cutting down an 800-year-old tree is not harvesting; it's slaughter (Beth Schultz, WA Conservation Council spokesperson, cited in Malan, 1998: 15).

These utterances employ vivid imagery and rhetoric as the speakers passionately give vent to their emotions about the south west forests.

SPIRITUAL FRAME

It became part of the tree's spirit (Dennis Eggington, 1998)
The final frame is a spiritual one: a frame which tends to be related to an Aboriginal narrative in Australia. However, there seems to have been little Aboriginal involvement in the RFA processes and public texts are few. Aboriginal voices are thus unfortunately marginalised in my story through their marginalisation in the RFA. Aboriginal concerns tended to be relegated to the issue of preservation of their cultural heritage rather than their current economic and social interests (see also Lane, 1999).

Most available Aboriginal utterances appear to be strongly opposed to the logging of native forest:

> After the death of a family member, traditional Nyoongars committed the dead person's spirit to a tree where it became part of the tree's spirit. Logging for Aboriginal people was like destroying graves in Karrakatta Cemetery (Dennis Eggington, Chief Executive, Aboriginal Legal Service, WA, cited in Capp, 1998b). With strong belief in reincarnation, Bibbulmun people felt the ancient trees contained their ancestors' spirits (Ken Colbung, Aboriginal Elder, cited in Jones, 1998).

Even these utterances, however, perpetuate the minimalist 'misrepresentation' (Rangan and Lane, 1999) of Aboriginal groups as dedicated to the preservation of nature rather than exemplifying the full range of frames and values which Aboriginal people hold.

Other actors who invoke a spiritual frame for the forests are members of the 'New Age' population in WA and, in particular, the neo-pagans. Neo-paganism has flourished in WA in the 1990s, especially among younger, feminist women. It is a nature-drenched goddess mythology, the representation of interconnectedness and the sense of human incorporation into a web of natural objects: 'she is in nature, and she is nature' (Luhrmann, 1993: 224).

Several neo-pagans have lived in the forest rescue camps in south west WA for almost three years. It is these people whom the media and government politicians typically label as 'feral'. They are given little opportunity to present their views for themselves in the media, generally being depicted in newspaper photographs and TV news bulletins as colourful 'oddities' or 'freaks' rather than as the predominantly middle-class tertiary-educated they are, with their own legitimate points of view.

The spiritual frame is a marginalised frame within the RFA debate.

REPRESENTATIONS AS SYMBOLIC PACKAGING

Representations of the forest become symbols with which actors identify and around which they gather: 'Greenies versus Greedies' (Rees, 1999: 14).

The anti old-growth logging campaign has been supported by doctors, academics, scientists and thousands of others who consider it their moral duty to protect the native old-growth forests of south west WA. In the absence of strong Aboriginal voice/s in the debate, middle-class, non-indigenous, predominantly urban-based residents have adopted the moral imperative of protecting the old-growth forests. They claim scientific, aesthetic and even spiritual value for the forests. Yet, as Proctor (1996: 288) eloquently writes: 'the ancient forest they strive to protect is as much a reflection of their own particular view of nature as it is some primeval ecosystem under siege by logging'. The passion of all those who have written letters, rallied, sung and danced is inevitably enmeshed in a socially based construction of the forests. Viewed from a different frame or social construction (that of the resource commodification of the government and the timber industry), an entirely different set of preferred policies and outcomes emerges.

The south west forests are a contested discursive terrain. The trees are passive actors caught in the crossfire between agencies of governance attempting to maintain capitalist accumulation from the commodification of forests as wood by socially regulating industry access to the forests, and environmental interests attempting to reinterpret the forests as biotic tree species and cultural icons and to resist their felling. Processes of place construction (such as the RFA process) are intrinsically embedded in symbolic realms. Actors utilise symbolic packaging (Eder, 1996) to create collective representations/images of themselves and of the forests. For example, the conservationist symbolic package combines a romantic aesthetic representation of trees as nature with a scientific notion of biotic nature as species of flora and fauna. The symbolic imagery used is that of tall trees, often contrasted with images of clearcut. Some actors symbolise pro-logging parties using imagery of greed (e.g. Rees, 1999).

The resource package combines a commodity representation of trees as wood products with a scientific notion of sustainable levels of harvesting. Conservation of forests is regarded as 'willful waste. To have a place like that locked up when it could be roaded and made some use of' (Watson, 1990: 64). Actors from the timber industry symbolise the environmentalists as 'ferals' and 'greenies'.

The Forest Industries Federation (FIF) and the Forest Protection Society have also entered the 'war' of photographic images. The FIF (WA) has sponsored a photographic competition for pictures of regrowth forest and has widely publicised a romantic photograph of the Boorara forest titled 'New Forest'. The implicit argument is, for city-dwellers whose main experience of the forests is vacational, what they value is not old-growth forests *per se*, but rather the mental state of awe at the sight of beauty. The argument follows that if the 'need' for old-growth forest is simply the desire for such experiences, then such feelings can be represented by some substitute: a regrowth forest, a 'forest park' or a forest-experience centre.

The old-growth forests are a social construction, the identity of which is contested: 'there are indeed multiple meanings of places, held by different social groups [and] the question of which identity is dominant will be the result of social negotiation and conflict' (Massey, 1991: 278). There can be no one reading of place or of the environment. The environment is spatially and socially embedded. It embodies organic, technical, mythic, textual, social, economic and political processes in often conflicting but inseparable ways. It has no fixed meaning, but a variety of meanings attributed to it through representation. As such, the meanings of nature become a contested domain as the same site may be read and represented very differently, both over time and by different actors.

I have attempted to highlight the various interests and their issue frames which have been mobilised and articulated in the construction of the discourses, frames and story-lines represented in the complex interplay of the RFA debate. The WA RFA story shows the meaning of the forests to be socially contested, but in ways that draw in wider issues of individual and group identity, of civil–state society and of global–local relations. The story exemplifies how the progressive globalisation of production and openness of WA to international capital flows has served to exacerbate environmental tensions and contradictions over forests. The WA Liberal government, timber industry and citizen-workers tend to utilise shorter-term resource and personal income frames and seek to maximise the income that they derive from the forests. Environmental groups, tourism operators and 'concerned individuals' tend to use environmental preservation frames and scientific, romantic and conservation story-lines in attempts to protect native old-growth forest areas.

Actors from both sides in the debate use science to classify nature. The definitions of old-growth forest and sustainable yield used by CALM become the regulative principles of the appropriation of nature. Environmental organisations, such as WAFA, also use scientific story-lines in seeking to persuade the public and government of the merits of their case. Science debates science.

With regard to the RFA, however, there exist other, non-governance, often highly differentiated discursive frames and story-lines such as the use of romantic images of tall, sun-dappled trees contrasted with the non-aesthetic 'devastation' of clearfelled forests.

Symbolic packaging is important in communicating frames and stories to the public, and hence to the government. In the media world of column centimetres, photographs and soundbites, symbolism and dramatic action give 'sensationalism' and popular interest to a predominantly urbanised middle-class public for whom a romanticised celebration of forested nature and beauty offers the promise of a haven from the everyday realities of work and stress.

ACTOR-NETWORKS AND INTERMEDIARIES

To this point I have concentrated on the content of discursive story-lines. Their context is also important. In what is essentially a contest over the meaning and use of old-growth forests, set within an institutional framework of the government-driven RFA process, organisations have sought to persuade public opinion to their viewpoints.

In WA there is a strong professional network which has traditionally been involved in policy decisions about the south west forests. This network comprises the state government in the guise of CALM and its associated scientists in both its conservation and forestry arms. An intergovernmental network of Commonwealth and state departments was involved in production of the RFA. The producer network comprised the timber industry and, to a lesser extent, the forestry arm of CALM. The RFA policy community comprised CALM, the timber industry (especially the large companies involved) and, to a limited extent, the FIF (WA).

The WA state government, as a member of both producer networks and policy communities, utilises a series of regulatory processes to enrol others to its representation of the forests. (See Hillier, 2000c, for detailed analysis of the RFA process through a lens of regulation theories.)

The RFA process was tightly regulated by the state. Policy discussion and decision-making were kept as far as possible confidential from the wider public. The RFA Steering Group consisted entirely of governance bureaucrats; the Steering Group met in secret; most of the 'expert' reports commissioned and produced in haste as part of the RFA have not been made public; assumptions underlying the options set out in the Public Consultation Paper (PCP) were not fully explained; the PCP omits evaluation or discussion of several key issues (e.g. environmental and economic costs and benefits of non-use of old-growth forests and a shift to a plantation-based industry) and details of public submissions were not published before the RFA was signed by the Commonwealth and state governments. Information was largely released only on a supposed '"need-to-know" basis, with the assumption that the general public didn't need to know' (public participation consultant, pers. comm.).

Social regulation also involves using intermediaries to regulate the sphere of conscious political calculation in ways which modify actors' understanding of their options and alternatives. It is to this aspect that I now turn.

The government (CALM) communicated its frame to the public via a series of intermediaries of published texts, including scientific documents, reports and associated media releases on assessment criteria, results of assessments and, in particular, the Public Consultation Paper which proposed a 'benchmark' for timber harvesting and three options for discussion.

The 'benchmark' and three options offered in the RFA Public Consultation Paper (CALM, 1998b) appear extremely limited in coverage. According to the WAFA (WAFA, 1998b), the paper 'presents three narrow and "biased" approaches, all of which entail ongoing widespread destruction of old-growth and other high conservation and value forests'. Moreover, WAFA claims that: there is no discussion of the employment and economic benefits of protecting old-growth forests, but an emphasis on the alleged costs and job losses; there is no discussion of the ability of the plantation-based industry to meet timber requirements and provide employment; there is very little discussion of biodiversity, heritage and tourism requirements. In addition, non-use values of forests are barely addressed.

In this way the Public Consultation Paper 'attempts to close off debate' (WAFA, 1998b: 1) about other options, exactly as Mitchell (1994: 10) foresaw in 'the exercise of control, ... the willing closing off of perspective'. The government/timber industry policy community acted to set the agenda and to prevent other institutions and alliances from doing so.

The RFA process has been co-opted into a dominant developmentalist, commodification paradigm, 'with virtually no effort to seriously investigate "no development" options or alternative regional trajectories. ... Diverse voices are replaced and *dis*placed by a generalised and homogenised interpretation in which diversity is devalued in favour of the common currency of jobs, revenue and trade as measures of success' (Howitt, 1995: 389–90, emphasis in original).

The benefits of old-growth logging and the disadvantages of preservation are regarded as self-evident when presented in terms of state and national revenue, contributions to GDP and GSP, direct and indirect employment, economic multipliers, etc. The resources of the native hardwood forests are of 'unique' international significance for woodchipping.

The many consultants who contributed to the Comprehensive Regional Assessment (CRA) methodology on which the WA RFA was based, were also regulated by state guidelines in what they could include in their reports (intermediaries). One such consultant, engaged to produce a non-indigenous cultural heritage report, expressed doubts about the value of the restrictive methodological approach ordained. She asks:

> to what extent does such a system ensure that all views and perspectives are recorded, represented and acknowledged, and following from that, does such an itemised approach to assessment lead to an adequate or accurate representation of the area under examination? (O'Connor, 2000: 1).

Her conclusion is that

> the restrictive nature of the CRA with its so-called 'scientific' approach based on categories and criteria, was not able to fully take into account the full range of values held for the south west forests, nor did it permit the public to articulate their own conceptualisation of the region. ... Such parameters are an unnatural artifice that conflicts with the holistic way in which people regard their landscape (O'Connor, 2000: 10–11).

An assumption that the RFA was premised on independent unregulated scientific understanding is disingenuous. Economic and political processes have shaped the guidelines and, in turn, the evidence provided by the government's consultants and their perceptions of what was required from them.

In attempting to enrol the lay public of WA into its representation of the south west forests, the government took pains to emphasise the extensive use of scientific data in its report:

> ABARE has previously developed a model – FORUM (Forest Resource Use Model) – to simulate such impacts. FORUM is a regional linear programming model of production forestry (CALM, 1998a: 87–98).
> Senator Hill (Federal Environment Minister) rejected criticism that the RFA was unscientific. ... There is a difference between scientific rigour and scientific debate (Capp, 1998a: 4).

An often-attempted method of closing off or regulating debate is to blind lay readers with science. The benchmark figure (the estimated outcomes of implementing the controversial Forest Management Plan 1994–2003) is never questioned, despite concerns expressed by agencies of governance and environmental organisations that the 'harvesting' quantities in the plan are unsustainable and should be reduced (Mallabone, 1998b: 13). The outcomes of implementing the three RFA options as measured against the benchmark are expressed as a morass of barely intelligible numerical statistics, which are seemingly very impressive if the besieged reader skips the detailed verbiage and relies for information on the summary table (CALM, 1998b, Box 4.4: 50) where *all* the proposed options would appear to surpass the benchmark in virtually all aspects.

Governmental reports, on close scrutiny, however, are found to be somewhat 'economical with the truth' as telling figures are omitted:

> Of the total area of approx. 2.45 million ha of public native forest managed by CALM, timber harvesting is permitted only on a portion of the multiple-use forests within State forest and timber reserves (CALM, 1998a: 41).

That 'portion' is 64 per cent (CALM, 1998a: 25).

Data assumptions are unstated:

> The current sustainable level (of harvesting) is ... 1,360,000 m^3 of jarrah (of which 490,000 m^3 are first and second grade sawlogs) (CALM, 1998c: 1).

The 'current sustainable level' for jarrah first and second grade sawlogs, however, as stated in the CRA document (about which the above statement is part of a media release) is 'approximately 300,000 m^3 per annum, based on current specifications, harvesting practices and conversion technologies' (CALM, 1998a: 42), while the Report of the 'Expert Panel' on which the first RFA was based recommends a sustainability level of 286,000 m^3 (Turner *et al.*, 1999).

Such an apparent contradiction has been the subject of much acrimonious public debate (Mallabone, 1998b: 13). Data in the RFA process have become an intermediary which can be manipulated and interpreted in accordance with economic and political objectives. By invoking the authoritative canons of scientific reasoning and methodology, as demonstrated in several of the utterances cited above, CALM seeks to legitimate the rationality of its position, thereby enrolling others into its representation.

The state also used the definition of old-growth forest itself as an intermediary. Recall the government's definition of old-growth forest as 'ecologically mature forest where the effects of disturbances are now negligible' (NFPSIS, 1997: S6.2.1). There are three vital points of regulation in this one definition: ecologically mature, forest and disturbances. All act to serve the state's economic purpose of enabling the larger, more profitable trees to be logged.

For example, 'ecologically mature' trees are deemed to be 'senescent' or 'over-mature' (CALM, 1998a: 33) and will soon die. In colloquial terms, since they are approaching their 'use-by' dates, they might as well be logged for economic return.

Second, 'disturbances' include clearing for agriculture or mining, grazing, dieback infection and logging. Following rejection of a moratorium on old-growth logging during the RFA process, the media has reported several instances of logging 'disturbance' taking place in what was previously regarded (but subsequently excluded under the definition) as old-growth forest:

> a decision made by Environment Minister Cheryl Edwardes to approve logging of an interim heritage-listed section of old-growth forest (120 ha of the Wattle block) (Mallabone, 1998a: 12).
>
> logging has been brought forward before Christmas (132 ha of the Kerr block) (Rechichi, 1998: 11).
>
> Promises from the Environment Minister Robert Hill that the conservation value of Hilliger forest would be assessed fully under the RFA had come too late to save the block (which) had been logged (Rose, 1998: 34).

Recent (2000) relaxation of dieback control has also had the effect of substantially increasing the amount of old-growth forest susceptible and subject to this form of 'disturbance'.

Finally, there is the definition of 'forest' itself. Taking the RFA definition of forest as 'a vegetation type dominated by woody vegetation having a mature or potential mature stand height exceeding 5 metres, with an overstorey canopy cover greater than 20 per cent' (CALM, 1999a: 3), over one third (around 350,000 ha) of the total land set aside for reserves in the RFA actually comprises non-forest vegetation and landforms. It consists of coastal heath, scarplands, rocky outcrops, sand dunes, sedgelands, swamps, an exotic tree park, land cleared for agriculture, a prison farm and even gravel pits and rubbish tips.

As Peter Robertson, convenor of WAFA, commented, 'there are the forests that the RFA should have protected, but instead avoided in favour of wetlands, rocky outcrops, sand dunes, cow paddocks and non-commercial woodlands' (cited in Burns, 1999b: 3). Even Don Spriggins (Chair of the WA Institute of Foresters) conceded that 'all of the twenty-seven forest ecosystems identified in the RFA are important. While some may not contain much forest …' (1999: 14).

However, the WA Minister for the Environment outwardly remained confident in her scientific advisors:

> The scientific assessment and mapping has been very explicit. We are absolutely sure about what it is that we have included. If they ['the reasonable person in the street'] were to go down to the forest they would see that it would

construe [*sic*] of swamps and rocky outcrops and that is the life of the forest,
the biodiversity. That's what they enjoy (Burns, 1999d: 18).

If gravel pits, rubbish dumps and a prison farm are all 'scientifically' forests, when is
a tree a tree?

State regulation uses science to classify the forests. It then utilises that classification as an intermediary to selectively shape attention and to structure
decision-making; to objectify, codify, and thereby manage, the forests. The definition
of old-growth forest is culturally regulated to create technical, cultural value-laden
'truths' which are used by governance to define 'reality' and become in turn the regulative principles of the appropriation of nature. They are 'implicated in
state-constructed measures to shape and control regional landscape, and to rationalise forestry spaces, which are ordered ... according to the logic of prevailing
systems of power' (Cline-Cole, 1998: 312).

Agents of governance also attempt to regulate the identity of those anti-old-
growth logging. Labels such as 'extremist', 'terrorist', 'feral' and even 'tree-hugging hippy
crap' (Wilson Tuckey, Federal Minister for Forestry and Conservation, depicted in *The
Australian*'s cartoon by Leak, 1999: 8) are examples of an intermediary of name-calling
aiming to discredit opponents in the minds of 'neutral' third parties.

The state government also utilised legislation as an intermediary. Jones (1998:
982) suggests that 'as the state is dependent on the accumulation process, when
its management is threatened, displacement tends to occur from the economic to
the political sphere'. This displacement is apparent in WA where the WA
Environment Minister has declared areas of old-growth forest as 'Temporary Control
Areas' in an exclusionary tactic of regulation. The implications of such designation
are that public access is temporarily denied to certain areas of Crown Land:

> Protesters could be fined $2,000 if they erect structures in a state forest. This
> could include a post, pile, stake, pipe, chain or anything that is fixed to the land
> [to] ensure the safety of protesters (Capp, 1998b: 10).
> Police prepare to arrest protesters illegally camped in state forest. The blockade
> has breached a Temporary Control Order (Lane block) (Capp, 1998d: 10).
> Five arrests as war restarts in forests (Rechichi, 1999: 10).
> 80 people facing 139 charges arising out of protests (Rose, 1999: 10).

People who protest thus became equated with criminals in the minds of third-party
'neutrals'.

The WAFA is itself a network, comprising some twenty or so environmental
groups together with several thousand unaffiliated individuals who logged on to its website. WAFA has also used scientific intermediaries to communicate its representations
of the old-growth forests to the public and to government.

Whilst the discourse of scientific reasoning marginalised the discourse of pop-ular political opposition during the 'official' consultation period in 1998, populist discourses have come to the foreground more recently. Environmental agencies have sought to utilise the intermediary of the media (and thereby capture public attention) through organising rallies in the Perth CBD ('Stop the Chop') and in front of the WA Parliament, concerts ('Calmageddon'), and asking difficult questions at Wesfarmers shareholders' meetings. Romanticised photographic images of tall trees were produced, in contrast with the devastation of clearcut areas. Local artists produced CDs, poetry, novels and works of art.

WAFA has also supported blockades of old-growth forest blocks about to be logged. By what they regard as civil disobedience (now criminalised under Temporary Control Orders), protesters set up forest rescue camps and occupy tree platforms and tripods, handcuff themselves to logging machinery, perform the Latvian elm folk dance and chain themselves to concrete blocks and car bodies. Contact with the state-wide media is constant and actions provide strong photo-graphic images.

The RFA process has witnessed temporal and temporary alliances between actor-networks of people who are generally driven by different logics of action. In this instance the timber industry, trade unions, the state and big business have become allied, whilst class, race, age and gender barriers have been breached in oppositional alliances between doctors, academics, rural lifestylers, Aboriginal elders and young environmental activists, many of whom have never before been involved in demonstrations.

In the RFA debate, however, the traditionally accepted resource-dominated rep-resentation of forests has not been undermined or remoulded into an environmentally based representation. Whilst amendments made to the RFA may offer some 'added-on' concessions to environmentalists – CALM, as such, has been split into the Department of Conservation and the Forest Products Commission, responsible to dif-ferent Ministers; Bunnings Forest Products has been renamed the Southern Timber Company (SoTiCo) and mostly sold to the Japanese company Marubeni; and the Forest Protection Society has become Timber Communities Australia – the transfor-mation in rhetoric does not appear to have translated into a transformation in practice (although the incoming Labour administration does seem to be making a difference). As Healey perspicaciously writes, 'unless the reframing of policy discourses touches these deeper levels of policy assumptions, the power of new strategic frames to move from rhetoric to real effects ... is likely to be limited' (1999b: 40).

LOBBYING – INSIDER VERSUS OUTSIDER STRATEGIES

Cracknell (1993) and Jordan and Maloney (1997) distinguish between insider and out-sider strategies of action. Whereas these authors regard insider activities to be those which take place within formally established processes, and outsider activities to include lobbying or direct action, I consider lobbying to also include traces of what might be called insider *and* outsider behaviour. For example, I would term as 'insider', internal lobbying activity between members of a producer network or policy community.

Such insider–outsider activity in the RFA debate included lobbying of key members of the WA Parliament and of CALM by representatives of the large timber companies active in the south west forests. Lobbying is known to have taken place during establishment of the original RFA in WA and before the Liberal government's 'backflip' (pers. comm.). This form of lobbying fits neatly the resource mobilisation model as explained earlier.

In contrast, the WA section of the Australian Conservation Foundation openly decided not to participate in the formal RFA process because of a perceived 'stack-ing' of the Steering Committee (with agents of governance) to meet predetermined ends. The ACF, as part of the WAFA, then engaged in lobbying agents of state gov-ernance, but relied to a much greater extent on enrolling the lay WA public to its representation and for public pressure to lobby the government much more effec-tively. To this effect, WAFA used the media strategically.

The media relishes images of confrontation as police arrest protesters, typi-cally depicted as young, oddly clothed and 'feral'. In order to counterbalance this imagery more middle-class environmental supporters have organised their own actions, including the Men and Women in Suits telephone blockade of the WA Premier's office to demonstrate 'passion for the old-growth forests – albeit in a con-trolled, civilised manner' (anon, 1998b: 11); the whole-page adverts in *The West Australian* placed by doctors (19 June 1998: 32 and 21 December 1998: 34) and the various adverts placed by groups of professional individuals in the press.

Official responses have been shown to be out of touch with the public mood. The WA government and its CALM advisers were caught out initially by the scale, intensity and cross-political party nature of the anti old-growth logging protests. Having made rel-atively minor amendments to the RFA, the government was then subjected to the intense physical lobbying presence of the pro-logging Forest Protection Society.

The choice of 'outsider' strategies by anti old-growth logging groups, and more recently by the timber workers (the FPS), may reflect a realistic assessment of the improbability of achieving their objectives through the RFA consultation process of written submissions, or through dialogue with Ministers or civil servants. In these instances lobbying can be seen as an outlet for feelings of frustration and alienation with the RFA process and with its outcomes.

No one can doubt, however, that the issue has not been aired in the public sphere, with newspaper editorials, TV and radio segments devoted to the old-growth debate.

In 2000 some 87 per cent of the WA population was surveyed as being against old-growth logging. The state government was forced to reframe the RFA debate from an economic to a political standpoint. As stated above, however, the Liberal administration lost control in WA in February 2001 partly because of its poor handling of the RFA process. Perhaps democracy might work after all!

CONCLUSION

THE SHADES AND LIGHTS OF CHIAROSCURO PRACTICE

What have the two chiaroscuro halves revealed? I have demonstrated the importance of representation. Representations are always of something, rather than the thing itself. Whether land on the urban fringe or old-growth trees, representations are re-presentations. Representations are social constructs and as such reflect the interests, values and ideals of those who use them. Planning practice often involves contests of representations.

In the North East Corridor aesthetic values and representations of spaciousness and rural lifestyles were eclipsed by economic values and representations of returns on investment and tourism potential. In the RFA debate, in contrast, representations of old-growth forests as pristine, natural environment, as 'a sacred cause, a fundamentally constitutive element of the human condition' (Clegg and Hardy, 1996: 682) politically overcame economic resource-based representations of trees as predominantly a timber commodity. Representation did not simply form a context for the local definition of social power, but was 'crucial to the terms of reference of such negotiations' (Jacobs, 1994: 770). Debates which appear on the surface to be about urbanisation or resource management are actually much more complex, and are about identities and meanings, values and power: about politics.

Politics, in WA as elsewhere, have become far less centred, less easily contained and brokered. Politics have become a

> micro-politics based on the cultural manufacture of identities – which themselves are no more than convenient summaries of difference – rather than a macro-politics based upon fixed entities having an ontological status because they reflect the social divisions that made the modern world (Axford, 2001: 23).

The original forms of governance have shifted and become more fluid and more fragmented. Governance is practised through shifting producer networks and policy communities, influenced often by issue networks, all of which may be cross-sectoral coalitions and networks organised at a range of spatial scales (Amin and Thrift, 1995a). Empirically grounded analyses of the two practice stories above allow understanding of such actor-networks.

Examination of the struggles for translation of representations by different actor-networks unpacks the social production of power and illustrates how 'knowledge' is produced as particular representations become accepted as 'legitimate' by actors and determine outcomes. We learn that outcomes cannot be structurally determined as the structures themselves are created by contingent and mutable social practice. Gibson-Graham (1996) argues that power configurations and the institutions by which they are reified can only be provisionally hegemonic. Therefore, as McGuirk (2000: 654) suggests, 'within every collectively performed interaction, there is the possibility for realignment, transformation and redefinition of the network and its outcomes'.

Actor-network theory illuminates the power-plays which various actors utilise in order to 'persuade' or enrol others to their viewpoint. Power-plays include the use of 'expert' scientific discourses in textual intermediaries imprinted with the dominant frames and power relations of the institutional structure and practices from which they emerge, and legislative intermediaries which create exclusionary boundaries around what is legislated to be appropriate and inappropriate behaviour.

Other power-plays involved informal negotiation and lobbying of key actors which often proved to be more effective in influencing outcomes than did participation in formally established processes of decision-making. 'It is the backstage power-play ... which is the real politics of planning' (Flyvbjerg, 1998a: 8).

Although permitting members of the public to have some influence over the decision outcomes, it would appear that lobbying activities further serve to marginalise the already marginalised in society. Lobbying favours those who have connections and who are articulate, who tend to be the wealthier groups in society (Schlozman, Verba and Brady, 1999). In addition, as Fiorina (1999) demonstrates, lobbying may allow small unrepresentative groups of people with intense commitments to extreme causes to influence outcomes which are deleterious to the rest of society. (I take up the questions of whether lobbying has the potential to undermine the capacity of planners to plan and what action planners could take in such circumstances in Part 4.)

A key feature of lobbying is that it cannot be formalised into rules or procedures. It is reliant on the political opportunity structure and the existence or otherwise of opportunities to lobby and on the capacity, the motivation and skills and connections of the individuals and networks involved. As such it remains lodged in an informal arena.

Networks are relational and fluid. They form and transform according to the issues under consideration. Network activities involve relationships with and responses from other actors, who in turn are drawn into focusing attention on the issue and into reshaping their own identities, representations and perhaps even commitments. Identities are inherently relational, both at an individual level, but also in respect of collective group or actor identities.

Actor-network theory facilitates the deconstruction of power-structures, decision-making and the resultant decisions. Through actor-network theory we can begin to unpack the social production of place. Place is constructed out of a particular constellation of relations, articulated together as a particular locus. As Massey (1993: 66) writes, place is 'constructed out of particular interactions and mutual articulations of social relations, social processes, experiences and understandings, in a situation of co-presence'. Places are processes.

PRACTICE STORIES AND COMMUNICATIVE INTERACTION

How do the practice stories relate to communicative interaction and/or the model of discursive democracy presented in Part 2? Both practice stories narrate instances of community participation: in the North East Corridor a Habermasian-inspired communicative process and in the RFA a controlled consultation process, in both of which agencies of government offered lay people only 'accommodative voice' (Sampson, 1993), intending to accommodate the public by letting people have their say, although power relationships were to remain unchanged.

Both stories illustrate the wide diversity of stakeholders in planning decisions, some of whom are power-full and others relatively power-less; some have the authority of governance, some do not; some are resource-full, possessing wealth, education, articulateness, connections, others are not. Habermasian communicative action, as we have seen, utilises a standpoint of the generalised other, a universalist identity of the moral self such that 'each individual is a moral person endowed with the same rights as ourselves' (Benhabib, 1992: 10). By abstracting from the concrete individual identity of the other participants, everyone is able to treat all others as equal rational beings entitled to the same rights and duties as they would wish for themselves. 'The moral dignity of individuals derives not from what differentiates them from all others, but from what, as speaking and acting agents, they have in common with all others' (Benhabib, 1992: 151). Participants are accorded a definitional identity which annuls differences (of identities, values, feelings, motives, etc.) between people. Difference is something which must be transcended because it is partial and divisive, and inhibits intersubjectivity or reversibility of perspectives. Although Habermas (1993, 1994) identifies a plurality of participants' lifeworlds and expounds a need for value pluralism, he generalises this all away in his attempt to seek some universal basis of participant equality on which communicative action can stand. Participants thus become equal by bracketing difference.

Habermasian communicative action, therefore, treats different people by the same standard. Treating people equally, however, is inherently unequal (e.g. sole use of the English language in participation programmes when many participants have a non-English speaking background). According to Habermas, this may be the best we can do. It represents 'an attempt to exclude violence, if only to reproduce some sort of violence internally again but in a criticisable fashion' (Habermas, 1992: 479). But I do not think this is good enough. We can and we must do better to accommodate difference.

Both practice stories also illustrate the role of power and politics in influencing agendas and decision-making. Discussion of Habermas' distinction between communicative action and instrumental or strategic action is relevant at this point.

Instrumental or strategic action involves actors bringing about a desired outcome by selecting an appropriate means to deliver success. Such means may involve the manipulation or strategic distortion of communication and/or other ways of using power to influence the decision. (See Phelps and Tewdwr-Jones, 2000, for more detail and an empirically grounded analysis of Habermasian action forms.) Instrumental action is political.

My task now is to attempt to introduce the 'political' aspects of direct action/lobbying into the more 'moral' theoretical framework of procedurally just communicative action outlined earlier. It is impossible to depoliticise planning decisions and we must recognise not only the formal political role in the planning process of elected representatives, but we should also 'scratch the surface' (Phelps and Tewdwr-Jones, 2000) to reveal how social actors are increasingly organising and mobilising outside of the formal procedure. Direct action/lobbying has become part of decision-making behaviour.

As Mouffe (1996) suggests, social objectivity is constituted through acts of power. It is ultimately, therefore, political and exclusive. It is hegemonic. Power is not an external relation between already constituted identities, but in fact constitutes the identities themselves in a contingent and precarious terrain. The purely constructed nature of social relations is thus based in power. Power is legitimated in order to impose itself. In any analysis of or attempt to understand empirical decision-making behaviour 'it therefore becomes meaningless, or misleading ... to operate with a concept of rationality in which power is absent' (Flyvbjerg and Richardson, 1998: 5).

This is a different reading of power to the Habermasian view of power as illegitimate. In Habermasian communicative action legitimacy is grounded purely in rationality and the force of the better argument. By eliminating other expressions of power, communicative action is unable to recognise the essential relationship between power and legitimacy.

We need to recognise and understand the crucial role of antagonism and conflict in decision-making between different viewpoints and interests. In fact, as Mouffe (1996: 8) asserts, 'one cannot take seriously the existence of a plurality of legitimate values without recognising that they will conflict and that conflict may well be ineradicable. We should not, therefore, assume that conflicts can easily be mediated or accommodated without violence to some or other views and actors. There will always be losers.

The key problem with Habermasian communicative approaches to decision-making is that they still rely on *rationality*. They are still essentially *moral*. In reality, however, as my practice stories demonstrate, politics often intervenes, pushing notions of rationality and morality into the realms of the utopian. I am here at odds with Habermas (1994: 109) who, despite recognising that 'significant political issues ... touch on questions of justice', then subsumes the political into 'what they are, as moral and practical questions'. I believe there is a fundamental difference between moral and political considerations, a difference noted by Tewdwr-Jones and Allmendinger (1998: 1981) who state that communicative action is inherently unable to 'guarantee that all participants will act in an open and honest manner all the time'.

It is rather politics and the transformation of actors' political identities, often using rhetoric as a tool of persuasion, which are important. There are also many issues which simply defy universal comprehension (e.g. indigenous peoples' spiritual issues) and which therefore cannot be resolved at a rational level. The above considerations fall clearly outside of the Habermasian model.

In the North East Corridor decision, communicative rationality yielded to strategic action and power. As some actors' positions became more entrenched, some withdrew from the formal participation process in frustration and confusion and others engaged in direct action outside of the formal process. These 'categories' were by no means mutually exclusive. At present in Western Australia, as the two stories indicate, it appears to be somewhat more of a 'fight with few holds barred than ... a contest under well-defined rules' (Gamson, 1995: 142), with the odds heavily weighted in favour of the already advantaged groups in society. The North East Corridor story demonstrates how alliances/advocacy coalitions are an important aspect of the rationality of power and how groups which did not form strategic alliances, whose members' core policy beliefs were not in consensus, or who did not possess effective networks which they could call upon, were unable to influence the decision outcome. Those stakeholders with fewer, less strong network contacts were left to participate predominantly through the hierarchical rational formal structure, or not to participate at all, placing them in an inevitably weak position. If these actors form what Fraser (1992) and subsequently Habermas (1996) referred to and advocated as a 'weak public',[14] they are very weak indeed.

The local authorities and state planning departments were also left on the decision margin, being unable to engage in overt strategic action and 'naked power-play' (Flyvbjerg, 1998a: 233). The tensions and conflicts between the institutional constraints of traditional managerial, hierarchical ways of working of officers of governance and the horizontal networks of other actors were worked through, not by communicative action, but by power-plays. Foucauldian analysis of power offers much to the understanding of both stories.

Both practice stories demonstrate that contemporary civil society appears to have fragmented into a range of diverse public spheres, some of which are gaining considerable amounts of power. At the same time, the Habermasian-type political public sphere appears to be losing its influence and significance at the expense of some of the more cultural spheres (Sassi, 2001). As Sassi writes, 'both civil society and the public sphere appear today as more plural by nature than before, revealing a more agonistic realm consisting of extremes in movements and groups hostile towards each other' (2001: 100). Such contradictions would seem to emphasise the need for a non-coercive, discursive arena for actors to work through policy disputes.

The North East Corridor and RFA stories also clearly demonstrate that participation does not necessarily lead to consensus formation, an important issue to which I return in Part 5.

On the plus side of communicative or discursive action, however, some actors did listen to the representations and arguments presented and did, as a result, change their opinions and sometimes their activity. The most notable instance of persuasion through the force of argument in the RFA instance was the conversion of Dame Rachel Cleland, founder member of the WA Liberal Party, to the anti old-growth logging cause and her subsequent formation of a new political party, Liberals for Forests, which played a significant role in toppling the sitting Liberal regime.

Barker (1999: 11) lists elements of change brought about through communicative action as including not only altered opinions, but also a sense of changed personal and collective identity, altered forms of public speech and ideas, a sense of self-empowerment, the de-legitimation of existing authority and the creation of new informal and formal institutions and networks. Perhaps the most famous instance of a person undergoing profound change through discussion is Gusty Spence. Former regional leader of the Ulster Volunteer Force, a paramilitary Protestant loyalist organisation in Northern Ireland, imprisoned for the murder of a Catholic barman, Spence talked at length with imprisoned members of the Irish Republican Army (IRA). Backing this discussion with seminars with academic visitors and extensive reading, Spence came to view violence as counter-productive and espoused the cause of reconciliation with the Catholics. Since his release from prison, Spence has devoted himself to community politics and the development of peace in Northern Ireland (Garland, 2001).

The key to Spence's transformation was his search for areas of 'common ground' with the Catholic prisoners, and the investigation of 'radical ways forward' (Garland, 2001: 202–3). Unfortunately, despite Spence's achievement of increased dialogue and cooperation amongst the prisoners, such attitude transformations were not taken up by the higher media profile 'petty politicians [who preferred] scor-

ing sectarian points' (Spence, in Garland, 2001: 197) and whose purposes negotiation did not suit.

As Spence concluded, 'one has to be prepared to take that extra step – it's
known as *compromise*' (Garland, 2001: 198, emphasis in original). Spence men-
tions compromise, not consensus, although as will be seen in Chapter 12,
Habermas has recently entertained the idea of compromise as a possible outcome
of communicative action.

I have mentioned Gusty Spence at some length because his conversion from
the instrumental force of might to communicative force of the better argument is per-
tinent to my planning-related cases. In addition, a similar situation to Spence's
frustration with higher profile actors was found during the RFA debate. Local people
from various 'sides' in the south west of WA were working together to reach common ground and a negotiated settlement of the dispute, including environmentalists,
business leaders and wives of timber workers. Political posturing by union leaders,
elected members and others based in Perth, however, prevented such local initiatives from gaining wider influence and momentum.

The North East Corridor and Regional Forest Agreement stories also illustrate
clear discrepancies between different perspectives on and representations of the
nature of particular issues. Discrepancies between professional planning staff and
other agents of governance and affected stakeholders are especially moot. This
points to the importance of participatory planning, of having people define their own
problems in a forum wherein they are given voice and listened to with respect.

With regard to my shades of chiaroscuro, power is seen to reside in the relationships between actors. Networking, both through formal processes of
participation and informally, has the potential to change the dynamic equilibrium
within and between these relationships and also opens up new circuits of power or
colourings which *can* benefit all concerned.

Interactive governance and participatory planning may take several forms, as
illustrated in the stories above. In some instances, we have seen that participatory
planning may get 'hijacked' (Healey, 2000: 527) by powerful actors. As Healey notes,
this potential for manipulation and takeover places a premium on an inclusionary
ethics, ' a commitment by those in governance positions to attend to the range of
relations through which people …, in diverse ways "inhabit" and give meaning'
(2000: 527) to place. Such an ethics of light needs to infuse all rather than spotlight
some of the regulatory practices through which material resources and opportunities
are planned, managed and distributed, but also the ways in which relational
resources are developed.

Methodologically, an inclusionary approach is required which facilitates the
kind of open discussion essential to a participatory context. However, as Fischer
(2001: 260) astutely comments, actual realisation of such an approach (rather then

simply its illusion – see McInroy, 2000) involves more a question of attitudes translated into practices than matters of technical methodology. It is here that Foucault's
work helps us understand that knowledge production is intrinsically a matter of
power relations.

In this part I have revealed the two halves of light and dark shades in two practice stories, plus Habermasian and Foucauldian concepts of communicative action
and power as applied to planning practice. As in successful chiaroscuro painting,
tenebrism and sfumato should be applied as circumstantially appropriate rather than
formulaically, painting-by-numbers. Can anyone imagine, for example, the Mona
Lisa's enigmatic smile (sfumato) represented tenebristically (as perhaps in
Caravaggio's *Raising Lazarus*?). The result would be akin to a leer or a grimace,
lending an infinitely different meaning to the work.

Returning to planning, the capacity for local planners to engage the empowering potentialities of participatory, communicative planning practice is inevitably
dependent on the time- and place-specific congruence of political, institutional,
socio-cultural, economic and discursive opportunity structures available (McGuirk,
2000) together with planners' own instincts of appropriateness.

In Part 4 I further explore this theme of instinct, examining how planning officers and elected representatives may be inscribed into the various interpretive
schemes of governance. To assist such exploration I take a more fine-grained ethnographic approach to questions of local planning and local planning politics.

PART 4

SHADOW NEGOTIATIONS

CHAPTER 8

THE SHADOW OF EXPERIENCE: the habitus

INTRODUCTION

In this part I continue exploration of the ways in which different actors' values and mind-sets affect planning outcomes and relate to systemic power structures. I concentrate on the activities of planning officers and elected representatives (ERs) and attempt in particular to fill the gap between officer recommendation and elected representatives' decisions by opening up the hidden transcripts of the politics of decision-making, the very logic of democratic practice. These communicative behaviours which precede and are construed in the ritualised formal process of political decision-making form a shadow of power in which practitioners and theorists work. I attempt to cast light on such shadows in order that planning practitioners may be more able to understand the 'real world' in which they work, to anticipate actions and reactions and to improvise accordingly.

As Albrechts writes, 'the whole apparatus of adverse bargaining, negotiation, compromise and deadlock which normally *surround* the planning process is undervalued' (1997: 8, emphasis added). Concentration on the mechanics of the process itself misses vital aspects such as these.

The capacity for planning officers to 'harness the empowering potentialities of governance is dependent upon the place-specific and dynamic confluence of political, institutional, socio-cultural, economic and discursive settings within which opportunities are embedded' (McGuirk, 2000: 668). As such there is a need to examine the micro-level of planning practice to discover how, in various circumstances, actors may be associated and inscribed into the interpretive schemes of networks of governance. Only actual participants themselves possess such knowledge. I therefore adopt a fine-grained ethnographic approach to the politics of planning and present narratives of practice told by planning officers and elected representatives. I am firmly of the opinion that by listening to practice stories planners can enhance their understanding of the social production of power in planning decision-making. This understanding may then become a crucial part of both identifying and enabling a more powerful mediating role for local planners.

Recent work in planning theory (e.g. Healey, 2000a; 2000b; 2002) recognises the importance of power dynamics of policy relations and policy agendas and the need for analytical tools to help identify how such relations are played out in specific

instances 'and how far this reinforces or challenges and maybe even changes established power relations and material outcomes' (Healey, 2000b: 919).

It is this fine-grained analysis which I attempt in this paper: to narrate stories
from local authority elected representatives and planners, to explore the adage that
'politicians make policy, civil servants administer',[1] to uncover any distinctive sorts of
criteria (or 'administrative politics' (Blowers, 1980: 26; Albrechts, 1999)) which
elected representatives and planning officers might bring to bear on discussions of
public issues, and to identify whether they could be said to have a certain 'cultural
style'. As such, I link analysis of the stories to the work of both Habermas and
Foucault. I also turn to Pierre Bourdieu's concept of the habitus in seeking theoretical explanation.

If planning theory is to be of real use to practitioners it needs to address practice
as it is actually encountered in the worlds not only of planning officers but also of
elected representatives. Analysis of instances where officer recommendations are
ignored, or where elected representatives change their minds, suggests that actual
decision-making may be exercised in ways which are contingent, complex and organised with little distinct or overt logic. I seek to uncover the communicative behaviours
which form a shadow of power that may remain invisible to practitioners and theorists.
Such instances of communication form the hidden transcripts of decision-making.
They constitute the functioning of habitus and the logic of democratic practice.

Practitioners' habitus – schemes of perception, appreciation and action –
enable them to perform acts of practical reasoning based on the identification and
recognition of certain stimuli, including an anticipation of political will and potential
decision outcomes. Kolb and Williams (2000) refer to this activity as 'shadow negotiation'. Planners with a sense of the game of practice may exercise an anticipated
adjustment of habitus to the probabilities presenting themselves.

I demonstrate how Bourdieuian habitus adds to planning theory some concepts of a political economy of practice, which helps an understanding of the
double structure of negotiations, of strategic interplays and the ways in which
elected representatives and planners may act in shaping land-use decisions.

EXPERIENCING SHADOWS

As outlined in Part 2, Habermas recognises the importance of experience in people's lives. His concept of the lifeworld concerns the 'shared, taken-for-granted
presuppositions of social action that enable actors to interpret each others' actions
and to participate in common institutions' (Bohman, 1999: 73). The lifeworld
encompasses the cultural structure of social situations or processes. It forms con-
text/s of action, generally inherited from the past and experience, which provide a

basis for shared understanding and which serve to constrain beliefs and actions in some manner/s without necessarily determining them.

Cook (2001) identifies three broadly defined structural components of the life-world which are reproduced symbolically by communicative action: culture, interpersonal relations and personality. These components are reproduced through socialisation processes of family status, the education system and the legal system. People acquire socialised 'generalised capacities for action' (Habermas, 1987: 137) and act in accordance with the values and norms they have acculturated. As Habermas wrote:

> how could anyone focus on moral intuitions and reconstruct them, before having them – and how do we get them? Not from philosophy, and not by reading books. We acquire them just by growing up in a family. This is the experience of everyone. … There can't be anyone who ever grew up in any kind of family who did not acquire certain moral intuitions (1986: 171).

Of importance to my argument, Habermas notes that there is an ineliminable difference between 'what we always claim for our rationality and what we are able to explicate as rational' (1985b: 195); a point which Flyvbjerg's (1998a) later work demonstrates. Habermas argues that in situated praxis, actors command a practical assurance that even the most rigorous set of arguments fails to supply. Practical assurance is a product of social habituation. There is thus a distinction in Habermas' mind between habituation and rational argument.

In contrasting, yet complementary fashion, Michel Foucault also places a primacy on an analysis of experience and habit. Foucault is more concerned than Habermas, however, with critically analysing what he describes as a 'history of the present' (1977a: 31) in order to explore, expose, challenge and perhaps transform 'those things that continue to exist and have value for us' (1977b: 146). Foucault's intention is to expose

> how that-which-is has not always been; i.e. that the things which seem most evident to us are always formed in the confluence of encounters and chances, during the course of a precarious and fragile history. … It means that they reside on a base of human practice and human history; and that since these things have been made, they can be unmade, as long as we know how it was that they were made (1983: 206).

Knowledge of how things were/are made, especially how people's subjectivity has been constituted and their conduct influenced, is possible through reflection on experience. Foucault regards experience as a place to glimpse the outside of discourse and hence the production of knowledge. In *The Thought From Outside* he wrote:

> A thought that stands outside subjectivity, setting its limits as though from with-
> out, … and that at the same time stands at the threshold of all positivity, not in
> order to grasp its foundation or justification but in order to regain the space of
> its unfolding, the void serving as its site, the distance in which it is constituted
> and into which its immediate certainties slip the moment they are glimpsed – a
> thought that, in relation to the interiority of our philosophical reflection and the
> positivity of our knowledge constitutes what in a word we might call 'the thought
> from the outside' (1987: 15–16).

This thought from outside is the locus of power and real space (Brown, 2000). It is the space of experience.

Foucault's work aims to help us come to understand ourselves through a jux-taposition of knowledge and experience. This juxtaposition results in an enhanced comprehension of the competing discourses and the fields of power which they construct and enable. Through such experiential knowledge and understanding we can position ourselves more effectively with regard to the power relations in which we find ourselves: 'knowledge as a means of surviving by understanding' (Foucault in Kritzman, 1988: 7).

Despite the insights of Habermas and Foucault, the problem remains of how to relate experience, lifeworlds and their discourse formations to the actual lives of the individual people who enact such experiences and discourses. The theorist who possibly provides the most useful way forward in working through this dilemma is Pierre Bourdieu. It is to his work which I now turn.

ON HABITUS

One of the questions with which Pierre Bourdieu's work has been concerned is 'what motivates human action?'. Do people act in response to external stimuli? To what extent is people's reasoning about how they act influenced or determined by structural factors?

For Bourdieu, 'social practices neither represent the working out of objective social laws operating, as it were, behind the scenes, nor stem from the independent subjective decision-making of free human beings' (Painter, 2000: 242). Bourdieu proposes a structural theory of practice which connects structure and agency in a dialectical relationship between culture, structure and power. He recognises the social relations among actors as being structured by, and in turn, contributing to the structuring of, the social relations of power among different positions (of class, gen-der, etc.). It is this theory which forms the basis for Bourdieu's concept of habitus, a notion not totally unlike Habermas' conception of habituation and lifeworld and Foucault's experiential history described above.[2]

Habitus is defined as 'a system of durable, transposable dispositions, structured structures predisposed to function as structuring structures, that is, as principles which generate and organise practices and representations' (Bourdieu, 1990c: 53). Habitus is thus a sense of one's (and others') place and role in the world of one's lived environment. As the stories in this part and others clearly demonstrate, habitus is an embodied, as well as a cognitive, sense of place.

Painter (2000: 242) describes habitus as

> the mediating link between objective social structures and individual action and refers to the embodiment in individual actors of systems of social norms, understandings and patterns of behaviour, which, while not wholly determining action … do ensure that individuals are more disposed to act in some ways than others.

Bourdieu's concept thus leaves room both for individual reason-based action and for social determination.

Habitus is the product of history. As such, it is 'an open system of dispositions that is constantly subjected to experiences, and therefore constantly affected by them in a way that either reinforces or modifies its structures' (Bourdieu and Wacquant, 1992: 133). The dispositions of habitus serve to predispose actors to choose behaviour which appears to them more likely to achieve a desired outcome with regard to their previous experiences, the resources available to them and the prevailing power relations; 'the relation to what is possible is a relation to power' (Bourdieu, 1990c: 4). Actors undertake a practical evaluation of their and others' potential behaviour. However, as will be demonstrated in the following chapters, such a practical evaluation is often not a conscious pattern of rational thought, but rather an intuitive practical reaction to a situation based on experience – an embodied sensibility which leads to structured improvisation (Calhoun, 2000: 712). This is not to say, of course, that structured improvisation is entirely determined by factors outside the control of the individual, or that no reason has gone into the acquisition of particular sensibilities/dispositions. But it is to say that habitus is not outwardly deliberative.

Bourdieu believes that human action is interested. Unlike rational actor theorists (such as Habermas), however, he regards interestedness as being generally a pre-reflective level of awareness which develops over time. Schwartz (1997: 19) asks whether different types of conduct vary in their levels of interestedness. For example, might some forms of behaviour respond more directly to perceived needs of survival than others? It would appear that Bourdieu's answer to this question is affirmative. When faced with entirely new situations, strategic calculation may be fully conscious, becoming unconscious with time as the same or similar situations are repeatedly encountered.

Habitus is constituted in practice and 'always oriented to practical functions' (Bourdieu, 1990c: 52). Bourdieu regards habitus as an open concept since actors' dispositions are constantly subjected to a range of different experiences. The dispositions that comprise habitus may be affected by these experiences in terms of being either reinforced or modified. Although Bourdieu anticipates that most experiences will serve to reinforce actors' habitus (as people are more likely to encounter situations and interpret them according to their pre-existing dispositions rather than to modify their feelings), he does accept that changes may occur. Habitus 'is durable but not eternal' (Bourdieu, 1996: 133).

FIELDS AND GAMES

Bourdieu terms the socially structured space in which actors play out their engagements with each other a 'field'. Each field possesses its own unique history and logic. It is a 'relational configuration endowed with a specific gravity which it imposes on all the objects and agents which enter in it' (Wacquant, 1992: 17).

A field is also a space of unequal relations and of conflict and competition as actors struggle to achieve their objectives. As Bourdieu writes, 'even in the universe *par excellence* of rules and regulations, playing with the rule is a part and parcel of the rule of the game' (1990b: 89).

A field, then, is a space of play within a network of objective relations between positions. These positions are objectively defined in the determinations they impose on actors and institutions, by their situation in the structure in the distribution of power.

Bourdieu frequently employs the analogy of a game when conveying the sense of activity/ies within a field.[3] To be successful in a game situation requires not just understanding and following the rules, but having a sense of the game. It requires constant awareness of and responsiveness to the play of all the actors involved. It requires assessment of the resources, strengths and weaknesses of one's own team-mate/s and also of the opponent/s. It requires improvisation and flexibility and above all, it requires use of anticipation as to what one's team-mate/s and one's opponent/s will do. Behaviours cannot be reduced simply to theoretical rules. As Lipstadt writes, 'it is past experience, or the habitus, that orients the choice of strategy, a pragmatic playing to the jury [Council/public], or a flagrantly rule-bending solution' (2000: 34).

There are few talented newcomers to games who have the abilities described above. More often, insight and a sense of the game – a habitus – develop with experience. Players learn from experience about what is possible and what is not, about how to work effectively within existing practices in the field and about how the rules might be modified. Players' activities are constructed, therefore, both by the external limits of rules and regulations, and also by their own internalisations and placing of limits on what they think they can do or what they want to do in the circumstances.

Habitus, therefore, offers an insightful way of understanding social interactions. Actors' behaviours will be related to their position *in* the field (in legal terms, and also in terms of the sense of their place and those of other actors in the field). Their behaviours will also be related to the resources available to them, and to their view *of* the field, including their ideological viewpoint and their perception of which issues are worth fighting for, this last being constructed from their position in the field.

As Bourdieu indicates, an actor's practical relation to the future, which defines their present behaviour, consists of the relationship between the habitus, 'constructed in the course of a particular relationship to a particular universe of probabilities' (1984: 64), and the opportunities offered to them. The relation to what activity is possible is a matter of whether it is within the power of the individual. This in turn depends on what position an individual occupies within the field. The 'sense of the probable future is constituted in the prolonged relationship with a world structured according to the categories of the possible … and the impossible' (1990c: 64). Habitus is thus the selective perception of a situation which generates a response according to the practical potential of satisfying the desire/s of the actor/s.

CAPITAL AND POWER

The concept of the field is closely linked to that of capital: 'capital does not exist and function except in relation to a field' (Bourdieu and Wacquant, 1992: 101). Capital is effectively the resources which actors take to the field.

Capital should be regarded not only as having its more usual, economic, connotation, but as also having applicability to resources such as status, power, personal contacts and formal and informal forms of knowledge. Bourdieu identifies three types of capital as follows:

- Economic capital or material wealth and concomitant power.
- Social capital, which may be defined as the resources and power which people obtain through their social networks and connections.[4]
- Cultural capital, which refers to knowledge and skills which actors acquire either through formal examination or through less formal means of education. Cultural capital often relates to prestige and status and includes resources such as articulateness, persuasiveness, aesthetic preferences and cultural awareness.

Bourdieu suggests that cultural capital exists in three different states. The first is an embodied state, since cultural goods can only be 'consumed' by understanding their meaning, unlike material goods. Cultural goods include music, works of art, scientific formulae, professional jargon, religion, etc.

Second, cultural capital exists in an objectified form as objects, such as books, scientific instruments, works of art, etc. which require specialised cultural abilities for their use.

Third, cultural capital exists in an institutionalised form, most often represented by educational, and/or professional, credentials.

To these three forms of capital can be added a fourth: linguistic capital (Bourdieu, 1993; Chouliarki and Fairclough, 2000). Linguistic capital manifests itself as a style of speaking/writing which not only 'constitutes the given', but does so in a way which gives credibility to that particular representation of the world.[5]

Bourdieu recognises the importance of the symbolic dimensions of capital. His term, symbolic capital, incorporates the other four forms of capital as it represents 'the form that the various species of capital assume when they are perceived and recognised as legitimate' (Bourdieu, 1989: 17). Bourdieu thus recognises the links and potential conversions between the various forms of capital and their relationship to power. Symbolic capital is a form of power that is not necessarily perceived as power as such, but as legitimate demands for recognition, deference, obedience or the service of others (Schwartz, 1997: 90).[6] The exercise of power through symbolic exchange (often of communication) rests on a foundation of shared belief about the relative positions of the agents involved: for example, of the planning officer as technical expert compared with local authority elected representatives, or the mayor or high priest or family head as 'natural' leader.

The key to symbolic power is thus that it is a legitimating form of power which involves the consent or active complicity of both dominant and dominated actors. Dominated actors are not passive bodies to whom power is applied, but rather people who believe in both the legitimacy of the power and the legitimacy of those who wield it. Bourdieu (1987) regards symbolic power as 'worldmaking power' due to its capacity to impose a legitimised vision of the social world.

CONCLUDING HABITUS

'Social life requires our active engagement in its games' (Calhoun, 2000: 710). It is impossible to live as an outside observer. Actively engaged we obtain a huge amount of practical knowledge. This knowledge, however, is filtered by the embodied understanding of our habitus, which reflects and affects our understanding of what is taking place in various situations and shapes how we practically engage with those situations.

Determining a preferred course of action in any situation requires an actor to employ insight and understanding. In many instances, simply playing by the rules and putting formulae into effect will not suffice. There is a need for the practical wisdom of Aristotelian phronesis,[7] Platonic *orthè doxa*[8] or the 'cunning intelligence' of Scott's (1998) *mètis*[9] too. As Taylor (1999: 41) suggests, 'the person of real practical wisdom is marked out less by the ability to formulate rules than by knowing how to act in each particular situation'. There is a vitally important 'phronetic gap' between the rule or formula and its enactment. Practice, therefore, may be regarded as a 'continual "interpretation" and reinterpretation of what the rule really means' (Taylor, 1999: 41).

There thus exists what Lipstadt (2000) calls a 'professional habitus' (Bourdieu uses the term 'cognitive habitus'). This is akin to an organisational culture when possessed by a group of people such as elected representatives or planning practitioners as will be demonstrated below.

In summary, Pierre Bourdieu's theorising of fields and habitus gives substance to the insight which Jürgen Habermas captures slightly differently in his theorisation of the uncoupling of systems and lifeworld and which Michel Foucault implies in his theorising of power and resistance. The strength of Bourdieu's work at what Thrift (1996a: 48n11) terms 'the Foucauldian limit', in comparison with Habermas and Foucault, is that the differentiation of fields and habituses more readily allows empirical investigation of the dynamics of social practices than do the more general and abstract notions of the other authors (Chouliarki and Fairclough, 2000: 101). Taking practice seriously then implies that we view society through the lens of what actors are trying to do. I therefore turn to stories of the worlds of planning practice as seen through the lenses of elected representatives and planning officers.

CHAPTER 9

NEGOTIATING THE GAP

INTRODUCTION

> Never assume that the feelings of people are unchangeable (Teck, 1997: 55).

Whilst attempting to pay attention to the important theory–practice gap, most recent theories of collaborative planning lack fine-grained analysis of what actually takes place and how arguments become convincing in deliberative dialogue. Moreover, collaborative planning theories tend to focus on the coordinating role of planning officers in attempting to achieve some form of consensus, eliding the vital gap between officers' recommendations and elected members' decisions – the gap between the authority of professional planners and the politics of public authorities. It is this gap on which I concentrate.

I seek to bring into hearing various dialogical techniques and devices of communication, modes of authority and subjectifications and the telos of strategies and ambitions. I go beyond simplistic statements that planning is political and attempt to uncover 'the real principle behind strategies' (Bourdieu, 1987: 76), or as Bourdieu terms it, 'a feel for the game (*le sens du jeu*)'. Outcomes from public participation strategies, however consensual they may be, tend to be advisory only (Innes and Booher, 1997: 2; Pløger, 2001). They enhance the functioning of representative democracy not replace it (Bloomfield *et al.*, 2001: 501). Planning officers and elected representatives both have the opportunity to 'translate' such outcomes into what they themselves prefer.

My aim in this chapter is to add some sense of the political to planning theory. I seek to uncover the how and why of those seemingly errant decisions when increasingly assertive[10] elected representatives ignore officer recommendations or change their minds. I focus on the mechanisms through which politics influences what elected representatives want, 'what they regard as possible and even who they are' (Edelman, 1964: 20). I do not pretend to offer an exhaustive range of possible reasons. However, I believe that if planning practitioners are to act effectively they cannot afford to ignore or to misconstrue the contingent and dynamic nature of political habitus. They may then also be able to gain a feel for the game, to anticipate reactions to their recommendations and to take steps accordingly.

The state of the debate: from Habermas to habitus

Habermasian communicative action normatively calls for the creation of political institutions in which discursive processes have a central role in decision-making. In his recent work, Habermas (1998) has specified the basic shape which such political institutions should take for his concept of deliberative democracy to be practical. The cornerstone is public reason, which Habermas demonstrates in his model of the circulation of power. I am interested here only in the arc in which information generated in the public sphere is transformed through democratic procedures of governmental will-formation into communicative power. The rationality of decision outcomes should ideally be a function of the reasons proposed (the force of the better argument), assured through legally prescribed procedures of deliberation and decision-making designed to ensure sufficient approximation to ideal conditions of discursive openness under limitations of time and information. 'The state's *raison d'être* ... [lies] in the guarantee of an inclusive process of opinion- and will-formation in which free and equal citizens reach an understanding on which goals and norms lie in the equal interest of all' (Habermas, 1998: 241).

Habermasian communicative action has influenced the approaches to planning theory developed by Patsy Healey (e.g. 1992b, 1996a, 1997a), Judith Innes (e.g. 1995, 1996b, 1998) and others. These authors have emphasised that good planning policy decision-making should be a collaborative, deliberative process, in which actors reciprocally share knowledges and meanings. Knowledge claims are validified through inclusionary argumentation in institutional consensus-building processes.

Leonie Sandercock's (1998) implicitly Habermasian-grounded work stresses inclusion and the recognition of difference in her 'epistemology of multiplicity for planning practice'. The goal of her radical model of planning practice is to collectively empower the systematically disempowered whilst working towards structural transformation of systematic inequalities (1998: 97) in a more democratised process.

John Forester's (e.g. 1989, 1993a, 1999a, 1999b) theorising explicitly acknowledges how the counterfactual ideas of Habermasian critical theory help us unpack 'practical and institutional contingencies, ... political vulnerabilities' (Forester, 1993a: x) as we listen to the actors' interpretations and representations of self and other. Habermas' ideas remind us that decision-making is shaped through arguments, by claims which may be rational or irrational. Forester's work is strongly grounded in empirical practice stories. He reads Habermas 'sociologically as a critical pragmatist' rather than as a 'Kantian moral theorist' (1999a: 204) to probe the production of meaning and its interpretation '*in the political and ethical work* of ... developing practical judgement' (1999a: 6, emphasis added).

Forester's emphasis on the politics of planning work is particularly important, making the crucial link between practical reasoning and political motivation.[11] Forester acknowledges that the role of politicians/elected representatives and their tendency to strategic posturing can 'regularly undermine [planners'] collaborative problem solving' (1999a: 2) and that 'the distance between rational public policy and political will can be substantial' (1999a: 87). Forester indicates how planning practitioners must be able 'to search not just for what is good in some abstract sense but to find what is good in the political sense' (1999: 47). In order to do this successfully, planners must be able to understand politics and how it works. We may know this intuitively, but what Forester offers is an analysis of what it implies for effective practice.

In the 'game' of planning decision-making, a certain number of regular patterns of behaviour result from conformation to codified, recognised rules. However, other, generally political, patterns of decision behaviour do not appear explicable either by the invocation of codified rules or in terms of brute causality. It is here that Pierre Bourdieu's concept of the habitus intervenes as a 'feel for the game' or 'practical sense'.

Practical knowledge can only be acquired in practice and can only be expressed in practice. While Bouveresse (1999: 52) asserts that 'there is no proof that all practical knowledge can be reconstructed in the form of an implicit knowledge of a corresponding theory', John Forester's work gains its strength from its grounding in the stories of planning practitioners themselves. In similar vein, this chapter is grounded in the practice stories of elected representatives. By reading such stories planners can learn about what may be important to politicians, to what practitioners could pay attention and what may be really at stake behind the fictions of rational decision-making.

WHERE ARE THE GAPS?

A concentration on traditional planning policy-making and decision-making ideas of survey–analysis–plan or officer recommendation–council decision–implementation obscures the complexity of the process. Such theories assume that policy- and decision-making proceed in a relatively orderly, unidirectional, stepwise, instrumental process towards a finite end point. They are too deterministic, however, to serve as adequate theories of reality and leave huge gaps.

First, there is what Hindess (1997: 80) terms the 'democratic deficit', an absence of consideration of the role of democracy in, for example, public participation prior to the officer recommendation, public influence in the council decision, Ministerial ratification and so on. Second, as Yanow (1996) indicates, there is a

huge gap between decision and implementation. Third, the work and recommendations of planning officers are traditionally perceived to be technocratic and value
neutral. As I will indicate, this is not the case in practice.

I attempt to represent in Figure 9.1 what I believe to be some of the possible
gaps in current planning theorising, applicable at a local authority scale.[12] I deal here
only with the 'gap' between officer recommendation to the local authority planning
committee and the council decision, what Bohman and Rehg might term 'the relation between reason and politics' (1997: xviii).[13]

John Forester (1999a: 253) terms the committee stage/s of decision-making
'enacted political drama'. Indeed, watching elected representatives in action, or listening to tapes of meetings, one can easily recognise the validity of dramatic or even
sporting metaphors. Committee and council meetings are like games in which
actors/players often reject any stance of objectivism and/or the rules. Meetings
become a performance and practices are seen as no more than the acting out of
roles; the habitus.

METHODOLOGICAL CONTEXT

I seek to theorise practice; to step down from an objectivist viewpoint to situate
myself in 'real activity', in practical relation to the world of local planning decision-making. In order to do this I have 'returned' to practice, and though unable to tell stories
through participatory observation as an elected representative in the tradition of
Altshuler (1965), Blowers (1980) and Throgmorton (1990, 1996), I have conducted

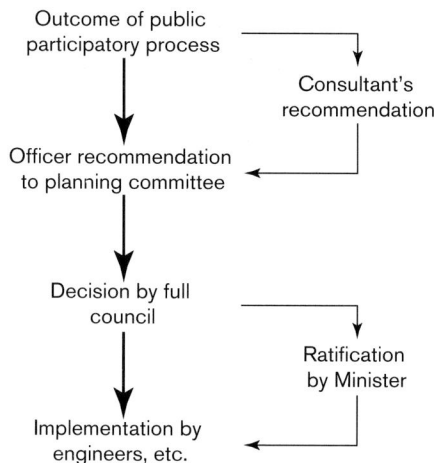

Figure 9.1 Gaps in planning theorising (Source: Hillier, 2002: 148)

conversational interviews ('looking inwards' (Kitchen, 1997)) with several currently serving and ex-politicians at local government level in Western Australia from metropolitan and country town authorities, in capacities ranging from member or chair of the planning committee to mayor[14] of their jurisdictions.[15] I attempt to hold together what Bourdieu calls a 'twofold truth; both the points of view of the agents caught up in local decision-making and my own inevitable agency in relating the elected representatives' position-takings to the positions from which they are taken' (Bourdieu, 2000: 189). I hope that, in this way, the stories which elected representatives tell can reveal 'political judgements about opportunities and constraints, about more and less responsible efforts, about more and less supposedly legitimate mandates, about relevant history to be respected and learned, relevant concerns, interests, and commitments to be honoured' (Forester, 1999a: 47).

I have also interviewed several current and former public planning officers in senior positions from metropolitan authorities ('looking outwards'), who are widely regarded as exemplars of astute practitioners with integrity and participatory track records, and who are motivated by concerns for social justice. My analysis also includes reference to published stories by ex-planners including Clavel (1980), Krumholz (1990) and Kitchen (1997).

For a contextual understanding of local planning practice in WA, I include key information in point form:

- The Town Planning & Development Act 1928 (amended) requires local municipal authorities to produce/review Town Planning Schemes (TPSs) every five years.

- TPSs regulate land-use zones and set the development standards which are the basic tool of development control within a municipality. They contain information on the physical form of developments, such as setbacks, plot ratios, parking bays, etc. The TPS must be approved by the state West Australian Planning Commission (WAPC) and the Minister.

- Councils are able to delegate power to planning officers to approve/refuse development proposals which do/do not comply with selected aspects of the TPS. The extent of delegated authority varies according to the amount of control the elected representatives wish to retain. For example in WA, East Fremantle has delegated 0 per cent of its authority to the planners, Stirling and Albany have delegated approximately 90 per cent, the City of Fremantle 50 per cent. The WA average is about 60 per cent.

- Local authority planning decisions must be taken on sound planning principles. Aspects of market competition, impact on property values, morality, compassion, etc. are not deemed planning principles.

- Applications to subdivide land are decided at state level by the government-appointed WAPC, not at municipality level.
- Appeals against planning decisions at the time of this research can be made either directly to the Minister for Planning or the Town Planning Appeal Tribunal. Ministers are not compelled to give reasons for their judgements. Ministerial Appeals information is not available through Freedom of Information legislation.
- Conduct of planning officers and elected representatives is bound by the Local Government Act 1995 which includes provisions for:
  - the roles of the council, councillors, the mayor, etc. in representing the interests of the whole district and all its electors, ratepayers and residents;
  - disclosure of financial interests in matters affording local government decisions and extent of subsequent participation and voting in decision-making meetings.
- Most, but not all, local authorities in WA have open planning committee and full council meetings at which the public is given opportunity to speak.
- Mayors may be elected either directly by the public or from the ranks of elected representatives by the council itself.
- Voting in local government elections is non-compulsory and non-politically aligned.

As stated above, I am concerned here only with those decisions of planning committees and full council which are taken contrary to planning officers' recommendations and those which represent an endogenous change of mind between the decision of the planning committee and its 'ratification' by full council. Given the percentage of decisions taken under delegated authority and the norm of agreement between officer recommendation and elected representatives, we are concerned, therefore, with a very small amount of planning decisions, a figure Kitchen (1997: 86) estimates at about three per cent of total strategic, policy and development control decisions.

I seek to uncover the 'hidden transcripts' (Scott, 1990) which influence elected representatives behind the scenes and those less hidden acts of communication which take place in public committee meetings, the transcripts of which result in what would appear on the surface to be largely irrational decision-making. In what follows I am not going to be judgmental. I tell the stories as I heard them, at face value. I do this so that, in John Forester's (1999a: 34) words, 'these stories might nurture a critical understanding by illuminating not only the stance of the rational and the idiosyncratic, but also the particular values being suppressed through the euphemisms, the rationalisations, the political theories and "truths" of the powerfull'.

I attempt to uncover the various types of frames through which elected representatives might view issues, but make no claims as to its being anywhere near an exhaustive list.

FILLING THE GAP?

Decision first, rationalisation after (Flyvbjerg, 1998a: 20).

Planning is the art of persuasion. Whether it is officers persuading elected representatives of a technical recommendation or constituents persuading their representatives of a particular opinion, the constructive use of persuasion is important. Persuasion involves 'the proper framing of arguments, the presentation of vivid supporting evidence, and the effort to find the correct emotional match with your audience' (Conger, 1998: 86).

I am not interested in instances of large-scale lobbying by interest groups[16] nor in exposing corruption.[17] I acknowledge that corruption in political decision-making may be widespread and probably accepted to a certain extent throughout the democratic world.[18] In Australia, it appears that elected representatives are almost expected to be corrupt. Their depiction in the popular media (e.g. the movie *Muriel's Wedding*, the soap opera *Sea Change*) and in novels such as Thea Astley's *Reaching Tin River* almost universally underscores that Australia 'from its very beginnings, has been built and thrives on scam and corruption' (Astley, 1990: 186). Indeed, Astley talks about political crooks having 'a respectability this country has learned to tolerate' (1990: 130). With specific regard to planning, there have been recent inquiries in WA into activities at the cities of Wanneroo and Cockburn respectively.

In what follows I distinguish between what I term public and private actions. Public actions take place in open committee and council meetings which set the stage for performances and drama. Private actions take place backstage, often informally via meetings, telephone or email conversations. The public transcript of the committee or council decision, then, tells not the whole story. It ignores the hidden transcripts of backstage communication. It is to these which I turn as I outline possible reasons for elected representatives' behaviour.

PRIVATE: PERSONAL GAIN

I term as personal gain those decisions in which an elected representative directly stands to gain financially or has other interests in the outcome. I emphasise that my research suggests that such behaviour by late 1999 had become limited in WA: 'it's not pecuniary interest on the whole. Few come on council specifically for that' (Mayor, rural LA).

However, the Inquiry into the City of Cockburn (1999–2000) has been particularly concerned that 'the council has allowed itself to be manipulated by [the
mayor], a dominant personality who had been pursuing his own interests' (Hunter,
1999a: 33) over development of a parcel of land owned by his family company, of
which he is a director. Evidence was also given to the inquiry that a motion had been
adopted by the council to delete certain items from its Code of Conduct. The
deleted items included:

> Councillors will ensure that there is no actual (or perceived) conflict of interest in
> the impartial and independent fulfilment of their civic duties [and] Councillors
> (staff) will not take advantage of their position to improperly influence (other)
> Councillors or (other) staff in the performance of their duties or functions, in order
> to gain undue or improper (direct or indirect) advantage or gain for themselves or
> for any other person or body (Department of Local Government, 1999: 11).

Such deletions would appear to accord with Larmour and Wolanin's (2001: 5) definition of corruption as 'some kind of intrusion or distortion which prevented
something from being as it should'. However, since the Cockburn and earlier
'Wanneroo Inc.' inquiries in WA, it would appear that instances of elected representative direct manipulation of decisions for personal gain have declined significantly:

> People are far more cautious (Mayor, metropolitan LA).
> I had X into my office, showed him the Cockburn summary and told him to sub-
> stitute his name for that of Councillor G. He went absolutely white and withdrew
> the development application (Mayor, rural LA).

Clearly some elected representatives do put pressure on planning officers to make
recommendations in their interests or persuade their council colleagues to overturn
officer recommendations accordingly, but these are in a small minority. More difficult
to discern is the receipt of gifts.

PRIVATE: GIFTS

The issue of gifts is complex.[19] It is linked with the sections below on favours and on
culture. There is no simple 'black and white' manner in which to regard elected representatives' receipt of gifts from local residents and ratepayers or developers.
Bourdieu (1990c: 100) suggests that receipt of a gift implies 'the possibility of a
continuation, a reply, a riposte, a return gift' as part of the very functioning of some
forms of habitus 'and the logic of practice that proceeds through a series of irre-
versible choices, made under pressure and often involving heavy stakes'.

The notion of reciprocity is important. Reciprocity denotes gratitude for the gift
received and often acknowledgement of its cultural meaning and implications. Gifts
assign symbolic meaning to fundamental dimensions of personal relationships. Iris

Marion Young (1997a: 355) points out, however, that the equality and mutual recognition of gift-giving is of a different order from the equality of contracts and exchange and the inequality of bribes. A gift is usually a token. Its value lies in the spirit in which it is given rather than its material worth. It is undemanded, given openly rather than in secret. A true gift should not expect something in return or any consideration of the recipient 'owing' the donor. It is an altruistic transfer with no expectation of a material reward (Rose-Ackerman, 1999: 93).

This latter would seem to be the way in which most of the elected representatives interviewed regard gifts. They prefer not to receive gifts, or, if they cannot refuse, the gifts (such as artworks) are taken as donations to the local authority in general and put on display, given to charity, but 'certainly not touched' by the individual or their family (Mayor, metropolitan LA).

Whether this type of sentiment is true or either an individual or part of some collective self-deception, it is open to interpretation as a twofold truth. If, as Bourdieu (2000: 192) suggests, 'a gratuitous gift is impossible', gift-giving to elected representatives may be regarded as an 'anti-economic economy … based on the denial of interest and calculation' in which no one is really unaware of the logic of exchange, but no one fails to comply with the rule of the game, which is to act as if one does not know the rule. Bourdieu (2000: 192) uses the term 'common miscognition' 'to designate this game in which everyone knows – and does not want to know – that everyone knows – and does not want to know – the true nature of the exchange'.

It is, then, as Bourdieu (1990c) comments, all a matter of style. The choice of occasion, timing, cultural circumstances, etc. of the gift and the personal relations between the giver and receiver, can have different implications and meanings, which the elected representatives themselves need to understand. 'One person's bribe is another person's gift' (Rose-Ackerman, 1999: 5).

PRIVATE: FAVOURS

Doing favours for another may be related to gift-giving in that there may be some expectation of reciprocity. Favours are often deemed to be part of an exchange. It seems in WA that elected representatives might occasionally perform favours of permitting/refusing a particular development application, for example, for people in the community who have supported them in some manner in the past or who might be called upon some time in the future:

> a standing in good stead – in case – you know. Future favours (Mayor, rural LA).

There would appear to be almost a logging or 'clocking up' (metropolitan LA planning officer) of favours in certain instances.

Favours might take the form of votes traded between council colleagues:

you scratch my back and I'll scratch yours (ex-elected representative, metropolitan LA);

part of the pervading business culture of exchange of favours and corporate
dealings (ex-elected representative, metropolitan LA)

or favours performed for the wider community:

the Freemasonry connection, etc. (Mayor, metropolitan LA).

Pressure for favours is even greater in small, close-knit rural communities where
everyone knows and may even be related to almost everyone else. In such circumstances the need for decisions to be made on valid planning reasons increases:

there is constituent pressure, neighbour pressure, especially when they're personal friends, but I remind people of the Acts and the sections on valid planning
reasons and impartiality (Mayor, rural LA).

With applications from friends, however,

You obviously try to help, you know. You might give them quiet advice on how to
improve their application or to withdraw it (Mayor, rural LA).

Whether 'doing future favours' is reciprocated or not is difficult to determine.
Entrepreneur Alistair MacAlpine (2000: 55) warns against performing such favours
and cites Machiavelli as advising that 'friendships that are obtained by payments
and not be greatness or nobility of mind, may indeed be earned, but they are not
secured and in time cannot be relied upon'.

Careful elected representatives seem to know how to act in each situation.
They actively engage with the habitus.

PRIVATE: FACTIONS

There are factions, alliances or caucuses in many groups and institutions. As
Flyvbjerg (1998a: 138) writes, 'alliances are an important part of the rationality of
power', and Roelofs (1967: 252–3) defines a caucus as being 'usually private, certainly informal, and often marked by that somewhat stylised *bonhomie* typical of
relations between men who, even if not friends, know that they need each other'.
Bourdieu (2000: 145–6) writes of an implicit collusion, or *esprit de corps*, between
agents, an agreement which does not presuppose a contractual decision, but which
is the basis of a 'practical mutual understanding'. Such a *collusio* is based on habitus,

spontaneously produc[ing] behaviours adapted to the objective conditions and
tending to satisfy the shared individual interests, thus enables one … to account
for the appearance of teleology which is often observed at the level of collectives
and which is ordinarily ascribed to the 'collective will' (Bourdieu, 2000: 146).

Factions cross partisan lines of political party, ethnicity and gender. Communication is private, often by untraceable meeting or telephone call. Its aim is 'a deal, not an appeal' (Edelman, 1964: 146).

In WA, 'Purple circles' (ex-planning officer, metropolitan LA) exist in most local authorities, in which there are 'tacit agreements' to vote similarly, even to the extent that

> people go against their own ideals to vote with the faction (ex-planning officer, metropolitan LA).
>
> It's their 'duty' to go along (ex-elected representative metropolitan LA).
>
> There's logrolling. Any particular development is automatically good if it's supported by one of the inner sanctum (ex-elected representative metropolitan LA).

What matters in coordinating 'beliefs' and votes is not what those beliefs are, but rather who holds them. The issue is exacerbated if the faction leader is also the local mayor. Several department of local government investigations in WA have revealed this to be the case. Mayors have been found to dominate proceedings rather than being impartial chairs, which thus 'denies the community fair, proper and open debate' (DLG, 1999: 20). In this manner 'power easily becomes an end in itself, to be sought by any means that can be rationalised or concealed, a perversion of Machiavellian strategy' (Edelman, 1988: 58, resonating with the advice in MacAlpine's best-selling book *The New Machiavelli: The Art of Politics in Business,* 1988).

PRIVATE: CULTURE

Australia is a multicultural country and WA is no exception. Apart from a large Angloethnic population, there are significant communities of Italian, Serbian, Croatian, Chinese and increasingly Vietnamese, Iraqi and Afghani people living in WA. Each community may have different cultural personal values and ways of working. In some Asian cultures, for instance, the significance of gift-giving as a mark of respect is important. Such gifts are not intended as bribes, but are a cultural aspect of business relationships.

People's life experiences can also shape the ways they interact with elected representatives and officers of governance. Many migrants have arrived in WA from countries which do not have democratic systems in the Western sense. Ballot-boxes and elected representatives are unfamiliar, if not alien concepts, as are open committee and council meetings to people who have never had opportunities to publicly voice their concerns. Other migrants have arrived from countries which did not have a planning system. Such people tend to hold certain expectations that they can do whatever they like with their land. Having to submit planning applications which are then refused can be confusing and bewildering.

Migrants from certain cultural backgrounds may also actively suppress conflict in the interest of social harmony, unquestioningly obey authority and carry out perceived role obligations (Tyler, Lind and Huo, 2000). Such behaviour is followed, even though resulting outcomes may not be in the migrants' best interests, as they themselves often recognise.

Local residents may thus find themselves in 'liminal limbo' (Meerwald, 1999), caught in an interstitial position between two or even more cultural ways of working. It should not be surprising, therefore, that people from particular cultural groups should seek out any elected representatives on council from that group, irrespective whether that person is the relevant ward councillor or not; that some people give elected representatives gifts as a token of respect for those in authority, and that elected representatives from different cultural groups tend to 'look after their own' (elected representative, metropolitan LA).

It was also suggested that migrants (especially second generation and later) are keen to be involved either in development:

> development equals progress in a new life (ex-elected representative, metropolitan LA)

and/or as elected representatives themselves as a means of affirming their Australianness as equal citizens and displaying loyalty to both Australia and their own culture through helping to protect the interests of their kin (Lee, 1999).

My argument is that elected representatives from such cultural groups may not believe that they are acting unethically in receiving gifts, helping kinspeople and so on. The Mayor of Cockburn, a Croatian, 'did not believe that he was doing anything wrong' (Hunter, 1999b: 37) in using his position to influence council decisions. The British-based planning system in WA is

> culturally insensitive to various ethnic needs (Mayor, metropolitan LA).

At the same time, however, members of frustrated cultural minority groups see apparent favours and privileges given to

> the old school tie, Western suburbs' private school 'mates' (Mayor, metropolitan LA)

who seem to work covertly in similar fashions:

> That's the *real* Mafia (Italian constituent, metropolitan LA).

The WA planning system is 'a template which doesn't fit local needs' (Mayor, metropolitan LA). Elected representatives are often not deliberately acting wrongfully but are resisting an inappropriate system. Whether the way forward is to change the system or to 'educate' elected representatives and the public as to what constitutes correct and incorrect conduct is a matter for debate.

PUBLIC: POSTURING, GRANDSTANDING, BENEVOLENCE AND VOTE-WINNING

In public arenas such as planning committees and full council meetings, elected representatives often use hortatory language, appealing for public support for their positions. Political debate is overtly rhetorical and emotional on all sides, including elected representatives and members of the public gallery. Symbols and stories are frequently used in the framing of issues.

Elected representatives tend to be guilty of political impression management; posturing and 'grandstanding in front of the public' (Mayor, rural LA), especially in the lead-up to local elections, when they are eager to create a good image as concerned, involved representatives worthy of being voted back into office. One ex-metropolitan planning officer commented that:

> committees are like circuses [as elected representatives] bend to the whims of the most vocal element, ... [to] whoever turns up or who they happened to hear from last.

Politics is performance wherein participants perform roles through which they enact their positions, as humble petitioner, as oppressed victim (members of the public) or as all-powerful and/or benevolent provider (elected representatives). Meetings come to resemble Bakhtinian carnivalesque or Debordian spectacles. Yet, as Debord points out, the spectacle is also 'the locus of illusion' (1994: 12) where, 'in a world that really has been turned on its head, truth is a moment of falsehood' (1994: 14).

Elected representatives generally like to be seen supporting their ward constituents. In particular, they seem keen to appease the local Ratepayers' Association, which is often their powerbase in the constituency:

> If the Ratepayers' Society says jump, they jump (planning officer, metropolitan LA).

This may involve, as Kitchen (1997: 41) indicates, speaking out against something or voting against an application, even when they know that in terms of council policies, which they themselves approved, it should be accepted.

Public perceptions of benevolence lead to the accumulation of Bourdieu's symbolic capital, including making the elected representative/s involved feel good about themselves: 'a kind of continuous justification for existing' (Bourdieu, 2000: 240). Politicians would appear to be 'suckers for hearts and flowers arguments' (Mayor, metropolitan LA) and virtually every interviewee recalled stories of people in the public gallery winning over elected representatives on decisions contrary to officer recommendation. Whether it is the small child with a ventilator in a wheelchair, the elderly grandmother silently weeping or the attractive young blonde woman bursting into tears, elected representatives seem to change their minds about

issues, often to the frustration of planning officers whose reasoned, technical arguments get discarded. As one officer grumbled:

> grovelling is good, tears are good, but tight jeans are better.

Members of the public who play emotional strategies are often successful. They may
use potent symbols of helplessness, such as wheelchairs and tears, to achieve their
own goals. These goals may well be contrary to the good of the majority of the local
population or of more marginalised groups in society.

Sometimes, however, people's strategies may misfire and serve to antagonise
elected representatives rather than inveigle them. Behaviour such as making force-
based threats and name-calling is counterproductive, as is dogmatically telling
elected representatives that they are wrong:

> grovelling is good, begging for mercy is good, telling them they're wrong is not
> good (planning officer, metropolitan LA).

Such activities may generate 'planning by petulance' (Mayor, metropolitan LA) or
Machiavellian-style revenge, against the people concerned. This may also result in
decisions taken against officer recommendation and serve to reinforce elected representatives' feelings of omnipotence.

It could appear from the above that 'parochialism and populism rule OK' (ex-planning officer, metropolitan LA) in WA, but I emphasise that it is only a small proportion of
predominantly development application-related planning decisions which are influenced in these ways. Kitchen (1997) estimated that in his British local authority, it was
in only twenty per cent of cases where public speaking rights had been exercised that
the planning committee decision was different from that of the officer recommendation.

POLITICAL WILL: 'THERE GOES THE MOB! I AM THEIR LEADER, I MUST FOLLOW THEM'

Are elected representatives simply puppets of populism or can we begin to discern
more about the exercise of political will? Is there a political culture in the field of local
government decision-making in which elected representatives' interests and options
are shaped by the prevailing values, beliefs and practices of the society: the habitus?

Elected representatives may be swayed by rhetoric rather than argument. The
presence of an audience in the public gallery may lead to posturing and acts of
benevolence or petulance. The spectacle of the committee meeting becomes a self-
portrait of power.

Local politicians like the symbolic capital, the status and social prestige their
position invokes, but as Baxter (1972: 106) suggests, 'possibly more important is

the prestige it brings to a councillor in his [*sic*] own eyes – the satisfaction of feeling important'. This may be through helping family, friends, constituents or cultural kin. Decisions are taken according to an often impulsive 'feel for the game' which is being played out in public and/or in private. Elected representatives tend to 'conduct themselves according to imagination and not prudence' (Ivison, 1997: 58).

There is a need to consider new theoretical conceptions of planning decision-making, those which account for the gap between officer recommendation and council decision. Political decision-making involves far more than rationality, far more than simple marketplace trading. I offer the narrative examples above to begin the work of recreating theory, turning the gap of 'in-between space' of elected representative decision-making into something more tangible. Unless planning practitioners begin to understand the complexities which take place on- and off-stage, they will continue to be frustrated and confused by seemingly irrational decisions which ignore their hard-worked recommendations.

CHAPTER 10

PLANNERS AS MISSIONARIES OR CHAMELEONS?

INTRODUCTION

> Despite the fact that planners have little influence upon the structure of owner-
> ship and power … they can influence the conditions which make citizens able
> (or unable) to participate, act, and organise effectively regarding issues affecting
> their collective lives (Forester, 1982: 67).

Planners have important roles to play in land-use decision-making because every
decision negotiation is really two negotiations in one: a negotiation with colleagues
and elected representatives about content – the issues at hand and a recommended path of action; and also a negotiation about relationships – the shadow
negotiation. As will be revealed by the practice stories which follow,[20] the quality of
actors' relationships and the meanings of their moves may be shadowy, which, as
Forester (2000a: 149) suggests, may not be a bad thing!

The recent research from which the stories below have been taken has been
inspired by a line from John Forester's book, *The Deliberative Practitioner*, that the
'morally improvising planner who ignores the suppression of citizens' voice or data
weakening the claims of the powerful would be wilfully blind' (1999a: 237), and also
by Jim Throgmorton's (2000: 14–15) complaints, as an elected representative generally regarded to have a minority view on council, that 'the [planning] staff often
massaged their own advice so that it would correspond with what it believed the
Council majority expected' and that he 'could not always count on the staff to provide the information needed'. I wanted to discover whether planners in WA are as
'wilfully blind' as those in Iowa appear to be.

In this chapter I attempt to build on Forester's (1999a, 2001) exploration of
the crucial link between practical reasoning and political motivation. I address local
planning practice as it is actually encountered, with its practical and institutional
contingencies and political vulnerabilities. Whilst I agree with Forester's suggestion
with regard to 'wilful blindness', his work tends to presuppose that planners both
actually want to help the marginalised in society and that they care about the outcomes of their recommendations.

Evidence from planners' practice stories in WA suggests that whilst some
planners may adopt a missionary position of social justice, many others adopt an
equally missionary position of development facilitation. Others again may indeed be

'wilfully blind', serving, like chameleons, their elected representatives' political predilections. The stories demonstrate certain similarities of behaviour in that no officer can be said to act 'rationally' in the Habermasian sense. Their actions are politically shaped as they themselves are political agents, exercising some forms of power and resisting others in various ways. Indeed, as Tewdwr-Jones (2002: 65–6) writes,

> the position of the individual planner, with his or her motivations, ways of think-
> ing and styles of acting and communicating, employing personal and
> professional goals, seems to be pivotal in the adoption of more inter-personal
> relations between different planning actors.

Having listened to the stories of elected representatives in the previous chapter I turn to the question of how might planning practitioners dilute the 'rogue' voices which occasionally dominate planning decision-making? How might they take 'practical action in a messy political world' (Forester, 1999b: 184)?

We need to know how thinking, active practitioners attempt to counteract elected representatives' use and abuse of power. We need to learn from their stories of effective responses, and in particular, how they *anticipate* and pre-empt the vagaries of political will. As Forester (1999b: 185) states, 'we should illuminate not only where progressive efforts get stuck, but how clever practitioners can get unstuck'.

Albrechts' (1999) valuable work in Belgium clearly indicates that planners have to explore political feasibility, to build alliances, to negotiate, to mobilise support, to lobby and to bargain if they are to push through controversial decisions. Albrechts' focus on the highly political role of planning officers helps to debunk the mythology of rational planning and its so-called technocratic neutrality.

In WA, interviews with several 'clever practitioners' revealed some strategies which it is useful to consider.

METHODOLOGICAL CONTEXT

I seek to theorise practice, to step down from an objectivist viewpoint to situate myself in 'real activity', in practical relation to the world of local planning decision-making. In order to do this I have 'returned' to practice, and though unable to tell stories through participatory observation as a local planner in the tradition of Catanese (1974, 1978, 1984), Reissman (1975), Clavel (1980), Krumholz (1990) or Kitchen (1997), I have conducted conversational interviews with twelve people who are, or who have served as, senior planning officers at local government level in

WA from a range of metropolitan authorities. This was not a random sample of practitioners. Rather, the twelve are personally known to myself as having different
approaches to interactions with elected representatives.

In conversational interviews, I asked respondents about their perceptions of
the role of land-use planning and that of local government planning officers. We
spoke of planners' interactions with elected representatives, particularly those councillors on planning committees, and what considerations planners use to frame their
activities and recommendations. We discussed the quotation from John Forester
cited earlier with regard to examples of hypothetical applications for an Aboriginal
hostel or policy proposals for increasing residential densities and also a further
Forester quotation: 'practitioners without insight will be callous, barely competent, if
not altogether ineffective' (1999a: 143).

In penetrating inside the 'black box' of government (Healey, 2000b: 919), I
seek to unpack what Dobel (1999) has termed the triangle of judgement of planning
officers trying to hold together the complex domains of personal responsibility, institutional obligations to office and political prudence. In so doing, I endeavour to
report my conversations in as non-judgemental manner as possible, cognisant of
Bourdieu's 'twofold truth' (2000: 189) outlined above.

PRACTICAL ACTION, POLITICAL VISION?

> It is the preliminary backstage power-play, not the plan's rubber-stamping by the
> City Council, which is the real politics of planning (Flyvbjerg, 1998a: 83).

The *Report of the Inquiry into the Operations and Affairs of the Town of East
Fremantle* in WA (DLG, 1999: 51–2) defined the role of a town planner as being 'to
increase the welfare of all people in the community by creating a more healthy, efficient, convenient and attractive environment that provides a greater level of choices
for the individual'. As such, 'the town planner has a prime responsibility to pursue the
public interest in matters relating to town and regional planning'. The problem, however, as Preston (2000: 17) points out, is that 'public interest' is an elusive term,
open to various interpretations. Who is or are the public/s? What is in their best
interest? If elected representatives represent the public, then should planning officers defer to the wishes of elected representatives? How do planners act when
they regard elected representatives as likely to make a decision not perceived to be
'in the public interest'?

Dobel (1999) lists three models which may describe planning officers'
actions:

- the legal institutional model – emphasises the officer's subjection to legal and institutional authority, or 'the book' (e.g. Finer, 1941). Catanese (1974, 1984) describes this as taking an apolitical–neutral role.
- the personal-responsibility model – argues that personal responsibility should be incorporated in officer's judgements (e.g. Thompson, 1987).
- the effectiveness model – highlighting the political dimension of judgements, the model posits the need to use power to act effectively (e.g. Long, 1996). Catanese labels this an overt or covert activist role.

It is important to remember that planning practice, even within the local government sector, is comprised of individuals who have their own ideas of what types of behaviour and what outcomes are 'right' or 'wrong', 'good' or 'bad', about their 'duty' and about the 'public interest'. Different individual planning officers will inevitably bring different preferences to bear in particular contexts and still consider themselves as acting with integrity. Issues of integrity are not clearcut black and white, but tend to be blurred by personal values such as concerns with social justice, environmental issues and/or a belief in unfettered economic or market forces (O'Toole, 2000; Pratchett, 2000).

As Allmendinger writes:

> there is an assumption ... that planners are benign and imbued with liberal conceptions of democracy and that they all agree on what is the 'public good'. This is clearly not the case. Planners are people like everyone else; they have their own agendas, grudges, desires and idiosyncrasies and these are reflected in day-to-day practice (1996: 231).

The issues at hand in this chapter include: do local planners care about the outcomes of their recommendations; to which of Dobel's three models do they relate; and how, and finally if and when, do planning officers act against their best judgements? (Arpaly, 2000). By unpacking planning officers' practice stories we can begin to distinguish between what Forester (2000b: 914) terms 'enabling' from 'disabling' practice: practices which actively seek to enable particular outcomes to be achieved or those wherein planners passively allow process to take precedence and elected representatives to take whatever decision they might wish.[21]

In this chapter I use a simple ideological framing device as a basis for understanding planning officers' actions. I believe that an ideological framework enables greater understanding of *why* planning officers act as they do in addition to how they act.

I have chosen to regard planning officers, such as those whom Throgmorton appears to have encountered, as *chameleons*, and those who actively attempt to achieve outcomes which they believe to be 'in the public interest' as *missionaries*.

CHAMELEONS

The notion of planning officers as value-neutral, apolitical technocrats working 'by the book' was underpinned by classic planning texts (e.g. Keeble, 1952). The notion appears to be still alive in Britain at least, where a recent survey by Campbell and Marshall (1998, 2002) found strong evidence of allegiance to professional auton-omy and 'independent professional judgement'.

Such planners believe in the objectivity of technical knowledge and the ability of strict application of legislation to transcend interests. When asked to justify their recommendations, they will take pains to emphasise their technical knowledge, referring to the procedures and legislation which compose the cultural capital of their professional expertise.[22] In this manner, the planners transform their cultural capital into symbolic capital.

Throgmorton's (2000) example of planning officer behaviour would appear to owe more to political expedience than simply playing by the book, 'feeding' as they do, the elected representative decision-makers' information and recommendations which it is anticipated they want to receive. Such behaviour represents a continua-tion of the practice which Altshuler described as eschewing 'all but the most noncontroversial values' (1966: 356).

Cook and Sarkissian (2000: 116) tell of a South Australian planner who left a position in which 'I had a lot of pressure from the councillors to make recommenda-tions which took into account their values and their ways of interpreting the provisions and I also had a lot of pressure from the CEO'. In WA, three of the four 'chameleons' interviewed mentioned some form of 'pressure from above' to produce information and recommendations in line with what elected representatives would anticipate receiving.

In WA, some instances were recalled of pressure to approve or do something contrary to the current plan being applied directly by elected representatives:

> Council instructed the department to come up with new guidelines. You have to do what they want or they'll employ consultants to do it (A).
> If I tell Council that 'you can't do that by the rule', they tell me 'change the rule then' (A)

and sometimes by the local authority CEO:

> The CEO guides decisions the way he wants the outcome (B).
> There is a level of pampering to the Minister of the day by the CEO who's on a performance contract and to the CEO by the Executive Managers who're also on performance contracts (C).

The neo-corporatist management style prevailing in WA authorities, with staff on three- to five-year contracts and performance measurement, appears to influence CEOs' and planners' behaviour.[23] If officers' futures are to be determined by their 'superiors' measuring 'performance' then it is likely that officers may well act as requested and seek to please those carrying out the measuring – ultimately councillors.

Chameleon-like behaviour results from a desire to maintain a salaried job, which desire takes precedence over caring about particular planning outcomes:

> I'm not going to risk my job for going out on a limb (C).
> Sit down and shut up and take the money (B).
> Go with the flow. I keep quiet (B).
> You need to understand what system you're operating in. There's no room for ideology (A).
> There's no point in trying to stymie council decisions as it gets up councillors' noses (A).
> I can't say 'you're not doing the right thing by the people' or the councillors will tell me to go away and just do my job. You learn to suck your breath in (A).
> If you don't do what they want you'll lose your job (A).

Whether 'sucking your breath in' or just 'keeping quiet', it seems that these officers have learned 'to understand where people are coming from. It makes it much easier … to work with them' (A).

It is important to these planning officers not to upset either the CEO or the elected representatives. They talk about gaining the 'respect' of council by 'giving them consistent advice' (D), by 'remembering that you're employed by the Council' (A) and 'learning why your reports are changed' (C). As C states, 'continuity [in the position] gives you a certain level of wisdom. Continuity is a skill in itself.'

Some chameleons find it easiest on themselves to rely on the legislation and a professional ethos of technological neutrality. They

> play it as straight as I possibly can (A).
> do sufficient research to justify the recommendations (D).
> need to have your bases covered (C)

but the key strategy is that of flexibility:

> I've not got the killer instinct. I go with the flow (B).
> Conditions change so your approach is going to change (D).
> You've got to be flexible (D).
> … know which side your bread is buttered (A).
> manoeuvrable (A).
> You need flexibility (A)

and ducking for cover when required:

deflect the problem onto someone else (D).

farm difficult problems out to consultants (D).

defer decisions – use administrative reasons not to make a decision (D).

Several of these senior officers remarked that they had not always acted in such a manner. One in particular told of how they had been a frustrated idealist junior planner who had chosen to become 'more sophisticated at working with people' . 'I've got less ideological. I know how to write better' (C). This officer regards himself as a sophisticated game player who has 'become cunning over time to survive' (C). Another officer had simply 'gravitated to areas where you don't have to make choices' (B). Intervention and non-value-neutral planning was regarded by these officers as something 'devious' (B, D), undertaken as 'mercenary advocacy' (B).

What I did find surprising, however, was that three of the four officers interviewed expressed some degree of bitterness with their planning lives. They told of painful experiences, which may well be related to their retreat into chameleon-like behaviour. The last respondent, the youngest of the four, seems proud of his survival skills, boasting of his 'insight' and 'cunning':

> You need a clever twist. If you write what's wanted, it's less pain for you (C).

IN THE MISSIONARY POSITION

Allmendinger (2001: 2) indicates that, 'the whole apparatus of planning was built around the notion of a benevolent elite working towards common goals', epitomised by Davies' (1972) notion of the 'evangelistic bureaucrat'. In times when goals are not that 'common', officers may find themselves acting as Catanese's (1974, 1984) activists in either overt or covert ways. As Miles Rademan, former director of community development for Crested Butte, Colorado, wrote, 'we must absolutely shake off our image as faceless technicians and be prepared to dirty our hands and should in the hurly-burly political arena' (1985: 42).

John Forester (and many other academics, including myself) trust that planning officers will act as missionaries for *social justice*: 'one needs to ensure, for the sake of justice, that the minorities are properly heard, and that they play their necessary part in the process' (Hampshire, 2000: 47). Yet working in a climate of neo-economic rationalism, social justice may be a much harder 'barrow to push' (H).

In WA the officers interviewed who could be regarded as missionaries for social justice expressed a *need* to become involved. For example:

> It's not possible to be completely neutral (F).
>
> Those who are most effective give a damn about what's going on. If you
> become mechanical, there is no need for a planner, as you could be replaced by
> an administrator (F).

These officers regarded their job as one of 'managing conflict' (F, E) between various sets of ideals and saw 'conflict as a natural part of a dynamic urban area' (F).
However, they agreed with McClendon and Quay (1988: xix) that 'to be an effective
champion [of social justice], we must win'.

Applbaum (2000) describes the types of strategies which officers utilise in
terms of civil disobedience. He suggests that in order to counter what is believed to
be either a violation of the rights of some minority (justice-based disadvantages) or
a mistake about what is in the public interest (common-good-based disadvantages),
actors engage in persuasive strategies aimed at changing decision-makers' minds
about what justice demands or what is in the common good.

Like several of the respondents from WA, Applbaum regards intervention akin
to 'a game of chess' (K) where one 'play[s] the game' (E). In a section subtitled 'how
to play? the strategies of discretion' (2000: 123), Applbaum considers three
classes of strategies which a public official might employ: persuasive, incentive and
deceptive.

Persuasive strategies seek to change 'in good faith, the beliefs, values, and
interests of other political players through deliberation or symbolic action'
(Applbaum, 2000: 124). Persuasive strategies are public and act openly on the
rational faculties of their audience. In this way, planning officers present evidence at
planning committees and/or council meetings, for example, of how a particular
development proposal is or is not in accordance with the local plan and/or policy.
The cultural capital of professional protocol is utilised as a useful rhetorical device:

> your recommendation is based on the scheme, policies and standard planning
> practice (F).

Discussions may be summarised and resulting maps drawn in ways which persuade
readers to a certain viewpoint[24] (see Iedema, 1997, 2000). The officer translates
individual understandings, governmental regulations, institutional rules, etc. into a
text with a particular message. Professional protocol becomes a political tool.[25]

Incentive strategies seek to alter the costs and benefits to political authorities
of certain actions. Strategies include giving *veiled threats and warnings*.

When committee deliberations wander into territories of non-planning decision
rationales, officers may remind elected representatives of the consequences of not following 'due process' or they may make reference to the WA Cockburn or Wanneroo
inquiries into the conduct of elected representatives. Officer reminders of 'due process'
tend to be couched in legalese, by reference to the appropriate statutes. On the other
hand, plain mention of Cockburn or 'Wanneroo Inc.' in WA at present is seemingly sufficient to remind elected representatives of their digressions. With such warnings
planners pragmatically attempt to get elected representatives to think through for themselves the possible consequences of their potential actions and decisions.

Planners may thus introduce an element of uncertainty into elected represen- tatives' minds (Forester, 1999, pers. comm.). As a planning officer explains,

> councillors have a simplified view of the situation and the legislation and tend to have and to want too much certainty. The role of the planner is to introduce uncer- tainty by making councillors aware of what they might lose, of the possibility, for example, of losing credibility (H)

– and, by implication, votes.

In telling a story of an application to turn an area of undeveloped land into urban residential accommodation, this planning officer recalled how he managed to reduce his degree of uncertainty and to push the uncertainty onto the councillors

> by making them think twice about what they thought would be a black and white situation ... in terms of the ramifications of the decision in general, for the flora, and for them in terms of opposition and votes.

In this way, the planner shaped attention (shaped a tension?) round the issues involved and was able to facilitate a less environmentally harmful outcome whereby the council pushed the uncertainty onto the proponent/developer via imposing con- ditions on development and a required increase in provision of public open space.

Another planner interviewed was adamant that

> certainty isn't and shouldn't be a core value of planning (J).

Deceptive strategies work through elements of omission and manipulation. Officers learn to frame problems in ways which serve their purpose and direct elected repre- sentatives' attention to certain aspects of the issue for discussion. They use the symbolic power of their 'expert' status. As Flyvbjerg writes, 'power defines what counts as knowledge and rationality' (1998a: 27).

Heading them off at the pass

One planner revealed that when he writes his officer reports and recommendations for the planning committee, especially on issues concerning facilities for marginalised groups, such as Aboriginal people, he attempts to anticipate the reaction from the elected representatives. One possible strategy is to 'head them off at the pass' by

> making my proposal more left wing so that the right wing elected members can nibble at it and you end up with something that's centre left (H).

He refers to this as a strategy of 'damage limitation'.

Distortion/disclosure of information

One of the planners interviewed asked the question:

> sometimes is it not 'better' to not do the 'right democratic thing' by process to
> get an outcome for the marginalised? (H).

He suggested that in instances such as the location of a remand hostel or Aboriginal drop-in centre, where one could anticipate resistance from neighbouring residents and a fairly right-wing council, that strategies such as minimal publicity and writing reports 'blinding the elected representatives with science' might be useful. Omission, evasion and silence (Ramsay, 2000). Not, the planner was at pains to stress, that he had personally done so.

This planner also wondered whether

> if by making an area 'nicer' ends in its gentrification and pushing out of poor
> people by the middle class, is this what we should be doing? (H).

A difficult question, which I subsequently raised with other practitioners. One felt that

> bending the rules for social justice is democratically unethical. The suggestion
> argues that a coherent technical interpretation of planning should override plan-
> ning decisions, but there's no rational basis to this argument as it overturns
> democracy. If you get caught doing it then the council won't trust you and they'll
> want to deal with everything and take away your delegated authority (I).

Despite describing a strategy of 'bending the rules' as democratically unethical, this planner continued by saying that a more successful strategy would be to lobby elected representatives 'through the back door'.

> Planners need connections too. You try to get tacit agreement of the key faction
> councillors for what you want (I).

These narratives suggest ways in which planners may be able to counteract anticipated decisions which they believe could operate to the disadvantage of the already disadvantaged.

Sager (2001: 765) suggests that if decision-makers are 'manipulated', 'fooled or tricked' by planning officers into making their choice, then the decision lacks legitimacy. Is this necessarily so, however? Is such 'manipulation' always objectionable?

John Forester discusses issues of 'distorted communication' or 'misinformation' at length in *Planning in the Face of Power* (1989). He argues that 'planners themselves sometimes participate in distorting, and, in special cases, may be justified in doing so' (1989: 29). The crucial questions are 'when can misinformation be ethically justified?' (1989: 42). When should one tell freedom's necessary lies? My answer is that planners should anticipate the outcomes which might follow in circumstances with and without their 'mis'information (e.g. in the Aboriginal drop-in case) and make their own judgements. Politically necessary actions decided by prudent evaluation of the consequences to which they are likely to lead are, according to Ramsay (2000: 12), overwhelming moral considerations.

Other elements which interviewed officers reported as operating in their interest include consistency and integrity, and delegated authority.

Consistency and integrity
Planning practitioners require personal credibility to be effective when giving information to the public and to elected representatives. Several respondents stated that if planners appear reasonable and pragmatic and confident about their knowledge, then elected representatives are more likely to act on their advice.

> You need to be consistent in your approach and process as this removes any argument of favouritism to any particular group (F).
> You get better results and develop better relationships with community and councillors. People can tell you're trying to provide a consistent framework (F).
> You're setting the ground rules and they know what to expect. You get more respect in doing that. They know I'm consistent (F).

Delegated authority
Councils may delegate officers the authority to approve/refuse applications concerned with certain aspects of the local authority's planning scheme. Several WA authorities have delegated up to ninety per cent of the decisions to officers. Planning committees simply receive a list of the applications and the officer decisions to 'rubber stamp'. Officers are understandably keen to receive delegated authority over as many applications as possible, as this decreases the potential for political will to intervene.

The planning officers whose stories are reported above would fit Catanese's category of covert activists. Only one would wear the overt activist tag. This officer believes that he has 'built up a reputation' (J) for holding a certain ideological viewpoint which he does not attempt to hide.

Blunt-speaking, he believes in a need for 'a degree of Machiavellianism on behalf of the planner' to achieve what he considers to be good outcomes. In this regard he listed strategies which he would consider using, including:

> talking to prominent councillors,
> recommending to the applicant that they talk to councillors,
> suggesting the applicant talks to local residents to convince them about the application,
> coming up with a very tight set of conditions for council to impose, which you know won't be kept,
> choosing not to push too hard for something,
> do absolutely nothing. Let the application go through quietly. If I talk to them with my reputation as 'socialist J', it may put them off (J).

(These last two are instances of negative symbolic capital.)
    But, he stresses,

> I'm not belligerent.

J also engages in persuasive strategies with elected representatives:

> They comprehend easily things like traffic problems but not the broad issues of
> planning like addressing a street frontage. I try to use dramatic examples and
> expressions that councillors can relate to to help them understand.

Acting as a missionary for social justice in a predominantly neo-economic rationalist
climate is difficult, however. All of the planning officers interviewed who fell into this
category spoke of stress and frustration:

> You go through the emotional wringer (F).
> I've toned it down a tad. It's a survival mechanism. I still keep my values and integrity
> but I need to buffer [myself] a bit to physically and emotionally sustain myself (F).
> Taking planning as being the conservation of amenity rather than just a set of
> numbers makes the job more difficult and you get more heartache (J).
> You open a Pandora's box for everything (J).
> It's like permanently trying to row a barbed-wire canoe upstream (J).
> It wears you down (J)

and felt that the introduction of performance-related contracts 'left them exposed'
(F). Some planners felt that the contracts were

> seen by councillors as a weapon – agree with us or go (F).

On the other side of the ideological fence, some planning officers completely agree
with the extension of *market rationale* into planning and its bureaucracy. The public
sector is 'liberalised' in a 'triple agenda of corporatisation, commercialisation and
privatisation' (Gleeson and Low, 2000: 99). The private sector is regarded as showing the way to economic transformation through imaginative physical development
(Healey, 1997: 151).
    Market missionaries employ virtually the same strategies as do those for social
justice, using their cultural capital and symbolic power in persuasive strategies
aimed at persuading elected representatives of the merits of a particular option:

> ... have briefing sessions with councillors about potentially controversial stuff
> right up front. It enables clarification of what you're trying to do and what should
> be the outcome (M).
> They see you as having the statutory knowledge so you remind them of their
> statutory duty and the legislation (M).

They also use incentive strategies:

> warning councillors of the rationale behind the report. You warn councillors of what might happen (M).

Two of the keys to being an effective 'missionary' are anticipation:

> You need to have good links with the councillors. That way you know where they're coming from. … You can then frame your response according to the councillor (F).
> Knowing the councillors is vital. If you want to pre-empt councillors saying x, then you put a comment in your report so they know where we've addressed it (K). … pre-empt problems (K).
> If you don't listen, you won't see it coming (K)

and a sense of timing:

> Planning is being able to take advantage of serendipity when it presents itself (J). The door might only open for a short time. You need to act then (J).
> Councillors don't want to get pinged. Don't put them in a hard decision-making situation just before an election (M).
> Don't put stuff up at certain times. Planners need to think their approach and strategy through the political process – this includes timing (M).
> Communities need to understand if you've got a good strategy, it's worth implementing. It may take ten years. You look for opportunities (M).

Both anticipation and timing are often linked with experience. Together they make up what respondents generally agreed to be insight:

> The difference between those who are good at planning and have a longer future is they're those who are not naïve but have insight (F).
> how to play the complex balancing act (J).
> losing one's naïveté (K)

or 'political nous' (M):

> you develop political antennae (M).
> nous is knowing the councillors, the timetable and playing accordingly. It's having a feel for the game (M).

Metaphors of games and war were frequently used:

> Planning is a series of battles. Don't expect to win it all on day one. You don't have to win the battle to win the war (M).
> The planner's in the front line (K).

... a game of chess (K).
play the game (K).

WHAT DOES IT ALL MEAN?

From the interviews with chameleon and missionary planners, several common themes emerge. Both groups regard planning practice as a sort of game or even a war in which officers need to show consistency and to justify their actions. Planning was regarded as being highly stressful, with most respondents losing the sharper edges of their idealism over time. Some continued to act as missionaries for social justice, predominantly covertly, while others act as missionaries to facilitate development and market freedom. For these officers, strategic use of the symbolic capital of their expertise, anticipation, timing and a feel for the game or political nous, are vital.[26] Others, the chameleons, retreated into planning 'by the book' or gave elected representatives the information they thought they wanted to hear. Virtually all respondents complained of the constraints imposed on them by performance-measured contracts, both for themselves and the CEO.

Planners thus find themselves caught between the 'Scylla of expediency and the Charybdis of moralism' (Dobel, 1999: 193). In a debate over relativism versus absolutism, the missionaries would argue that getting 'dirty hands' is necessary to achieve a desirable end for the public good. None of the missionaries regarded their actions as unethical (although chameleons tended to view it as 'devious'), echoing Walzer's (1973: 174) suggestion that 'it is easy to get one's hands dirty in politics and it is often right to do so'.[27]

There are several labels which might be applied to public officials on this question:

*   the obedient servant versus the political realist (Applbaum, 2000: 115)
*   orthodoxist versus heretic (Bourdieu, 1993; drawing on Weber's opposition between priests and prophets)
*   chameleons versus missionaries (in this volume), and
*   wilfully blind versus ? (Forester, 1999a).

Findings from interviews with a selection of planning practitioners in WA mesh with those from the whole of Australia in suggesting that 'the kinds of people who self-select onto planning in Australia do not necessarily seek change actively. Rather, they are, in general, the sort of people who support the status quo and value compliance' (Cook and Sarkissian, 2000: 129). This is very much a Weberian view of public service: that one should act impartially and overcome one's preferences to provide conscientious service and one should implement the laws and policies even if one personally disagrees with them (Weber, 1988).

However, Dobel (1999) proposes that officials who confuse their own interests with the defence of office and who give up their personal integrity become 'institutionally embedded and malignantly obedient', accepting practices without thinking of their moral content. Dobel's suggestion that people's motives for 'malignant obedience' may stem from advancement, a desire to be perceived as loyal, a need to retain one's job or a fear of reprisal, appears borne out by the WA interviews, as does his statement that institutional embeddedness and malignant obedience resolve the tensions of work:

> Once individuals deny personal responsibility and transfer it to others or the
> institution, the tensions lessen. ... They can participate in policies, satisfy the
> demands of superiors, meet the requirements of competence and promotion,
> and still maintain a reasonable and human illusion of integrity (Dobel, 1999: 44).

Although the respondents would not think that keeping a 'low profile' is a form of 'dirty hands' (or 'deviousness' as they termed it), it could be suggested that playing by the book or telling elected representatives what they want to hear can also justify criticism. As McClendon and Quay write: 'Hell's bells! What's more unethical than collecting a paycheck in the guise of promoting or protecting the public interest while having no real influence or impact on anyone or anything?' (1988: 95).

Pierre Bourdieu suggests that:

> the congruence between signifier and signified, between the representative and
> the represented, doubtless results less from the conscious question to meet the
> demands of the clientele [elected representatives] or the mechanical constraint
> exerted by external pressure [performance-measurement, contracts, etc.] than
> from the homology between the structure of the political field and the structure
> of the world represented (1992: 182).

Chameleon planners play the game of organisational survival. Such 'gun-shy' 'caretaker' planners (McClendon and Quay, 1988) are not interested in innovation or change. Their goals tend to become more negative than positive. They are more interested in avoiding blame than in assuming responsibility. Their operative silence becomes a form of complicity with the established relations of political–economic power.[28]

Most of the missionary planners interviewed, in contrast, provide good examples of Catanese's covert activists: planners 'who remained inherently professional but [were] aware of the political process and the way that it affects decision-making for planning' (1978: 185). Missionary planners are prepared to dirty their hands, to work within the system, for what they believe to be better public outcomes.

As Bourdieu writes:

what is at stake in the game is, on the one hand, the monopoly of the elaboration and diffusion of the legitimate principle of division of the social world …
and, on the other hand, the monopoly of the use of objectified instruments of
power (objectified political capital) (1996: 181).

The game thus

takes the form of a struggle over the specifically symbolic power of making
people see and believe, of predicting and prescribing, of making known and
recognised, which is at the same time a struggle for power over the 'public powers' (state administrations) (1996: 181).

Missionary practice becomes what Bourdieu would term a 'double game' of playing
a game within the wider game of planning practice.

The discourses produced by missionary planners are thus 'doubly determined'
as they are affected by a 'duplicity' which results from 'the duality of fields of reference and from the necessity of serving at one and the same time the esoteric aims of
internal struggles and the exoteric aims of external struggles' (Bourdieu, 1996: 183).

Those planning officers who are missionaries in the cause of social justice
argue that their strategies are necessary to mitigate the potentially worst excesses of
minority interest group politics (Campbell and Marshall, 2000b) and of elected representative whims (see Hillier, 2002). After all, if planners are supposed to represent
the public interest, does not the wider public interest take precedence over the nar-
rower? As one respondent said, 'leverage is important. Planners need leverage to do
good work' (J). In this way, they become justified (to themselves at least) in doing an
act (e.g. manipulating information to 'manufacture consent') which inelinably has a
part which would be wrong to do on its own, but is acceptable in the circumstances
when done in doing what is right.[29] As Sorell writes, 'some elements of democracy
may have to be acted *against* by morality' (2000: 83, emphasis in original).

Whilst these planners may not produce reports for elected representatives
which are, as a Birmingham City councillor complained in the 1970s, 'a subtle blend
of bullshit and flannel and making sure that things go their way' (Newton, 1976:
156), they do use the cultural capital of their 'discretion' as legitimate means to
achieve political ends (Arendt, 1968b: 4–5) in instances when giving full information might cause internal resistance by elected representatives, potentially
sabotaging what are judged to be worthwhile and important projects (e.g. the
Aboriginal hostel and density issues used as examples in the WA interviews).

I would argue that all of the missionary planning officers interviewed in WA
have personal integrity: consistency between their inner beliefs and their public
actions. Not only that, integrity also involves having the reflective capacity to make a
commitment and the courage to act on it, linking their roles as planning officers to

their central web of values (see Dobel, 1999). These individuals make recommendations first on the basis of how a proposal fits the appropriate law, rules and policy
and then on the basis of the regime values behind an anticipated reaction to the proposal. Personal ideology remains a background condition of critical evaluation rather
than a foreground directive for action.

These officers exemplify John Forester's morally improvising planners who
have developed 'an astute practical judgement to deal with far more than "the facts
at hand"' (1999a: 3). Through 'political nous', intuition or judgement, they transform
their knowledge into power[30] and 'interfere purposefully' (Albrechts, 1997: 10) in
the interests of a broader public good.

Important elements of astute practical judgement include anticipation and timing.

Anticipation

The stories above suggest that planning officers 'need by turns to be an expert, a bit
of a politician, an assistant negotiator or broker of community differences, a stickler
for procedure ["due process"], and a stoic who can accept disappointment with
equanimity' (Minson, 1998: 60). In political policy- and decision-making environments, 'clever' (Forester, 1999a) planning officers anticipate how the issue at hand
might appear both to the local public and to the elected representatives, and temper
their 'expert advice' accordingly.

Forester (1999a) echoes the importance of anticipation to enable responses
to foreseeable relationships of power and domination. The practice stories he nar-
rates show how such anticipation requires 'imagination and emotional
responsiveness, the capacities to empathise with other parties *and* to remain politically critical at the same time' (1999: 12, emphasis in original).

Of course there will be events which planners cannot anticipate, especially
those instances when private deals and favours may have been struck. Overall, however, I believe that the predictive abilities of 'practical anticipations of ordinary
experience' (Bourdieu, 1987: 96) should form a strong basis for effective practice.

Experienced practitioners should be able to reflect in action on the frame conflicts which might arise in relation to various development applications or policy
suggestions. Schon and Rein (1994) stress the importance of practitioners 'getting
into the heads' of likely actors (elected representatives, local residents, developers,
etc.) to anticipate their reactions. This should then facilitate practitioners in designing their own actions (moral improvisation) so as to communicate the lessons they
wish the other actors to draw, shaping their attention accordingly.

Timing

'In public policy the three most important factors are timing, timing, timing' (Frantzich,
1999: 199). Timing is key to the success of improvisation. Missionary planning officers are prepared to wait until 'the door opens' (J), even if, for some big-picture ideas,

'it may take ten years' (M). Added together, these elements constitute what I have termed elsewhere as prudence (Hillier, 2002), derived from the Latin verb meaning 'to see ahead'.[31] Prudence also entails exercise of practical judgement or a Bourdieuian feel for the game.

It could be argued that chameleon planners also engage prudence, anticipating the mood and reactions of elected representatives and giving them information selected accordingly and/or using their practical judgement to lie low on potentially controversial issues. They, too, have a feel for the game, but it is a different game to that played by the missionary planners. Both types of planner have schemes of perception, appreciation and action which enable them to perform 'acts of practical knowledge, based on the identification and recognition of conditional, conventional stimuli to which they are predisposed to react' (Bourdieu, 2000: 138): i.e. a habitus. The planners' habituses, albeit different, 'make it possible to adapt endlessly to partially modified contexts, and to construct the situation as a complex whole endowed with meaning, in a practical operation of quasi-bodily *anticipation* of the immanent tendencies of the field' (Bourdieu, 2000: 139, emphasis in original).

Bourdieu explains the difference between acting as one should according to one's habitus and acting as one should according to rules of conduct, legislation, etc. He suggests that there is no rule which does not leave some degree of play or scope for interpretation and improvisation: a 'phronetic gap' (Taylor, 1999: 41). Practice is a continual interpretation and reinterpretation of what a rule really means. Whereas chameleon planners tend to conceive of rules as rigid underlying formulae, and play 'by the book', in what could potentially be a 'wilfully blind', 'scientifically disastrous … travesty in practice' (Taylor, 1999: 42–3), missionary planners interpret rules in light of the 'game' in progress, in the relationship between the structure of the hopes or expectations constitutive of a habitus and the structure of probabilities which is constitutive of a social space (Bourdieu, 2000: 211).

FROM HABERMAS TO HABITUS: WHAT DOES THE CONCEPT OF HABITUS OFFER PLANNING THEORY?

In theorising about the actually existing world of planning practice, that 'messy, political world' (Forester, 1999b: 184) we need to 'learn from practice' how planning officers think and react in the theoretical 'gap' (Hillier, 2002) between planning recommendation and decision-making.

Bourdieu's exploration of interrelationships between agency and structure, through his concept of the habitus, can help us to unpack not only the behaviour of elected representatives (Hillier, 2002), but also that of local authority planners. An understanding of habitus helps us recognise the complex interplay between structuring

forces and the use of agency in shaping policy proposals and decision recommendations. It enables an understanding of individual action which comes closer to the real
complexity of practice than rational-actor or structural theories which attribute action to
either rational choice or external constraints alone. Bourdieu brings us the notion that
action is generated by the interaction of the opportunities and constraints of situations
with actor dispositions (their habitus).

The modes of understanding, representations and proclivities which planning
officers and elected representatives bring to decision-making together with the
structure of institutions (of society in general and planning in particular) which contain and constrain actors' actions are, for Bourdieu, 'the stuff of social reality'. He
suggests that to understand what is really happening in any social situation or interaction (such as planning decision-making), we should ask: what game/s are the
actors playing? What is at stake?

In the political games of planning practice, actors may be seeking power, status, popularity (elected representatives), a stress-free life, outcomes of social justice
or market facilitation (planning officers). The stakes of different games, what could
be gained or lost, also shape the ways in which actors attempt to set boundaries on
the field – of who can 'play', what rules/regulations will be invoked and so on.

The habitus appears in one sense as each individual's characteristic set of dispositions for action. As Calhoun writes, 'it is the melting point between institutions and
bodies' (2000: 713). Within the field of land-use planning decision-making, planning
officers and elected representatives occupy specific positions at any one point in time.
The position of an individual planner or member is shaped by the network of relationships which connect them to other officers and members of governance and to the
wider community of local residents. The actual position the person occupies, however,
is only one of an enormous range of different positions – they could have done many
other things with their lives. In this manner, the planner's or member's body/biography
describes a trajectory through space of positions in the field. Their particular trajectory
is produced partly by material factors and partly by choices and the way the actors
played the various games into which they entered (Calhoun, 2000).

Bourdieu's theorising goes beyond that of Habermas, which has had such an
influence on planning theory. Bourdieu suggests that 'grounding reason in the trans-
historic structures of consciousness or language partakes of a transcendentalist
illusion' (Bourdieu and Wacquant, 1992: 47) as discourses are often *politically*
charged. Political reasoning requires a kind of practical and circumstantial judgement that cannot be directly derived from moral imperatives. Bourdieu adds political
reasoning to the moral reasoning of Habermas' actors. Whereas Habermas priori-
tises 'the right' over 'the good', Bourdieu seeks to rebalance the practical and
cognitive dimensions of discourse and action. The issue is not one of 'truth' versus
'relativity', of validated knowledge versus unvalidated opinion, as Habermas tends to

present it, but of the truth of generality versus the truth of specificity, or truth at the level of abstract principle versus truth embedded in practical circumstances.[32]

Bourdieu thus stops short of accepting the universality of reason. He demands a *Realpolitik* of reason which would permit thinking universally without presupposing universal reason (Poupeau, 2000). Whereas Habermas presupposes both the universality of reason and the existence of universalisable interests in order to achieve rational consensus formation, Bourdieu begins with the uniqueness of social interaction and from there he examines the conditions under which universals and rationality may emerge.

Bourdieu's concepts of habitus, field and capital include consideration of *power relations*. Whereas Habermasian rational consensus includes a 'liberal "grammar" of equality' (Mouffe, 2000: 44), which tends to bracket power-plays and exclusionary action, Bourdieu recognises the power of organisations and individuals who come to the 'decision-table', to exclude those who 'lack the necessary competence to compete effectively' (Bourdieu, 2000: 112) , whether this 'competence' is an invitation to participate, membership of a representative organisation, time, gender, income, expertise, etc. Bourdieu indicates how scientific discoveries (*pace* planning arguments, visions and policy interpretations) are accepted by 'society' according to who makes the discovery rather than what that discovery might be.

Relations of power, therefore, are also relations of symbolic force. Bourdieu suggests that what clashes in the field (of planning decision-making) are competing social constructions and representations which claim to be grounded in a 'reality' which imposes its verdict 'through the arsenal of methods, instruments and … techniques collectively accumulated and implemented, under the constraint of the discipline and censorship of the field and also through the invisible force of the orchestration of habitus' (2000: 113). Speakers tacitly adjust what they say to the relations of power between themselves and their audience.

Bourdieu analyses speech-acts in communicative exchanges, therefore, in a different way to Habermas. Whereas Habermas examines speech-acts to disclose a rationally motivating force at work, Bourdieu's concern is to demonstrate that whatever power speech-acts possess, it is power ascribed to them by the social institution of which the utterance of the speech-act is a part. 'Speakers' (authors) can performatively act on the real through words because they act on those representations of the real which their situated authority allows them to impose. As Poupeau (2000: 80) indicates, 'communication is then not exempt from relations of power, which are born from differences of status between speaker and listeners'. The Habermasian suggestion that conditions could exist in which communication would be unaffected by social constraints (the ideal speech situation) is, according to Bourdieu, a 'fictitious elision of the social conditions of language use' (Thompson, 2001: 10). For Bourdieu, linguistic competence alone is insufficient. It is necessary to have a 'situated competence' (Bourdieu and Wacquant, 1992: 146).

Habermasian analysis of speech-acts fails to recognise that communicative meanings go beyond the words and ideal speech conditions of truth. Bourdieu suggests that analysis should be concerned not simply with the conditions of truth (the ideal speech situation), but with determining the value of truth. Such analysis involves examining the relationship between actual speakers rather than just between 'words and things' (Poupeau, 2000: 80). Habermasian speech-act analysis neglects investigation of the concrete interactions between speakers and therefore omits a fundamental aspect of the production of meaning.

MacCallum's (2001b) detailed case study demonstrates how examination of speaker interactions is vital to fully understanding the meanings invoked. Her work presents an excellent example of members of a land-use planning 'community panel' wresting power of the agenda from the panel's executive through strategic transformation of linguistic capital into symbolic power. That the panel members were able to succeed stems from the relationship both between the members themselves and between the members and the executive; a relationship which created belief in the legitimacy of the words and of the person/s who uttered them and a recognition by the executive of the symbolic force or violence of the utterances.

The symbolic violence exerted by the performative acts of the panel members' words, as indicated above, is far from rational. Bourdieuian analysis adds the *social dimensions of language* and the *concrete aspects of communication* to the linguistic sphere of Habermas.

Bourdieu complains that a Habermasian communicative situation in which participants would engage in reciprocity, seeking to understand the viewpoints of others and giving them the same weight as their own, ignores 'that the force of arguments counts for little against the arguments of force ... and that domination is never absent from social relations of communication' (2000: 65). Bourdieu claims that Habermas subjects social relations to a 'twofold reduction', a depoliticisation of political power relations to relations of communication (force of the better argument), from which he has in practice already removed the power relations that take place. Nevertheless, with reference to academic debate, Bourdieu does suggest that conflictual, but regulated cooperation may lead to the subordination of the selfish interests of individual actors and a dialogic confrontation with others which may induce a move to greater reflexivity (Bourdieu, 2000: 121).

Overall, Bourdieu's theorising more nearly approaches the agonistic conception of democracy favoured by Mouffe (1993, 2000) and of planning decision-making by Hillier (2000a). The conflicts and struggles of groups and individuals are viewed in Bourdieuian theory as strategic confrontations not of the actors, but of their habituses. Individuals and groups, guided by their respective schemes of thought, perception and action, are agents of their social conditions, their habitus.

CONCLUSIONS

> Democracy suggests that the best technical advice in the world is the wrong
> decision if elected representatives vote against it (ex-planning officer, metropoli-
> tan LA).

Traditional theories of planning policy- and decision-making tend to conceptualise a
unidirectional, incremental, instrumental process in which council decisions follow
planning officer recommendations. Such theories bracket the gap which exists in
reality between recommendation and decision, a gap containing hidden transcripts
of private and public deals, favours, cultural traditions, demagogic posturing and
omnipotent acts of benevolence or vindictiveness.

Is planning practice a world of 'moral attrition' where 'ideals and integrity cor-
rode under the acid of power, ... frustration, imperfection, and constraint' as Dobel
(1999: xi) suggests; a world in which elected representatives prioritise popularity
above land use and in which planning officers do not care about the outcomes of
their work or who, wilfully blind to the outcomes, take the expedient path of feeding
their elected representatives the information which the officers anticipate they will
most appreciate? Or are some missionary planners able to make a difference, anticipating elected representatives' behaviour and improvising accordingly?

John Forester's stories from planning practitioners begin to fill the gap in
demonstrating the vulnerability of planners' efforts to the messiness of politics. My
stories from elected representatives and planning officers serve to both corroborate
Forester's material and to add to our understanding of those seemingly irrational
decisions when elected representatives ignore officer recommendations or change
their minds between one meeting and the next. I emphasise the contingent nature of
relations and the importance of the personal dynamic (Tewdwr-Jones, 2002)
between planners, the public and elected representatives and the role of the habitus
in helping planners to anticipate actors' reactions to recommendations. By exposing
the potentially hidden transcripts of the habitus, the social traditions, presuppositions and strategies of actors' social worlds, their political 'culture', I hope to provide
a 'tool of liberation' (Schusterman, 1999: 12) for planning practitioners unable to
make sense of the often unarticulated workings of these worlds and the apparently
irrational decisions which result.

In presenting a range of possible 'reasons' for elected representatives' and
planning officers' actions I raise the caveat of intellectualism: the hermeneutic danger that I may have substituted my relation to practice, for the practical relation to
practice itself. The picture I draw is 'that practical rationality depends far less on for-
mulas or recipes than on a keen grasp of the particulars seen in the light of more
general principles' (Forester, 1999a: 33). Planning decision-making is a complex

mixture of hybrid processes – technical, collaborative and political[33] – involving a range of values and ideals competing for decision-makers' attention.

Do my stories present planning as an exercise in actor-centred moral reasoning, as Habermas might suggest, or a more Bourdieuian feel for the game of practice? Bourdieu (2000: 72–3) warns us against the two extremes of excluding reason and admitting reason only. Clearly, reason is, or has been, an important part of most of the officers' decisions to work towards planning outcomes in which they firmly believe, or to simply survive without too much stress. However, we must also consider the *Realpolitik* of reason, which, to be effective, cannot be limited to the regulated confrontation of rational dialogue which recognises no force other than that of argument. The issue of whether strategies are pursued consciously or unconsciously becomes less important once it is recognised that they are driven by the interrelations of elected representatives' and officers' habituses with the particular conjuncture of the field of local authority decision-making, i.e. a practical feel for the game. 'Habitus is what you have to posit to account for the fact that, without being rational, social agents are *reasonable*' (Bourdieu and Wacquant, 1992: 129, emphasis in original).

As Bourdieu has written more recently, habitus is a 'can-be', tending to produce behaviour 'adjusted to the possibilities, in part by orienting the perception and evaluation of the possibilities inscribed in the present situation' (2000: 217). Strategies of action are thus not abstract responses to abstract situations, but take place in response to prompts which 'speak' to those elected representatives and officers characterised by possession of certain cultural and symbolic capital and a certain habitus.

EXTENDING MY MODEL OF DISCURSIVE PLANNING DECISION-MAKING

Bourdieu's theorising adds the possibility of exploring the broader power structures and legitimisation dynamics within which land-use planning agencies act, an addition much called for by authors such as Yiftachel (1998, 2001) and Yiftachel and Huxley (2000).

Thrift (1996a) points out the similarities and differences between Bourdieu's work and that of Giddens (1976, 1977, 1979, 1981), Bhaskar (1979) and Layder (1981), to which I add Sztompka (1990, 1991, 1993) as depicted in Figure 10.1.

I have no space here to engage at length with the four authors besides Bourdieu, save to point out (after Thrift, 1996a: 67–72) that:

- For all, except Bhaskar, social structures are characterised by their duality. Constituted by human practices, social structures are also the medium of this construction. Humans can, through their practices, thus reconstitute or transform the structure. Structure and agency are interdependent.

Bourdieu	Bhaskar	Giddens	Layder	Sztompka
Structure	Structure	Structure	Structure	Structure
↕	↕	↕	↕	↕
Habitus	Position–practice system	System	Organisations/institutions	Agency-praxis system
↕	↕	↕	↕	↕
		Institutions	Interactions	
↕	↕	↕	↕	↕
Practices	Practices	Practices	Practices	Practices

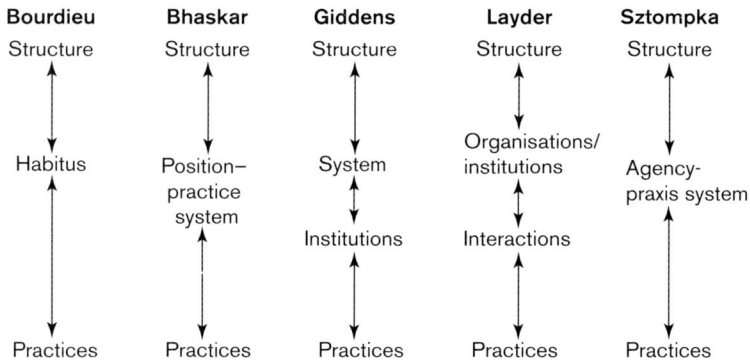

Figure 10.1 Mediating concepts between structure and agency (after Thrift, 1996a: 69)

- All authors introduce the idea of a mediating concept between structure and agency. Bourdieu uses the habitus; Bhaskar offers a position–practice system in which positions are places, functions, rules, rights, etc. and practices are the activities in which humans engage; Giddens refers to the 'system' as reproduced and regular social practices, in turn mediated by 'institutions'; Layder suggests an objective substantive structure of institutions and an inter-action structure within which human interaction takes place; Sztompka's theory of social becoming posits a level of agency–praxis in which structures as capacities for operation and agencies as capacities for action meet.

- All authors present theories of practical action related to practical reason: when people 'act, often in situations of stress or bewilderment, and they ... act only in terms of their most taken-for-granted understandings and expectations' (Glendinning, 2001: 11). As outlined previously, practical action, phronesis or prudence is an essential and invaluable part of planning practice. It is linked to anticipation and the shaping of actors' expectations and orientations towards the future: 'the real ambition to control the future ... varies with the real power to control that future, which means first of all having a grasp on the present' (Bourdieu, 2000: 221).

- All authors recognise that time and space are central to the construction of social interaction. 'Practices are defined by the fact that their temporal structure, direction and rhythm are constitutive of their meaning' (Bourdieu, 1977: 9).[34]

Could the structure/practices of Bourdieu et al. above correspond to the system and lifeworld of Habermas? My suggestion is in the affirmative. As such, the habitus provides us with a site of mediation between systems and lifeworld and an analytical focus on communicative interaction which recognises Foucauldian-type notions of power.

The point common to Bourdieu, Habermas and Foucault is that each provides a critical perspective on practice – critical in the political sense of being a critique of domination and an analysis of its manifestations in society. The three perspectives all combine an analysis of the nature of domination and the mechanisms by which it is enacted and legitimated. Whilst differing in their interpretations of relationships between power and meaning, there are nevertheless interesting convergences and complementarities between the authors' views.

For Foucault and Bourdieu, for example, reason has a history. Being is history. In fact, as Poupeau (2000) points out, there is a double historicity: that of 'socially constituted mental structures and that of the social structures which shape them'. Given Habermas' concessions towards an historically shaped lifeworld and habituation, the issue of consensus in the model of discursive democracy must be questioned, and is taken up in the next part.

Second, a new domain of understanding is opened up by the addition of Bourdieuian theory to Habermas' and Foucault's assessment of discursive and persuasive power. This is the domain of a *Realpolitik* of reason, which gives us a more adequate theory of political judgement. Reason is not context-dependent. It is a socially constituted contested entity. Deliberation by itself is not enough. We need to consider the power-plays which are carried out in both formal and informal settings. Planning is an activity often undertaken in the shadows of power.

Third, there is the addition of prudence. Planning officers are constantly drawing on prudence as they make practical judgements based on a *bricolage* of limited information, perceived values and anticipation of potential actions and their consequences. With the addition of prudence, the theory makes the important transition from ethics or morals to politics, thereby gaining a higher degree of correspondence with the realities of planning practice.

The discursive dimensions of planning practice allow for critical analysis of local decision-making interactions as sites of struggle between competing and contradictory representations. Framed within an analysis of field (local land-use planning), habitus and forms of capital, we can unpack the communicative behaviours of particular agencies/actors and begin to understand the expressions of power and the power-plays invoked.

> The mind working in search of a strategy is not simply recalling past methods.
> … Nor is it performing simply an intellectual or rational thought process. … It is
> only possible through continuous practice, deep meditation (reflexivity) and long
> deliberation (Teck, 1997: 17).

PART 5

OUT FROM THE SHADOWS

CHAPTER 11

ASSOCIATING WITH SHADOWS

INTRODUCTION

In this part, I explore processes which offer the flexibility to be issue-dependent, to include those groups and individuals affected by the context and which welcome, rather than attempt to suppress, conflict. In so doing, I examine the implications of Benhabib's (1996a) distinction between associational space as a space in which people work together in concert, and agonistic space, which she regards as competitive space. If, as Mouffe (1996) suggests, all space is inherently conflictual and agonistic once we go beyond the moral to consider the political dimension, does this imply that associative democratic decision-making is impossible? Does it mean that there is always 'more than reason', and that insider (associative democratic) and outsider (informal action) strategies should be legitimated to take place in parallel?

IDENTITY AND INTEREST REPRESENTATION

As I have developed in the previous two parts, 'identity – our sense of ourselves as individuals and as social beings – is constructed through social processes rather than being innate or pre-given' (Bondi, 1993, cited in Pred, 1997: 124). We see the world and give identity to place through our particular self-identities and reimagine our identities as we see and interpret our relation to the world.

Identities of self and of place are intrinsically related. Moreover, identities of both are complex and dynamic – multiple identities or multiple subject positions, each of which is subject to political transformation and change. As Massey (1991: 278) writes, 'there are indeed multiple meanings of places, held by different social groups, [and] the question of which identity is dominant will be the result of social negotiation and conflict'. There can be no one reading of place. Planners have traditionally sought to 'balance' readings, but have often brought to the very act of 'balancing' particular mindsets which have, perhaps unconsciously, biased the scales.

Planners may also underestimate the importance of residents' attachment to their local areas and how it comprises a vital component of their social identity. A threat to their physical environment thus becomes a threat to the self.[1] Traditional forms of planning decision-making have tended to convey a message of place as identified and controlled by outsiders (the planners). Plans and policies are loaded with material, ideological and political content which may perpetuate injustices and do violence to those values, images and identities which have not been traditionally recognised. Instead of regarding places as areas with particular boundaries, they should be imagined as 'articulated moments in networks of social relations and understandings' (Massey, 1991: 28).

> it cannot be otherwise that identity repeatedly becomes undermined, problem-
> atic, an issue, something to be reworked, reconstructed, retrieved, or struggled
> over in order to reanchor (Pred, 1997: 126).

Place becomes one of the terms of reference for the negotiation and articulation of identity. The social practices of discourse and communication are vital components of deliberation. It is therefore important to consider how the discourse of planning functions ideologically to shape attention and rationalise policy decisions, how it 'mediates among the choices made available to us, the values we collectively espouse, and our ability to act ... about how we should live and invest, where and with whom' (Beauregard, 1993: 5–6).

In addition to the discourse of planners we need to pay attention to the ways in which other people verbalise their places in the world, their values and identities. Meanings may become more important than facts in policy deliberation. The result-ing plan becomes 'a reworking of everyday narratives to find a potentially truer, more comprehensive one ... Planning commands time by taking the narratives we have in mind and refashioning them' (Krieger, 1981: 141).

Planning requires giving voice, ear and respect (Healey, 1992b) to all partici-pants and their representations, values, images and identities. It means understanding the subjective nature of identity and how 'identifications emerge from the social relations we participate in and the discourses ... that give them meaning' (Gibson-Graham, 1995: 276). These social relations and discourses may serve as barriers or offer opportunities for identity-building. The process of the planned trans-formation of place is thus both formative and disruptive of identity.

Since the late 1960s in the Western world, waves of interest-focused citizen activism have led to what has been termed the rise of civil society (Cohen and Arato, 1992).[2] Interests have been represented through relatively formal processes of pub-lic participation in planning, such as making written submissions or attending public meetings, through advocative processes such as lobbying (Hillier, 1997), or through intimidatory processes (Smith, Nell and Prystupa, 1997) such as civil disobedience.

As Smith et al. (1997: Fig. 1; 141) diagrammatically illustrate, convergence towards a form of interest representation which facilitates participation, in the inter-ests of accountability and empowerment, and generally what are regarded as more efficient processes (such as environmental dispute resolution), has gradually over-come bureaucratic constraints such as reluctance to share power and technocratic inertia.[3] However, as Abram (1998) demonstrates, increased citizen participation in planning has not necessarily led to more consensus, nor to popular planning decisions being made, but has often led to more vocal objections and raised expectations for governance to respond to local demands.

LAYING THE FOUNDATIONS FOR BUILDING NEW THEORY

I am concerned with issues of social justice and giving more than simply voice to the voiceless in the interstices of society, with regard to interest representation in land-use planning decision-making processes. Building on the results of empirical research into the power and influence of informal direct action (Part Three) and the interactions of planning officers and elected representatives on local planning decisions (Part Four), I am concerned in this part with attempting to build inductive theory addressing issues of both: legitimation of informal direct action by opening up planning processes and public protest to all, and also 'institutionalisation' of community mobilisation through forms of associative democracy. 'Both approaches are valuable and necessary' (Young, 2001: 671). I attempt an initial reconciliation and subsequent critique of the two in a conception of associative/agonistic planning which incorporates both informal action and institutionalised practices.

Figure 11.1 represents a tentative attempt at illustrating this diagrammatically. The vertical axis represents a political distinction between institutionalised community mobilisation and informal direct action. The horizontal axis represents two types of space: associational/consensus and agonistic. Within the diagram I offer some possibilities for types of action which might be represented in each area (recognising the non-exclusivity of each domain) and point out that *within* individual networks there may also be activities/behaviours taking place which are institutionalised – informal and consensus–agonistic in nature. Any patterns in practice would be extremely messy, containing various levels and intensities of networks nesting inside/overlapping each other.

In this chapter I lay the foundations for building new planning theory. I challenge practice goals of the Habermasian notion of consensus and suggest that con-sensus, a 'feeling or sensing together', rather than agreement, might be more practically appropriate.

I diagrammatically represent the general fuzzy area in which planning activity appears to me to take place and lay the foundations for its theoretical development by exploring the constituent aspects of interactive networks, new social movements, direct action and associative democracy. I then examine the inherent paradox of liberal democracy, the democratic system within which most Western planning operates. The value of individual liberty epitomised by liberalism is at odds with the egalitarian and majoritarian nature of democracy. Consensus-building cannot equate all values since any decision will prefer some value/s over others. I conclude the chapter by suggesting that the philosophy and practices of agonistic democracy may offer a fruitful alternative to attempting to reach consensus.

POLITICS:
INSTITUTIONALISED

Neocorporatism	Associative democracy
Policy networks	Radical pluralism
e.g. tenants' associations	e.g. small reciprocities/fixing
development coalitions	

SPACE:

ASSOCIATIONAL	**AGONISTIC**
'CONSENSUS'	
Issue networks	Direct action
e.g. coping networks	e.g. resident action
	groups, environmental
	movements

INFORMAL

NB Within individual groups/networks, etc. there may also be institutionalised–informal and consensus-agonistic activity

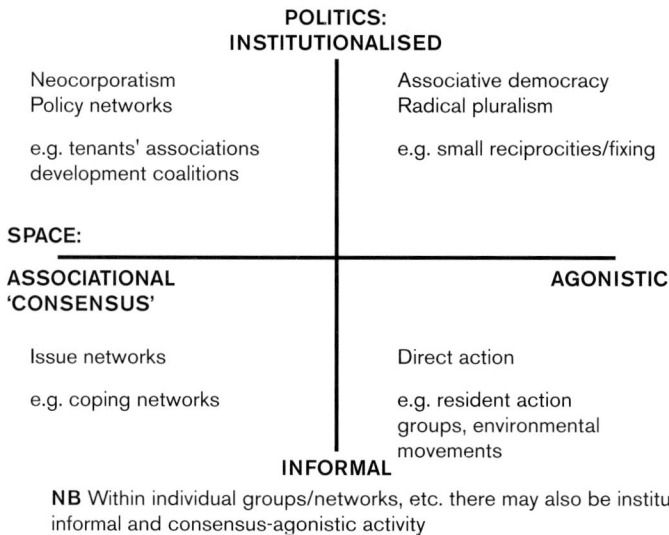

Figure 11.1 Organisational landscape of participatory processes in planning (Source: Hillier, 2002b: 116)

THROWING LIGHT ON THE PROBLEMATICS OF CONSENSUS: A CONTEXT

My previous chapters have deconstructed processes of public participation in local land-use planning decisions to identify a variety of events chained together by the expectations, interests, fears and desires of the actors involved. These chains are communicated along networks as energy flows of varying intensities and power. The political opportunity structure[4] in place at a particular point in time may act to determine the relative intensity of the various approaches to interest representation which are utilised.

I have identified that networks of actors are contingent and dynamic as associations and coalitions form and disband according to the issue under consideration.[5] Traditionally antagonistic actors may work together, for instance, in the face of some other, mutual threat. As different forms of interest representation take place contemporaneously, planning processes may become replete with conflict and antagonism.

Judith Innes in particular (Innes, 1995, 1996, 1998, 2000; Innes and Booher, 1997, 1998b, 1999a, 1999b; Innes and Gruber, 1999) suggests that 'consensus-building has become a way of bridging across groups and interests, and it provides the opportunity to explore for new approaches to seemingly intractable issues where conventional analyses and decision processes have proven inadequate'

(Innes and Booher, 1997: 2). However, the idea of consensus is a highly contested goal. As Smith (2000) asks, is it a regulative of deliberation (as for Habermas) or a dangerous ideal in the name of which conflict is suppressed?

Participation programmes which allow people to speak out, but colonise their lifeworlds in this latter manner, give people only 'accommodative voice' (Sampson, 1993), whereby those in power accommodate the public by permitting people to have their say, although power relationships remain unchanged. Simply giving other participants more voice will not work if planners do not listen to and understand their meanings and claims. There should be a change in the social discourse of public participation. Planners would need to challenge traditional assumptions, practices and forms of knowing and develop new practices of dialogical encounter which enable communicative interaction within and between actor-networks in which everyone can 'justify, convince, defend, criticise, explain, argue, express (their) inner feelings and desires while interpreting those of others' (Chambers, 1995: 242). Understanding the representations of others and the recognition of common ground is important.

As Habermas suggests, we need to go beyond traditional knowledges and values, facts and norms, to develop a praxis of social decision-making able to incorporate difference and oppositional representations and ways of knowing, and which is informed by principles of equality and justice – a praxis in which people take responsibility for others, 'being for' and 'being with' them (Bauman, 1993).

It is in this way, Healey (1994) suggests, that planners can engage in strategic consensus-building. However, is an objective of reaching consensus at the same time as respecting and valuing difference unattainably utopian? Participants in public participation programmes often hold diametrically opposed views as indicated in the stories narrated above. Can we do justice to all values, images and identities and still negotiate consensus?

I suggest not in the traditional meaning of the term consensus, nor in the accepted Habermasian sense of the achievement of 'agreements which terminate in the mutuality of intersubjective understanding' (Habermas, 1979: 3).[6] We need to include in our notion of consensus the possibility that differently formulated identities and representations may find any common links extremely precarious, and that there may well be substantive and even intractable disagreements over basic issues. Mouffe (1992) argues that decisions taken in a conflictual field generally imply the repression of some representations. Therefore, any consensus cannot exist without a 'constitutive outside', the exterior to the consensual community. I, then, would prefer to adopt Love's (1995: 62) version of con-sensus, spelled with a hyphen, carrying a meaning of 'feeling or sensing together', implying not necessarily agreement, 'but a "crossing" of the barrier between ego and ego, bridging private and shared experience' (Holland, cited in Belenky et al., 1986: 223). Con-sensus involves a respect for the views of others and an attempt to understand them: 'a harmony simultaneously disrupted and ordered. The contrapuntal themes are not at war or in conflict, but they come together without becoming the same' (Love, 1995: 62).

Con-sensus would enable local participants in participatory decision-making programmes to resist the colonisation of their lifeworlds by systemic power structures and to replace them with a new consciousness, an 'epistemology of multiplicity' (Gomez-Pena, 1993: 38). We would need to consider reconstitution of the Habermasian concept of the public sphere as one which allows for the creation of local autonomous public spheres as appropriate, to which all the public has access as relevant and which guarantees respect of differences, freedom of expression and the right to criticism.[7]

In an earlier chapter (Chapter 6) I demonstrated a case in which, through astute channelling of energies, a small group of actors successfully lobbied elected representatives and utilised the media to manipulate a new situation definition away from what would have been a better technical planning response to a 'solution' which suited themselves. This actor demonstrated clearly that 'strength is *interven*tion, *inter*ruption, *inter*pretation and *inter*est' (Callon and Latour, 1981: 292).

Empirically there exists a complex array of actors/actants which each temporally exhibit various qualities from several of the domains depicted in Figure 11.1. I attempt to indicate, in Figure 11.2, a representation of the general fuzzy area in which planning activity appears to me to take place.

Citizen interest representation through direct action has the potential to undermine dramatically the capacity of planners to plan. Is this necessarily a 'bad thing', however? If informal direct action is taken by the otherwise voiceless, is it not a legitimate means of obtaining voice through making 'public noise' (Young, 2001: 673)? Although unlikely to take to the streets in demonstration, planners do have fewer *public* opportunities to 'gain the ear' of elected representatives.

What action should planners take in circumstances when their recommendations for a technically sound policy are opposed by an influential network of articulate actors with a less viable, self-interested alternative? Can and should planners use what powers they have (and their networks) to fight for an outcome in which they believe? Should they fight fire with fire and engage in informal leaks and direct action? This raises no small matter of ethical questions.

My research, and the work in Europe of Louis Albrechts (1997) and Bent Flyvbjerg (1998a, 1998b), help to expose the clientelistic tendency of governance systems[8] and the informal activities of actors which both underpin and undermine such structures. Clearly, 'the whole apparatus of adverse bargaining, negotiation, compromise and deadlock which normally surround the planning process is undervalued' (Albrechts, 1997: 8) in both practice and theory. Such pragmatic considerations should be integrated into theory which aims at eventual implementation or praxis. The question is how? Direct action/lobbying has become part of decision-making behaviour. I certainly do not advocate its abolition. I firmly believe

POLITICS:
INSTITUTIONALISED

Neocorporatism
Policy networks

Associative democracy
Radical pluralism

SPACE:

ASSOCIATIONAL
'CONSENSUS'

AGONISTIC

Issue
networks

Direct
action

INFORMAL

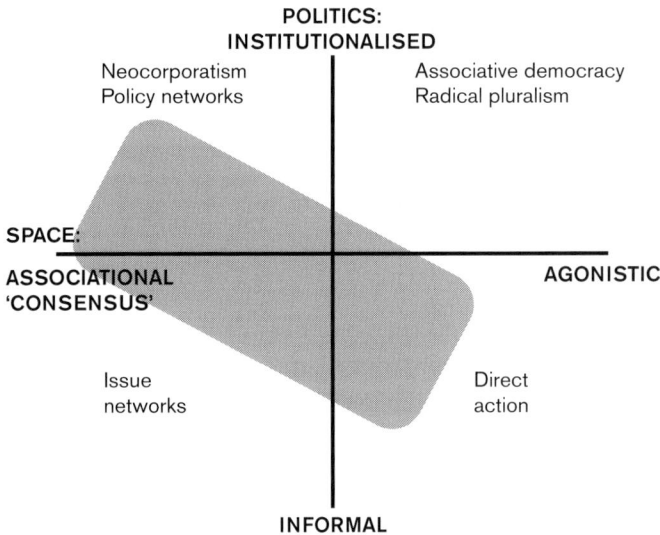

Figure 11.2 Participatory planning activity in practice

that preserving people's right to lobby is important. Yet at present (in WA at least) it appears to be somewhat more of a 'fight with few holds barred than ... a contest under well-defined rules' (Gamson, 1995b: 142), with the odds heavily weighted in favour of the already advantaged groups in society.

Do we want to impose some formal institutional structure, therefore, on what is essentially an interpersonal framework? Can we as planners really not feel comfortable (less vulnerable?) unless there is 'an awesome and incontestable authority' (Bauman, 1991: 251) hanging over everything? Even if this means inventing and imposing an artificial order?

Melucci (1989, 1996) and Young (2001) are strong advocates of conducting debate in public spheres independent of the institutions of governance, in order to provide guarantees of non-corporatism, non-tokenism and non-cosmeticism to local people, and to ensure that society's issues, demands and conflicts are subjected openly to negotiation. Non-institutionalised public spheres, Melucci argues, make possible a 'democracy of everyday life'.

There are strong arguments for the encouragement and legitimation of informal direct action as a means of giving voice to the traditionally voiceless in planning decision-making processes. The implicit assumption, which runs through much of my analysis above, that if public protest takes place, the formal participation processes have failed ('campaigns are the currency of unsuccessful groups' (Richardson and Jordan, 1979: 123)) is open to question. An open process, in which all actors can protest publicly, could be an alternative.

If we are aiming to overcome a situation in which the more affluent and well-connected are able to exercise greater power over planning decision-making, and to give voice and power to the voiceless, we need to consider the relative merits of

- opening up the decision processes to outsider strategies of direct action eschewing deliberation;
- attempting to restrict deliberative decision processes to institutionalised insider strategies;
- enabling insider and outsider strategies to take place in parallel.

We may well need to consider introducing new affirmative principles which aim to avoid the mere institutionalisation of effectively mobilised networks of power, power which is then legitimately exercised over weaker, less able networks. We would require new arenas which are perhaps less rule-directed than rule-altering/reflexive. To what rules could we switch? How might we create a 'form of articulation between individual freedom and civic participation' (Mouffe, 1992: 231) which respects the priority of the socially just over the socially and economically powerful?

I believe that people should be able to speak for themselves in inclusionary methods of decision-making, but that we could need some forms of affirmative action, perhaps, to ensure that marginalised and less articulate voices are not only given opportunities to be heard, but that they are listened to with respect and considered with affirmative weighting. In so doing we would need not only to *give* voice by democratising existing networks, but moreover to *build* voice by building alternative networks or 'subaltern counterpolitics' in which the hitherto excluded have a viable stake, and to make these networks accessible to and resourceful for such groups threatened by the powerful networks of the articulate.

So, how could we do this? Who would be likely to gain and who to lose?

I am confident that we would need to think about local strategies, which would be contextually appropriate, rather than centralised solutions.

Before I explore the possibilities outlined above in detail, however, I offer a brief theoretical foundation to the key concepts of interactive networks, new social movements (NSMs) and associative democracy.

INTERACTIVE NETWORKS

The theoretical bases for the concept of interactive networks may be found, according to Burns and Taylor (1997) in the three separate discourses of civil society (Cohen and Arato, 1992), communitarianism (Etzioni, 1996) and social capital (Putnam, 1993, 2000; Cox, 1995).

'Networking is the process by which relationships and contacts between people or organisations are established, nurtured and utilised for mutual benefit'
(Gilchrist, 1995: 2). Networking thus involves developing and using human relationships. Networks, or institutional webs of relationships, both formal and informal, are
becoming increasingly recognised as playing a major role in decision-making
processes (see Castells, 1996, 1997, 1998; Amin and Hausner, 1997). Networking
enables actors to maintain their own identities and yet to work together, creating
potential for energies of information and influence to flow across institutional and
identity boundaries. In this way, not only powerful, but also more marginalised actors
may access resources, support and arenas of debate and negotiation which might
not otherwise be available (Skelcher *et al.*, 1996). The Darwinian notion of 'survival
of the fittest' thus becomes, as Kropotkin (1914) identified, not necessarily the
physically strongest, nor the Machiavellian most cunning, but those who learn to
combine in mutual support. More recently, Milofsky (1988), Tarrow (1994) and
Gilroy and Speak (1998) and others (e.g. Innes, 1994; Healey, 1997a, 1997b;
Hillier, 1997b; Flyvbjerg, 1998a) have outlined the importance of networks and
exchange of energies in building and maintaining social, political and informational
capital.

Networks are 'socially constructed rationalities, tied up with the specificities of
time and place' (Amin and Hausner, 1997: 8). They are dynamic and contingent on
their particular contextual circumstances. Networks vary in size, degrees of formality,
in the strength of their ties, and in their power dimensions. Amin and Hausner
(1997: 10) identify spectra of regressive/progressive, closed/open, adaptable/non-
adaptable, deliberative/non-reflexive and centralised/decentred networks. Similarly,
Odrillard (1997) distinguishes between reactive, cognitive and creative networks, in
which differences in behaviour reflect differences in sedimented rationality (substantive, procedural and complex). Locations of networks along these spectra will
reflect their respective governance logics, some of which may assist and others hinder their operational success. (See also Skelcher *et al.*, 1996: 54.)

Governance activity may be aimed at sustaining networks or at transforming
them. As Gilroy and Norwood (1997) comment, spatial planning efforts, as an example of governance activity, are inherently drawn into such processes. They may
reinforce or obstruct and fragment organised coping mechanisms which planners
simply cannot see.

If we fail to understand how such networks and webs operate, and the associated power structures and energy flows within and between them, we as planners
may remain blind both to possibilities of working interactively with communities and
to dangers we would wish to avoid.[9] As Geoff Mulgan has convinced the Blair
administration in the UK, 'the defining feature of this world is connexity' (Mulgan,
1997: 20).

Informal and formal networks or webs and perceptions of common purpose provide the underpinnings for what may be termed new social movements.

NEW SOCIAL MOVEMENTS

The term New Social Movement (NSM) has gained wide currency in the West since the mid-1970s. Cohen and Arato (1992: 523) claim that NSMs 'construe the cultural models, norms, and institutions of civil society as the main stakes of social conflict'. NSMs show a dual organisational logic, seeking to exert influence on political society and policy-making for both offensive and defensive reasons (e.g. resource mobilisation, defence of identity). It is the institutional potentials which, therefore, comprise what Cohen and Arato (1992: 511) call the 'stakes of struggle'.

Cohen and Arato (1992), Weir (1993) and Buechler (2000) provide a critical analysis of the earlier work of Tilly (1978, 1986, 1995) and Tarrow (1989, 1992, 1994) on rational interaction and NSMs. They also critique the theoretical approaches of Habermas (1982) and Touraine (1981, 1985) as not encompassing the dualistic internal logic of NSMs. Following work by Keane (1988) and Scott (1990), Cohen and Arato (1992) then attempt to provide a theoretical framework which can accommodate both offensive and defensive logics.

Fainstein and Hirst (1995: 181) rather circumspectly define social movements as 'collective social actors defined by both their (dis)organisation and their aims'. Yet, situated as NSMs tend to be at the intersection of Habermasian system and life-world, the public and private, they often challenge the role of governance with regard to uneven distributions of power and resources. They therefore challenge 'urban meaning' (Castells, 1983: 319–20), threatening or breaking down the material and social hierarchies which structure urban life. Although it is widely acknowledged that most NSMs tend to be fragmented, parochial and of limited duration and effectiveness, if successful they have the potential to expose power relationships and operations and to overturn stereotypes and traditions and reframe ideas and practice into more participatory and negotiable models. I, therefore, prefer to use Castells' (1997: 3) definition of social movements as 'purposive collective actions whose outcome, in victory as in defeat, transforms the values and institutions of society'.

Gamson (1992, 1995a, 1995b) suggests that collective actions tend to be framed by one or more aspects of injustice, agency (potential empowerment) and identity. A group of people attempt to do something about a perceived injustice perpetrated against humans/nature. NSMs often go beyond a concern with the economics of class, despite Eder's (1990) insistence that nature represents an object of class struggle dominated by the petit bourgeois 'new middle class'.

According to Melucci (1989, 1996, 2000) NSMs articulate three main forms of symbolic challenge to the ways in which development is conceived and identities and needs defined: prophecy, or the announcement of alternative frameworks of meaning; paradox, or the exaggeration of the irrationality and violence of dominant codes; and representation, or the retransmission of contradictions of the system. Conflicts are shifted towards goals of reappropriation and reversal of meanings pro-duced by seemingly distant and impersonal structures (such as planning practice) which operate according to instrumental rational rationales. NSMs, therefore, 'pose new issues, shape consciousness, and open new arenas of political discourse' (Wekerle and Peake, 1996: 265).

Public spheres become conflictual arenas in which NSMs wage 'a critical struggle against the representation of the world served up by the dominant models, denying their claim to uniqueness and challenging the symbolic constitution of poli-tics and culture' (Melucci, 1996: 357). Traditional modi operandi are broken down and symbolic orders are threatened and reversed as NSMs signify, name and act in new ways ranging from revolution to milder forms of civil disobedience. There is a potential to develop new forms of praxis which could possibly transform larger insti-tutional practices.

However, as Boggs (1986) illustrates, since the 1970s, where the bureau-cratic state and capital, working in tandem, have managed to arrange deals among organised privileged minorities, the state has often left as its legacy 'an atomised mass consciousness that combines elements of passivity, cynicism, and privatism' (Boggs, 1986: 28). More recently, Pearson (1998) has suggested that the rise of Pauline Hanson's One Nation Party in Australia, supported by predominantly working-class people of Anglo-European origin,[10] is a direct reflection of their perception that 'minority' interest groups (representing, for example, single mothers, Aboriginal peo-ple, etc.), have 'warped' public policy against the interests of themselves, the 'majority'. As Cruikshank (1994: 48) states, with regard to the USA, 'many people were far less concerned with the apathy and inaction of the poor than with their mobilisation'.

We could anticipate that different strategies would probably be opera-tionalised by some NSMs to confront the transformative effects of others in an attempt to close off rather than enlarge their influence. Yet, Canel (1992) and McNeish (1999) make a distinct point when they suggest that we should not be overly judgemental, as the very existence of NSMs should perhaps be considered a gain in itself in terms of their latent emancipatory political potential and their opening up of the public arena to wider debates.

OPENING UP DIRECT ACTION

Residents rage at rash development (Sutton, 1997: 2–3).

Mayer (1995: 230) argues that 'rather than demanding specific third sector or community representation, social movements will need to use their own chip within the system of the new bargaining system'. This 'new bargaining system' is becoming increasingly accepted by actors as involving lobbying and direct action (Chapters 6 and 7).

The concept of direct action embraces various forms of action including marches, demonstrations, sit-ins, refusal to pay taxes and other acts of civil disobedience which Routledge (1997) terms the postmodern politics of resistance. Yet, as Cohen and Arato (1992: 566) ask, is there any justification for activities which bypass existing procedures and institutions for expressing (planning) concerns? Do acts of civil disobedience violate the rights of elected members to make binding law, thus challenging both liberal and democratic principles?

According to Melucci (1996: 183) the message is the action itself rather than what the actors may claim verbally 'because they often do not even *ask* (for goods, advances, reforms), they *bring* (make visible new meaning through their practice)' (emphasis in original). It is these new meanings which planning policy-makers may have overlooked (such as Aboriginal symbolic value, aesthetic value, etc. – see Chapters 6 and 7), which may well have important ramifications for planning decisions.

Direct action is located at the seam between system and lifeworld, in the interstices between the boundaries of insurrection and institutionalised political activity. As such, it may offer the traditionally marginalised and planning-voiceless the opportunity to participate and to speak. It therefore 'expands the range and forms of participation open to private citizens within a mature political culture' and presents a valuable means to citizens to attempt to 'exert influence on members of political society and to ensure that professional politicians remain responsive to public opinion' (Cohen and Arato, 1992: 567).

Empirical evidence of direct action in planning debates (see Part 3) suggests that most activity is aimed at either providing information about ramifications of a certain policy and/or attempting to persuade decision-makers to a particular course of action. The logic of direct action is to discursively gain decision-makers' attention and to make them consider alternative arguments and options rather than to seize political power. Direct action may often be 'the last chance to correct errors in the process of realising democratic principles or to set in motion innovations for the average citizen who is not endowed with privileged opportunities for influence in the political system' (Cohen and Arato, 1992: 601).

Although in certain circumstances direct action may be a strategy of last resort as Cohen and Arato suggest, research in the planning (Hillier, 1997) and community development (Tilly, 1975; Ostrom, 1992) fields, indicates that it can also be regarded as an 'up front' activity, a valid and normal political resource to be used by actors in pursuit of their objectives.

Melucci (1988) and Young (2001) are strong advocates of the encouragement and legitimation of direct action as a means of giving voice to the traditionally voiceless. By speaking out or acting directly in public spheres which decision-makers cannot ignore, one avoids the problems of corporatism which may arise with panel or committee membership or associative democracy (see below) which essentially operate under the constrained alternatives that are produced by and support the structural inequalities which activists are attempting to fight. Formal deliberation forums thus 'make it nearly impossible for the structurally disadvantaged to propose solutions to social problems that might alter the structural positions in which they stand' (Young, 2001: 654). Open processes, in which all actors can protest publicly, could be an alternative.

The practical difficulties of operationalising such activist public spheres and ensuring they are just, are problematic, however. How do we overcome situations in which the more affluent, articulate and connected are able to generate greater 'noise' and to exercise greater power over decision-making?

Not everyone is prepared to take direct action in a political culture which generally operates to produce quiescence and passivity (through family, school, workplace and law and order disciplinary traditions). Those who participate tend not to be the disenfranchised, the marginalised and excluded, but those able to devote resources (time, money, contacts, etc.) to the 'cause'. 'The first to rebel are not the most repressed and emarginated of groups, but, instead, those who perceive an intolerable contradiction between an existing collective identity and the new social relationships imposed by change' (Melucci, 1996: 295–6). I disagree, however, with Melucci regarding the necessity of a pre-existing collective identity as many groups (Friends of …, Residents and Ratepayers', etc.) develop around a perceived new threat or issue.

There are important questions of inclusion and exclusion. If direct action favours some individuals and groups over others, who misses out? Does direct action simply 'buttress many relations of inequality' (Mouffe, 1993: 151)? How can the interests of the majority be protected in the face of vociferous minorities? Not everyone is happy:

> there seems to be some self-proclaimed spokesmen [sic] for the 'community' who manage to spread great anxiety and distress among our vulnerable population. Certain fears are being introduced and considerably reinforced by these

scaremongers, who elevate themselves to a superior level and present themselves as the medium between a worried community and the powers that be ...
They are destructive, counterproductive and can be outright dangerous (Stengel,
1997: 28).

Should populism be allowed to reign? If we open up planning policy decision-making processes to outsider strategies and 'encourage' the use of direct action –
public protests, media coverage, informal lobbying – it could be socially unjust.

Furthermore, my argument so far has concentrated on citizen action. What
about planning officers? My research (Hillier, 2000a and Chapter 6 of this volume)
indicated planners to be irritated and frustrated by citizens taking direct action. Some
regarded it as 'unfair' and 'going round the back' of formal participatory processes,
even 'cheating'. Yet, these planners clearly overlooked the traditional practice of officers writing or summarising reports to suit preferred ends, or having a discrete 'word
in the ear' of key elected members such as committee chairs and Ministers.

Albrechts' (1997) valuable work has brought such activities into the public
arena for probably the first time. Referring to the Flanders Structure Plan, Albrechts
demonstrates the *necessity* of planning officers engaging in 'delicate lobby work
(talking to members of parliament, to several ministers, leading civil servants, leaders
of the trade-union, ... consultants, the press)' (1997: 17–18), or what he terms
'making friends' in order to progress work. The planners lobbied members of political parties and 'used them to keep the Structure Plan on the political agenda, ... to
give voice to the ideas reflected in the plan in closed party meetings, to put pressure
on their ministers in the government' (Albrechts, 1997: 20). The planning team also
engaged in 'bargaining' with government departments and pressure groups and
'informing' the broader public in what Albrechts (1997: 23) admits as an explicit
strategy of 'using knowledge as power'.

Occasionally, as Albrechts indicates, stronger measures of leverage were
required. 'We refused to sign the contract ... Without us and our planning team the
process would have come to an end, this would provoke major discontent with
(some) important actors in society' (1997: 18).

Albrechts' focus on the 'highly political role' (1997: 24) of planners and
Flyvbjerg's (1998a) depiction of the 'stroking strategy' which officers of the Technical
Department in Aalborg employed with the local Chamber of Industry and Commerce,
raise the question of how planners can justify their own lobbying activities as legitimate whilst condemning those of citizens' groups as illegitimate, and undermining
their capacity to plan. It may be a matter of perception: that the planners interviewed
(in Hillier, 1997) perceived the public displays of influential actants to have been successful and that such public displays were not a course of action open to themselves.
Planners are unlikely to carry placards and march on Parliament.

If direct action is taken by the otherwise voiceless, is it not a legitimate means of obtaining voice, however? Although unlikely to take to the streets, planners do have several less public opportunities to 'gain the ear' of elected representatives. Whilst regarding direct action as a legitimate attempt at decision-making influence, I nevertheless stop short of concurring with Cohen and Arato (1992: 566) that 'civil disobedience ... is a key form that the *utopian* dimension of politics can assume' (emphasis added) for reasons of its social injustice.

I agree with Mansbridge (1995b), Berry *et al.* (1993) and Healey (1996b, 1997a) among others, that the power of the strongest interests needs some regulation to prevent too great a distortion of the wishes of the majority of citizens. Direct action has 'brought to light the ineffectiveness of the traditional institutions of political representation' (Melucci, 1996: 113). We need to consider issues of rights and responsibilities, and to whom, and of rules which 'force the "powerful" to pay attention to the rest of us' (Healey, 1996b: 215). The evidence of legal and institutionalised rights giving the traditionally marginalised a foothold in the system and a catalyst for collective action is well demonstrated by the environmental racism actions enabled by civil rights legislation in the US (see e.g. Bullard, 1993).

We also need to recognise that

> the more conflicts of interests there are the more it is important to have procedural solutions of conflict adjudication through which parties whose interests are negatively affected can find recourse to other methods of the articulation and representation of their grievances (Benhabib, 1996a: 73).

We should, therefore, consider developing new debating and decision-making forums and arenas, outside, perhaps, of formal politics, in which marginalised groups have voice and power, a more socially structured setting than is available by means of communicative action alone:

> a medium of loosely associated, multiple foci of opinion formation and dissemination which affect one another in free and spontaneous processes of communication ... *a plurality of modes of association* in which all affected can have the right to articulate their point of view (Benhabib, 1996a: 74, 73, emphasis in original).

It is to the notion of associative democracy that I now turn.

ASSOCIATIVE DEMOCRACY

Network and NSM theories help us to understand power-plays and challenges in collective policy-making activities. Intersections and conflicts between the needs and interests expressed by various networks and movements and public sector policy formation and implementation are matters of some concern to planning praxis. As such, theoretical (and empirical) research into forms of associative democracy may offer us a potential avenue of investigation in seeking new structures to realise collaborative strategy-making in more procedurally and socially just manners.[11]

I am not concerned here with those conceptions of associative democracy which call for direct democratisation and the decentralisation of governance responsibilities to voluntary and self-governing associations as argued typically by Martell (1992), Hirst (1994) and Schmitter (1995), but rather with the development of Cohen and Rogers' (1995) interventionist approach aimed at fostering the organised representation of presently excluded interests by means of government subsidies, taxes and legal instruments, and at encouraging deliberative reciprocity between associational members (see also work by Amin, 1996).

Wright (1995: 2) explains the concept of associative democracy as

> invigorating secondary associations[12] in ways which enable them to be, on the one hand, effective vehicles for the representation and formulation of the interests of citizens, and on the other, to be directly involved in the implementation and execution of state policies.

Ideas for associative democracy have arisen in response to concerns about the bias of the 'interest group system', and lobbying activities in particular, in favour of wealthier citizens and what Cohen and Rogers (1992) term the 'feudalisation' of the administrative state through the capture of its agencies by organised interests. Associative democracy seeks to curb the mischiefs of faction and to encourage forms of less factionalising group representation using public powers – or what Hirst (1997: 19) terms 'governance through choice and voice'.

Amin and Thrift (1995b) stress a set of four orientations for success. These orientations include a negotiated 'interactive' approach rather than an 'imperative' approach in which

> the central authority initiating and directing the changes, takes on the role of participant and treats the other participants as independent agents, whose behaviour can only change as a consequence of mutual interaction. The task of the central authority ... does not involve establishing certain new systemic rules, forcing the participants to respect them; rather it is to stimulate the process of defining and formulating these rules, thus allowing the participants to satisfy their needs and realise their interests (Hausner, 1994: 1).

Other orientations are that the practical agenda produced as a result of associative deliberation should be context-dependent, it should be a process of institutional 'filling-in' through negotiation, affording agency to communities, and it should aim at intermediate forms of collective governance of the socio-economy (Amin and Thrift, 1995b: 54–5).

Planning practice in WA in the 1990s, despite its lip-service to public participation strategies, generally accords certain groups a distinctly secondary (if not lower) role in policy decision-making. Planners are often suspicious of the information which such groups provide, regarding them as being self-seeking vested interests. Planners may also lack the courage to move from a traditional decide–announce–defend approach to one of greater deliberation and negotiation. Associative democracy could develop intermediate structures to link the opinions of all stakeholders more strongly to the policy-making process.

What might associative democratic strategies infer? I have identified in earlier chapters how power and persuasion/influence play important roles in planning decision-making. Associative democracy, through the politics of associations of interest groups, may open up ways through which the exercise of power and persuasion can meet democratic norms, regulating the more wealthy and larger interests and enhancing the voices (and theoretically the influence and power) of the less articulate and smaller interests.

Associative democracy would thus build on already existing interest groups and the potential for interest groups to form in response to planning issues. It also theoretically enables those people who do not tend to join groups (especially the poor – see Hillier and van Looij, 1997) to form their own associations. Associative democracy therefore recommends promoting the organised representation of presently excluded interests.[13]

It would also theoretically encourage the organised to be more other-regarding in their actions and recommends a more direct and formal governance role for groups (Cohen and Rogers, 1992; Bader, 2001). This last point is important. There would be a need for new institutions if associative democracy were to succeed. Political and socio-economic strategies alone are unlikely to serve the interests of the disadvantaged. There would be a need for judicial strategies. 'The state must basically perform the role of a partner enabling other actors–partners to perform their own roles; and in some cases it might even have to create these roles' (Amin and Hausner, 1997: 18). None of this can be accomplished without using political power to redistribute resources and to underwrite and subsidise (financially, with time, personnel, etc.) associational activities (Walzer, 1995).

Mathews (1989: 12–13) thus argues that a drastically different perspective is needed, organised round the following:

- The highest priority must be given to democracy at all levels.

- The emphasis needs to be on collective activity, via existing associations, to release the energy and imagination of the membership, while bringing their collective strength to bear on political issues.
- The state needs to be seen as a supporter and coordinator of the process of change.
- The movement needs to shift ideologically from a culture of protest to a culture of the responsible exercise of power.
- Policy needs to be formulated round the notion of transformation from within, rather than regulation from without.
- There needs to be a respect for pluralism of associations at the political level, conceiving of the state as the orchestrator of the process of 'political exchange' between associations.

'It is one thing to have the opportunity to … lobby and petition; it is quite another to be involved in establishing priorities for local policy-making' (Lowndes, 1995: 167). Rather than being allowed voice in an arena where planners simply 'count their interests in deciding what to do, while keeping [our] fingers crossed that those interests are out-weighed' (Cohen, 1996: 101), associative democratic procedures may offer citizens, and especially traditionally marginalised groups, an arena in which they have real voice in local policy-making, voice which is respected and which has influence over the final decision, voice in open and 'dialogic' governance (Amin and Graham, 1997: 424).

I believe that the concept of associative democracy could potentially embrace the four core concepts of the reflexive state which Amin (1996) identifies:

- decision-making pluralism
- a combination of authority with consensus (or con-sensus)
- processual, dialogic rationality and interactive governance
- concertation or decision-making through negotiation.

Local governments embodying these concepts should operate transparently, openly empowering local citizens and other stakeholders in a negotiation situation or 'sub-altern counterpublic' (Fraser, 1992: 123) which regards their views and interests as of equal, if not affirmative, validity with each other (Lake, 1994).

The advantages of an associative democratic framework in which context-specific interactive networking and negotiation can take place can be listed as follows:

- They constitute environments of action which allow questions of fairness and mutual obligation to be raised (Offe, 1992: 83).
- Assuming fair conditions of discussion and an expectation that the results of deliberation will regulate subsequent action, the participants would tend to be more other-regarding' (Cohen and Rogers, 1995: 260), i.e. an advantage of reciprocity.

- Discussion in the context of enduring differences between participants should lead to more reflectivity and imagination in their definition of problems and policies (Cohen and Rogers, 1995: 260).
- A requirement of trying to find outcomes to which others can agree (con-sensus) should drive argument and policies in directions which respect and further a wider range of interests (Cohen and Rogers, 1995: 260).
- Frameworks allow participants to be 'shielded from unreasonable expectations and the risk of standing alone with the "right" kind of action' (Offe, 1992: 83).
- Frameworks reduce the fear of exploitation by others (Offe, 1992: 84).
- Traditionally marginalised groups are more likely to be effectively activated in circumstances where other actants are visibly and transparently participating (Offe, 1992: 85).
- Mutual monitoring of policy implementation should be a consequence of such decision-making (Cohen and Rogers, 1995: 260).
- Frameworks stabilise expectations and give confidence that the policy outcomes will form a lasting agreement valid into the future (Offe, 1992; Healey, 1997a; Lake, 1994; Amin and Graham, 1997), i.e. they decrease uncertainty.
- Given reasonable progress there should be increased confidence among participants in the possibility of future cooperation (Cohen and Rogers, 1995: 260).
- Frameworks generate as a by-product, from a 'social, substantive and temporal point of view, the assurance of stability and conditions of trust' (Offe, 1992: 83).

As Baum (1997) indicates, transparent operation and empowerment and consensus decision-making may be a reasonable expectation in arenas when differences are relatively small, actors share overlapping interests and conflicts are either mild or infrequent. However, when differences are greater and actors less transigent, the idea of negotiating openly may discourage some people from pressing their views forward and they may either acquiesce to something with which they do not really agree or leave the process.

Several other important problematic issues should also be noted.

PROBLEMS OF REPRESENTATION

Is it inevitable, as Mulgan (1997: 204) suggests, that 'representation separates citizens from decisions' or is it physically possible for *all* stakeholders to have a voice? What about the non-human (Eckersley, 1999; O'Neill, 2001), the not-yet-present (Dryzek, 2001; O'Neill, 2001), the deceased and those (such as gypsies) who gain specific advantages from 'living on the edge' (Sibley, 1998: 99) and who may suffer from incorporation into a regulatory system? These problems, and those of size, will necessitate some absences from the negotiating arena and some form of representation. Yet, as is now generally recognised (Dyrberg, 1997; Hillier and van Looij, 1997; Laclau, 1996; Young 1995, 1997b), it is impossible to represent accurately anyone or anything else. Representation is indeed re-presentation. It is structured around the constitutive gap between performance and semblance and involves imaginary and symbolic dimensions (Dyrberg, 1997). The act of re-presenting confers power on the representer to act in the name of an absent totality, to stand firm or to concede points of debate. In other words, the conditions of possibility of the system (i.e. representation) are also the conditions of its impossibility (see Laclau, 1997.)

Furthermore, as Phillips (1995: 155) points out, in the light of persuasive argument at the negotiating table, representatives should not be able to 'just take it into their heads to abandon the commitments they brought with them'. There should be some mechanism by which representatives can either take ideas and proposals back to their groups[14] or be fully accountable for their actions.[15]

A fundamental problem of representation raised by Pløger (2001) and alluded to in Part 4 above, may serve to undermine the entire model of discursive democratic decision-making for Western representative-based systems. In circumstances in which participatory–deliberative agreements are merely recommendations to elected representatives without a binding mandate for their acceptance, Pløger argues that the participants have no power, only a voice: 'claims and suggestions only work if those in power agree or (less likely) feel obliged to respect the claims of their citizens to safeguard their party loyalty, political legitimacy, or political credibility' (2001: 234). Whilst I agree that this gap between planning recommendation and decision does exist, I have demonstrated in Chapter 10 how certain 'missionary' planners can act to persuade the elected representatives to confirm the community-agreed recommendation.

There are also important problems of achieving representation of traditionally less articulate, less organised groups as compared to those who tend to lobby and take direct action in any case. 'For many people in excluded communities, joining a formal organisation is not a natural thing to do' (Burns and Taylor, 1997: 10). Outreach mechanisms (Healy and Walsh, 1997) may be crucial to achievement of fair representation.

In addition, in what Cohen and Rogers (1995: 65) term the 'Frankenstein issue', some groups, once endowed with quasi-public status, may continue to exercise power after the policy decision has been taken, use that power to freeze their position and work to distort future debate and opportunity.

ARTIFACTUALITY

Associational activity is artifactual. It is subject to change and manipulation by different powerful actors. Young (1995: 211) regards artifactuality as a problematic tendency, yet without some institutional support (information, transport, finance?)

and encouragement for disadvantaged groups to establish and participate, I believe that policy-making situations would change very little, with power still often blurring a dividing line between rationality and rationalisation (see Flyvbjerg, 1998a). The need is for social solidarities to be formed and develop naturally rather than be conveniently fabricated or rationalised.

ACCEPTANCE

Although Burns and Taylor (1997) discuss informal mutuality in socially excluded populations rather than associative democracy as a means of giving people voice, their work does offer us a valuable perspective on tensions which associative democratic debate should avoid if it is to be successful. Burns and Taylor identify three public sector attitudes towards mutuality: compatible with formal systems; forming part of a continuum between formal and informal systems; and conflictual with formal systems, threatening the ability of officials, such as planners, to function. Associated with these three attitudes are found mainstream strategies of toleration, encouragement or repression.

In order for associative democracy/mutuality to fulfil its potential as a springboard (Burns and Taylor) or participatory resource for marginalised groups, it would have to be accepted in good faith by the 'mainstream' (officers of governance, elected members, organised interest groups, etc.) without attempts at neutralisation by co-optation and incorporation into a highly bureaucratic, jargonistic, technocratic system.

How might associative democratic forums be established? Cohen and Rogers (1992, 1995) propose a deliberate use of public powers to promote the necessary organisational bases, involving the construction of temporary, context-related 'new arenas for public deliberation that lie outside conventional political arenas' (Cohen and Rogers, 1995: 250). There should be active promotion of organised representation of presently excluded interests, including, where appropriate, facilitation of group formation through a process of active listening for latent agency and nurturing its evolution (Gamson, 1995b).[16]

Burns and Taylor (1997), in this vein, identify the need for creation of 'social relays' to link actor-networks to one another and activate dormant links. The importance of state support for groups through mediating mechanisms rather than by direct state intervention (interference) cannot be overemphasised. Critical analysis of empirical examples of operation (albeit short-lived) of intervener funding in Ontario, Canada, and the Resource Assessment Commission in Australia, may offer valuable insight into how associative planning policy decision-making may be practised.[17] In particular, stories from Canada demonstrate the necessity of establishing a robust legal basis as a foundation for association. In such a way might the well-documented problems of the British City Challenge partnerships be avoided, namely:

- power holders failing to relinquish power
- power holders pre-deciding strategic outcomes and allowing participatory debate of minor issues only
- key actors quitting the debate forum.

As Amin and Graham (1997: 425) note, such participatory experiments have often 'degenerated into undemocratic and unaccountable networks serving highly particularistic or dominant local interests'. Traditionally disadvantaged groups have yet again been marginalised.

Real 'democratic associationalism' would entail far more than the 'currently fashionable but nebulous idea of stakeholder democracy' (Amin and Graham, 1997: 425), exemplified by most 'partnership' arrangements. If planners were to proceed in this manner, I would support Amin's (1996) interpretation of associative democracy and emphasis on the importance of commencing with the socially excluded, as the greatest potential for innovating change lies in the interstitial spaces of society – those spaces which often resist mainstream interference and establish their own networks of mutuality, interaction, dialogue and negotiation.

However, organising political life using associationality as a regulatory principle of freedom and empowerment can itself involve a sort of imposition, becoming 'traditional politics' "bigger brother"' (Roßteutscher, 2000: 176). We here encounter Connolly's (1991) paradox of difference, that some form of social order is necessary, but any social order is repressive to some. Would associative democracy be simply another form of Foucauldian normalisation, its so-called 'empowerment' merely another instance of governmentality, with marginalised people participating in their own further subjectification by exercising power over themselves, tying themselves to some form of definitional logic of who they are? Would associative democracy be little more than neocorporatism, a way of managing 'the pressures of interests on the state' (Wilson, 1990: 150) in an institutionalised framework of bargaining which renders conflict 'tolerable' by domesticating and neutralising any potentially serious challenge to the requirements of capitalist rationalisation?

Should attempts at associative democracy prove to be a means of institutional manipulation, as above, I would envisage them to also produce its own countertendency – pushing social conflict outside of the associative democracy arena, back into direct action, resignation or apathy.

Models of associative democracy raise many questions, including what sort of planning-related functions and decisions are appropriate for voluntary associations and what are not. Should associative democracy be considered as a form of organisation to cover all aspects of planning practice or as one among many policy tools? If local authorities decide to organise and/or subsidise associations, how could this be undertaken (adapted from Young, 2000: 193)?

Yet, as Young (2000) suggests, despite the many problems with associative democracy, it would be a mistake to dismiss the idea completely. Should public sector planners consider implementation of some aspects of associative democratic participatory planning (such as citizens' juries in Britain, Germany and USA and Canadian Round Tables) they would do well to bear in mind the relative advantages and disadvantages of such a framework. In particular, Young (2000) and Roßteutscher (2000) counsel recognition of the inherent tensions. Tying civic associations strongly to authoritative state procedures and imperatives reduces the ability for citizens to independently hold state institutions accountable. Alternatively, if deliberation and decision-making authority are dispersed widely across voluntary associational interests and perspectives, they may well lose the bigger picture of society, be highly unequal and/or be torn apart by institutional anarchism.

THE DEMOCRATIC PARADOX

> Democracy is the pride and hope of modernity. It also contains danger. The danger does not flow merely from forces hostile to democratic institutions. It resides within the ideal itself (Connolly, 1987: 3).

> Modern governmental rationality is simultaneously about individualising and totalising: i.e., about finding answers to the question of what it is for an individual, and for a society or population of individuals, to be governed or governable (Foucault, in Gordon, 1991: 36).

Liberal democracy is ambiguous. It is based on a constitutive tension simultaneously differentiating and harmonising individuality and commonality. The value of individual liberty epitomised by liberalism intersects in liberal democracy with the apparent 'incompatible rationality' (Dunn, 1979) of a majoritarian view of the public good in an attempt to combine a respect for human freedom at the same time as organising society in a manner of which the majority approves (Touraine, 1994).

A fundamental problem, therefore, with Habermasian and other ideals of consensus is the structure of the liberal democratic system within which it rests. As Hobsbawm has recently written: 'there is no necessary or logical connection between the various components of the conglomerate which make up what we call "liberal democracy"' (2001: 25) and even Habermas himself notes that 'political philosophy has never really been able to strike a balance' (2001b: 116) between the principle of democracy, or 'popular sovereignty', and human rights or private liberty.

Each strand has classical antecedents. Aristotle and the Renaissance humanists prioritised public autonomy over the private liberties of citizens, while John Locke championed the priority of private rights over the dangers of tyrannical majorities. This tension between the democratic logic of equality and the liberal logic of liberty, is, as Mouffe (1993) points out, an inherent struggle within liberal democracy.

We can diagrammatically represent this struggle as a combination of two continua: of political ideology from structuralism through republicanism/pluralism to liberalism, and of the location of power from concentrated centralised power through collective power to individualism (Figure 11.3).

Liberal democracy is apparently committed to delivering its subjects the incompatibility of enforcing both their own individual views together with the majority democratic decision. As Wuthnow (1999: 33) writes: 'the most serious challenge facing democratic liberalism is to reconcile its libertarian strands with the intervention required to ensure that its egalitarian ideals are also upheld'. Interventions aimed at generating greater equality of voice should not submerge the voices of oppressed minorities beneath the numerical superiority of their oppressors. Similarly, how does a state deal with those of a minority view whose commitment to their beliefs is so strong as to override acceptance of the legitimacy of the state implementing and enforcing a democratically upheld majority decision?

Most of the theorists mentioned so far in this book privilege the democratic aspect. Habermas defines democracy as a discursive and argumentative process which shapes a common will. He argues that democratic institutions and the sovereign power of the people should take precedence over individual rights. Yet, as Touraine (2000) and others (e.g. Nelson, 2000; Young, 2000) point out, voters often act not out of reciprocity, or out of recognition of the other, but from self-interest and/or defensive tactics based on uncertainty, fear and animosity. An aggregative

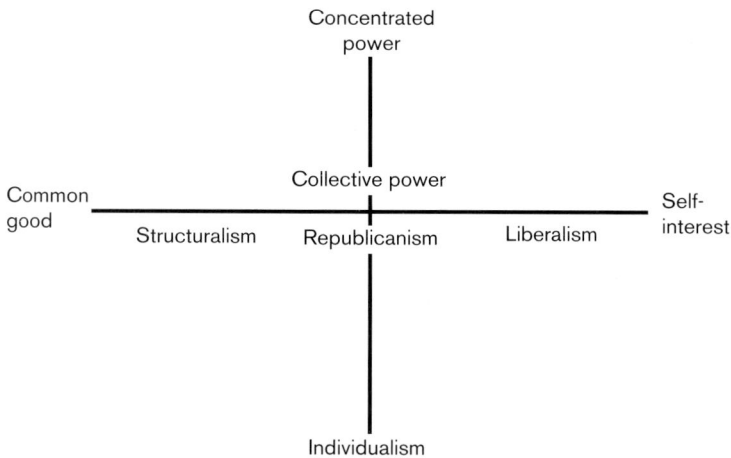

Figure 11.3 The democratic paradox (after McArdle, 1999)

democracy offers no way of distinguishing between these motives. It is highly unlikely that an aggregative democratic outcome will be fundamentally a rational outcome. The Liberal democratic framework therefore reduces politics to the calculus of interests (see Mouffe, 1995; Forester, 1999b: 180). In Brittain's words: 'direct democracy by the majority can jeopardise the civil rights of minority or other powerless groups' (1996: 441).

Democracy empowers governments to authorise compulsion: for instance, to regulate the private behaviour of consenting adults (in 2001, homosexuality remains illegal in WA for males aged under twenty-one); to keep people in jail (in WA Aboriginal people are twenty-one times more likely to be imprisoned for a minor offence than are non-indigenous people (ABS, 2000)); to fine the poorest in society for breaking their welfare obligations of 'mutual respect' and to redistribute that money indirectly to the wealthy (through tax relief, road building, etc.) (Salvation Army, 2001). Such actions are the results of voting rather than of the reasons why people voted.

I do not mean to infer that democracy is a defective ideal, but to recognise that there will always be a tension between democratic inequality and reality in a world of inequality, injustice and oppression. In such a world, liberalism, defined by Dean (1999: 210) as 'a philosophy of limited government that respects the rights and liberties of citizens and employs the rule of law' to discipline those deemed not to exercise 'responsible autonomy' (i.e. those who interfere with the liberties of others), reached its apogee in Britain under Prime Minister Margaret Thatcher who famously commented that 'there is no such thing as society' (1987: 10).

Maximising the liberty of individuals and organisations to pursue their own ends as the primary principle of liberalism is thus at odds with democracy, and, from a planning perspective, with achieving social justice (Hoch, 1992). Whereas planners (those acting as missionaries for social justice) might seek to redistribute a market allocation of services and facilities towards those in society who are least well off, liberalists such as Robert Nozick (1974) claim that all humans are unique and cannot be compared to each other for purposes of redistribution. State intervention in a market system constitutes interference with individual liberty. There should be no assumption that some people have a right to assistance (Nozick in van Erp, 2000: 152).

SOME PROBLEMS

Both liberal and democratic aspects of liberal democracy are abstracted from actually existing social and power relations, from language, culture and 'the whole set of practices that make agency possible' (Mouffe, 2000: 95). They effectively evacuate the political. As Mouffe has more recently stated, when a society lacks diversity of democratic political identifications, the terrain is open for other non-political identifications to take their place, using a range of non-democratic outlets to express their opinions and values. The real threat to liberal democratic institutions thus lies in the growing marginalisation of entire groups of people unable to identify with democratic decision-making (Mouffe, 2002).

There is a need to overcome the antipolitical character of much theorising influenced in particular by Habermasian communicative action. The hollowing out of the political realm in such theorising both tends to presuppose that agents are already committed to reaching mutual agreement and to constrain discussion and decision-making by juridical and institutional formulae, reducing procedures to a form of 'liberal legalism' (Habermas, 1996: 445–6). One of the reasons why Habermas appears to favour juridical procedures may be their perceived effectiveness in engendering legitimacy. As Baird (2001) demonstrates, in Germany people place more trust in legalistic procedures than in political procedures. People expect and trust 'courts' to make more procedurally just decisions even if in reality they do not. The legalistic model, therefore, 'may be comforting to those who believe that a right answer for our conundrums in politics exists' (Baird, 2001: 344) and who choose to overlook the messy logrolling, bargaining and political compromises which take place. Thus, if we recognise that relations of power are constitutive of the social and cannot be legislated or ruled out, we need to accept that perfect transparency and/or perfect harmony are unrealisable.

Power is an omnipresent relation in planning policy decision-making. If we recall both Bourdieu and Foucault, power is an endless and open strategic game:

> At the very heart of the power relationship, and constantly provoking it, are the recalcitrance of the will and the intransigence of freedom. Rather than speaking of an essential freedom, it would be better to speak of an agonism' – of a relationship which is at the same time reciprocal incitation and struggle; less of a face-to-face confrontation which paralyses both sides than a permanent provocation (Foucault, 1982b: 221–1).

The trend of communicative action/deliberative democratic theories to conflate politics with morality in rationalist and universalist terms, erases this agonistic dimension, which, as argued strongly by Mouffe (1993, 1995, 1996, 2000, 2002) and others, is ineradicable in political decision-making. As Mouffe writes:

> this leads them to miss a crucial point, not only about the primary reality of strife in social life, and the impossibility of finding rational, impartial solutions to political issues, but also about the integrative role that conflict plays in modern democracy (2002: 95).

Mouffe suggests in fact that well-functioning democratic decision-making calls for a 'vibrant clash of political positions' rather than an avoidance of confrontation and an emphasis on consensus-building.

CAN WE MAKE ETHICAL DECISIONS?

If we follow the train of thought above and abandon belief in universal moral decision rules, then the question remains of how we can act ethically. Bauman (1992) refers to this question as the ethical paradox of modernity. It would appear that in our post-modern world of value pluralism, where ideas of value and rationality are historically conditioned (such as in Bourdieu's concept of habitus), answers are influenced by the multiplicity of cultural discourses (see, for example, Tully, 1995).

Whilst I agree with a need for taking value pluralism seriously, we should avoid the twin dangers of naturalising and legitimating given inequalities in a set of rights and of being guilty of relativism. Habermas (2001b) links the expression of popular sovereignty with the creation of a system of rights. Yet, by protecting human rights and the right of peoples to espouse different values, we leave a loophole for some groups to 'legitimately' exploit others. Lyotard's (1985: 74) example of Naziism is to the point: 'after all, since there was near unanimity upon it, from where could one judge that it was not just? This is obviously very troublesome'.

Pluralism must be distinguished from relativism. Value pluralists recognise the existence of a wide range of qualitatively heterogeneous 'goods' which are distinguishable from 'bads'. Relativists, alternately, deny that there are any definitive 'goods', but that the definition of 'goods' is internal to particular cultures or to individual subjectivity (see Galston, 2000).

Habermas and his followers would argue that both the above dangers might be overcome through deliberation: 'discussion about a shared conception of the good and a desired form of life that is acknowledged to be authentic' (Habermas, 1994: 113). Such discussion entails participants engaging in reciprocity or at least a responsibility to others, affording them voice, recognising their integrity and attending to their needs (see Ralston Saul, 1997). We should, however, be mindful of Touraine's (2000) assertion that democratic discussion often results not in the formation of a general will but in the recognition that everyone has a space in which to speak. Touraine's comment appears to be borne out by Campbell and Marshall's analysis of public participation programmes in the Bay area of California that a 'focus on the right of individuals or communities to articulate their self-interests appears to reduce local democracy to confusion and noise' and to 'virtually paralyse the decision-making process' (2000: 340).

Vested interests vie with each other in a politics of turf. Such antagonism should not be unexpected in participatory attempts to make planning decisions in the public interest. As Gamble (2000: 92–3) astutely points out, there is a key distinction between a liberalist conception of the public interest as the aggregate of individual interests and the public good. The public good is theoretically something objective and knowable through the exercise of reason (accessible by an elite, such as planners). In such a notion of the public good there is no place for public interest.

As the public interest, therefore, cannot be derived from an objective conception of the public good and is unlikely to be easily derived from an aggregate of often oppositional private and vested interests, it generally tends to be determined by the relative strengths of different factions, and overall, by politics. Where do planners stand, then, when faced with rejection of the public good in deference to a public interest of the majority or a powerful few; when the shadows of power fall over planning decisions, 'to the detriment of good technical planning' (planning officer (021), Western Australia, pers. comm.)?

In democratic participatory processes, the technically determined public good may lose out to a politically determined public interest. A technically 'good' participatory process offering voice to all stakeholders may result in a technically 'bad' outcome, as we saw in Chapter 6.

> The bad outcome was not the fault of the process (planning officer (102), WA,
> pers. comm.).
> In the end it was not the most technically correct planning solution for the area,
> but compromises had to be made for broader community issues (planning offi-
> cer (113), WA, pers. comm.).

In such circumstances, is there, as Galton (2000: 262) suggests, 'a case for insulating the experts against the vagaries of democracy'? Can the violation of democratic norms be justified by experts who purport to understand the interests of the public better than the public, as in the case of the WA Minister for Planning, Grahame Kierath, who declared 'the public got it wrong' when he ordered the demolition of old grain silos against public opinion? Or do such actions open the door to the abuse of technical knowledge and discretion in the direction of tyranny?

The ambivalence which planners may feel about a tension between technically sound and democratically or politically sound outcomes reflects their subconscious respect for the ambiguity of the paradox of liberal democracy in practice. So, what does the prudential planner do?

Charles Hoch's (1992, 1994) stories of planning officers in practice suggest that planners should acknowledge these inherent tensions in the contingency of their work and seek 'neither the power of rules or the mastery of political persuasion' (1992: 214). Such action could entail planners reporting a community preference to elected representatives together with an explanation of why such preference might not be the best planning outcome. Should pressure be subsequently brought to bear directly by the community on elected representatives so that they select a poor planning outcome, the officer/s could nevertheless claim to have performed their duty. On the other hand, missionary planners, as described in Chapter 10, might take more active involvement in attempting to persuade elected representatives to the merits, or otherwise, of a particular outcome.

PARADOXICALLY SPEAKING IN CONCLUSION

Most democratic discussion and negotiation is not and cannot be based on visions of a consensual, harmonious outcome. Conflicting differences between different groups' conceptions of the 'good' are not negatives to be eliminated but rather diverse values to be recognised in decision processes. Referring to the struggle between the need for an outcome which acts in the name of the whole community and the particularism of interests, Laclau (1991, 1994) proposes that the struggle is not produced by democracy, but that it precedes democracy. Rather, it is exactly what makes democracy possible.

Several authors (e.g. Laclau, Mouffe, Connolly, Touraine, Zizek) assert that division and disharmony are constitutive of the human condition and that what democracy needs is disharmony. They call for a new democratic culture. Combining post-structuralism and post-Marxism with a blend of subject theory (Torfing, 1999: 3) they turn to the work of Jacques Lacan and, in particular, his seminar on *The Ethics of Psychoanalysis* (1959–60) to articulate an 'ethics of disharmony'. The argument may be briefly summarised as:

- Exclusion and antagonism are constitutive of all identity.
- All identity is constituted as difference, i.e. that which one is and is not.
- All systems of social relations are constituted through acts of antagonism or power between different identities. Such systems are thereby ultimately political and show traces of the exclusion which govern their constitution: 'the choice of A always involves the forceful repression of B, C and D' (Torfing, 1999: 68) – i.e. B, C and D become the 'constitutive outside', whether they are options or the stakeholders who support those options (Laclau, 1996; Mouffe, 1993). Since what is repressed can no longer be what it 'is', the subversion of the alternative options also implies the subversion of the identity of the stakeholders who identify themselves with these options. Therefore, the only thing which can constitute the system of social relations and possibilise these identities (i.e. exclusion), is also what subverts them. The conditions of possibility of the system are also its conditions of impossibility. It is present through its absence.
- This means that all differential identity will be constitutively split between the logic of difference (the particular) and the logic of equivalence (the universal). Since the universality of society is unachievable, it tends to be replaced by particulars in a hegemonic role.
- Difference and particularisms are therefore the necessary starting point for the relative universalisation of values which form the basis for a popular hegemony.

Planning practice in a liberal democratic system, while fostering value pluralism, cannot equate all values in consensus-building since decisions require some form of

ordering of values which prefers some values to the relative repression and/or exclusion of others. The 'consensus' arrived at thus cannot exist without an 'outside'
which leaves the decision open to challenge.

Planning decision-making in a plural democratic society has to come to terms
with this dimension of conflict and antagonism which is a consequence of the irreducible plurality of values. This may entail planners recognising stakeholders'
commitments to values to be a matter of historical contingency and loyalty (habitus)
rather than rationality. It may also entail development of contingent, circumstantially
appropriate procedural principles of just treatment of stakeholders which serve to
domesticate antagonism.

Detailed discussion of a Lacanian contribution to my theoretical model and
agonistic decision-making will be developed in the following chapter. Such decision-
making is grounded less in rational choice, but more in the limits of rational choice –
limits imposed by the choices stakeholders may be constrained to make among values
that are both 'inherently rivalrous (and often constitutively uncombinable) and sometimes incommensurable, or rationally incomparable' (Gray, 1995: 116). Agonistic
decision-making requires the indeterminacy and contingency which characterise
political discourse and practice. Liberal legalistic projects, such as those of
Habermas, are generally unrealisably utopian on anything but a small scale. They
'abolish' or 'sterilise' politics (Gray, 1995: 126) and replace politics by laws.

Philosophy and practices of agonistic decision-making may offer 'a fruitful
alternative to rationalist liberalism' (Mouffe, 2002: 98–9). As Mouffe continues, such
modes of decision-making afford central roles to practices, and can therefore be
developed in a way which

> highlights the historical and contingent character of the discourses that con-
> strue our identities and constitute the language of our politics; language that is
> constantly modified, that is entangled with power and needs to be apprehended
> in terms of hegemonic relations.

I therefore take my diagrammatic and conceptual foundations forward into the following chapter where I seek to theorise 'beyond consensus' and to develop a robust
explanatory theory of local planning practice.

CHAPTER 12

ON SLIPPERY ICE: BEYOND CONSENSUS

INTRODUCTION

> We have got on the slippery ice where there is no friction and so in a certain
> sense the conditions are ideal, but also, just because of that, we are unable to
> walk; so we need friction. Back to the rough ground (Wittgenstein, 1958: 46).

In this chapter I ask whether an objective of reaching deep or thick consensus rather
than simply superficial or thin consensus is unattainably utopian. Does a proposal
become so diluted in becoming consensual that it loses meaning? Are actors' interests not transformed *per se* through collaboration but rather submerged or induced
into conformity with group norms (Allmendinger, 1999)? Are some actors acculturated to acceptance of others' arguments and decisions as a natural aspect of the
social order (Brockner *et al.*, 2001)? Do some actors' cultures lead them to withdraw from communication rather than engage in conflictual debate in public
(Crawford, 1990)? Does consensus thus create merely a false sense of closure and
an illusion of stability (Bloomfield *et al.*, 2001)?

Even pro-consensus authors such as Judith Innes accept that there are occasions when a consensus reached will be so 'thin' as to be almost meaningless. She
recognises the dangers of achieving 'a plan which everyone bought into because
there was something in it for everyone rather than because it was regarded as a
solution or even the best approach' (Innes and Gruber, 1999: 13), but retains
strong faith in a collaborative approach to decision-making.

What is there 'beyond consensus'? I shed Lacanian light onto the shadows of
practice in development of a theory seeking to account for the practice terrain in
which there exists contestation of views and values, of formality and informality. I
refuse to close off options in theorising the undecidable decision-world of agonistic
planning practice. 'The challenge of democratic deliberation is not to avoid, transcend or displace conflict but to deal with practical difference in and through
conflictual settings' (Forester, 1999a: 84).

MORE THAN REASON

In the previous chapter I examined the potential for associative democracy, or 'democratic associationalism' (Amin and Graham, 1997) to build voice for those hitherto

disenfranchised from planning policy decision-making and to enable conflicts of values and interests to be aired, respected and debated rather than suppressed. Not only does the concept of associative democracy raise practical operational problems, but there are also considerable philosophical problems which would need to be resolved were associative democracy to become part of planning praxis.

I believe that planning theorists need to recognise that differently formulated associations, identities, values, claims and arguments may find any common links extremely precarious and that there may well be substantive and even intractable disagreements over basic issues (see Hillier, 1998a). The key issue concerns the implications of a distinction between what Benhabib (1996b) terms associational space (consensual space in which people work together in concert) and agonistic space (competitive space). Associational or consensual space is essentially a moral space of interactive rationality based in Habermasian communicative action. As Benhabib emphasises:

> it is through the interlocking net of these multiple forms of associations, net-
> works, and organisations that an anonymous 'public conversation' results. It is
> central to the model of deliberative democracy that it privileges such a public
> sphere of mutually interlocking and overlapping networks and associations of
> deliberation, contestation and argumentation (1996a: 73–4).

Such deliberation, contestation and argumentation take place in situations similar to those identified by Innes above as necessary for consensus-building, of universal moral respect and egalitarian reciprocity to speak, to initiate new topics, to question other actors and to challenge the rules as well as the agenda of public debate (1996a: 78–9).

Reciprocity, or 'recognition of the other as one in whose place I can put myself' is essential as the 'core of democratic principles and practice' (Gutmann and Thompson, 2000). However, as is practically recognised by Throgmorton (2000), and persuasively argued by Young (1995, 1997b), reciprocity is unlikely in situations where differences are well entrenched and where there is mistrust and suspicion. Benhabib's associational space is counterfactual. It is a utopian ideal which excludes the possibility of power-plays and of politics and which conceals the impossibility of its own realisation.[18] It lacks an awareness that 'for humans, resistance, transgression, and agonism are fundamentally vital' (Coles, 1995: 32) and that dissent is as important in dialogical relationships as the idea of agreement.

Agonistic space is 'a competitive space, in which one competes for recognition, precedence and acclaim' (Benhabib, 1992b: 78). It is the view of space engaged by Nietzsche (1954), Arendt (1958) and Foucault (1982c, 1984b) and by subsequent authors such as Connolly (1991), Mouffe (1992, 1993, 1996, 1999), Young (1995, 1997b), Mansbridge (1995b) and Wolin (1996).

Foucault, in particular, expresses the idea of discursively articulated power as agonism. He describes agonism as 'a gymnastic relation characterised by a play of interpretations and anticipations' (1994b: 238), which exactly fits the planning officers' behaviour as described in Chapter 10. Foucault continues, moreover, that 'the art of the game is not to dominate an opposing actor, but to anticipate and exploit its interventions, and thus to make one's own intervention of (counter-)strategies' (Pottage, 1998). As such, local planning practice, in WA at least, would appear to be definitely agonistic.

Given the above, Foucault is convinced that there cannot be a mediating horizon between actors which would make strategies either communicable or commensurable, rather only a 'continuous incorporation of contraries'. Construction of consensus in such a situation would be, according to Foucault, 'a reign of violence' (1994b: 236) as it would suspend the active autonomy of the actors involved. The only reciprocity which Foucault allows is that of 'reciprocal incitation' (1982b: 222).

Foucault, however, denies that his agonistic conception of power is fatalistic. He suggests that the agonistic contest between autonomous actors is 'incessantly political', a problematic of interrogation, engagement and negotiation (Connolly, 1998).

Agonistic space, therefore, is a political space embracing legitimate and public contestation over access to resources (Wolin, 1996). Its pluralism is axiological, recognising the impossibility of ever adjudicating without contest and without residue between competing visions (Mouffe, 1996). Conflict between different viewpoints, interests and values is inescapable.

Mouffe (1996) regards a belief in the final resolution of conflicts to be a dangerous and simplistic illusion. She argues that 'acting in concert' requires the construction of a 'we', a political unity, but that a fully inclusive political unity can never be realised since wherever there is a 'we', there must also be an excluded 'them', a constitutive outside. Any agreement reached will thus be partial, based on acts of social regulation and exclusion. The 'surplus of meaning' (Dyrberg, 1997: 196) which remains uncontrolled is liable to challenge from the excluded other.

For Connolly (1991) and Mouffe (1997, 1998, 1999), a pluralist democracy must allow the expression of dissent and conflicting interests and values. Since we cannot eliminate antagonism, we need to domesticate it to a condition of agonism in which passion is mobilised constructively (rather than destructively) towards the promotion of democratic decisions which are partly consensual, but which also respectfully accept unresolvable disagreements. Whilst agonism is generally construed as a struggle against, it may also be construed as a struggle for. Hence, Foucault's (1984b: 379) remark that 'one must not be for consensuality, but one must be against nonconsensuality'.

Agonistic space, then, does not eliminate power by subordinating it to rationality in a search for consensual agreement. There is always 'more than reason' with
regard to strategic policy-making, whether this be contestations of power, non-
negotiable and axiomatic value differences, or the never-ending assertions of
competition, conflict and alterity (Mouffe, 1996; Walzer, 1999). Once we consider
the political dimension of deliberative policy-making we may find that rational (rather
than rationalised) outcomes are impossible to achieve. 'Why use the force of the
better argument when force alone will suffice?' (Flyvbjerg, 1998a: 80). What does
this imply for democratic decision-making and planning?

Since attempts to establish a rational consensus may result either in a thin
agreement at the lowest common denominator on the few issues about which parties can concur and/or be simply a 'front' (Allmendinger, 1999: 12) for powerful
interests to maintain influence and capacity to get what they want whilst seeming to
act more deliberatively, we need to understand and incorporate power into our
framework. We need to provide channels of expression in which conflicts can be
expressed whilst limiting the use of abusively confrontational antagonistic behaviour; channels which enable participants to move beyond potentially entrenched
rights-based positions to constructively uncover each side's interests and expectations from outcomes and what aspects are critical to them; channels which offer
more in various ways than participants might otherwise obtain by pursuing their
interests in legal, political or other arenas. Competition and cooperation are often
inextricably entwined in deliberative processes, as Innes' (1999b) empirical work
confirms. The two often cannot be separated and 'neither denial nor discomfort will
make it disappear' (Lax and Sebenius, 1986: 30).

In the philosophical sense we need 'a deliberative vision of democratic politics
which can also do justice to the agonistic spirit of democracy' (Benhabib, 1996a:
9). Benhabib, however, fails to achieve such a vision, finding associational and agonistic space theoretically incompatible. Similarly, Gutmann and Thompson (1996,
1999, 2000) struggle to include antagonism and disagreement in what is essentially a moral deliberative paradigm. Despite acknowledging the existence of
disagreement, they still seek consensus, however: 'deliberative democracy seeks
not consensus for its own sake but rather a morally justified consensus' (1996: 42),
proposing six universalist principles to be achieved: reciprocity, publicity, accountability, basic liberty, basic opportunity and fair opportunity. Of these, reciprocity, with
all its problems, is regarded as key.

Given these moral conditions, mutually acceptable reasons for unresolvable
disagreements are permissible. Gutmann and Thompson term such outcomes,
when there is agreement to disagree, as 'moral or deliberative disagreement'. Their
prescription for deliberative democracy is thus that citizens should 'deliberate with
one another, seeking moral agreement when they can, and maintaining mutual

respect when they cannot' (Gutmann and Thompson, 1996: 346), a concept similar to Connolly's (1998) notion of agonistic respect.

It is in this area of moral disagreement (which, together with that of disagreements governed by self-interest, I would regard as political disagreements) that Gutmann and Thompson (1996, 2000) call for prudence, whose 'distinctive method' is bargaining. They suggest that bargaining is justifiable when the universals governing moral deliberation fail: 'bargaining is a legitimate way of resolving political conflicts that would otherwise remain unresolved' (Gutmann and Thompson, 1996: 71). It should, however, be a strategy of last rather than first resort, not the principle of least effort. Habermas (2001b: 117) has recently distinguished between bargaining as a process in which actors strive for a balance of different interests and consensus as a process of actors arriving at shared opinions by mutually convincing each other. Bargaining is considered second-best behaviour, based as it is in self-interest and conflict rather than reciprocity and consensus, yet Gutmann and Thompson (2000: 175) suggest that if the consequences of bargaining can be shown to be mutually justifiable to the people bound by them, 'then instituting self-seeking bargaining in place of deliberation can satisfy the principles of deliberative democracy'.

Gutmann and Thompson have attempted to deal with agonism by separating it out from their theory of moral deliberation and incorporating it through bargaining in special circumstances of moral disagreement or immutable self-interest.[19] I would argue, however, that such a conception is of relatively limited use to the highly politicised activities of planning practice. Elster's (1998) consideration of bargaining, however, is different from that of Gutmann and Thompson and may offer us a way forward. Elster (1998: 5) identifies three different modes of decision-making in conditions of unreachable consensus: arguing, bargaining and voting. Importantly to my argument here, he suggests that *political* decision-making usually involves all of the procedures in combination. Taking this issue further, Gambetta (1998) writes that it is sometimes difficult to separate bargaining from argument, although essentially he defines bargaining as involving negotiation through the exchange of promises and/or threats or warnings, whilst argument is an attempt to persuade others of the values of one's views.

By way of example, Aboriginal groups in Australia, who have a tradition of group-based society, of harmony between people and of decision-making by consensus (Oxenham, 2000), are increasingly negotiating directly with developers rather than the governmental planning system (Mr Robert Bropho, 1996, pers. comm.). The thinking behind such a strategy not only comes from an Aboriginal traditional dislike of confrontational negotiation in large 'public' meetings and a preference for negotiation on an individual basis ('rather gains were made by stealth and working the system – getting around people rather than direct confrontation'

(Crawford, 1990: 61)) but also that both groups have vested interests in achieving an outcome and therefore have a stimulus to negotiate (unlike planning officers of governance to whom the issue may not be so important). Although the participants may not like or respect each other and are unwilling to engage in reciprocity (imagining themselves in the other's position), communicative action or procedural justice, the necessary interaction between them for an outcome to be achieved is sufficient to stimulate negotiation: a transaction of enlightened self-interest (Rubin, 1991: 4) or coalition of convenience (Fenger and Klok, 2001) in which actors hold attitudes of 'I don't care what your values are, I don't have to like or trust you, but let's negotiate a compromise'.[20]

Can we do this philosophically? My Aboriginal example appears similar to Elster's (1998) and Gambetta's (1998) notions of bargaining. As such, we should be able to work through transactions of enlightened self-interest or bargain to reach a compromise. Here I stress the difference between *compromise* and *consensus*. Compromise is reached through a *transaction* or through *bargaining*. Consensus is reached through *argument* or *deliberation*. Both have elements of agreement and differences of viewpoints and values. Transacted or bargained outcomes may not be strictly 'moral' (following Gutmann and Thompson's reasoning), but they may, nevertheless, be socially just. 'A bargain is often the better part of political wisdom' (Walzer, 1999: 62).

Even Habermas has begun to acknowledge that complex processes of bargaining and compromise have a legitimate role to play in democratic decision-making, in deciding conflicts between interest groups about distributive problems 'without erasing legitimate oppositions' (2001a: 31). He recognises that understanding between actors will only be possible if they 'expect to be able to learn from each other' and that reciprocity should probably have 'the more modest goal of mutual respect for the sincerely attested power of opposed traditions' (2001a: 34–5). He accepts, moreover, that 'there can always be *reasonable* dissent' (2001a: 40, emphasis added) about ethical questions and that 'in the case of controversial existential questions arising from different world views even the most rationally conducted discursive engagement will not lead to consensus' (2001a: 43).

Conceding that it is 'reasonable to expect continuing disagreement' (2001a: 43) in such circumstances, Habermas suggests that a compromise is 'fair' if it provides advantages to each party, tolerates no 'free riders', and no one is exploited in such a way as to force them to give up more than they gain by compromise (1996: 165–7).[21]

In this section I have demonstrated that participatory processes of consensus-building can be counterproductive, especially if they are imposed hegemonically on actors who are more familiar with different styles and forms of negotiation and decision-making. There is, therefore, more than one dimension to the values at stake in collaborative planning. By concentrating only on the substantive, consensus procedures

may ignore critical sources of antagonism and conflict in the interpersonal and procedural dimensions. Little attention so far has been paid by planning theorists to
the roles of agonism, of bargaining and compromise in planning decision-making.
Yet such issues may well be central to planning practice.

CONSENSUS VERSUS AGONISM – A THEORETICAL RECONCILIATION?

The questions which remain are that if we conceive of planning policy-making as a
political medium through which the antinomies of difference are expressed and contested and we reject an Habermasian consensual teleocommunitarian morality as
utopian and counterfactual, can we achieve an agonopluralistic ethic in theory and
practice and what would agonistic democracy look like at an urban scale of decision-
making?

In order to examine the theoretical aspects of these questions, I return to the
work of Hannah Arendt whose ideas influenced both Habermas and Foucault to a
certain extent (as identified in Part 2). Whereas Habermas regards the consensus-
building force of communication aimed at agreement as an end in itself and takes this
as the basis for his theory of communicative action, Arendt regards not agreement,
but action and judgement as the ends in themselves. Arendt's process of cultivating
an 'enlarged mentality' through deliberation is a precondition for political action and
judgement. Her ideas thus 'give voice to plurality – to debate, deliberation, *and disagreement as well as consensus*' (Villa, 1996: 70, emphasis added).

By holding a disjunction of judgement and practical reason, Arendt preserves
the political dimensions of performance *and* persuasion, deliberation *and* initiation,
agonism *and* agreement (Villa, 1996: 71). Whilst being appreciative of the roles of
rational argument and agreement, Arendt emphasises that the real value of the public sphere lies in its capacity for never-ending political debate.

What ties the two dimensions together is a focus on public-spiritedness and a
care for the world. Where care is present, the world is humanised by the 'incessant
and continual discourse' (Arendt, 1968b: 30) of a plurality of opinions. Where care
is lacking and self-interest dominates, conflict reigns.

If we can understand the circumstances and conditions which tend to lead to
argument or bargaining in policy disputes, we may become more able to steer participants towards agonistic argument to the benefit of the traditionally marginalised.
I suggest that there may be three key variables involved: actors' values, their perception of the other actors and their outcome preferences.

Forester (1999) suggests that much hinges on actors' values; that value differences are sometimes irreconcilable, but that this should be the end-point of

negotiation rather than a presumption. We should be asking questions of what makes disputes irreconcilable? How do different value claims matter practically to participants and to all those affected by the decision? We need to tease out differences in participants' values between those which they simply like, want, need, have a commitment to and so on, i.e. between their core and *secondary* values. In this vein, Sabatier (1987) proposes that actors' value-systems have a three-fold structure, comprising a deep core of fundamental normative and ontological axioms, a policy core of basic choices, and secondary aspects which actors are more likely to compromise for various reasons.

I suggest, therefore, that participants are likely to reach consensus if large areas of their core and secondary values overlap/are commensurate, but that incommensurability of both will lead to situations of bargaining within the formal process and tactics of informal direct action outside. In circumstances where core values are incommensurable but there is agreement between secondary values, agonistic deliberation or argument may take place.

Forester (1999) also argues the importance of participants' perceptions of the other actors involved. He offers a four-box matrix in which one side either believes the other's value statements or suspects them of posturing, against whether the other side is actually expressing itself honestly or is bluffing. Whilst I argue that Forester's matrix should be multi-way rather than one-way, it does nevertheless, help us to understand more about conditions and circumstances in which positional bargaining is likely (suspicion on one side and bluff on the other), collaborative dialogue is possible (conditions of trust and sincerity), or anger, resentment and escalation of conflict is probable (suspicion on one side and honesty on the other).

Thompson and Tuden's (1959) typology of decision processes has been resurrected by Lee (1993) as it forwards comprehension of the important dimensions about participants' beliefs and outcome preferences. Thompson and Tuden (see Figure 12.1) suggest that irreconcilable conflict and direct action are likely when actors disagree over both their understanding of the causation of the dispute and their preferred outcomes. However, when there are levels of agreement on outcomes, bargaining may occur, while agreement as to causation makes negotiation more probable. Translating these ideas into my base diagram (Figure 11.1) gives Figure 12.2.

However, as Joe Springer (1998, pers. comm.) astutely commented, and Pruitt's (1991), Warren's (2001) and Young's (2001) work supports, my horizontal axis remains an inadequate explanation of reality. Not all actors choose to participate. Some may remain ignorant of the issue completely, some may be apathetic, unconcerned about the outcome, and others may be alienated by the process, the players or other considerations. Some participants may never enter the process, or may withdraw before its completion, to retire into inactivity or, at the other extreme, to ferment revolution outside of the formal process. (On this last issue of exit, see

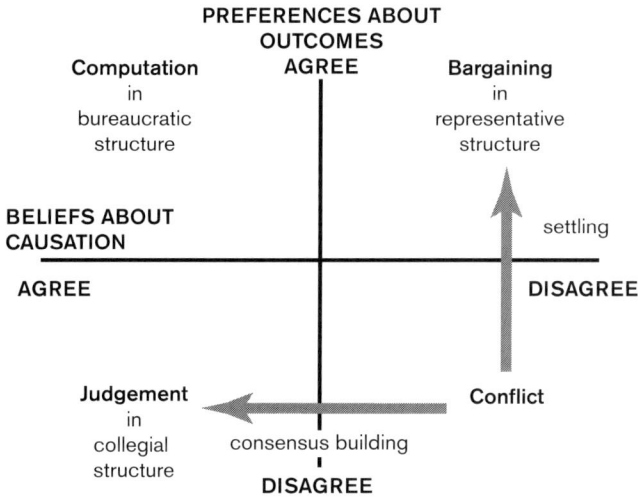

Figure 12.1 Social decision processes (Source: Thompson and Tuden, (1959), cited in Lee, 1993: 106)

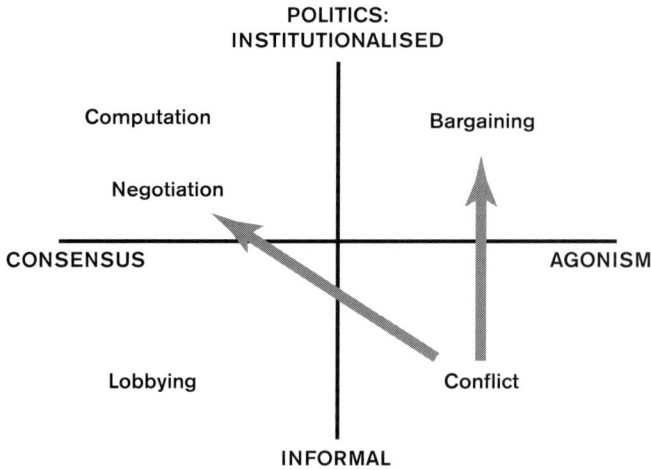

Figure 12.2 Social decision processes and participatory processes in planning (Source: Hillier, 2002b: 127)

the tactics of the Australian Conservation Foundation (ACF) in the Regional Forest Agreement example given in Chapter 7.)

As Young writes: 'individuals and organisations ... need *both* to engage in discussion with others to persuade them that there are injustices that ought to be remedied and to protest and engage in direct action' (2001: 689, emphasis in original). I affirm both strategies whilst recognising the tension between them.

My horizontal axis should therefore be extended to that depicted in Figure 12.3.

POLITICS
INSTITUTIONALISED
|

Associative
Deliberative   debate
argument/   Bargaining
negotiation

                                                           Non-Participation
              Participation

CONSENSUS   AGONISM   Antagonism   Apathy

                                                          Alienation   Ignorance

                                         Exit
Lobbying   Conflict
                                              Direct   Inaction
                                              action

                                                          Revolution
              INFORMAL

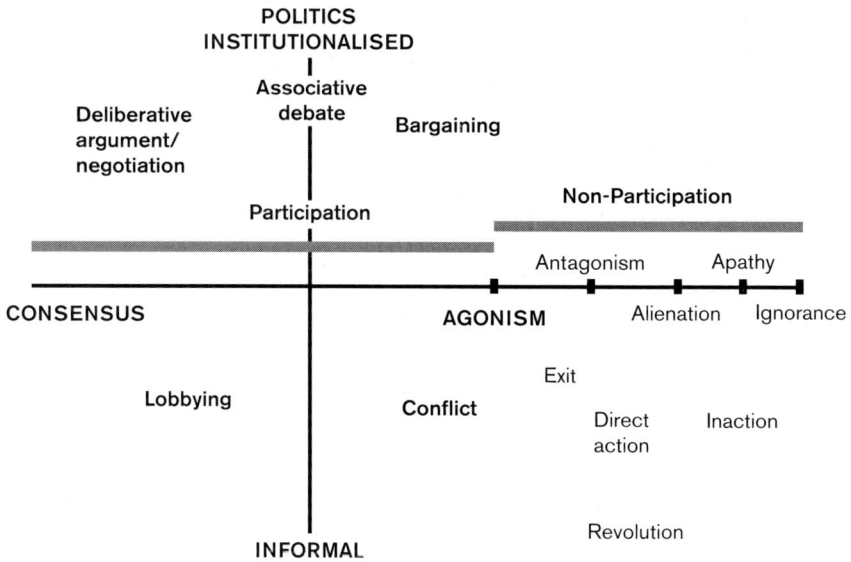

Figure 12.3 Participation in planning activity (Source: Hillier, 2002b: 127)

CONSENSUS VERSUS AGONISM – A PRACTICAL RECONCILIATION?

Consensus-building procedures described by Innes and Susskind *et al.* (1999) resemble the practical realisation of aspects of Cohen and Rogers' (1995) conception of associative democracy. Embracing as it does the four core elements of decision-making pluralism; a combination of authority with consensus; processual, dialogic rationality and interactive governance; and concertation or decision-making through negotiation (Amin, 1996), the conception of associative democracy is similar to Habermas' (1998) suggestion for a model of deliberative democracy, consisting of a public sphere of political communication whose institutional basis is provided by voluntary associations of civil society together with inputs of expert information.

It is not my task here to suggest normative institutional details for actualisation of associative democracy (see Amin, 1996; Amin and Hausner, 1997; Amin and Thrift, 1995b). I do, however, highlight some of the problems which may emerge to affect the potential of associative democratic, and by implication, consensus-building processes.

As demonstrated in the previous chapter, Young (1995) regards the necessary *artifactuality* of associative democracy as problematic and suggests a need for social solidarities to be formed and develop naturally rather than be conveniently fabricated or rationalised. Other important problematic issues discussed in Chapter 11 include those of *representation* and *acceptance*, together with the issue that using associationality as a regulatory principle of freedom and empowerment can itself be a powerful imposition.

Rather than associative democracy, therefore, my belief is that agonistic democracy as a model without fixed certainties but rather a contestation of multiple representations and interpretations through which identities and positions are formed, can incorporate elements of both associative debate and direct action; that insider (associative) and outsider (direct action) strategies are legitimate. But does this leave us in a political free-for-all in which the strongest, the most articulate, those with the most influential contacts, or the most violent win?

Is it impossibly utopian to realise an agonistic forum in an urban policy-making setting? Would it necessitate 'some fictive model of political agency that has never been instantiated anywhere' as Connolly (1998: 124) concludes? A political imaginary?

There cannot, and should not, be any 'model' of agonistic democracy as ways of working need to be contingent on circumstances, time, place and stakeholders. As Flyvbjerg (1998a: 234) writes, 'when we understand power we see that we cannot rely solely on democracy based on rationality to solve our problems'. For this reason I prefer a theory of democracy which incorporates both associative and agonistic aspects.

CULTURES OF POWER

I recognise that if any actors believe that they can improve their outcome through any potentially viable alternative to a negotiated agreement, they may be expected to try to do so. This means that agonistic democratic procedures will not alter fundamental power relationships in a society, no matter what our desires. Powerful actors may simply resort to using other powers (of connections, financial wealth and other forms of leverage) available to them instead of, or at the same time as, engaging in a collaborative, associative strategy of consensus-building decision-making.

In terms of institutional organisation, given the theoretical debate above and in the previous chapter, it follows that the practical nature of associative participation and the nature of procedural rules (Bohman and Rehg, 1997: xviii; Weber, 1998) would need to be articulated in such a way that the inherent agonism and undecidability (Dyrberg, 1997) of political/planning decisions is embodied in an institutional setting which offers all actors a realistic possibility of participating in planning policy decision-making and which recognises the ultimate non-consensual undecidability of decisions and hence makes it possible to disagree.

We need to recognise the messiness of politics and to 'reconfigure the political' (Walker, 1994: 669) in societies currently 'strangled by insidious webs of alliance between the dominant political, economic and social institutions' (Amin, 1996: 329). Is this possible? In societies where the performance of bureaucratic administrations is increasingly measured in efficiency terms, administrators are seeking to discover and undertake activities instrumental to the achievement of such ends. In addition, as Healey (2001) points out, some administrators (both officers of governance and elected representatives) retain traditional cultural habituses of mindsets and practices (including 'educating' local communities rather than listening to them) despite deep changes in the spatial economics and social natures of the populations they determinedly plan *for*. As such, the nature of administrative power would appear paradoxical to, and perhaps incommensurable with, the logic of communicative power, based on relations of mutual recognition and respect for differences.

Consensus-aiming deliberation may thus demand that participants adopt a fundamental change of attitude in the way in which they think about and use power. Rather than regarding power as 'power to' or 'power over' as unilateral control and 'winning the debate' in achievement of self-interest in often adversarial situations, participants would have to regard power as 'power with' – the power of association, a focus on common goals and a joint approach to working through problems on a 'level playing field'. Some actors may find such a transformation impossible to realise. It may well be just 'wishful thinking' (Kohn, 2000: 422).

There is, as Ravetz (1999) describes, a 'natural tension' between mainstream institutions with statutory and/or fiduciary responsibilities and actors with interests of individual property values, environmental protection, etc. Ravetz' diagram (1999: 339), reproduced here as Figure 12.4, charts several possible pathways through the political chain of constituencies, institutions, 'hegemonic projects', processes and outcomes.

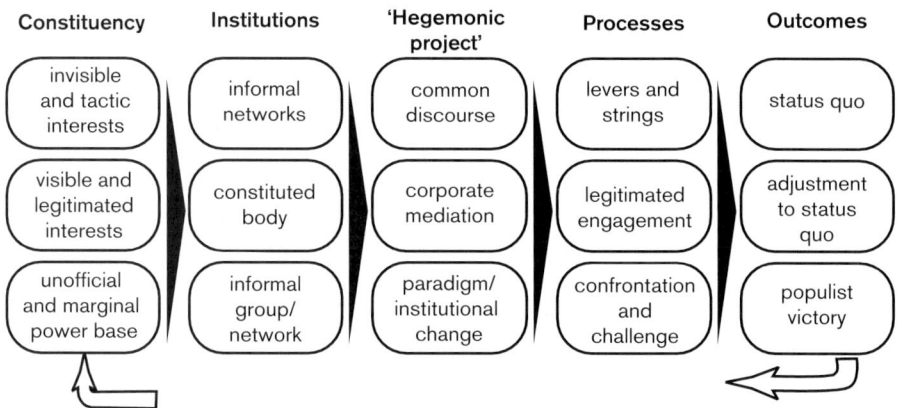

Constituency	Institutions	'Hegemonic project'	Processes	Outcomes
invisible and tactic interests	informal networks	common discourse	levers and strings	status quo
visible and legitimated interests	constituted body	corporate mediation	legitimated engagement	adjustment to status quo
unofficial and marginal power base	informal group/ network	paradigm/ institutional change	confrontation and challenge	populist victory

Figure 12.4 Contrasting approaches of tacit, legitimate or marginalised participation (adapted from Hajer, 1995 and Gidens, 1984) (Source: Ravetz, 1999: 339)

As can be seen in Figure 12.4, one pathway involves informal networks and contacts who pull strings (e.g. the Friends of the Valley in Chapter 6). Another pathway flows from visible and legitimated interests who act through formal processes to reach a consensual outcome of adjustment to the status quo (the Habermasian ideal). A third pathway leads from the marginalised power bases through group networks towards confrontation and challenge, resulting in a paradigm shift and populist victory (e.g. the West Australian Forest Alliance in Chapter 7). Each is a valid pathway. Since, as Kohn (2000) suggests, evidence indicates that the outcomes of formal deliberative processes are more heavily weighted in favour of articulate elites, it would appear that marginalised groups in society have greater chance of victory if they select an informal pathway of strategic action.

In addition, when deliberation often becomes stuck at actors' positions stated in rights-based terms, there is little opportunity for negotiations to move forward. The conditions for a communicative rather than an antagonistic style of interaction cannot be automatically produced by the simple creation of an inclusive deliberative forum.

We would also need to remember that whilst new institutional forms may offer previously ignored interests an opportunity to enter planning debates, the pattern of the institutional form constrains the changes it enables (see Morone, 1990). Furthermore, we would need to remember the essentially political rather than moral nature of much of what will take place. An emphasis on reciprocal deliberation alone attends too little to the degree to which disagreements are shaped by political differences of interest and power (Shapiro, 1999). It is all too common to see collaborative round-tables disintegrate from being forums of cooperation, deep democracy, individual dignity and personal fulfilment to virtual battlefields of competition, domination, control and greed (McArdle, 1999: 38–9).

PROBLEMS OF CLOSURE

For Smith (2000) the very idea of deliberative decision-making institutions is paradoxical in that tensions may exist between the need for a decision outcome and the institutionalisation of deliberation. Decisions tend to imply the end of a process, but deliberation in principle is ongoing. Reaching mutual understanding takes time, often longer than planners and politicians can allow. The problem becomes one of closure, and as Chambers (1995: 255) suggests, 'the closer and more final is that point of closure, the more participants will be motivated to act strategically rather than discursively'.

Rubin (1998) points a distinction between *resolution* of a debate, denoting an outcome which involves participants' attitudinal change and agreed issue resolution, and *settlement* of a debate in which the underlying attitudinal bases of conflict may not have been addressed. He also notes a shift in practice from a focus on resolution to settlement, which is generally regarded as being much easier and faster to achieve.

It would appear that Mouffe's (and Laclau and Mouffe's, 1985) conception of agonistic democracy will tend to result in outcomes of settlements rather than issue resolution. Privileging contestation over consensus, agonistic democratic processes allow actors within a coalition to maintain their autonomy and differences from the others as far as compatible with the common project.

Given that in many questions of public policy-making there will exist deep core value differences and the chances of consensual agreement are extremely slim, does agonistic democracy bring planning practice sufficiently out from the shadows of power that decisions may be reached in a fuller light of understanding? I turn to this question below. Meanwhile I consider the issue of whether the Lacanian philosophical foundations of agonistic democracy mentioned in Chapter 11 are compatible with those of the discursive theory which I am developing.

LACANIAN LIGHT IN THE SHADOWS?

If we follow Mouffe's lead above that achieving consensus is impossible in most instances of complex land-use planning decisions; that there will always be a constitutive outside; and that conditions of agonism are 'as good as it gets', what does the introduction of Lacanian thought mean for my theory of discursive democratic decision-making and for planning practice?

Lacanian thought suggests that any conception of the socio-political institution of society as an harmonious totality or of a public sphere with complete information is no more than a fantasmatic mirage. The ideas of complete information, an harmonious society and of consensus are the Lacanian impossible Real rather than actual lived reality.

Reality serves as the 'external boundary' of our lived experience which enables us to make out of it a close and coherent system. It is the social reality of actual people/actors. The Real is its '"inherent limit"; the unfathomable fold which prevents it from achieving its identity with itself' (Zizek, 1991: 112). The Real is thus the inexorable 'abstract' spectral logic which determines what goes on in social reality (Zizek, 1999: 276). In other words, the Real is impossible to know. It escapes knowledge and, specifically, linguistic representation. It is beyond language.

It is the traumatic moment of attempting to know and to encounter the Real which initiates a process of symbolisation and the 'ever-present hegemonic play between different symbolisations of the Real' (Stavrakakis, 1999: 74). It is this 'play' which leads to the emergence of politics between the different symbolic viewpoints of what the 'world' should look like and to the political institution of a new fantasy (decision/accepted viewpoint, etc.) in place of a dislocated one.

Slavoj Zizek (1997) points out that an encounter with the Real is always traumatic as there is always an unbridgeable gap separating the participants from it. With
regard to information availability, Dean (2001) indicates the lack between reality and
the Real of complete information. This lack is the realm of 'secrets': withheld or
unknown information. Whilst there are secrets, there cannot be meaningful consensus.

Dean (2001) also demonstrates the gap between the fantastic universal Real
of the public supposed to (or having a right to) know and the reality of the public
supposed to believe. Provision of information and public involvement in participatory
strategies thus holds out the possibility of good decision-making to the public supposed to believe. Yet lack of information/the secret conceals the gap between the
public supposed to know and the public supposed to believe. Reality is 'a reductive
acceptance of the way things are instead of a utopian embrace of the way things
might be' (Dean, 2001: 630).

Reason and Understanding are also problematised. Reason, in itself, cannot exist.
What we have, in reality, is Understanding. However, as Zizek (1991: 159–60) indicates, 'the fundamental illusion of Understanding is precisely that there is a Beyond
eluding its grasp. ... Reason is simply Understanding *minus* what is supposed to be
lacking ... – in short: what appears to it as its inaccessible Beyond' (emphasis in original). What hope is there then for Habermasian theory if Reason is unattainable?

Zizek compares his Lacanian interpretation of consensus with that of a
'Habermasian "ideal speech situation" in which participants theoretically speak truthfully'. Yet truth is simply a fiction: 'there is a domain "beyond Truth" that is not simply
the everyday domain of lies, deceptions and falsities, but the Void that sustains the
place in which one can only formulate symbolic fictions that we call "truths"' (Zizek,
1999: 161). Similarly, Badiou (1988) claims that 'community' remains an 'unname-
able surplus', a 'fundamental fantasy' (cited in Zizek, 1999: 167). Zizek suggests that
the Habermasian version of communicative action is 'lacking': 'without the element of
the Real of *jouissance*,[22] the Other [of consensus] remains ultimately a fiction, a
purely symbolic subject of strategic reasoning exemplified in "rational–choice theory"'
(1997: 25). Since information cannot be complete since there is no 'truth'; since language cannot totally convey what actors feel, and the unexpressed lack is the kernel
of actors' subjectivity, meaning must always be a distortion of the Real. That meaning
is a distortion, however, is unthinkable for Habermas.

No social fantasy of consensus or harmony can fill the lack around which society is always structured. The political, therefore, is not and cannot achieve the Real
per se, but is rather one of the modalities in which we attempt an encounter with the
Real and its constitutive lack. As Stavrakakis writes: 'the political is associated thus
with the moment of contingency and undecidability marking the gap between the
dislocation of one socio-political identification and the creation of the desire for a
new one' (1999: 75).

Consensus has become the totalising moment of much participatory planning theory and practice. However, the ultimate paradox of consensus is that society is 'held together' by the very antagonism that forever prevents its closure in an harmonious, rational whole (Zizek, 1991). Consensus functions, in its very absence, however, as a point of reference enabling us to locate participatory decision-making. Consensus is Real, in the Lacanian sense: 'an impediment which gives rise to ever-new symbolisations by means of which one endeavours to integrate and domesticate it … but which simultaneously condemns these endeavours to ultimate failure' (Zizek, 1991: 100).

The Real of consensus is thus an impossible harmonisation with a fetishised Other. 'To "understand the Other" means to pacify it, to prevent the meeting with the Other from becoming a meeting with the Real that undermines our own position' (Zizek, 1991: 102). In such a manner, actors are able to preserve the unproblematic identity of their own subjective positions. Paradoxically, however, the Real of consensus has become the driving force of much participatory communicative planning practice. What is achieved in practice is *reality*. The resulting plan or policy statement is a symbolic expression of the incompleteness of consensus. It is important to recognise the difference between the two and the gap between Real consensus and its clumsy, incomplete imitation in reality. Reality, therefore, is always threatened by an encounter with impossibility (the Real) – that which is always located outside of the field of construction and has the ability to dislocate it by revealing its limits.

It is Habermas' 'fetish-like' (Torfing, 1999: 61) concentration on information and consensus and his failure to maintain the split between the public supposed to know and the public supposed to believe which makes agonism and the secret the keys to democratic decision-making. The public supposed to know relies on knowledge/information, unerring judgement, reciprocity, dialogic reason, consensus and certainty. The public supposed to believe involves ritual and mystery. Habermas believes that the process of critical debate transforms the latter into the former. Deliberation is 'a kind of purification' (Dean, 2001: 639) which leads to consensus and certainty through critical reflection. But we know that this is impossible. Are participatory planning strategies then merely a search for the thing that can best stand in for consensus, the lost object of desire? Are inclusive stakeholder meetings the Lacanian *objet petit a*[23] which condense the impossible, the 'deadly' 'Thing' of consensus, serving as its stand-in and thereby enabling us to entertain a liveable relationship with it? Attempting it may be, as Dean (2001: 642) suggests, simply 'Habermasochism'.

If we attempt to eliminate or negate the possibility of agonism in order to grasp consensus with its 'intact purity' of the Real, Torfing (1999: 128–9) proposes that we are simply being guided by an illusion. What is negated is always already negated (Zizek, 1990). There is a force of negativity that is prior to social antagonism. This force is antagonism as Real, the traumatic kernel which resists symbolisation, compared with the reality of antagonistic fight. Negating the reality of antagonism, therefore, leads not to the harmony and consensus of a fully constituted 'we', since antagonism is constitutive of social identity itself. We then tend to misrecognise the true cause of our failure. Thinking that they are missing some kind of 'golden rule', planning theorists attempt to find and to follow normative 'golden rules' closely. Yet, as Zizek (1996) would suggest, referring to the work of Pierre Bourdieu, what such theorists misrecognise is that 'the mysterious X' which accounts for Real consensus cannot be pinpointed to a specific symbolic feature.

Lacanians would suggest that within planning practice what should differentiate democratic from other forms of decision-making would be the legitimisation of conflict and the refusal to eliminate it through the establishment of an *authoritarian* harmonious consensus. Additionally, we should not act *as if* we believe in perfect information or consensus. 'No inclusion, whether of groups or information, people or issues, will provide enough legitimacy to justify what is claimed in the name of the public' (Dean, 2001: 646). Within a Lacanian framework the agonistic diversity between different conceptions of the good is not regarded as something to be eliminated but as something to be 'valued and celebrated. This requires the presence of institutions that establish a specific dynamic between consensus and dissent' (Mouffe, 1996: 8) rather than simply a Habermasian regulative idea of free unconstrained and perfectly informed communication.

However, Lacan is generally accepted as being a post-structuralist, unable to incorporate a complete understanding of capital, class, gender, race, etc. in structuring actions. Where does this leave the *Realpolitik* of planning practice? Is there hope for planners? Lacanians such as Zizek and Mouffe suggest that there might be. Zizek (1997) points out that the condition of impossibility is at the same time the condition of possibility; that the very condition which prevents us from achieving Real consensus is, at the same time, a positive condition of our attempting to achieve it. The lack of completeness of our understanding is a component in our striving for a range of Realities in praxis. The aim is rather to establish some form of agreement within an environment of conflict and diversity, to create a 'doubtful society, beset by productive self-doubt' (Stavrakakis, 1999: 112), to create an ethos of practice associated with the mobilisations of passions and sentiments, the multiplication of practices, institutions and language games (Mouffe, 1996: 5–8) which accepts the impossibility of reaching the consensual Real, but which strives to accommodate conflicting desires as the reality being sought. As Stavrakakis (1999: 112), asks, 'isn't it something worth fighting for?'

Assuming the answer to Stavrakakis' question is 'yes', we need to think about theory without agreements rather than agreements without theory. Some groups in society relate through conflict (Baum, 1997). Whilst associational democracy may be morally preferable, it still may not be possible. The rules are not the game.

CONCLUSIONS

Planning practice is 'a field where interests and social groups meet and clash under conditions created by the interaction of multiple forces' (Melucci, 1996: 92). Planning practice will always be agonistic: a system of shadow negotiations and 'interweaving opposites, of ambivalences, of multiple meanings which actors seek to bend to their goals so as to lend meaning to their action' (Melucci, 1996: 95). Whilst recognition of agonistic reality is important, as Benhabib (1996c: 8) points out, without some form of agreement or settlement to an outcome of the debate, it is impossible to be sure that the (planning) decision will not be 'unjust, racist, fickle, and capricious', a victory for the most organised, vociferous or 'best' connected, as in my Western Australian examples.

Grounded in traditions of networking, through associative/agonistic practice, we may nevertheless make relational links, across cultural barriers, organisational divisions and fractures in the distribution of power (Healey, 1997a: 311). Whilst actors may never reconcile fundamental differences, they may, nevertheless, be able to balance interests and compromise (Habermas, 1998: 245), to convert relations of antagonism to those which Mouffe (1999: 756) terms 'conflictual consensus', Meyerson *et al.* (1996) name 'swift trust' and which Connolly (1998: 122) calls 'agonistic respect': 'a social relation of respect for the opponent against whom you define yourself even while you resist its imperatives and strive to delimit its spaces of hegemony'.

All the above involves opening up the opportunity structure for involvement in planning policy-making. To achieve this, stakeholders with vested interests and established mindsets (elected representatives, private sector entrepreneurs, planners and other officers of governance and even public sentiment) need to be persuaded of the benefits of collaboration and that it is concerned with 'engagement and negotiation, not a political doctrine of ... consensus and resolution' (Connolly, 1998: 123). We also need to recognise that networking means far more than having contacts; that cooperation and collaboration mean far more than knowing people or sitting on the same committee (Marilyn Taylor, 1997, pers. comm.).

Any associative/agonistic practice must be context-contingent (in terms of place, time, representation, resources, etc.). There would inevitably be problems with attempts at associative/agonistic democratic policy-making. It is likely that local citizens would either expect to achieve too much, ignoring the inertia of actors' vested interests, or mistrust governance intentions and refuse to participate. Formalisation of networking could actually serve to destroy the informal coping systems of marginalised communities. There may well be attempts by some actors at exclusivity, at cooptation and corporatism, particularly if the public sector is providing financial support and infrastructure for the practice. We would need to be careful not to create yet another system which serves to colonise people's lifeworlds. There will

almost certainly be direct action or bargaining activity taking place contemporaneously with associative debate.

Is this last necessarily a bad thing? I think not. Planning officers should relax
their need for control and certainty. They need to learn to live with incompleteness,
inconsistencies, contradictions and the fact that some actors will refuse to be 'main-
streamed' as they regard it, remaining 'outsiders by choice' (Maloney et al., 1994),
whilst others will place their bets both ways, participating in associative forums and
in direct action:

> in a world where negotiation, instrumental trade-offs, and strategic bargaining
> are the most common routes to reaching collective 'agreement', and resolving
> disputes, it is plausible that the most serious barrier [to associative debate] can
> be found in the conversational habits that citizens have become used to
> (Chambers, 1995: 247).

After all, if planning officers themselves engage in lobbying elected members and negotiating trade-offs with developers, why should they begrudge others the practice?[24]

The 'message' from this chapter for planning officers is threefold:

- to recognise the difference between the unapproachable Real of consensus
  and its reality;
- to accept that there will be policy questions for which there is no 'right' answer
  and where actors' views will continue to be agonistic and to begin to anticipate such questions;
- to recognise the difference between settlement and resolution of an issue and
  to accept that settlement may be all that can realistically be hoped for.

Associative/agonistic practice, as conceptualised and represented in Figure 12.3,
could recognise the inherent undecidability of decisions and accept unresolvable
differences of values and opinion without passing moral judgement on them. There
should be freedom of dissent as well as of agreement. Where consensus cannot be
achieved through negotiation, bargaining or transactions may take place to reach
compromise agreements. As Mouffe (1999: 755) comments, 'compromises are
possible; they are part of the process of politics'.

Practice should be open to agonistic struggle and resistance to totalising
hegemonic 'solutions'. Obviously, there is no guarantee that any outcome/s, produced by resistance and direct action, will be 'better' for traditionally marginalised
peoples than other outcomes. There will always be losers from planning decisions.
As such, this is a tragic view of political life and its possibilities with regard to planning in that it recognises the inevitability of conflict and the experience of imposition
on those whose wishes are denied. My ambition is to realise situations in which it is
not usually the powerless and marginalised who lose.

It may well be that the creation and survival of any associative forums would be less important than their role in the development of networks which can hold 'organisational intelligence' (Milofsky, 1987) and the 'stirring up' of actors to respond to particular opportunities and challenges. If attempts at associative/agonistic democratic policy-making establish a tradition of forms of action which mobilise in an emancipatory way those actors in the interstices of society who are directly affected by a planning issue and who might be unnoticeably excluded from a consensual process, then I would regard the experiments as having been successful.

Planning decision-making in practice is replete with overt and covert network activity, as people activate political networks, intra- and inter-organisational networks and 'local residents" networks to further their own purposes. What I have attempted to do in this part is to engage in the theoretical struggle for a new discursive terrain of planning activity, with new principles of legitimacy of agonism (incorporating direct action) contesting the old principles of formal participation processes.

I have attempted to mark momentary convergences but also fundamental divergences between teleocommunitarian approaches to associative consensus-building and an agonopluralistic ethic. I have suggested that the two approaches can live together in a 'mixed-game' (Mouffe, 1999: 756), in part collaborative and in part conflictual. Because public spheres are arenas in which symbolic mediating processes shape public opinions, it is important to address both the consensual aspects of opinion and also the agonistic resistances to domination and attempts to enrol other actors to certain views (Lara, 1998).

Some form of radical pluralism and forums for expressing similarities, negotiating agreements or bargaining compromises would be necessary. Yet planners should be aware of the existence of intractable opposition and resistance as well as searching for agreement. Denial of opposition does not make it disappear. By 'stirring up' stakeholders to action, we may encourage airing of a fuller range of views and knowledges than would otherwise take place.

We should refuse to close off the options that direct action and other forms of 'resistance' might make available. For some agonal subjects, direct action may be the only form of representation and empowerment open to them. As in Nietzsche's (1954) agonistic contest, the point is to prevent the solidification of strategic relations into states of domination.

> The problem is not of trying to dissolve [relations of power] in the utopia of a perfectly transparent communication, but to give ... the rules of law, the techniques of management, and also the ethics ... which would allow these games of power to be played with a minimum of domination (Foucault, 1988: 18).

It is my hope that

> out of a shift towards a more hybrid democracy in some places a type of planning
> emerges that expands practical democratic deliberations rather than to restrict
> them, that encourages diverse citizens' voices rather than to stifle them, that
> directs resources to basic needs rather than to narrow private gain. This type of
> approach uses public involvement to present real political opportunities, learning
> from action not only what works but also what matters (Albrechts, 2001b: 2).

My diagram of potential planning activity represents the terrain hosting the contest
between two urges: the one, of direct action, seeking a site of untrammelled freedom beyond all limits, and the other, of formal associative democratic structures,
representing the safety of life rendered meaningful by its inescapable limits. It
enables theorisation of Innes and Gruber's (1999) 'hybrid' planning processes
(partly collaborative, partly political) without the stultifying boxes of their typology of
planning styles. It is a terrain of experimentation and diversity in which a contestation
of views can occur and in which new coalitions and alliances, of friends and some-
time adversaries, can form for limited and localised initiatives in order to be able to
walk forwards out of the shadows across both slippery ice and rough ground.

PART 6

SHADOW PLAY

CHAPTER 13

'COMING EVENTS CAST THEIR SHADOWS BEFORE'

INTRODUCTION

Lochiel's Warning, written by Thomas Campbell in 1802, provides a fitting introduction to this final chapter. Although a forewarning of doom for Lochiel, the quotation in the title above refers to the importance of prophecy or anticipation and improvisation of one's actions accordingly. If we can interpret the shadows we may be better able to influence 'coming events'.

Retaining my chiaroscuro metaphor in this chapter, I reprise key themes and issues from the preceding parts: shadow talk, the shades and lights and chiaroscuro styles of planning practice before coming, in transition, out from the shadows to identify some of the remaining shadows hanging over planning practice.

I began my inquiry for a new explanatory discursive theory of local planning decision-making practice by following authors such as John Forester, Patsy Healey and Judith Innes who have referred to Habermas' theory of communicative action in order to address issues of the design and operation of democratic institutions of planning governance. In much of the recent and current debate about communicative theory and consensus-building, discussion has centred on its *ideal* forms of expression. This has tended to lead to stand-offs between champions of the participatory ideal and those who would regard themselves as 'realists'. I have attempted to temper the ideal with the real as observed/narrated in practice stories in order to provide what I hope will be a relevant, meaningful explanatory theory of discursive democratic planning practice at a local level which can facilitate understanding of participants' actions and enable planning practitioners to themselves act in a more reflexive manner.

I have emphasised the importance of contingency, fluidity and performativity in planning practice. As Baum (1999: 5) writes, 'planning depends on making sense of the world in ways that simultaneously appreciate contingency and imagine possibilities of acting'. Participants' identities themselves are contingent, destabilised by the existence of the Other, and, like their representations of place, depend on the particular circumstances, the issues under discussion and the role/s they choose to perform.

PUBLIC SPHERES

The role of public spheres as forums for debate and negotiation is also emphasised. Whilst I agree with Dean's (2001: 645) Lacanian/Zizekian view that the public sphere, in a strict Habermasian sense, cannot exist, that such a conception 'rests on the constitutive impossibility of a politics without, outside of, and beyond power, a politics where decision is postponed in favour of a consensus that has already been achieved' (through power-full intervention), I do believe in local arenas where stake-holders are able to discuss planning issues. I believe in a multiplicity of public spheres rather than *the* public sphere of Habermas.

Moving planning decision-making away from a tightly rule-governed process of decide–announce–defend towards a focus on broader, effective citizen participation, means engaging with the idea of inclusive, autonomous public sphere/s. In a public sphere, people can discuss matters of mutual concern and learn about facts, events and the representations, opinions and interests of others. There exists a multiplicity of 'minipublics': the communicative and associational networks of society, from resident action groups (RAGs), clubs of various kinds and religious organisations to simple socialising activities in cafes and pubs. Public spheres are therefore 'a decentred anonymous matrix of communication about common concerns, comprising the full gamut of networks and modes of communication that allow for the contestatory, agonistic and rhetorical as well as deliberative expression and formation of public opinion/s' (Cohen, 1999: 266).

Contestation between groups/movements appears rife, and increasingly hostile in the early twenty-first century. There would seem to be a continuing need for 'spaces' for the non-violent, communicative, democratic settlement of disputes, both on a formal and an informal basis. Such inclusive distributive settings should perhaps be, as Young (2001: 685) proposes, outside of and opposed to ongoing settings of official policy discussion.

Habermas (1996) understands a public sphere as a dialogic 'space', a social phenomenon rather than an institution, an organisation or a system. It is a 'network for communicating information and points of view' (1996: 361). Habermas recognises the importance of informal deliberations which 'uncover topics of relevance to all of society, interpret values, contribute to the resolution of problems, generate good reasons and debunk bad ones' (1992: 452).

Public spheres are thus performative. They come into existence through the acts of their participants and are maintained and reproduced in a sequence of performances or meetings. They are also contingent spaces, open to different, perhaps unpredictable actions: 'what it will become depends on how the participants themselves utilise the space' (Rättilä, 2000: 49).

This is active democratic citizenship in its most liberal sense. Habermas' commitment to the realisation of liberal democracy incorporates a strategy of extending the realm of democratic institutional arrangements, norms and values throughout society. At a localised level of planning practice this strategy entails all stakeholders being possessed of the will and the capacity to agree on a shared conception of the 'common good'. Consensus is achieved through participatory discussion, through which the diverse needs and wants of stakeholders (local communities, planners, developers, environmentalists, infrastructure providers, etc.) are recognised, respected and mutually adjusted to one another through the weight of the better argument.

Experience of such participatory decision-making theoretically transforms participants psychologically. By engaging in reciprocity, taking into consideration the interests of others, participants become more socially responsible, they generate feelings of belonging and a willingness to accept decisions which may not favour them by virtue of their being arrived at in a procedurally just manner.

More recently, Habermas has specified the need for legal 'rules' and procedures for the actualisation of communicative action. His representation of communicative decision-making has now been criticised as 'legalistic utopia' (Kohn, 2000). It has become what Michel Foucault termed a 'juridico-discursive' view of government, and Slavoj Zizek (1999) has called 'para-politics': the 'attempt to de-antagonise politics by formulating clear rules to be obeyed so that the agonic procedure of litigation does not explode into politics proper' (Zizek, 1999: 241).

POWER AND POLITICS

Foucault's power-full critique of Habermas' theory, as described in Chapter 3, is especially valid for planning decision-making practice. As Foucault suggests, we cannot have a theory of power *per se*, but can only 'analyse the specificity of mechanisms of power, locate the connections and extensions and build little by little a strategic knowledge' (1980: 145). In order to do so, I have narrated a series of stories from practice, some considered from the perspective of outsider theorist and others from the perspective of participants inside the realm of action, both planning practitioners and elected representatives. My practice stories reveal Habermasian communicative theory to be profoundly utopian in that it does not reach down to the reality of day-to-day practice lives and concerns of participants.

My practice stories (Chapters 6, 7, 9 and 10) demonstrate that networks of power and power-plays may have distinct and important influence on planning outcomes. The stories are intended to indicate the kinds of things practitioners could think about as they act. Through use of narrative, examples and case-based knowledge I have attempted to help practitioners recognise, understand and eval-uate the games of various participants.

I thus introduce the dimension of politics into communicative theory, agreeing with Yiftachel (2000: 253) on the importance of treating the public regulation of space as a 'contingent political phenomenon'. Political 'rationality' is always bound up with substantive rationality in planning practice (Marris, 2001).

I attempt to bring together selected Habermasian and Foucauldian perspec-tives in a complementary manner in a theoretical model which seeks to describe what is actually involved in the procedures of democratic local planning decision-making, bearing in mind the irreducibility of planning practice to either moral idealisation or legalistic codes or rules of practice. Planning practice is far more than a set of mechanisms for decision-making.

CONSENSUS VERSUS AGONISM

I challenge an assertion that stakeholder regard for a 'common good' is necessarily conducive to the consensual achievement of the common good through commu-nicative discussion. A consensus approach in which universalism, altruism and dialogue are privileged over particularism, self-interest and wheeler-dealing (Minson, 1993) fails to represent the reality of most messy local planning decisions. It is important to appreciate the limitations of consensus-building and to recognise the presence of an element of 'friend–enemy relations' (Mouffe, 2000) or agonism in vir-tually all politicised society.

> It is only when we acknowledge this dimension of 'the political' and understand
> that 'politics' consists in domesticating hostility and in trying to defuse the
> potential antagonism that exists in human relations, that we can pose the funda-
> mental question for democratic politics (Mouffe, 1995: 263).

This 'fundamental question', which applies to planning as a democratic political practice, is, for Mouffe, not how to arrive at a rational consensus, not to eliminate passions from decision-making, but to mobilise those passions towards 'democratic designs' (Mouffe, 1995, 2000).

What such 'designs' would comprise is inevitably circumstantially contingent. There cannot and should not be any 'model' of agonistic democracy as ways of working need to be contingent on circumstances, time, place and stakeholders. Yet, as Connolly (1991: 193) writes: 'agonistic democracy, where each of these terms provides a necessary qualification to the other, furnishes the best political medium through which to incorporate strife into independence and care into strife'. Whilst my postmodern sensibility baulks at use of the word 'best', I believe that agonism reminds us that a public sphere is as much, if not more than a stage for conflict as a set of Habermasian procedures designed to achieve consensus.

I addressed the issue of agonism and planning decision-making in Part 5 in which I posed the following questions:

- What potential do concepts of associative democracy offer us, or do they attempt to force stakeholders into a formalised neocorporatist structure with all its possible disadvantages for the already marginalised?

- What about outsider strategies of lobbying and informal action which have long offered a means of empowering various groups in society?

- If agonistic democracy means both of the above − that insider and outsider strategies are legitimate − does this leave us in a political free-for-all in which the strongest, the most articulate, those with the most influential contacts, or the most violent win?

- Is it impossibly utopian to realise an agonistic forum in an urban policy-making setting? Would it necessitate 'some fictive model of political agency that has never been instantiated anywhere' as Connolly (1998: 124) concludes? Or can there be some sort of agonistic respect among differences irreducible to a rational consensus?

In seeking theoretical robustness for a 'reconciliation' of agonism and consensus, I returned to the work of Hannah Arendt whose thinking has influenced authors on both sides. Arendt's work is important in that she also recognises the inherent paradox of political action: that the moment of 'clearing' in which a space of freedom emerges is also the moment of its disappearance.

I introduced the Lacanian Real into the discussion of the impossibility of complete information, of consensus and of the ineradicability of conflict. The gap between the Real of consensus and its reality is antagonism, the constitutive lack around which human experience is organised. In planning practice, 'consensus decision-making offers a fantasy solution' (Baum, 1997: 145) to deep-rooted problems. How to deal with this fantasy and with antagonism are the key questions with which theory and practice will 'for ever be confronted and for which there can never be a final solution' (Mouffe, 2000: 139).

I presented a diagram in Chapter 12 which attempts to incorporate the above aspects of agonism into a representation of planning practice. I include consideration of exit (that people might not want to participate in the planning process or might walk away from a process even though they may have resources of time, voice and power), of bargaining and of compromise as I recognise these as strategies for domesticating antagonism to agonism. They may well be regarded as 'trade-offs' or 'second-best' outcomes (Blaug, 1999), but they are means of reaching decisions which it is incumbent on practitioners to do.

RELATIONAL NETWORKS: MULTIPLEX PRACTICE

We should not forget the wider context in which planning practice sits, an issue to which I return later. At this point I refer to the contextual change from govern*ment* to govern*ance*, as described by Bang and Dyrberg (2000) and the implications for policy-making which they emphasise. Moot for my discussion of planning practice is the tendency that politics cannot be confined within specific settings, but should be regarded as a network of both formal and informal components. 'Political domination is not only an issue of class power or state coercion, but also of exclusions from elite-governed networks' (Bang and Dyrberg, 2000: 150).

Second, the distinction between representative democracy and participatory democracy is beginning to break down at a local level. Local citizen 'activists' are increasingly being drawn into networks of governance and having greater influence on the design and implementation of planning policy decisions.

Finally, there is increasing emphasis placed on dialogue and collaboration between agents of governance and 'lay' persons. Whilst Bang and Dyrberg argue that such collaboration leads to a 'weakening of the state's ability to conduct efficient steering' (2000: 150), I would suggest that greater citizen involvement generally holds more benefits than disbenefits for planning practice.

All these tendencies reflect the actor-network theory related importance of networks and the extension of influence over planning decisions to a much broader 'community' than that of officers of governance and elected representatives. Planning practice needs to take such 'multiplexity' of decision-making seriously if it is to be effective. Planning decision-making is both ' a concentrated complex and a process of diverse relational webs' (Amin and Graham, 1997: 418).

Decision-making can be regarded as a nexus between relational proximity and time–space extensibility, where intense close relations (generally face to face) coexist with mediated flows of increasingly electronic communication over greater time–space distances. The Regional Forest Agreement example in Chapter 7 demonstrates how the West Australian Forest Alliance network enrolled actors from Perth, south west WA and internationally to its campaign against logging old-growth forests.

Particular sets of relationships are also unique to the decision circumstances. Networks are dynamic, complex and contingent on the issue under consideration. We should also recognise the importance of stakeholder heterogeneity, of difference – different habituses, mindsets, cultural ways of working, etc. All this implies that participatory collaboration and consensus-building tend to be confined to particular types of problem scenarios and particular types of decisions. Not all decisions are amenable to reaching consensus.[1]

Healey (2000) has identified a 'uniplex' conception of the city distinct from a 'multiplex' conception. Her uniplex city is self-contained, pivoting round the core, hierarchically ordered and internally integrated, although with separation of land uses. The multiplex city, by contrast, recognises the multiple relationships which transect urban space–time and beyond. Politics and governance cultivate these (inter)relationships, focusing on relations and processes rather than objects, and recognising that relations are dynamic and actively socially constructed.

I translate Healey's concepts from an application to urban systems to that of decision-making processes. I regard a uniplex way of working participatorily to be characterised by an approach of a panel or a committee organised by a central agency of governance, formally constituted with centrally set objectives and a defined outcome, with stakeholder representatives ordered to abide by certain non-negotiable rules, to keep to a strict agenda and to vote on issues. The role of the committee is to comment on a plan or suggestions already drafted by the agency which acts as the committee's executive.

In contrast, a multiplex way of working would be characterised by a participatory approach of a committee, established perhaps in response to request/s from local stakeholders. The committee structure is loose, flexible and non-hierarchical, with a remit to try and resolve certain conflictual issues through discussion rather than to develop a definitive 'plan'.

Empirical research into the effectiveness of these different ways of working is in its infancy. MacCallum's (2001a, 2001b) pioneering work in Western Australia, however, is illuminating. Her discourse analysis of a uniplex committee's meetings indicates a mistrust on the part of non-executive participants of the centralising and dominant role of the government executive and increasing frustration with a way of working which relegated the committee members to supposed 'balance and objectivity' rather than being able to state particular interests and concerns. Not surprisingly, this became a process of hard negotiation rather than collaboration.

By the third committee meeting, the tension between the executive and the membership had come to the surface. Some of the non-bureaucrat committee members successfully challenged the executive and reframed the practice in which they were engaged 'from a "neutral" bureaucratic one, in which the executive held most of the cards, to a political one in which they felt more powerful' (MacCallum, 2001b: 5). The membership achieved an 'unprivileging' of bureaucratic modes of practice in their planning task and a consequent significant alteration in the power relationship between the membership and the executive. At the time of writing the committee deliberations were still ongoing, so the duration of the power shift and its consequences are as yet unknown. I would anticipate a counter-challenge by the executive in some manner. There appears to be an increasing level of irritation at 'interference' by the membership and a reluctance to carry out certain committee recommendations.

In contrast, MacCallum's (2001a) discourse analysis of a multiplex committee working in a similar geographical location, with similar issues for consideration to those of the uniplex committee, indicates an entirely different committee atmosphere. The nature of the multiplex committee was accidentally fortuitous, established by an officer of local governance with little experience of such committee work. Having ensured all various interests were represented on the committee, collaborative discussion took place, during which the committee objectives were derived, representing the meanings given by committee members to a series of issues and tasks. As MacCallum (2001a: 15) states, the objectives 'were not intended as a final outcome, but as a "reprogramming device" for the committee's ongoing work. They belonged to the committee.' As such, the focus of committee conversation was working through the contentious elements of the objectives themselves rather than challenging how they came into being as in the uniplex case.

In the multiplex committee there is no strict control over an 'agenda'. Discussion is loosely structured and not overly focused on ends. Meetings generally begin with unstructured 'chat' amongst participants who do not often meet each other. The result to date has been that once-antagonistic participants have developed a rapport with each other. They now listen to each other's point of view with respect and take each other seriously. The committee members act collaboratively rather than adversarially. Similarities between the multiplex way of working and that of indigenous peoples are striking (see Chapter 12).

These examples highlight the importance of regarding planning decision-making as a complex of performative relationships and networks and the existence of a political practice opportunity structure which allows multiplex ways of working to develop. There is no big picture, as such, only a set of 'constantly evolving sketches' (Thrift, 1996b: 1485).

THE ROLE OF HABITUS

The importance of a conducive opportunity structure cannot be overemphasised. Evidence to date suggests a definite reluctance on the part of agents of governance to relinquish the perceived power, control and comfort of a uniplex structure (Healey and Vigar, 1996; McGuirk, 2000; Phelps and Tewdwr-Jones, 2000; Albrechts, 2001; Healey, 2001; Holt-Jensen, 2001; Howitt, 2001).

Planning officers may become 'prisoners of their own past practices', demonstrating 'strategic hesitancy' to 'build relationships in a shared-power world' (Healey and Vigar, 1996: 13). As the authors explain, 'the result is sometimes an inward-looking defensiveness which closes networks rather than expanding them'.

Rose (1999) links such behaviour to power and suggests that the governance pole of Self refuses to receive information or feedback that would cause it to change itself. This, she suggests, lays the foundations for a dangerous self-deception out of tune with wider reality.

> The self sets itself within a hall of mirrors: it mistakes its reflection for the world, sees its own reflections endlessly, talks endlessly to itself, and, not surprisingly, finds continual verification of itself and its world view. This is monologue masquerading as conversation, masturbation posing as productive interaction; it is a narcissism so profound that it purports to provide a universal knowledge when in fact its practices of erasure are universalising its own singular and powerful isolation. The pole of 'self' is both a deformed and deforming power: deforming because it seeks to bend all else to its will, and understands all else only in terms of itself; deformed because it thinks (or gambles) that its will is the will of the universe (Rose, 1999: 177).

The institutional and political embeddedness of officers of governance and elected representative decision-makers, illustrated above and by the practice stories in Part 4, demonstrates the power of a presiding policy discourse and mindset/s in organising concepts, claims and values for attention. Planners' and elected representatives' discourses and behaviours are embedded in a, or several, habitus/es which frame and limit options.

The introduction into my theory of Pierre Bourdieu's concepts of the habitus, field and capital help us to unpack the *Realpolitik* of reason and provide a 'sensible third path between universalism and particularism, rationalism and relativism, modernism and postmodernism' (Calhoun, 1993: 62). The schemes of perception and action of the habitus invalidate a Habermasian assumption of an ahistorical universal rationality. For Bourdieu, as for Foucault, there is an understanding that subjectivity is constantly being constructed out of the material and historical structures with which people and objects interact. The habitus emphasises the importance of practical wisdom (phronesis) in social action and the role of tradition or institutional mindsets in the practical outcomes of planning.

A weakness of the habitus has been Bourdieu's previously relatively passive view of agency and the ability of agents to take conscious, rational action, especially with regard to managing change (Bridge, 2001). However, Habermas' focus on transformation through communicative dialogue and Foucault's emphasis on the role of power offer mechanisms to link such dispositions (habituses) to intentional actions as both an explicit as well as an implicit or intuitive process (see Bourdieu, 2000: 227–36).

Bourdieu's theory (and public practice) are both informed by a desire for a just society. As the practice stories of my missionary planners for social justice indicated

in Chapter 10, an understanding of the concept of habitus can help planning officers
unpack and anticipate potential reactions to an application or policy. Planners may
then be able to improvise in order to facilitate more socially just outcomes than might
otherwise transpire. 'The mind working in search of a strategy is not simply recalling
past methods. ... Nor is it performing simply an intellectual or rational thought
process' (Teck, 1997: 1). It is constantly anticipating and improvising.

PRUDENCE/PHRONESIS

The role of prudence, practical reason/wisdom or phronesis is vital to planning practice. Throughout this book I have made the case for the indispensable role of
practical knowledge, informal as well as formal processes, and improvisation as
planners work in the shadows of power. Ways of working which exclude or suppress reflection on experience, knowledge and potential for improvisation risk
ineffectiveness. Even the chameleon planners in Chapter 10 who chose to 'keep
their heads down' reflected on their past experiences, 'reasoning in context'
(Fischer, 2000) their preferred actions or inactions.

In addition to anticipation, 'political nous' and a sense of timing, or alertness to
turning points, are vital to effective 'missionary' practice. These may well be 'innate'
skills of habitus, 'the art of assessing likelihoods; ... of anticipating the objective
future' (Bourdieu, 1990: 60), enabling actors to 'grasp intuitively that *decisive*
moment' (Teck, 1997: 343, emphasis in original).

Bourdieu refers to the 'specific logic of practical sense' in interpreting the
'rules' of a game. Such sense is unarticulated and local, taking its cues from local
contexts with their particular ensembles of discourses and practices. Nevertheless,
practical sense is often sophisticated: 'a world in which "I think" (*cogito*) is inseparable from "I can" (*practico*)' (Thrift, 1996a: 102). Intellectual learning and
experiential learning merge in praxis.

Way (1995) elaborates on this linkage between thought and action. He suggests that individual actors filter information which comes from both the linear reality
of cause and effect or the multi-dimensional reality of opportunity. Actors both intel-
lectualise and 'feel' information. This information is then 'processed' according to
the actor's belief system or habitus which then translates into decisions and actions
(Figure 13.1). Although grossly oversimplified into essentially a straight line, ignoring
the multiple relational networks of actors and the dynamism of time, such a process
reflects the multiplexity of planning reality.

The concept of prudence as phronesis has been most notably related to planning practice by Bent Flyvbjerg (1993, 1998a, 1998b, 2001). Flyvbjerg expands
the original Aristotelian concept to include explicit consideration of power. He does

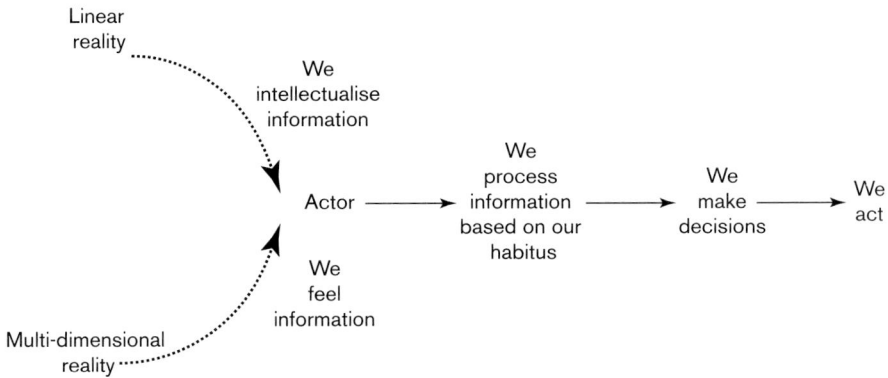

Figure 13.1 Linear and multi-dimensional thinking (after Way, 1995: 21)

not, however, expand the original concept to combine legislation and deliberation as does McAfee (2000), who suggests that the phronesis of political legislative decisions should involve interpretation and deliberation.

Phronetic planning practice would lose its 'programme' approach of prescribing and controlling, driven centrally, considering outcomes first in a grand plan developed by outsiders of where the local community should be (Muirhead, 2001). It would incorporate Ife's (1995) five components of understanding (analysis), awareness, experience, learning from others and intuition. More recently, Ife has suggested a series of questions on which planners could beneficially reflect before launching into action. I list these questions below as food for thought for prudent, phronetic planners: 'what matters … is asking the right questions' (Fourny, 2000: 4).

- Am I prepared for others to change me in ways I want to change them?
- Do I privilege my expertise over those whom I'm working with?
- Am I clear about my objectives and outcomes? (If so, should I not be practising in this manner? I should welcome a journey of discovery and uncertainty.)
- Who is controlling the agenda – them or me?
- Am I doing this for them or me? Whose needs are we meeting?
- Will I know when to let go?
- Am I involved in skill/knowledge sharing and transfer or am I doing to others rather than with them?
- Am I encouraging both vertical dialogue (with agencies of governance) and horizontal dialogue (across cultures and communities)?

(Ife, 2000, pers. comm.).

FROM LEGISLATORS TO INTERPRETERS

I borrow Zygmunt Bauman's (1987) title as it encapsulates the practice transition of planning officers from Muirhead's programme approach of the planner as expert legislator, controlling land use and space, ordering action and designing society, to the planner as prudential interpreter of the relational multiplexities of society. Each approach is upheld by the habitus/es and beliefs of a 'community of meanings' (Bauman, 1987: 4).

Habermas' recent work is still characterised by the role of 'planners' as legislators (see Chapter 2). His distinction between a weak public whose 'deliberative practice consists exclusively in opinion formation and does not also encompass decision-making' (1996: 50) and a strong public which takes institutionalised forms and is authorised to make binding decisions, firmly places planning officers as Bauman's legislators whose 'authority to arbitrate is … legitimated by superior (objective) knowledge' (Bauman, 1987: 4). Legislators follow universal procedural rules which assure the attainment of truth and the arrival at valid moral judgement (Bauman, 1987: 4–5).

Habermas' thinking may well reflect the legalistic German system of a strong state to which he is accustomed, and which may well require juridico-discursive rules or discipline to inhibit strategic action and encourage communicative rationality. Mouffe (2002), however, suggests that the juridical terrain becomes privileged predominantly due to the growing impossibility of envisaging societal problems in a political way and the lack of a democratic political public sphere where agonistic confrontation can take place. She accuses Habermas of conflating politics with morality, understood in rationalist and universal terms, and complains that he ignores the ineradicable dimension of antagonism which is the lack between reality and the Lacanian Real.

Whilst agreeing with Mouffe about the impossibility of finding rational, impartial solutions to political issues, I still suggest that there may be potential avenues of transformation, transgression and possibility in much of the Western world for planning officers to work within the system (see Chapter 10) to become interpreters rather than legislators. Interpreters, according to Bauman (1987), translate statements between communally based traditions so that they can be understood by all stakeholders. Interpreters facilitate communication between the actors involved. There are no clearcut rules of interpretation (Bauman, 1993).

Interpreters maintain a great deal of power or influence nevertheless. As demonstrated by the practitioners in Chapter 10, they can act to shape attention/a tension and expectations in several ways. In the final analysis, however, people must be convinced that there are good reasons for the recommended outcome. One of the ways of convincing them is to ensure that recommendation and decision processes are procedurally just (see Chapter 4).

FORMAL AND INFORMAL PROCESSES

'Planning is a political means from which [actors] will be tempted to withdraw, covertly or openly, whenever there is a better way of pursuing their advantage' (Marris, 1987: 65–6). Frustrated individuals and groups opt out of formal processes as we saw in the North East Corridor example in Western Australia (Chapter 6) and try other means of lobbying, etc. to get what they want through less formal channels. Other groups (such as the Australian Conservation Foundation in the Regional Forest Agreement debate, Chapter 7) calculate the risks of informal action against the potential costs of joining a formal process which they perceive that they would not 'win' and in which their integrity may be compromised. By being party to such a formal process, the group would legitimate that process and its outcomes. Even though the process and the outcomes may be potentially flawed, the participation of the group would lend them validity, possibly to its own discredit. A refusal to partic-ipate can thus be a strategy of self-preservation. By retaining its integrity the group reserves its potential to lobby and engage the media from a position of strength on the outside of a demonstrably flawed process.

We can learn much about informal ways of working from indigenous communi-ties. In Australia, tension and conflict within indigenous communities is contained by strong habitus. In addition, a multiplicity of social contexts provides 'innumerable opportunities to argue about social context, social responsibility and social action' (Rose, 1999: 180). Agreements tend to be reached informally and ratified by a for-mal gathering.

Indigenous people/s occasionally become involved in debate with non-indige-nous communities (planners, developers and so on) about issues over which there are deep-rooted core differences of opinion and for which there is little possibility of reaching consensus. In such circumstances they may engage in a transaction of ignorance, negotiating a compromise in order to achieve a necessary outcome. This is Hegelian reconciliation: 'a humble consent that "all is *not* rational", that the moment of contingent antagonism is irreducible, that notional Necessity itself hangs on and is "embedded" in an encompassing contingency' (Zizek, 1991: 169).

Practical reason thus encompasses a set of interconnected 'reasons', rang-ing from Habermasian communicative argument achieving consensus to compromise agreements reached through negotiated transaction or bargaining. Some of these 'reasonable' conversations will take place in formal arenas, but many of them will not.

In *Between Facts and Norms* (1996), Habermas writes about the public sphere as being a type of communication structure based in the multiplicity of overlapping communicative and associational networks of society. This repre-sents something of a shift for Habermas, in which he acknowledges that political participation can be effective outside of institutionalised politics. The public sphere has become, for Habermas, a dialogical space rather than an institution or a system – a 'social phenomenon' (1996: 360). Public spheres may emerge in simple, episodic encounters between social actors, becoming more complex the more encounters expand to constitute larger networks of communication within and between associations and other actors (Rättilä, 2000).

Habermas (1996) describes political public spheres as embodying processes of informal opinion formation uncoupled from decision-making institutions and operating in an inclusive but unstructured network of overlapping public spheres. As such they play an important mediation role between civil society and the administrative power of the procedurally regulated public sphere of public sector decision-making. Informal public opinions act as a 'signal' of problems and issues to be addressed by agencies of governance.

As Rättilä (2000: 49) points out, however, Habermas is realistic enough to suggest that the existence and possibility of public spheres do not guarantee democratic decisions. An open public sphere does not necessarily imply an egalitarian or impartial sphere. Habermas deals with this issue by distinguishing between the informal, or weak public, and the formal deliberations of decision-making institutions, and proposing that democratic systems need both levels of deliberation. He thus works within the existing system of Western representative liberal democracy rather than seeking to alter or replace it.

As demonstrated in Chapter 9, however, representative democracy may be anything but formal, procedurally just and impartial. Local authority planning committee meetings include elements of the relatively unregulated, disparate communication characteristic of Habermas' weak public. The difference is that outcomes are formalised. This offers a new 'take' on rationality. Rather than being a quality of an actor (their capacity to think rationally and offer good reasons in public debate), rationality might be regarded more generally as discursive deliberation. It thus allows different ways of voicing and performing representations and opinions and opens up theory to be inclusive of wider participatory activities such as lobbying. Habermas himself implies the extension of communicative action to include more than merely rational argumentation when he writes that the public sphere includes the 'dramatisation' of problems 'in such a way that they are 'taken up and dealt with by parliamentary complexes' (1996: 359).

Yet even Habermas' revised theory still says little about how different 'democratic' struggles challenge prevailing institutions, norms and relations of power in practice. Neither does he really come to terms with issues of core deep-rooted differences (or 'matters of the heart' (Williams, 2001)) and resulting antagonistic or agonistic conflicts. It is these gaps which I attempt to fill in this book.

Planning praxis needs to consider valuing and perhaps even initiating localised, informal acts, whilst preventing them from collapsing into predominantly regulatory and conservatising processes (Kunnen, 2001). Kunnen's work emphasises the role of both informal, incremental processes, such as an open, welcoming 'presence' in the community which could facilitate numerous opportunities for informal 'on-site' discussions of issues, and also of 'resistant relationships' (2000) whereby practitioners develop and maintain relationships with community members. In such manners, Kunnen argues that practitioners may be able to represent 'the experience of powerlessness' (2000: 11) in advocating the voices of the marginalised in a practice climate shaped by managerialist discourses which emphasise performance-based tangible outcomes and efficiencies.

Blanc (1995) also proposes a similar role for a '*passeur*' or 'smuggler'[2] who would negotiate on behalf of local people (or aspects of nature?). Isaac and Kissmann (1998) cite the example of Albuquerque's city planners in New Mexico, USA, who act in various ways, as community advocates, as 'brokers' between the community and the bureaucracy, as 'introducers' between different sectors of the community, and as political operatives. Adapting their style to their audience, they incorporate multiple voices and are able to 'speak' with greater effect.

Advocacy and relational networks 'go hand in hand in successful negotiation, and you establish the terms of both in the shadow negotiation' (Kolb and Williams, 2000: 22). Working in the shadows of power could thereby enable practitioners to build relationships across differences, to establish credibility for the representations, values and ideas of the traditionally marginalised and to lay the groundwork for building mutual respect. However, mutual respect does not necessarily mean building consensus. Mutual respect can help domesticate antagonism to agonism in which participants recognise the boundaries of what is and is not possible. 'Advocacy establishes your place at the table, but it also defines the limits you set' (Kolb and Williams, 2000: 250). If the power of advocacy lies in promoting one's interests effectively as these authors suggest, informal shadow negotiations are important in defining, interpreting and recasting issues under consideration. Relationships are not static. They can be confronted, resisted and modified by strategic acts by, or on behalf of, various stakeholders.

Advocacy is not without its problems, however. It has the potential to be both liberatory for those whose point is advocated, but also regulatory, in that it becomes a 'professional tool'. Planning practitioners who act as 'social ventriloquists' or 'pantomime proletarians' (Beilharz, 2000: 84) for others, can never represent the others' views faithfully even if they wish to do so.[3]

In addition, some practitioners face an 'insider/outsider' dilemma. They are inevitably 'insiders' to the planning system, occupying a particular structural location in the system and possibly having a particular 'angle of vision' or habitus. They are most probably 'outsiders' to the group for whom they are advocating, unable to be bodily embedded in the situation or to fully comprehend the issues involved. Some practitioners will wish to and/or be able to empathise with such groups more than will other practitioners. Additionally, to what extent would advocates be prepared to 'go the extra mile' for their groups? As 'public servants' they are statutorily unable to engage in media strategies and dramatic tactics of civil disobedience to affect popular opinion.

Advocacy, therefore, will always fail to fulfil the promise of inclusive participation. It may, however, be worth exploring in situations where individuals and groups are unable or unwilling to formally represent themselves, especially if advocacy enables making connections between ideas and people who would not otherwise be connected. What do Kunnen's resistant relationships, translating between Habermas' weak and strong publics, offer my deliberative theory? Their emphasis on the informal fits well with a Lacanian understanding of agonism. As one of Kunnen's respondents states, 'there's also the view ... that if something's real, it's got to be formal, and if it's not formal it's not real' (Kunnen, 2001). Is the Real informal?

Whether the unapproachable Real and its ineradicable chaos can be approximated by a looser, more relational, participatory way of working, as exemplified by MacCallum (2000, 2001), is yet to be demonstrated.

PROCESS, OUTCOME, STRUCTURE OR AGENCY

This book has focused on procedural aspects of local land-use planning decision-making in reflection of my belief that with greater understanding of activities taking place, planning practitioners may be more able to work towards what they regard as good planning outcomes. However, practitioners need to pay attention to both the how and the what of their decisions. Concentration on process may lose sight of the outcome. As Ife (1995: 192) suggests, an obsession with process can ignore the structural context and/or the wider implications of a decision. It is important, therefore, to locate processes in their wider structural contexts. Although I have not had the space to do so in this book for my practice stories, it is recognition of this need for contextualisation which is one of the main strengths which a Bourdieuian emphasis on the habitus brings to my theory.

Communicating honestly and building 'consensus' are insufficient to change the world without cognisance of the structural context in which the debate is located. Procedural ethics and consensus do not necessarily equate to a good planning outcome from a technical point of view. As one of my practitioner respondents commented in Chapter 9, 'democracy suggests that the best technical advice in the world is the wrong decision if elected representatives vote against it'.

To what extent should 'the people have a right to act wrongly' (Walzer, 1981: 385), or should public opinion be overruled? What if 'the public got it wrong' as an ex-Planning Minister announced in Western Australia? As Nelson (2000: 184) tellingly says, 'one can have the right principles, but not have a right to legislate them; and one can have the right to legislate, but exercise it wrongly'.

These are questions of power – the power to decide. Planning practice calls for decisions and therefore the establishment of an (explicit or implicit) hierarchy among representations and values. Planning, located within a liberal democratic regime in most Western nation-states, cannot equate all values, since liberal democracy's very existence as a form of society requires a specific ordering of values which precludes total pluralism. Planning is always a case of 'undecidable undecided' as Mouffe (1993) terms it, unable to exist without excluding some values, which remain as the 'constitutive outside'.

The process–outcome debate may turn into a largely barren debate between 'idealists' (such as Healey, Forester and others who sometimes regard process as being as important as outcomes) and 'realists' (such as Yiftachel, Huxley and others who regard planning outcomes of spatial distributions of material and symbolic resources to be more important than process).[4]

They are both important. The point is not that we should cease to judge between process and outcome, but that the provisionality of judgement be recognised. Practitioners must decide for themselves. Perhaps this is what Forester (1999: 236) implies by moral improvisation when he writes about the 'basic obligations of public-serving planning' and how 'good moral improvisers must respond to both overlapping goals and mandates, norms and obligations, and *also* to the uniquely significant particulars and details that make each case what it distinctively is' (1999: 225, emphasis in original). If so, I agree.

I shy away from questions of what is 'good' planning as every planning practitioner, property developer and member of the public will have different answers according to differing circumstances. Again, I leave the question for practitioners themselves to decide. I offer, instead, what I hope is an explanatory framework which will assist planners in making sense of their worlds so that they can act or improvise accordingly.

I am drawn to Bauman's (1987: 143) concept of the interpreter who engages in 'civilised conversation' with stakeholders whose values may be in permanent conflict. Decisions are aporetic: undecidable choices made between contradictory values, raising questions and exclusions, without necessarily providing answers. Planning practitioners are often forced to make political trade-offs, to seek settlements of compromise rather than resolutions of consensus in a world where 'interests and identities preclude attainment of the urban imaginary' (Body-Gendrot and Beauregard, 1999: 17).

Yiftachel and Huxley (2000) also emphasise that although theorists may evoke the need to repoliticise decision-making by opening up processes to be inclusive of all stakeholders, they tend to ignore the role of market relations and global capitalism which increasingly imposes itself as the fantasmatic Real accepted by all parties. Zizek (1999: 353) bemoans the 'radical depoliticisation of the sphere of the economy' and calls for its repoliticisation. I am in agreement with his statement that

> as long as this fundamental depoliticisation of the economic sphere is accepted, all the talk about active citizenship, about public discussion leading to responsible collective decisions, and so on, will remain limited to the 'cultural' issues of religious, sexual, ethnic and other way-of-life differences, without actually encroaching upon the level at which long-term decisions that affect us all are made (1999: 353).

Agency needs to be cognisant of the effects of structure and, where necessary, question and challenge the very basics of its anonymous logic.

CONCLUSIONS

> Shadow meaning identity. Shadow meaning substance (Le Carré, 1993: 129).

> Shadows will smile (Mexican saying, Subcomandante Insurgente Marcos, 2001).

I began this book with the Mexican proverbial expression 'in the shadow of power', suggesting that the power and power-plays with which planning practitioners are engaged are subtle, often hidden transcripts, working informally rather than through formal planning decision-making processes. Through the various chapters I have attempted to give the shadows of power some substance and identity so that practitioners may be able to better understand the circumstances in which they find themselves and may be able to act more prudently in what is in reality a messy, highly politicised planning decision-making practice.

I hope to have contributed in some small part to filling a gap in theory which tended to ascribe a practical role for planners abstracting them from a contextual understanding of power, discourse and habitus. In this regard I have attempted to clarify the potential contributions of Jürgen Habermas and Michel Foucault to planning theory and practice, developing in Part 2 a simplistic model of discursive planning. Grounded in practice stories, I then went on to integrate a theoretical appreciation of communication, representation and interpretation with practical planning and to introduce the relevance of Pierre Bourdieu's concept of the habitus for understanding practice. I examined what is involved, in effect, in seeing participatory democratic practices as comprising a habitus of local planning decision-making praxis.

Addition of agonism as a political advancement over the essentially moral nature of consensus brought with it a Lacanian understanding of the ineradicable and unreachable chaos of the Real. I set aside 'the dangerous dream of a perfect consensus, of a homogeneous collective will, and [attempt] the permanence of conflict and antagonism' (Mouffe, 1996: 20). Yet this is not to espouse a reductive acceptance of the way things are instead of working towards the way things might be, which is, after all, the very *raison d'être* of planning. My theory of planning practice thus grapples with performative and relational uncertainty, change and conflict. Planning practice is often a liminal space of shadow negotiations which act to settle rather than to resolve issues.

I have engaged a metaphor of chiaroscuro as a device for reading the book. The 'background' is constructed vertically, read from theory to practice and from practice to theory. As in art, tenebrism and sfumato add depth and movement to the narrative pictures. I offer no templates or blueprints. Instead, I counsel prudence, a deciphering of the shadows cast before potential 'coming events', an anticipation of what might transpire and the improvisation of practical wisdom. In this manner I hope to have provided a foundation for planning practitioners to act effectively in the shadows of power.

BIBLIOGRAPHY

Abram, S. (1998) 'Planning as metaphor', unpublished paper presented at Oxford Planning Theory Conference, Oxford: Oxford Brookes University, April.

Abram, S. (2000) 'Planning the public: some comments on empirical problems for planning theory', *Journal of Planning Education and Research*, 19: 351–7.

Agger, B. (1991) *A Critical Theory of Public Life*, London: Falmer Press.

Albrechts, L. (1997) 'The difficult art of getting public support', unpublished paper presented at ACSP congress, Fort Lauderdale.

Albrechts, L. (1999) 'Planners as catalysts and initiators of change: the new Structure Plan for Flanders', *International Planning Studies*, 7, 5: 587–603.

Albrechts, L. (2001a) 'From traditional land use planning to strategic spatial planning: the case of Flanders', in L. Albrechts, J. Alden, and A. da Rosa Pires, (eds) *The Changing Institutional Landscape of Planning*, Aldershot: Ashgate.

Albrechts, L. (2001b) 'Enhancing public involvement', unpublished paper presented to WPSC, Shanghai.

Albrechts, L. and Denayer, W. (2001) 'Communicative planning, emancipatory politics and postmodernism', in R. Paddison (ed.) *Handbook of Urban Studies*, London: Sage.

Alcoff, L. (1991) 'The problem of speaking for others', *Cultural Critique*, 20, Winter: 5–32.

Alexander, E. (2001) 'The Planner-Prince: interdependence, rationalities and post-communicative practice', *Planning Theory and Practice*, 2, 3: 311–24.

Allen, B. (1998) 'Foucault and modern political philosophies' in J. Moss (ed.) *The Later Foucault*, London: Sage.

Allmendinger, P. (1996) 'Development control and the legitimacy of planning decisions: a comment', *Town Planning Review*, 67, 2: 231.

Allmendinger, P. (1998) 'Planning practice and the post-modern debate', *International Planning Studies*, 3, 2: 227–48.

Allmendinger, P. (1999) 'Beyond collaborative planning', unpublished paper presented at AESOP conference, Bergen.

Allmendinger, P. (2001) *Planning in Postmodern Times*, London: Routledge.

Altshuler, A. (1965) *The City Planning Process*, Ithaca: Cornell University Press.

Alvesson, M. and Sköldberg, K. (2000) *Reflexive Methodology*, London: Sage.

Amin, A. (1996) 'Beyond associative democracy', *New Political Economy*, 1, 3: 309–33.

Amin, A. and Graham, S. (1997) 'The ordinary city', *Transactions of the Institute of British Geographers*, 22: 411–29.

Amin, A, and Hausner, J. (1997) 'Interactive governance and social complexity', in A. Amin and J. Hausner (eds) *Beyond Market and Hierarchy*, Cheltenham: Edward Elgar.

Amin, A. and Thrift, N. (1995a) 'Globalisation, institutional "thickness" and the local economy', in P. Healey, S. Cameron, S. Davoudi and S. Graham (eds) *Managing Cities*, Chichester: Wiley.

Amin, A. and Thrift, N. (1995b) 'Institutional issues for the European regions: from markets and plans to socioeconomics and powers of association', *Economy and Society*, 24, 1: 41–66.

Anon (1998a) 'Forest protest says "save our jobs"', *Fremantle Gazette*, 3 July: 3.

Anon (1998b) 'Terrace phone jammers suited to eco-protest', *The West Australian*, 9 December: 11.

Applbaum, A. (2000) 'Democratic legitimacy and official discretion', in P. Rynard and D. Shugarman (eds) *Cruelty and Deception*, New York: Broadview.

Arendt, H. (1958) *The Human Condition*, Chicago: Chicago Press.

Arendt, H. (1963) *On Revolution*, New York: Viking Press.

Arendt, H. (1968a) *Between Past and Future*, New York: Viking Press.

Arendt, H. (1968b) *Men in Dark Times*, New York: Harcourt, Brace, Jovanovich.

Arendt, H. (1995a) *The Origins of Totalitarianism* (original 1951), New York: Harcourt, Brace and Co.

Arendt, H. (1995b) 'Philosophy and politics', *Social Research*, 57, 1: 73–103.

Armstrong, G. (1999) Timber workers take fight to the city, *The West Australian*, 10 August: 24

Arpaly, N. (2000) 'On acting rationally against one's best judgement', *Ethics*, 110: 488–513.

Ashenden, S. and Owen, D. (eds) (1999) *Foucault contra Habermas: Recasting the Dialogue between Genealogy and Critical Theory*, Thousand Oaks: Sage.

Atkinson, M, and Coleman, W. (1992) 'Policy networks, policy communities and the problems of governance', *Governance*, 5, 2: 154–80.

Australian Bureau of Statistics (2000) *Corrective Services, Australia, December quarter 1999*, catalogue no. 4512. 0, Canberra: ABS.

Axford, B. (2001) 'The transformation of politics or anti-politics?', in B. Axford and R. Huggins (eds) *New Media and Politics*, London: Sage.

Bader, V. (2001) 'Problems and prospects of associative demorcracy: Cohen and Rogers revisited', *Critical review of International Social and Political Philosophy*, 4, 1: 31–70.

Badiou, A. (1988) *L'Être et l'événement*, Paris: Éditions de Seuil.

Bagnasco, A. and Le Gales, P. (eds) (2000) *Cities in Contemporary Europe*, Cambridge, Cambridge University Press.

Baird, V. (2001) 'Building institutional legitimacy: the role of procedural justice', *Political Research Quarterly*, 54, 2: 333–46.

Bang, H. and Dyrberg, T. (2000) 'Governance, self-representation and democratic imagination', in M. Saward (ed.) *Democratic Innovation – Deliberation, Representation and Association*, London: Routledge.

Barber, B. (1984). *Strong Democracy*, Berkeley: University of California Press.

Barker, C. (1999) 'Empowerment and resistance: "collective effervescence" and other accounts', in P. Bagguley and J. Hearn (eds) *Transforming Politics*, Basingstoke: Macmillan.

Barrett, M. (1991) *The Politics of Truth*. Cambridge: Polity Press.

Barry, A., Osborne, T. and Rose, N. (eds) (1996) *Foucault and Political Reason,* London: UCL Press.

Baum, H. (1997) *The Organisation of Hope*, Albany, State University of New York Press.

Baum, H. (1999) 'Forgetting to plan', *Journal of Planning Education and Research*, 19: 2–14.

Bauman, Z. (1987) *Legislators and interpreters: on modernity, post-modernity and intellectuals*, Cambridge: Polity Press.

Bauman, Z. (1991) *Modernity and Ambivalence*, Cambridge: Polity Press.

Bauman, Z. (1992) *Intimations of Postmodernity*, London: Routledge.

Bauman, Z. (1993) *Postmodern Ethics*, Oxford: Blackwell.

Bauman, Z. (1997) *Postmodernity and its Discontents*, Cambridge: Polity Press.

Bauman, Z. (1999) *In Search of Politics*, Cambridge: Polity Press.

Bauman, Z. (2000) *Liquid Modernity*, Cambridge: Polity Press.

Baxter, R. (1972) 'The working class and Labour politics', *Political Studies*, 20: 92–107.

Baynes, K. (1995) 'Democracy and the Rechtsstaat: Habermas *Faktizität und Geltung*', in S. White (ed.) *The Cambridge Companion to Habermas*, Cambridge: Cambridge University Press.

Beauregard, R. (1989) 'Between modernity and postmodernity: the ambiguous position of US planning', *Environment and Planning D: Society and Space*, 7: 381–95.

Beck, U. (1992) *Risk Society: Towards a New Modernity*, London: Sage.

Beck, U. (1994) *Ecological Politics in the Age of Risk*, Cambridge: Polity Press.

Beetham, D. (1991) *The Legitimation of Power*, Basingstoke: Macmillan.

Beilharz, P. (2000) *Zygmunt Bauman: Dialectic of Modernity*, London: Sage.

Beiner, R. (1999) *Philosophy in a Time of Lost Spirit*, Toronto: University of Toronto Press.

Benhabib, S. (1990a) 'Communicative ethics and current controversies in practical philosophies', in S. Benhabib and F. Dallmayr (eds) *The Communicative Ethics Controversy*, Cambridge: MIT Press.

Benhabib, S. (1990b) 'Afterward', in S. Benhabib and F. Dallmayr (eds) The *Communicative Ethics Controversy*, Cambridge: MIT Press.

Benhabib, S. (1990c) 'In the shadow of Aristotle and Hegel: communicative ethics and current controversies in practical philosophy', in M. Kelly (ed.) *Hermeneutics and Critical Theory in Ethics and Politics*, Cambridge: MIT Press.

Benhabib, S. (1992a) *Situating the Self*, Cambridge, Polity Press.

Benhabib,S. (1992b) 'Models of public space: Hannah Arendt, the liberal tradition and Jurgen Habermas', in C. Calhoun (ed.) *Habermas and the Public Sphere*, Cambridge: MIT Press.

Benhabib, S. (1996a) 'Toward a deliberative model of democratic legitimacy', in S. Benhabib (ed.) *Democracy and Difference*, Princeton: Princeton University Press.

Benhabib, S. (1996b) *The Reluctant Modernism of Hannah Arendt*, Newbury Park: Sage.

Bernauer, J. and Rasmussen, J. (1988) *The Final Foucault*, Cambridge: MIT Press.

Bernstein, R. (1983) *Beyond Objectivism and Relativism*, Philadelphia: University of Pennsylvania Press.

Bernstein, R. (1991) *The New Constellation*, Cambridge: Polity Press.

Bernstein, R. (1992) 'Foucault: critique as a philosophical ethos', in A. Honneth, T. McCarthy, C. Offe and A. Wellmer (eds) *Philosophical Interventions in the Unfinished Project of Enlightenment*, Cambridge: MIT Press.

Berry, J. (1989) 'Subgovernments, issue networks and political conflict', in R. Harris and S. Milkis (eds) *Remaking American Politics*, Boulder: Westview Press.

Berry, J., Portney, K. and Thompson, K. (1993) *The Rebirth of Urban Democracy*, Washington, DC: Brookings Institution.

Best, S. and Kellner, D. (1991) *Postmodern Theory: Critical Interrogations*, London: Macmillan.

Bhaskar, R. (1979) *The Possibility of Naturalism*, Brighton: Harvester.

Blanc, M. (1995) 'Politique de la ville et démocratie locale', *Les Annales de la Recherche Urbaine*, No. 68–9: 99–106.

Bloomfield, D., Collins, K., Fry, C. and Munton, R. (2001) 'Deliberation and inclusion: vehicles for increasing trust in UK public governance', *Environment and Planning C, Government and Policy*, 39: 501–13.

Blowers, A. (1980) *The Limits of Power*, Oxford: Pergamon.

Body-Gendrot, S. and Beauregard, R. (1999) 'Imagined cities, engaged citizens', in R. Beauregard and S. Body-Gendrot (eds) *The Urban Moment*, Thousand Oaks: Sage.

Boer, B., Craig, D., Handmer, J. and Ross, H. (1991) *The Use of Mediation in the Resource Assessment Commission Enquiry Process*, Canberra: RAC, AGPS.

Boggs, C. (1986) *Social Movements and Political Power*, Philadelphia: Temple University Press.

Bohman, J. (1999) 'Habermas, Marxism and social theory: the case for pluralism in critical social science', in P. Dews (ed.) *Habermas: A Critical Reader*, Oxford: Blackwell.

Bohman, J. (2000) 'Distorted communication: formal pragmatics as a critical theory', in L. Hahn (ed.) *Perspectives on Habermas*, Chicago: Open Court.

Bohman, J. and Rehg, W. (1997) 'Introduction', in J. Bohman and W. Rehg (eds) *Deliberative Democracy*, Cambridge: MIT Press.

Bouchard, D. (1977) *Michel Foucault: Language, Counter-Memory, Practice*, Oxford: Blackwell.

Boulding, K. (1989) *Three Faces of Power*, London: Sage.

Bourdieu, P. (1977) *Outline of a Theory of Practice*, Cambridge: Cambridge University Press.

Bourdieu, P. (1984) *Distinction*, Cambridge: Harvard University Press.

Bourdieu, P. (1987) *Choses Dites*, Paris: Editions de Minuit.

Bourdieu, P. (1989) 'Social space and symbolic power', *Sociological Theory*, 7, 1: 14–25.

Bourdieu, P. (1990a) *In Other Words*, Cambridge: Polity Press.

Bourdieu, P. (1990b) 'Droit et passe-droit. Le champ des pouvoirs territoriaux et la mise en oeuvre des réglements', *Actes de la Recherche en Sciences Sociales*, 81/82: 86–96.

Bourdieu, P. (1990c) *The Logic of Practice* (trans. R. Nice), Stanford: Stanford University Press.

Bourdieu, P. (1993) *The Field of Cultural Production*, Cambridge, Polity Press.

Bourdieu, P. (1996) *The Rules of Art*, Cambridge: Polity Press.

Bourdieu, P. (1998) *Practical Reason*, Cambridge: Polity Press.

Bourdieu, P. (2000) *Pascalian Meditations*, Cambridge: Polity Press.

Bourdieu, P. and Wacquant, L. (1992) *An Invitation to Reflexive Sociology*, Cambridge: Polity Press.

Bouveresse, J. (1999) 'Rules, dispositions and the *Habitus*', in R. Shusterman (ed.) *Bourdieu: A Critical Reader*, Oxford: Blackwell.

Braaten, J. (1991) *Habermas' Critical Theory of Society*, Albany, NY: State University of New York Press.

Briand, M. (1999) *Practical Politics*, Urbana: University of Illinois Press.

Bridge, G. (2001) 'Bourdieu, rational action and the time-space strategy of gentrification', *Transactions of the Institute of British Geographers*, 26: 205–16.

Brittain, J. (1996) 'Direct democracy by the majority can jeopardize the civil rights of minority or other powerless groups', *Annual Survey of American Law*, No. 3: 441–9.

Brockner, J. *et al.* (2001) 'Culture and procedural justice: the influence of power distance on reactions to voice', *Journal of Experimental Social Psychology*, 37: 300–15.

Brown, A. (2000) *On Foucault*, Belmont: Wadsworth.

Bryson, J, and Crosby, B. (1992) *Leadership for the Common Good*, San Francisco: Jossey-Bass.

Buechlers, S. (2000) *Social Movements in Advanced Capitalism*, New York: Oxford University Press.

Bullard, R. (ed.) (1993) *Confronting Environmental Racism: Voices from the Grassroots*, Boston, Mass: South End Press.

Burns, A. (1999a) 'Court RFA backflip will cost 1500 jobs', *The West Australian*, 28 July: 1

Burns, A. (1999b) 'One-third of RFA reserves is not forest', *The West Australian*, 15 July: 3

Burns, A. (1999c) 'Edwardes pledges to correct reserves', *The West Australian*, 16 July: 5

Burns, A. (1999d) 'RFA credibility an endangered species', *The West Australian*, 18 July: 18

Burns, D, and Taylor, M. (1997) *Mutual Aid and Self Help: Coping Strategies for Excluded Communities*, York: Joseph Rowntree Foundation.

Butcher, H., Collis, P., Glen, A. and Sills, P. (1980) *Community Groups in Action*, London: RKP.

Butler, J. (1993) *Bodies that Matter*, London: Routledge.

Butler, J., Laclau, E. and Zizek, S. (2000) *Contingency, Hegemony, Universality*, London: Verso.

Cainzos, M. (1994) 'The actionalist turn in social theory', in P. Sztompka, (ed.) *Agency and Structure*, Amsterdam: Gordon and Breach.

Calhoun, C. (1992a) *Habermas and the Public Sphere*, Cambridge: MIT Press.

Calhoun, C. (1992b) 'Introduction: Habermas and the public sphere', in C. Calhoun (ed.) *Habermas and the Public Sphere*, Cambridge: MIT Press.

Calhoun, C. (1993) '*Habitus*, field and capital: the question of historical specificity', in C. Calhoun, E. Lipuma and M. Postone (eds) *Bourdieu: Critical Perspectives*, Cambridge: Polity Press.

Calhoun, C. (2000) 'Pierre Bourdieu', in G. Ritzer (ed.) *The Blackwell Companion to Major Social Theorists*, Oxford: Blackwell.

Callon, M. (1986) 'Some elements of a sociology of translation'. in J. Law (ed.) *Power, Action, Belief: A New Sociology of Knowledge?* London: RKP.

Callon, M. (1991) 'Techno economic networks and irreversibility', in J. Law (ed.) *A Sociology of Monsters*, London: Routledge.

Callon, M. and Latour, B. (1981) 'Unscrewing the big Leviathan: how actors macro-structure reality and how sociologists help them to do so', in K. Knorr-Cetina and A. Cicourel (eds) *Advances in Social Theory and Methodology*, London: RKP.

Callon, M. and Law, J. (1995) 'Agency and the hybrid collectif', *South Atlantic Quarterly*, 94: 481–507.

CALM (1997) *The Science of the RFA*, Nature Base website online: [http://www.calm.wa.gov.au/forest_facts/rfa_science.html]

CALM (1998a) *Comprehensive Regional Assessments and Regional Forest Agreement for Western Australia*, Vol. 1, Perth: CALM.

CALM (1998b) 'CRA snapshot of industries and people', *News on the RFA*, 6 February, Perth: CALM.

CALM (1998c) 'CRA boost for biodiversity', *News on the RFA*, 6/2/98, Perth: CALM.

CALM (1998d) Towards a Regional Forest Agreement for the Southwest Forest Region of Western Australia: a paper to assist public consultation, Perth: CALM.

CALM (1999a) *Regional Forest Agreement for Western Australia*, Perth: CALM.

CALM (1999b) *Regional Forest Agreement for Western Australia*, media release, 4/5/99, Perth: CALM.

Campbell, H. (2001) 'Planners and politicians: the pivotal planning relationship', *Planning Theory and Practice*, 2, 1: 83–5.

Campbell, H. and Marshall, R. (1998) 'Acting on principle: dilemmas in planning practice', *Planning Practice and Research*, 13, 2: 117–28.

Campbell, H. and Marshall, R. (2002) 'Values and professional identities in planning practice', in P. Allmendinger and M. Tewdwr-Jones (eds) *Planning Futures: New Directions in Planning Theory*, London: Routledge.

Campbell, H. and Marshall, T. (2000) 'Public involvement and planning: looking beyond the one to the many', *International Planning Studies*, 5, 3: 321–44.

Campbell, T. (2001) *Justice*, Basingstoke: Macmillan.

Canel, E. (1992) 'New social movement theory and resource mobilisation: the need for integration', in W. Carroll (ed.) *Organising Dissent*, Victoria: Garamond Press.

Capp G. (1998a) '12,000 letters send a message', *The West Australian*, 1 August: 4.

Capp, G. (1998b) 'Malthouse backed', *The West Australian*, 6 August: 34.

Carlson, C. (1999) 'Convening', in L. Susskind, S. McKearnan and J. Thomas-Larmer (eds) *The Consensus-building Handbook*, Thousand Oaks: Sage.

Castells, M. (1983) *The City and The Grassroots*, Berkeley: University of California Press.

Castells, M. (1996) *The Rise of the Network Society*, Oxford: Blackwell.

Castells, M. (1997) *The Power of Identity*, Oxford: Blackwell.

Castells, M. (1998) *End of Millennium*, Oxford: Blackwell.

Catanese, A. (1974) *Planners and Local Politics*, Beverley Hills: Sage.

Catanese, A. (1978) 'Learning by comparison: lessons from experiences', in A. Catanese and W. Farmer, *Personality, Politics and Planning*, Beverley Hills: Sage.

Catanese, A. (1984) *The Politics of Planning and Development*, Beverley Hills: Sage.

Cater, D. (1964) *Power in Washington*, London: Collins.

Centre for Aboriginal Studies (1991) *Ways of Working*, Perth: CAS, Curtin University.

Chambers, S. (1995) 'Discourse and democratic practices', in S. White (ed.) *The Cambridge Companion to Habermas*, Cambridge: Cambridge University Press.

Chambers, S. (1996) *Reasonable Democracy*, Ithaca: Cornell University Press.

Chouliarki, L. and Fairclough, N. (1999) *Discourse in Late Modernity*, Edinburgh: Edinburgh University Press.

Chowcat, I. (2000) 'Moral pluralism, political justification and deliberative democracy', *Political Studies*, 48: 745–58.

Clare, A. (2000) 'Language and disclosure: Habermas and the struggle for reason' in P. Corcoran and V. Spencer (eds) *Disclosures*, Aldershot: Ashgate.

Clavel, P., Forester, J. and Goldsmith, W. (eds) (1980) *Urban and Regional Planning in an Age of Austerity*, New York: Pergamon.

Clegg, S. and Hardy, C. (1996) 'Conclusion: representations', in S. Clegg, C. Hardy and W. Nord (eds) *Handbook of Organisation Studies*, London: Sage.

Cline-Cole, R. (1998) 'Knowledge-claims and landscape: alternative views of the fuel-wood-degradation nexus in northern Nigeria', *Environment & Planning D, Society & Space*, 16: 311–346.

Code, L. (1995) *Rhetorical Spaces*, New York: Routledge.

Cohen, J. (1999) 'Does voluntary association make democracy work?' in N. Smelser and J. Alexander (eds) *Diversity and its Discontents*, Princeton: Princeton University Press.

Cohen, J. and Arato, A. (1992) *Civil Society and Political Theory*, Cambridge: MIT Press.

Cohen, J. and Rogers, J. (1995) 'Secondary associations and democratic governance', in E. Wright (ed.) *Associations and Democracy*, London: Verso.

Coles, A. (1995) 'Introduction', in A. Coles and R. Bentley (eds) *Ex-Cavating Modernism*, London: Black Dog Press.

Commonwealth of Australia (1992) *National Forest Policy Statement*, Canberra: AGPS.

Commonwealth of Australia (1997) *Regional Forest Agreements: the Commonwealth Position*, Canberra: AGPS

Conger, J. (1998) 'The necessary art of persuasion', *Harvard Business Review*, 76, 3: 84–95.

Connolly, W. (1987) *Politics and Ambiguity*, Madison: University of Wisconsin Press.

Connolly, W. (1991) *Identity/Difference*, Ithaca: Cornell University Press.

Connolly, W. (1998) 'Beyond good and evil: the ethical sensibility of Michel Foucault', in J. Moss (ed.) *The Later Foucault*, London: Sage.

Conservation Commission (WA) (2001) *Forest Management*, online: [http://www.conservation.wa.gov.au].

Cook, A. and Sarkissian, W. (2000) 'Who cares? Australian planners and ethics', in P. Bishop and N. Preston (eds) *Local Government, Public Enterprise and Ethics*, Sydney: The Federation Press.

Cook, D. (2001) 'The two faces of liberal democracy in Habermas', *Philosophy Today*, 45, 1: 95–104.

Cox, E. (1995) *A Truly Civil Society*, Sydney: ABC.

Cracknell, J. (1993) 'Issue arenas, pressure groups and environmental agendas', in A. Hansen (ed.) *The Mass Media and Environmental Issues*, Leicester: Leicester University Press.

Crang, M. and Thrift, N. (eds) (2000) *Thinking Space*, London: Routledge.

Crawford, F. (1990) *Jalinardi Ways: whitefellas working in Aboriginal communities*, Perth: Centre for Aboriginal Studies, Curtin University.

Cruikshank, B. (1994) 'The will to empower: technologies of citizenship and the war on poverty', *Socialist Review*, 23, 4: 29–55.

Dahl, R. (1957) 'The concept of power', *Behavioural Science*, 2: 201–15.

Dalton, R. (1988) *Citizen Politics in Western Democracies*, Chatham, NJ: Chatham House.

Dalton, T. (1996) 'Participation: influencing policy in troubled times', in A. Farrar and J. Inglis (eds) *Keeping it Together*, Sydney: Pluto Press.

Davies, J-G. (1972) *The Evangelistic Bureaucrat*, London: Tavistock.

Davis, K. (1988) *Power under the Microscope*, Dordrecht: Foris.

Dean, J. (2001) 'Publicity's secret', *Political Theory*, 29, 5: 624–50.

Dean, M. (1999) *Governmentality*, London: Sage.

Debord, G. (1994) *The Society of the Spectacle*, New York: Zone Books.

Deetz, S. (1992) 'Disciplinary power in the modern corporation', in M. Alvesson and H. Willmott (eds) *Critical Management Studies*, London: Sage.

Deleuze, G. (1986) *Foucault*, Paris: Editions de Minuit.

Denzin, N. (1989) *Interpretive Interactionism*, Newbury Park: Sage.

Department of Local Government (WA) (1999) *Report of the Inquiry into Operations and Affairs of the Town of East Fremantle*, Perth: DLG.

Department of Local Government (WA) (2000) *Report of the Inquiry into the City of Cockburn*, Perth: DLG.

Deutsch, M. (1994) 'Constructive conflict resolution: principles, training and research', *Journal of Social Issues*, 50, 1: 13–32.

Dewar, D. (1999) 'Minister victorious on County housing', Planning, 12 February: 1 and 3.

Dewey, J. (1927) *The Public and its Problems*, Denver: Alan Swallow.

Dews, P. (1986) *Habermas, Autonomy and Solidarity*, London: Verso.

Dews, P. (1999) *Habermas: A Critical Reader*, Oxford: Blackwell.

Diamond, E. (1996) 'Introduction', in E. Diamond (ed.) *Performance and Cultural Politics*, London: Routledge.

Dobel, J. P. (1999) *Public Integrity*, Baltimore: Johns Hopkins University Press.

Donovan, M., Drasgow, F. and Munsan, L. (1998) 'The perceptions of fair interpersonal treatment scale', *Journal of Applied Psychology*, 83: 683–92.

Douglas, M. (1987) *How Institutions Think*, London: RKP.

Dreyfus, H. and Rabinow, P. (1986) 'What is maturity? Habermas & Foucault on "What is Enlightenment?"', in D. Hoy (ed.) *Foucault: A Critical Reader*. Oxford: Blackwell.

Driscoll, J., Sykes, R. and Crowley, P. (1998) *Intervenor Funding*, online: [http://www.geography.uoguelph.ca/45_421/group02.htm].

Dryzek, J. (1990) *Discursive Democracy*, Cambridge: Cambridge University Press,

Dryzek, J. (2000) *Deliberative Democracy and Beyond*, Oxford: Oxford University Press.

Dryzek, J. (2001) 'Legitimacy and economy in deliberative democracy', *Political Theory*, 29, 5: 651–69.

Dumm, T. (1988) 'The politics of post-modern aesthetics. Habermas *contra* Foucault', *Political Theory*, 16, 2: 209–28

Dunn, J. (1979) *Western Political Theory in the Face of the Future*, Cambridge, Cambridge University Press.

During, S. (1992) *Foucault and Literature*, New York: Routledge.

Dyrberg, T. (1997) *The Circular Structure of Power*, London: Verso.

Earley, P. and Lind, E. (1987) 'Procedural justice and participation in task selection', *Journal of Personality and Social Psychology*, 52, 6: 1148–60.

Eckersley, R. (1999) 'The discourse ethic and the problem of representing nature', *Environmental Politics*, 8: 24–49.

Economou, N. (1993) 'Accordism and the environment: the RAC and national environmental policy making', *Australian Journal of Political Science*, 28: 399–412.

Edelman, M. (1964) *The Symbolic Uses of Politics*, Urbana: University of Illinois Press.

Eder, K. (1990) 'The rise of counter-culture movements against modernity: nature as a new field of class struggle', *Theory, Culture and Society*, 7: 21–47.

Eder, K. (1996) *The Social Construction of Nature*, London: Sage.

Elster, J. (1983) *Sour Grapes*, Cambridge: Cambridge University Press.

Elster, J. (1998) 'Introduction', in J. Elster (ed.) *Deliberative Democracy,* Cambridge: Cambridge University Press.

Elster. J. (1990) 'Selfishness and altruism', in J. Mansbridge (ed.) *Beyond Self Interest*, Chicago: University of Chicago Press.

Engwicht, D. (1992) *Towards an Eco-city*, Sydney: Envirobooks.

Environment Forest Taskforce, (1997) *Information Sheet No. 1*, May 1997, Canberra: Environment Australia.

Etzioni, A. (1996) 'The responsive community: a communitarian perspective', *American Sociological Review*, 61: 1–11.

Ewald, F. (1992) 'A power without an exterior', in T. Armstrong (ed.). *Michel Foucault, Philosopher*, New York: Routledge.

Eyerman, R, and Jamison, A. (1991) *Social Movements*, Cambridge: Polity Press.

Fainstein, S. and Hirst, C. (1995) 'Urban social movements', in D. Judge, G. Stoker and H. Wolman (eds) *Theories of Urban Politics*, London: Sage.

Fenger, M. and Klok, P. J. (2001) 'Interdependency, beliefs, and coalition behaviour: a contribution to the advocacy coalition framework', *Policy Sciences*, 34: 157–70.

Finer, H. (1941) 'Administrative responsibility in democratic government', *Public Administration Review*, 1: 335–50.

Fiorina, M. (1999) 'Extreme voices: a dark side of civic engagement', in T. Skocpol and
    M. Fiorina (eds) *Civic Engagement in American Democracy*, Washington, DC:
    Brookings Institute.

Fischer, F. (1993) 'Citizen participation and the democratisation of policy expertise: from
    theoretical inquiry to practical cases', *Policy Sciences*, 26: 165–87.

Fischer, F. (2000) *Citizens, Experts and the Environment*, London: Duke University Press.

Fischler, R. (2000) 'Communicative planning theory: a Foucauldian assessment', *Journal
    of Planning Education and Research*, 19: 358–68.

Fisher, R. (1994) 'Generic principles for resolving intergroup conflict', *Journal of Social
    Issues*. 50, 1: 47–66.

Fishkin, J. (1992) *The Dialogue of Justice*, New Haven: Yale University Press.

Flax, J. (1992) 'Beyond equality: gender, justice and difference', in G. Bock and S. James
    (eds) *Beyond Equality and Difference*, London: Routledge.

Flyvbjerg, B. (1993) 'Aristotle, Foucault and progressive phronesis: outline of an applied
    ethics for sustainable development', in E. Winkler and J. Coombs (eds) *Applied
    Ethics: A Reader*, New York: Blackwell.

Flyvbjerg, B. (1998a) *Rationality and Power*, Chicago: University of Chicago Press.

Flyvbjerg, B. (1998b) 'Empowering Civil Society: Habermas, Foucault and the question
    of conflict', in M. Douglass. and J. Friedmann (eds) *Cities for Citizens*, Chichester:
    Wiley.

Flyvbjerg, B. (2001) *Making Social Science Matter*, Cambridge: Cambridge University
    Press.

Flyvbjerg, B. and Richardson, T. (1998) 'In search of the dark side of planning theory',
    paper presented at Planning Theory Conference, Oxford.

Forester, J. (1980) 'Listening: the social policy of everyday life', *Social Praxis*, 7, 3–4:
    219–32.

Forester, J. (1982) 'Planning in the face of power', *Journal of the American Planners
    Association*, Winter: 67–80.

Forester, J. (1989) *Planning in the Face of Power*, Berkeley: University of California
    Press.

Forester, J. (1991) 'Practice stories and the priority of practical judgement', unpublished
    paper presented to ACSP/AESOP conference, Oxford: Oxford Brookes University.

Forester, J. (1992) 'Critical ethnography: on fieldwork in a Habermasian way' in
    M. Alvesson and H. Willmott (eds) *Critical Management Studies*, London: Sage.

Forester, J. (1993a) *Critical Theory, Public Policy and Planning Practice*, Albany: State
    University of New York Press.

Forester, J. (1993b) 'Beyond dialogue to transformative learning: how deliberative rituals
    encourage political judgement in community planning processes', Haifa: Working
    Paper, Centre for Urban and Regional Studies.

Forester, J. (1995) 'Response: toward a critical sociology of policy analysis', *Policy Sciences*, 28: 385–96.

Forester, J. (1998) 'Reflections on the future understanding of planning practice', unpublished paper presented at AESOP Conference, Aveiro, Portugal.

Forester, J. (1999a) *The Deliberative Practitioner*, Cambridge: MIT Press.

Forester, J. (1999b) 'Reflections on the future understanding of planning practice', *International Planning Studies*, 4, 2: 175–93.

Forester, J. (2000a) 'Multicultural planning in deed: lessons from the mediation practice of Shirley Solomon and Larry Sherman', in M. Burayidi (ed.) *Urban Planning in a Multicultural Society*, Westport: Praeger.

Forester, J. (2000b) 'Conservative epistemology, reductive ethics, far too narrow politics: some clarifications in response to Yiftachel and Huxley', *International Journal of Urban and Regional Research*, 24, 4: 914–6.

Forester, J. (2001) 'An instructive case-study hampered by theoretical puzzles: comments on Flyvbjerg's *Rationality and Power*', *International Planning Studies*, 6, 3: 263–70.

Fornero, J. (1999) 'Sleep well, Mr. Court', *The West Australian*, 7 August: 12.

Foucault, M. (1975) *Surveiller et Punir* (trans. Discipline and Punish, 1977) New York: Pantheon.

Foucault, M. (1977a) *Discipline and Punish*, London: Allen Lane.

Foucault, M. (1977b) *Language, Counter-Memory, Practice: Selected Essays and Interviews* (D. Bouchard ed.), Oxford: Blackwell.

Foucault, M. (1980) 'Two lectures' in C. Gordon (ed.) *Power/Knowledge*, Brighton: Harvester.

Foucault, M. (1981) 'Omnes et singulatim: towards a criticism of "political reason"', in M. McMurrin (ed.) *Tanner Lectures on Human Values*, Vol. II, Salt Lake City: University of Utah Press.

Foucault, M. (1982a) 'The subject and power', in H. Dreyfus and P. Rabinow (eds) *Michel Foucault: Beyond Structuralism and Hermeneutics*, Brighton: Harvester.

Foucault, M. (1982b) 'Afterword', in H. Dreyfus and P. Rabinow (eds) *Michel Foucault: Beyond Structuralism and Hermeneutics*, Chicago: University of Chicago Press.

Foucault, M. (1982c) 'On the genealogy of ethics', in H. Dreyfus and P. Rabinow (eds) *Michel Foucault*: Chicago: University of Chicago Press.

Foucault, M. (1983) 'Structuralism and post-structuralism: an interview with Gerard Raulet', *Telos*, 55: 195–211.

Foucault, M. (1984a) 'The ethic of care for the self as a practice of freedom', in J. Bernauer and D. Rasmussen (eds) *The Final Foucault*, Cambridge: MIT Press.

Foucault, M. (1984b) 'What is enlightenment?' in P. Rabinow (ed.) *The Foucault Reader*, New York: Pantheon.

Foucault, M. (1989), *Resume des courses 1970–1982*, Paris: Julliard.

Foucault, M. (1991a) 'Governmentality', in G. Burchell, C. Gordon and P. Miller (eds) *The Foucault Effect*, Chicago: University of Chicago Press.

Foucault, M. (1991b) *Remarks on Marx: Conversations with Duccio Tombadori*, New York: Semiotext(e).

Foucault, M. (1994a) 'The ethics of the concern of the self as a practice of freedom', in P. Rabinow (ed.) *Michel Foucault: Ethics*, The Essential Works, Vol. 1, London: Allen Lane.

Foucault, M. (1994b) 'Le sujet et le pouvoir', *Dits et Ecrits*, 4: 222–43.

Foucault, M./Blanchot, M. (1987) *M. Blanchot: The Thought from Outside*, New York: Zed Books.

Fourny, J-F. (2000) 'Introduction', *SubStance*, 93: 3–6.

Fraser, N. (1981) 'Foucault on modern power: empirical insights and normative confusions', *Praxis International* 1, 3: 272–87

Fraser, N. (1989) *Unruly Practices: Power, Discourse and Gender in Contemporary Social Theory*, Cambridge: Polity Press.

Fraser, N. (1992) 'Rethinking the public sphere: a contribution to the critique of actually existing democracy', in C. Calhoun (ed.) *Habermas and the Public Sphere*, Cambridge: MIT Press.

Fraser, N. (1998) *Unruly Practices,* Minneapolis: University of Minnesota Press.

Freeman, J. L. (1955) *The Political Process,* New York: Random House.

Friedmann, J. (1987) *Planning in the Public Domain from Knowledge to Action*, Princeton: Princeton University Press.

Friedmann, J. (1992) *Empowerment*, Cambridge: Blackwell.

Galston, W. (2000) 'Democracy and value pluralism', *Social Philosophy and Policy*, 17, 1: 255–69.

Gambetta, D. (1998) 'Claro! An essay on discursive machismo', in J. Elster (ed.) *Deliberative Democracy,* Cambridge: Cambridge University Press.

Gamble, A. (2000) *Politics and Fate*, Cambridge: Polity Press.

Game, D. (1991) *Undoing the Social*, Milton Keynes: Open University Press.

Gamson, W. (1992) 'The social psychology of collective action', in A. Morris and C. Mueller (eds) *Frontiers in Social Movement Theory*, New Haven: Yale University Press.

Gamson, W. (1995a) 'Constructing social protest', in H. Johnston and B. Klandermans (eds) *Social Movements and Culture*, London: UCL Press.

Gamson, W. (1995b) *The Strategy of Social Protest*, Homewood, Illinois: Dorse Press.

Gans, H. (1962) *Urban Villagers*, New York: Free Press.

Geertz, C. (1973) 'Thick description: towards an interpretive theory of culture', in C. Geertz, *The Interpretation of Cultures*, New York: Basic Books.

Geertz, C. (1983) *Local Knowledge: Further Essays in Interpretative Anthropology*, New York: Basic Books.

Gelb, J. (1989) *Feminism and Politics: A Comparative Perspective*, Berkeley: University of California Press.

Gibson-Graham, J-K. (1996) *The End of Capitalism (as we knew it)*, Cambridge: Blackwell.

Giddens, A. (1976) *New Rules of Sociological Method*, London: Hutchinson.

Giddens, A. (1977) *Studies in Social and Political Theory*, London: Macmillan.

Giddens, A. (1979) *Central Problems in Social Theory: Action, Structure and Contradiction in Social Analysis*, London: Macmillan.

Giddens, A. (1981) *A Contemporary Critique of Historical Materialism*, London: Macmillan.

Giddens, A. (1984) *The Constitution of Society*, Cambridge: Polity Press.

Giddens, A. (1994) 'Living in a post-traditional society', in U. Beck, A. Giddens and S. Lash *Reflexive Modernisation*, Cambridge: Polity Press, 56–109.

Gilchrist, A. (1995) *Community Development and Networking*, London: Community Development Foundation.

Gilroy, R. and Speak, S. (1998) 'Barriers, boxes and catapults: social exclusion and everyday life', in A. Madanipour, G. Cars, and J. Allen (eds) *Social Exclusion in European Cities*, London: Jessica Kingsley.

Gittell, R. and Vidal, A. (1998) *Community Organising: Building Social Capital as a Development Strategy*, Thousand Oaks: Sage.

Gleeson, B. and Low, N. (2000) *Australian Urban Planning: New Challenges, New Agendas*, Sydney: Allen and Unwin.

Glendinning, I. (2001) 'Who's telling this story?' *The Australian's Review of Books*, March: 11–12.

Goffman, E. (1974) *Frame Analysis: An Essay on the Organisation of Experience*, Cambridge: MIT Press.

Gomez-Pena, G. (1993) *Warrior for Gringostroika*, St Paul: Greyworld Press.

Gordon, C. (1980) Michel Foucault: *Power/knowledge*, Brighton: Harvester, Wheatsheaf.

Gordon, C. (1991) 'Governmental rationality: an introduction', in G. Burchell, C. Gordon and P. Miller (eds) *The Foucault Effect*, Chicago: University of Chicago Press.

Gordon, C. (2000) 'Introduction', in J. Faubion. (ed.) *M. Foucault: Power. Essential Works of Foucault 1954–1984*, Vol. 3, New York: The New Press.

Grabher, G. (2001) 'Locating economic action: projects, networks, localities, institutions', *Environment and Planning A*, 33: 1329–31.

Gray, J. (1995) 'Agonistic liberalism', in E. Paul, F. Miller and J. Paul (eds) *Contemporary Political and Social Philosophy*, Cambridge: Cambridge University Press.

Gregory, D. (1997) 'Lacan and geography: the production of space revisited', in G. Benko, and U. Strohmeyer. (eds) *Space and Social Theory*, Oxford: Blackwell.

Griffith, E. (1939) *The Impasse of Democracy*, New York: Harrison-Hilton.

Gunder, M. (1997) 'Environmental phronesis, hermeneutics and planning education', unpublished paper presented to IAG conference, Sydney.

Gutmann, A. and Thompson, D. (1996) *Democracy and Disagreement*, Cambridge: Harvard University Press.

Gutmann, A. and Thompson, D. (1998) 'Deliberative democracy: the case of bioethics', *Liberal Education*, No. 1, Winter: 10–17.

Gutmann, A. and Thompson, D. (2000) 'Why deliberative democracy is different', *Social Philosophy and Policy*, 17, 1: 161–80.

Gutting, G. (ed.) (1994) *The Cambridge Companion to Foucault*, Cambridge: Cambridge University Press.

Habermas, J. (1970a) 'On systematically distorted communication', *Inquiry*, 13: 205–18

Habermas, J. (1970b) 'Towards a theory of communicative competence', *Inquiry*, 13: 360–75

Habermas, J. (1973a) *Legitimation Crisis*, Boston: Beacon Press

Habermas, J. (1973b) 'Wahrheitstheorien' in J. Habermas *Wirklichkeit und Reflexion: Walter Schulz zum 60*, Berlin: Neske.

Habermas, J. (1974) *Theory of Practice*, Boston: Beacon Press.

Habermas, J. (1976) *Communication and the Evolution of Society*, Cambridge: Polity Press.

Habermas, J. (1977) 'Hannah Arendt's communications concept of power', *Social Research*, 44: 3–25.

Habermas, J. (1979) *Communication and the Evolution of Society* (trans T. McCarthy) Cambridge: MIT Press.

Habermas, J. (1982) 'New Social Movements', *Telos*, 33–7.

Habermas, J. (1983) 'Hannah Arendt and the concept of power', in J. Habermas *Philosophical–Political Profiles*, Cambridge: MIT Press.

Habermas, J. (1984) *The Theory of Communicative Action, Vol. II, Lifeworld and System*, Boston: Beacon Press.

Habermas, J. (1985a) 'A philosophico-political profile', *New Left Review* 151 (May–June): 12.

Habermas, J. (1985b) 'Questions and counterquestions', in R. Bernstein (ed.) *Habermas and Modernity*, Cambridge: MIT Press.

Habermas, J. (1986) *Autonomy and Solidarity*, London: Verso.

Habermas, J. (1987) *The Philosophical Discourse of Modernity*, Cambridge: Polity Press.

Habermas, J. (1990) *Moral Consciousness and Communicative Action*, Cambridge: MIT Press.

Habermas, J. (1991) 'A reply', in A. Honneth and H. Joas (eds) *Communicative Action*, Cambridge: Polity Press.

Habermas, J. (1992) 'Further reflections on the public sphere', in C. Calhoun (ed.) *Habermas and the Public Sphere*, Cambridge, MIT Press.

Habermas, J. (1994) 'Struggles for recognition in the democratic constitutional regime', in A. Gutmann (ed.) *Multiculturalism*, Princeton: Princeton University Press.

Habermas, J. (1996) *Between Facts and Norms*, Cambridge: Polity Press.

Habermas, J. (1998) *The Inclusion of the Other*, Cambridge: Polity Press.

Habermas, J. (2001a) *The Liberating Power of Symbols*, Cambridge: Polity Press.

Habermas, J. (2001b) *The Postnational Constellation*, Cambridge: Polity Press.

Habermas, J. (2001c) 'Why Europe needs a constitution', *New Left Review*, 11 (Sep–Oct): 5–26.

Hajer, M. (1995) *The Politics of Environmental Discourse,* Oxford: Clarendon Press.

Hampshire, S. (1989) *Innocence and Experience*, Cambridge: Harvard University Press.

Hampshire, S. (2000) *Justice is Conflict*, Princeton: Princeton University Press.

Haraway, D. (1991) *Simians, Cyborgs and Women: The Reinvention of Nature*, London: Free Association Books.

Haraway, D. (1992) 'The promises of monsters: a regenerative politics for inappropriate/d others', in L. Grossberg, C. Nelson and P. Treichler (eds), *Cultural Studies*, London: Routledge.

Harvey, D. (1973) *Social Justice and the City*, London: Edward Elgar.

Harvey, D. (1993) 'From space to place and back again: reflections on the condition of postmodernity', in J. Bird, B. Curtis, T. Putnam, G. Robertson and L. Tickner (eds) *Mapping the Futures*, London: Routledge.

Harvey, D. (1996) *Justice, Nature and the Geography of Difference*, Oxford: Blackwell.

Harvey, N. (1996) 'Public involvement in EIA', *Australian Planner*, 33, 10: 39–46.

Hausner, J. (1994) 'Imperative vs interactive strategy of systematic change in Central and Eastern Europe', *Review of International Political Economy*, 1.

Healey, P. (1992a) 'In search of democracy', unpublished paper presented at Planning Techniques and Institutions conference, Palermo, September.

Healey, P. (1992b) 'Planning through debate', *Town Planning Review*, 63, 2: 143–62

Healey, P. (1993) 'Planning through debate', in F. Fischer and J. Forester (eds) *The Argumentative Turn in Policy Analysis and Planning*, London: UCL Press.

Healey, P. (1994) *Strategic Spatial Planning as a Process of Argumentation*, Perth: Curtin University, Centre for Architecture and Planning Research, Occasional Paper 23.

Healey, P. (1996a) 'The communicative turn in planning theory and its implication for spatial strategymaking', *Environment and Planning B, Planning and Design*, 23: 217–34.

Healey, P. (1996b) 'Consensus-building across difficult divisions: new approaches to collaborative strategy making', *Planning Practice and Research*, 11, 2: 207–16.

Healey, P. (1997a) *Collaborative Planning*, Basingstoke: Macmillan.

Healey, P. (1997b) 'An "institutionalist" approach to planning and its implications for "capacity building" within the planning community', unpublished paper presented to AESOP conference, Nijmegen.

Healey, P. (1997c) 'An institutionalist approach to spatial planning', in P. Healey, A. Khakee, A. Motte and B. Needham (eds) *Making Strategic Spatial Plans,* London: UCL Press.

Healey, P. (1997d) 'The revival of strategic spatial planning in Europe', in P. Healey, A. Khakee, A. Motte and B. Needham (eds) *Making Strategic Spatial Plans,* London: UCL Press.

Healey, P. (1998a) 'Building institutional capacities through collaborative approaches to urban planning', *Environment and Planning A*, 30: 1531–46.

Healey, P. (1998b) 'Institutionalist theory, social exclusion and governance', in A. Madanipour, G. Cars and J. Allen (eds) *Social Exclusion in European Cities*, London: Jessica Kingsley.

Healey, P. (1999a) 'Institutionalist analysis, communicative planning and shaping places', *Journal of Planning Education and Research*, 19: 111–21.

Healey, P. (1999b) 'Sites, jobs and portfolios: economic development discourses in the planning system', *Urban Studies*, 36, 1: 27-42.

Healey, P. (2000) 'Planning in relational space and time: responding to new urban realities', in G. Bridge and S. Watson (eds) *A Companion to the City*, Oxford: Blackwell.

Healey, P. (2002) 'Place, identity and governance: transforming discourses and practices', in J. Hillier and E. Rooksby (eds) *Habitus: A Sense of Place*, Aldershot: Ashgate.

Healey, P. and Hillier, J. (1996) 'Communicative micropolitics: a story of claims and discourses', *International Planning Studies*, 1, 2: 165–84.

Healey, P. and Vigar, G. (1996) 'Consensus-building and institutional re-design for regional development', unpublished paper presented to ACSP/AESOP congress, Toronto: Ryerson Polytechnic University.

Healy, K. and Walsh, K. (1997) 'Making participatory processes visible: practice issues in the development of a peer support network', *Australian Social Work*, 50, 3: 45–52.

Heclo, H. (1989) 'The emerging regime', in R. Harris and S. Milkis (eds) *Remaking American Politics*, Boulder: Westview Press, 300–20.

Hillier, J. (1993) 'To boldly go where planners …', *Environment and Planning Digests, Society and Space*, 11: 89–113.

Hillier, J. (1994) 'Discursive democracy in action', in R. Domanski and T. Marszal (eds) *Planning and Socio-Economic Development*, Lodz: Lodz University Press.

Hillier, J. (1995a) 'Planning rituals: rites or wrongs?', unpublished paper presented to AESOP Conference, Glasgow University, August.

Hillier, J. (1995b) 'The unwritten law of planning theory: common sense', *Journal of Planning Education and Research*, 14, 4: 292–6.

Hillier, J. (1996) 'SDC, or how to manipulate the public into a false consensus without really trying' in G. Dixon and D. Aitken (eds) *Institute of Australian Geographers, Conference Proceedings, 1993*, Melbourne: Monash Publications in Geography, No 45.

Hillier, J. (1997a) 'Values, images, identities: cultural influences in public participation', *Geography Research Forum*, 17: 18–36.

Hillier, J. (1997b) 'Going round the back? Complex networks and informal associational action in local planning processes', unpublished paper presented to ACSP conference, Fort Lauderdale, November.

Hillier, J. (1998a) 'Representation, identity and the communicative shaping of place', in A. Light and J. Smith (eds) *The Production of Public Space*, Maryland: Rowman and Littlefield.

Hillier, J. (1998b) 'Beyond confused noise: ideas towards communicative procedural justice', *Journal of Planning Education and Research*, 18: 14–24.

Hillier, J. (1998c) 'Paradise proclaimed? Towards a theoretical understanding of representations of Nature in land use planning decision making', *Ethics, Place and Environment*, 1, 1: 77–91.

Hillier, J. (2000a) 'Going round the back? Complex networks, informal action in local planning processes', *Environment and Planning A*, 34: 33–54.

Hillier, J. (2000b) 'Can't see the trees for the wood', *Planning Theory and Practice*, 1, 1: 59–79.

Hillier, J. (2000c) 'When is a tree not a tree?' unpublished paper presented at the Global Conference on Economic Geography, Singapore: University of Singapore.

Hillier, J. (2001) 'Diabolical images', in IAG Conference Proceedings, Dunedin: University of Otago.

Hillier, J. (2002a) 'Mind the gap', in J. Hillier and E. Rooksby (eds) *Habitus: A Sense of Place*, Aldershot: Ashgate.

Hillier, J. (2002b) 'Direct action and agonism in democratic planning practice', in P. Allmendinger and M. Tewdwr-Jones (eds) *Planning Futures: New Directions for Planning Theory*, London: Routledge.

Hillier, J. and van Looij, T. (1997) 'Who speaks for the poor?' *International Planning Studies*, 2, 1: 7–25.

Hillier, J. and van Looij, T. (1998) 'Spoken from nowhere? Pragmatic planning and the representation of Nature', Perth: Built Environment Research Unit, Curtin University, occasional paper.

Hindess, B. (1996) *Discourses of Power*, Oxford: Blackwell.

Hindess, B. (1997) 'Democracy and disenchantment', *Australian Journal of Political Science*, 32, 1: 79–92.

Hirst, P. (1994) *Associative Democracy*, Cambridge: Polity Press.

Hirst, P. (1997) *From Statism to Pluralism*, London: UCL Press.

Hobsbawm, E. (2001a) Bandits (second edition), London: Abacus.

Hobsbawm, E. (2001b) 'Democracy can be bad for you', *New Statesman*, 14, 646: 25–9.

Hoch, C. (1992) 'The paradox of power in planning practice', *Journal of Planning Education and Research*, 11: 206–15.

Hoch, C. (1994) *What Planners Do*, Chicago, APA.

Hohengarten, W. (1992) 'Translator's introduction', in J. Habermas *Postmetaphysical Thinking: Philosophical Essays*, Cambridge: Polity Press.

Hoggett, P. (1992) *Partisans in an Uncertain World: the Psychoanalysis of Engagement*, London: Free Association Books.

Holland, N. (1986) *Five Readers Reading*, quoted in M. Belenky *et al.*, *Womens' Ways of Knowing: the Development of Self, Voice and Mind*, New York: Basic Books.

Holt-Jensen, A. (2001) 'Pitfalls in communicative planning: the case of Landås township plan in Bergen, Norway', in L. Albrechts, J. Alden and A. da Rosa Pires (eds) *The Changing Institutional Landscape of Planning*, Aldershot: Ashgate.

Honneth, A. (1991) *The Critique of Power*, Cambridge: MIT Press.

Howitt, R. (1992) 'Industrialisation, impact assessment and empowerment', unpublished paper presented to the New Zealand Geographers Society/Australian Institute of Geographers, Auckland.

Howitt, R. (1995) 'SIA, sustainability, and developmentalist narratives of resource regions', *Impact Assessment*, 13, 4: 387-402.

Howitt, R. (2001) 'Frontiers, borders, edges: liminal challenges to the hegemony of exclusion', *Australian Geographical Studies*, 39, 2: 233–45.

Howlett, M, and Ramesh, M. (1995) *Studying Public Policy*, Toronto: Oxford University Press.

Hoy, D. (1986) 'Power, repression, progress: Foucault, Lukes and the Frankfurt School', in D. Hoy (ed.) *Foucault: A Critical Reader*, Oxford: Blackwell.

Hoy, D. and McCarthy, T. (1994) *Critical Theory*, Cambridge: Blackwell.

Hunter, A. and Staggenborg, S. (1988) 'Local communities and organised action', in C. Milofsky (ed.) *Community Organisations*, Oxford: Oxford University Press.

Hunter, T. (1999a) 'Call to sack Cockburn councillors', *The West Australian*, 21 December: 33.

Hunter, T. (1999b) 'Grljusich defends actions in land row with Council', *The West Australian*, 7 December: 37.

Huxley, M. (1998) 'The limitations to communicative planning: a contribution to the critique of actually existing practice', unpublished paper presented to Planning Theory Conference, Oxford Brookes University.

Huxley, M. (2000) 'The limits to communicative planning', *Journal of Planning Education and Research*, 19: 369–77.

Huxley, M. (2001) 'Governmentality, gender and planning', in P. Allmendinger and
    M. Tewdwr-Jones (eds) *Planning Futures*, London: Athlone Press.
Huxley, M. and Yiftachel, O. (2000) 'New paradigm or old myopia: unsettling the com-
    municative turn in planning theory', *Journal of Planning Education and Research*,
    19, 3: 101–10.
Iedema, R. (1997) 'The formalisation of meaning', *Discourse and Society*, 10, 1: 49–66.
Ife, J. (1995) *Community Development*, Melbourne: Longman.
Innes, J. (1995) 'Planning theory's emerging paradigm: communicative action and inter-
    active practice', *Journal of Planning Education and Research*, 14, 3: 183–9.
Innes, J. (1996) 'Planning through consensus building', *Journal of the American
    Planning Association*, 62: 460–72.
Innes, J. (1998) 'Information in communicative planning', *Journal of the American
    Planning Association*, 64, 1: 52–63.
Innes, J. (1999a) 'Evaluating consensus building', in L. Susskind, S. McKearnan and
    J. Thomas-Larmer (eds) *The Consensus-Building Handbook*, Thousand Oaks: Sage.
Innes, J. (1999b) 'Planning strategies in conflict: the case of the Metropolitan
    Transportation Commission', unpublished paper presented at the Association of
    European Schools of Planning conference, Bergen, July.
Innes, J. and Booher, D. (1997) 'Evaluating consensus building: making dreams into real-
    ities', unpublished paper delivered at ACSP conference, Fort Lauderdale.
Innes, J. and Booher, D. (1998a) 'Consensus building as role-playing and bricolage',
    unpublished paper delivered at ACSP conference, Pasadena.
Innes, J. and Booher, D. (1998b) 'Network power and collaborative planning: strategy for
    the information age', unpublished paper presented at ACSP conference, Pasadena.
Innes, J. and Booher, D. (1999a) 'Consensus building and complex adaptive systems',
    Journal of the American Planning Association, 65, 4: 412–23.
Innes, J. and Booher, D. (1999b) 'Consensus building as role-playing and bricolage',
    Journal of the American Planning Association, 65, 1: 9–26.
Innes, J. and Gruber, J. (1999) 'Planning strategies in conflict: the case of regional trans-
    portation planning in the Bay area', unpublished paper presented at AESOP
    conference, Bergen.
Isaac, C. and Kissman, S. (1998) 'The Albuquerque Community Planning Program: con-
    tradictions in planning for community identity', unpublished paper presented at
    ACSP conference, Pasadena.
Ivison, D. (1997) *The Self at Liberty: Political Argument and the Arts of Government*,
    Ithaca: Cornell University Press.
Jacobs, J. (1994) 'Negotiating the heart: heritage, development and identity in postimperial
    London', *Environment and Planning D, Society and Space*, 12: 751–72.
Janicaud, D. (1992) 'Rationality, force and power: Foucault and Habermas's criticisms', in
    T. Armstrong (ed.) *Michel Foucault, Philosopher*, New York: Routledge, 283–302.

James, M. (1998) 'Colonial culture rules at CALM, letter to the Editor', *The West Australian*, 14 December: 14.

Jennings, B. (1987) 'Interpretation and the practice of policy analysis', in F. Fischer, and J. Forester (eds), *Confronting Values in Policy Analysis*, Beverley Hills: Sage.

Jessop, B. (1990) *State Theory: Putting Capitalist States in their Place*, Cambridge: Polity Press.

Jessop, B. (1997) 'The governance of complexity and the complexity of governance: preliminary remarks on some problems and limits of economic guidance', in A. Amin and J. Hausner (eds) *Beyond Market and Hierarchy*, Cheltenham: Edward Elgar.

Johnson, P. (2001) 'Politicians and planners: making the relationship work without reducing democratic accountability', *Planning Theory and Practice*, 2, 1: 91–5.

Jones, M. (1998) 'Restructuring the local state: economic governance or social regulation?', *Political Geography*, 17: 959–988.

Jones, S-A. (1998) 'RFA threatens tradition', *The West Australian*, 27 July: 10.

Jordan, G, and Maloney, W. (1997) *The Protest Business*, Manchester: Manchester University Press.

Jujnovich, P. (1992) *A Resident's View of Urbanisation*, unpublished poem.

Kaldor, M. (1998) 'Reconceptualising organised violence', in D. Archibugi, D. Held and M. Kohler (eds) *Re-imagining Political Community*, Cambridge: Polity Press.

Kant, I. (1970) 'Perpetual peace', in *Kant's Political Writings* (trans. H. Reiss), New York, Cambridge University Press.

Kavoulakos, K. (1999) 'Constitutional state and democracy: on Jürgen Habermas's *Between Facts and Norms*', in *Radical Philosophy*, 96, (July–August): 33–41.

Keane, J. (1988) *Democracy and Civil Society*, London: Verso.

Keeble, L. (1952) Principles and practice of town and country planning, London: *Estates Gazette*.

Kelly, M. (ed.) (1994) *Critique and Power: Recasting the Foucault/Habermas Debate*, Cambridge: MIT Press.

Kim, J., Wyatt, R. and Katz, E. (1999) 'News, talk, opinion, participation: the part played by conversation in deliberative democracy', *Political Communication*, 16: 361–85.

Kitchen, T. (1997) *People, Politics, Policies and Plans*, London: Paul Chapman.

Klein, N. (2001) 'Getting to the heart of the world's problems', *Guardian Weekly*, 1–7 November: 23.

Knorr-Cetina, K. (1981) 'Introduction', in K. Knorr-Cetina and A. Cicourel (eds) *Advances in Social Theory and Methods*, Boston: RKP.

Kohn, M. (2000) 'Language, power and persuasion: toward a critique of deliberative democracy', *Constellations*, 7, 3: 408–29.

Kolb, D. and Williams, J. (2000) *The Shadow Negotiation*, New York: Simon and Schuster.

Komter, A. (ed.) (1996) *The Gift*, Amsterdam: Amsterdam University Press.

Kritzmann, L. (ed.) (1988) *Michel Foucault: Politics, Philosophy, Culture: Interviews and Other Writings: 1977–1984*, New York: Routledge.

Kropotkin, P. (1914) *Mutual Aid*, (second edition, 1972) New York: New York University Press.

Krumholz, N. (2001) 'Planners and politicians: a commentary based on past experience from the US', *Planning Theory and Practice*, 2, 1: 96–100.

Krumholz, N. and Forester J. (1990) *Making Equity Planning Work*, Philadelphia: Temple University Press.

Kunnen, N. (2000) 'Karaoke or fugue? Participation and community development', in J. Stephens (ed.) *Habitus: A Sense of Place*, conference proceedings, CD-Rom, Perth: Curtin University of Technology.

Kunnen, N. (2001) 'Karaoke or fugue? Participation and community development', unpublished PhD thesis, Perth: Curtin University of Technology.

Lacan, J. (1977) *Écrits: A Selection*, New York: Norton.

Lacan, J. (1992) *The Seminar, Book VII, The Ethics of Psychoanalysis 1959–60*, London: Routledge.

Laclau, E. (1991) 'God only knows', *Marxism Today*, December: 56–9.

Laclau, E. (1994) 'Introduction', in E. Laclau (ed.) *The Making of Political Identities*, London: Verso.

Laclau, E. (1996) *Emancipation(s)*, London: Verso.

Laclau, E. (1997) 'Subject of politics, politics of the subject', in R. Bontekoe and M. Stepaniants (eds) *Justice and Democracy*, Honolulu: University of Hawaii Press.

Lake, R. (1994) 'Negotiating local autonomy', *Political Geography*, 13, 5: 423–42.

Lane, J. (2000) *Pierre Bourdieu: A Critical Introduction*, London: Pluto.

Lane, M. (1999) 'Regional Forest Agreements: resolving resource conflicts or managing resource politics?' *Australian Geographical Studies*, 37, 2: 142–53.

Lara, M. P. (1998) *Moral Textures*, Cambridge: Polity Press.

Larmour, P. and Wolanin, N. (2001) 'Introduction', in P. Larmour and N. Wolanin (eds) *Corruption and Anti-corruption*, Canberra: Asia Pacific Press.

Latour, B. (1992) 'One more turn after the social turn…', in M. McMullin (ed.) *The Social Dimension of Space*, Notre Dame, IN: University of Notre Dame Press.

Law, J. (1992) 'Notes on the theory of the actor–network: ordering strategy and heterogeneity', *Systems Practice*, 5: 379–93.

Lax, D, and Sebenius, J. (1986) *The Manager as Negotiator*, New York: Free Press.

Layder, D. (1981) *Structure, Interaction and Social Theory*, London: RKP.

Le Carré, J. (1993) *The Night Manager*, Sydney: Hodder and Stoughton.

Lee, A. and Poynton, C. (eds) (2000) *Culture and Text*, Sydney: Allen and Unwin.

Lee, F. (1999) '"We have been given a second chance", a study of Chinese–Australian involvement in mainstream Australian politics and its effects in WA', unpublished paper presented to Curtin University 3rd Annual Humanities Postgraduate Research Conference, Perth: Curtin University.

Lee, K. (1993) *Compass and Gyroscope: Integrating Science and Politics for the Environment*, Washington, DC: Island Press.

Lefebvre, H. (1996) *Writings on Cities* (trans. E. Kofman and E. Lebas), Oxford: Blackwell.

Lemke, J. (1995) *Textual Politics: Discourse and Social Dynamics*, London: Taylor and Francis.

Leventhal, G. (1980) 'What should be done with equity theory? New approaches to the study of fairness in social relationships', in K. Gergen, J. M. Greenberg and R. Willis (eds) *Social Exchange: Advances in Theory and Research*, New York: Plenum Press.

Leventhal, G., Karuza, J. and Fry, W. (1980) 'Beyond fairness: a theory of allocation preferences', in G. Mikula (ed.) *Justice and Social Interaction*, New York: Springer-Verlag.

Lind, E. and Tyler, S. (1988) *The Social Psychology of Procedural Justice*, New York: Plenum Press.

Lindquist, E. (1992) 'Public managers and policy communities: learning to meet new challenges', *Canadian Public Administration*, 35: 127–59.

Lines, W. (1998) *A Long Walk in the Australian Bush*, Sydney: University of New South Wales Press.

Lippmann, W. (1955) *The Public Philosophy*, Somerset, NJ: Transaction Publishers.

Lipstadt, H. (2000) 'Theorising the competition', *Thresholds*, December: 32–6.

Long, N. (1996) 'Power and administration', in R. Stillman (ed.) *Public Administration Concepts and Cases*, Boston: Houghton Mifflin.

Love, N. (1995) 'What's left of Marx?', in S. White (ed.) *The Cambridge Companion to Habermas*, Cambridge: Cambridge University Press.

Lowi, T. (1964) 'How the farmers get what they want', *Reporter*: 34–6

Lowndes, V. (1995) 'Citizenship and urban politics', in D. Judge, G. Stoker and H. Wolman (eds) *Theories of Urban Politics*, London: Sage.

Luhrmann, T. (1993) 'The resurgence of romanticism: contemporary neopaganism, feminist spirituality and the divinity of nature', in K. Milton (ed.) *Environmentalism*, London: Routledge.

Lukes, S. (1974) *Power: A Radical View*, London: Macmillan.

Lukes, S. (1982) 'Of gods and demons: Habermas and practical reason', in J. Thompson and D. Held (eds) *Habermas: Critical Debates*, London: Macmillan.

Lynch, M. and Woolgar, S. (eds) (1990) *Representation in Scientific Practice*, Cambridge: MIT Press.

Lynn, S. and Wathern, P. (1991) 'Intervenor funding in the environmental assessment process in Canada', *Project Appraisal*, 5, 3: 169–73.

Lyotard, J-F. (1985) *Just Gaming*, Minneapolis: University of Minnesota Press.

MacCallum, S. (2000) 'When experts disagree: discursive dynamics underlying consensus in participatory planning', unpublished manuscript, Department of Urban and Regional Planning, Curtin University, Perth.

MacCallum, S. (2001a) 'Anxiety about stakeholder participation: can discourse analysis offer any comfort?', unpublished paper presented to School of Architecture, Construction and Planning seminar, Curtin University of Technology, Perth.

MacCallum, S. (2001b) 'Breaking the mould without breaking the rules: discursive struggles in a local land use planning committee', unpublished paper presented to Undisciplined Thoughts conference, Curtin University of Technology, Perth.

MacIntyre, A. (1988) *Whose Justice? Which Rationality?* Notre Dame: Notre Dame University Press.

Majone, G. (1989) *Evidence, Argument and Persuasion in the Policy Process*, New Haven: Yale University Press.

Malan, A. (1998) 'Forest fire far from friendly', *The West Australian*, 17 December: 15.

Mallabone, M. (1998a) 'Tuckey attack out of line: EPA', The West Australian, 16 December: 4.

Mallabone, M. (1998b) 'Labor attacks felling in block', *The West Australian*, 29 October: 12.

Mannheim, K. (1940) *Man and Society in an Age of Reason*, London: K. Paul, Trench, Trusner and Co Ltd.

Mansbridge, J. (1980) *Beyond Adversary Democracy*, Chicago: University of Chicago Press.

Mansbridge, J. (1995a) 'Feminism and democratic community', in P. Weiss and M. Friedman (eds) *Feminism and Community*, Philadelphia: Temple University Press.

Mansbridge, J. (1995b) 'A deliberative perspective on neocorporatism', in E. Wright (ed.) *Associations and Democracy*, London: Verso.

Marcos, S. I. (2001) *Our Word is Our Weapon*, London: Serpent's Tail.

Marris, P. (1987) *Meaning and Action*, London: RKP.

Marris, P. (2001) 'On rationality and democracy', *International Planning Studies*, 6, 3: 279–84.

Marsh, J. (2000) 'What is critical about critical theory?', in L. Hahn (ed.) *Perspectives on Habermas*, Chicago: Open Court.

Martell, L. (1992) 'New ideas of socialism', *Economy and Society*, 21, 2: 152–72.

Marx, K. (1970) *The German Ideology*, New York: International Publishers.

Massey, D. (1991) 'The practical place of locality studies', *Environment and Planning A*, 23: 267–82

Massey, D. (1993) 'Power-geometry and a progressive sense of place', in J. Bird, B. Curtis, T. Putnam, G. Robertson and L. Tickner (eds) *Mapping the Futures*, London: Routledge.

Mathews, J. (1989) *Age of Democracy*, Melbourne: Oxford University Press.

McAdam, D. (1996) 'Conceptual origins, current problems, future directions', in D. McAdam, J. McCarthy and M. Zald (eds) *Comparative Perspectives on Social Movements*, Cambridge: Cambridge University Press.

McAdam, D., McCarthy, J. and Zald, M. (eds) (1996) *Comparative Perspectives on Social Movements*, Cambridge: Cambridge University Press.

McAfee, N. (2000) *Habermas, Kristeva and Citizenship*, Ithaca: Cornell University Press.

McArdle, J. (1999) *Community Development in the Market Economy*, Melbourne: Vista.

McCarthy, T. (1976) 'Translator's introduction', in J. Habermas *Communication and the Evolution of Society*, Cambridge: Polity Press.

McCarthy, T. (1990) 'The critique of impure reason: Foucault and the Frankfurt School', *Political Theory*, 18, 3: 437–69.

McCarthy, T. (1992) 'Philosophy and social practice: avoiding the ethnocentric predicament', in A. Honneth, T. McCarthy, C. Offe and A. Wellmer (eds) *Philosophical Interventions in the Unfinished Project of Enlightenment*, Cambridge: MIT Press.

McClendon, B. and Quay, R. (1988) *Mastering Change*, Washington: Planners Press, APA.

McDonald, K. (1998) 'Forest fighters reject RFA options', *The West Australian*, 15 June: 10–11.

McGuirk, P. (2000) 'Power and policy networks in urban governance: local government and property regeneration in Dublin', *Urban Studies*, 37, 4: 651–72.

McInroy, N. (2000) 'Urban regeneration and public space: the story of an urban park', *Space and Polity*, 4, 1: 23–40.

McNeish, W. (1999) 'Resisting colonisation: the politics of anti-roads protesting', in P. Bagguley and J. Hearn (eds) *Transforming Politics*, Basingstoke: Macmillan.

Meerwald, A. (1999) 'Chinese subjectivities in liminal limbo', unpublished paper presented to Curtin University 3rd Annual Humanities Postgraduate Research Conference, Perth: Curtin University.

Melucci, A. (1988) 'Social movements and the democratisation of everyday life', in J. Keane (ed.) *Civil Society and the State*, London: Verso.

Melucci, A. (1989) *Nomads of the Present*, London: Radius.

Melucci, A. (1996) *Challenging Codes*, Cambridge: Cambridge University Press.

Melucci, A. (2000) 'Social movements in complex societies', *Arena Journal*, no. 15: 81–99.

Meyerson, D., Weick, K. and Kramer, R. (1996) 'Swift trust and temporary groups', in R. Kramer and T. Tyler (eds) *Trust in Organisations: Frontiers of Theory and Research*, Thousand Oaks: Sage.

Miller, J. (1993) *The Passion of Michel Foucault*, New York: Simon and Schuster.

Milofsky, C. (ed.) (1988) *Community Organisations*, New York: Oxford University Press.

Minson, J. (1993) *Questions of Conduct*, Basingstoke: Macmillan.

Mitchell, D. (1994) 'Landscape and surplus value', *Environment & Planning D, Society & Space*, 12: 7–30.

Moore, M. (1986) 'Realms of obligation and virtue', in M. Wachs (ed.) *Ethics in Planning*, New Jersey: Rutgers University Press.

Moore Milroy, B. (1990) 'Critical capacity and planning theory', *Planning Theory Newsletter*, Winter: 12–18.

Mouffe, C. (1991) 'Democratic citizenship and the political community' in Miami Theory Collective (ed.) *Community at Loose Ends*, Minneapolis: University of Minnesota Press.

Mouffe, C. (1992) *Dimensions of Radical Democracy, Pluralism, Citizenship and Community*, London: Verso.

Mouffe, C. (1993) *The Return of the Political*, London: Verso.

Mouffe, C. (1995) 'Post-Marxism: democracy and identity', *Environment and Planning D: Society and Space*, 13: 259–65.

Mouffe, C. (1996) 'Deconstruction, pragmatism and the politics of democracy', in C. Mouffe (ed.) *Deconstruction and Pragmatism*, London: Routledge.

Mouffe, C. (1997) 'Democratic identity and pluralist politics', in R. Bontekoe and M. Stepaniants (eds) *Justice and Democracy*, Honolulu: University of Hawaii Press.

Mouffe, C. (1999) 'Deliberative democracy or agonistic pluralism?', *Social Research*, 66, 3: 745–58.

Mouffe, C. (2000) *The Democratic Paradox*, London: Verso.

Mouffe, C. (2002) 'Which kind of space for a democratic habitus?', in J. Hillier and E. Rooksby (eds) *Habitus: A Sense of Place*, Aldershot: Ashgate.

Muirhead, T. (2001) 'A developmental approach – how is it different?', unpublished workshop paper, Perth: CSD Network.

Mulgan, G. (1997) *Connexity,* London: Chatto and Windus.

Mulgan, G, and Landry, C. (1995) *The Other Invisible Hand*, London: Demos.

Mumby, D. (1988) *Communication and Power in Organisations: Discourse, Ideology and Domination*, Northwood, New Jersey: Ablex.

Mumby, D. (ed.) (1993) *Narrative and Social Control: Critical Perspectives*, Newbury Park: Sage.

Murdoch, J. (1995) 'Actor-networks and the evolution of economic forms: combining description and explanation in theories of regulation, flexible specialisation and networks', *Environment and Planning A*, 27: 731–57.

Murdoch, J. (2001a) 'Ecologising society: actor–network theory, co-construction and the problem of human exceptionalism', *Sociology*, 35, 1: 111–33.

Murdoch, J. (2001b) 'The spaces of actor–network theory', *Geoforum*, 29, 4: 357–74.

Nagel, T. (1986) *The View from Nowhere*, New York: Oxford University Press.

National Forest Polict Statement Implementation Sub-committee (NFPSIS), (1997) *Nationally Agreed Criteria for the Establishment of a Comprehensive, Adequate & Represenative Reserve System for Forests in Australia*, Canberra: NFPSIS.

Natter, W. and Jones, III (1997) 'Identity, space, and other uncertainties', in G. Benko and U. Strohmayer (eds) *Space and Social Theory*, Oxford: Blackwell.

Nelson, W. (2000) 'The institutions of deliberative democracy', *Social Philosophy and Policy*, 17, 1: 181–202.

Nietzsche, F. (1901) *The Will to Power* (1968 edition), New York: Vintage Books.

Nietzsche, F. (1954) *Twilight of the Idols*, New York: Penguin.

Nozick, R. (1974) *Anarchy State and Utopia*, Oxford: Oxford University Press.

Nussbaum, M. (1990) *Love's Knowledge*, New York: Oxford University Press.

O'Connor, P. (2000) 'Heritage and landscape: a new role in CRAs', unpublished paper presented at Humanities Postgraduate Conference, Curtin University, Perth.

O'Neill, J. (2001) 'Representing people, representing nature, representing the world', *Environment and Planning C: Government and Policy*, 19: 483–500.

O'Neill, O. (1993) 'Justice, gender and international boundaries', in M. Nussbaum and A. Sen (eds) *The Quality of Life*, Oxford: Clarendon Press.

O'Toole, B. (2000) 'The public interest: a political and administrative convenience?' in R. Chapman (ed.) *Ethics in Public Service for the New Millennium*, Aldershot: Ashgate.

Oelschlaeger, M. (2000) 'Habermas in the "wild, wild west"', in L. Hahn (ed.) *Perspectives on Habermas*, Chicago: Open Court.

Offe, C. (1985) 'New social movements, challenging the boundaries of institutional politics', *Social Research*, 52, 4: 817–67.

Offe, C. (1992) 'Bindings, shackles, brakes: on self-limitation strategies', in A. Honneth, T. McCarthy, C. Offe and A. Wellmer (eds) *Cultural–Political Interventions in the Unfinished Project of Enlightenment*, Cambridge: MIT Press.

Olson, M. (1965) *The Logic of Collective Action*, New York: Schocken.

Ostrom, E. (1990) *Governing the Commons*, New York: Cambridge University Press.

Ostrom, E. (1992) *Crafting Institutions for Self-governing Irrigation Systems*, San Francisco: ICS Press.

Outhwaite, W. (1994) *Habermas: A Critical Introduction*, Cambridge: Polity Press.

Oxenham, D. (2000) 'Aboriginal terms of reference', in P. Dudgeon, D. Garvey and H. Pickett (eds) *Working with Indigenous Australians*, Perth: Gunada Press.

Painter J. (2000) 'Pierre Bourdieu', in M. Crang and N. Thrift (eds) *Thinking Space*, London: Routledge.

Pal, L. (1997) *Beyond Policy Analysis*, Toronto: Nelson.

Passerin d'Entreves, M. (1992) 'Hannah Arendt and the idea of citizenship' in C. Mouffe (ed.) *Dimensions of Radical Democracy*, London, Verso.

Pearson, N. (1998) unpublished address to University of Melbourne, Faculty of Graduate Studies, 6 August.

Phelps, N. and Tewdwr-Jones, M. (2000) 'Scratching the surface of collaborative and associative governance: identifying the diversity of social action in institutional capacity building', *Environment and Planning A*, 32: 111–30.

Pløger, J. (2001) 'Public participation and the art of governance', *Environment and Planning B, Planning and Design*, 28: 219–41.

Poster, M. (1992) 'Foucault, the present and history', in T. Armstrong (ed.) *Michel Foucault, Philosopher*, New York: Routledge.

Pottage, A. (1998) 'Power as an art of contingency: Luhmann, Deleuze, Foucault', *Economy and Society*, 27, 1: 1–27.

Poupeau, F. (2000) 'Reasons for domination, Bourdieu *versus* Habermas', in B. Fowler (ed.) *Reading Bourdieu on Society and Culture*, Oxford: Blackwell.

Pratchett, L. (2000) 'The inherently unethical nature of public service ethics', in R. Chapman (ed.) *Ethics in Public Service for the New Millennium*, Aldershot: Ashgate.

Pred, A. (1997) 'Re-presenting the extended moment of danger: a meditation on hyper-modernity, identity and the montage form', in G. Benko and U. Strohmayer (eds) *Space and Social Theory*, Oxford: Blackwell.

Preston, N. (2000) 'Public sector ethics: what are we talking about?' in P. Bishop and N. Preston (eds) *Local Government, Public Enterprise and Ethics*, Sydney: The Federation Press.

Proctor, J. (1996) 'Whose Nature? The contested moral terrain of ancient forests', in W. Cronon (ed.) *Uncommon Ground*, New York: Norton.

Pusey, M. (1987) *Jürgen Habermas*, London: Tavistock.

Putnam, R. (1993) *Making Democracy Work*, Princeton: Princeton University Press.

Putnam, R. (2000) *Bowling Alone*, New York: Simon and Schuster.

Rabinow, P. (1984) *The Foucault Reader*, New York: Pantheon.

Rademan, M. (1985) 'Viewpoint', *Planning*, October: 42.

Rajchman, J. (1988) 'Habermas's complaint', *New German Critique*, 45: 163–91.

Ralston, Saul J. (1997) *The Unconscious Civilisation*, Harmondsworth, Penguin.

Ramsay, M. (2000) 'Justifications for lying in politics': in L. Cliffe, M. Ramsay and D. Bartlett *The Politics of Lying*, London: Macmillan.

Rangan, P. and Lane, M. (2001) 'Indigenous peoples and forest management: comparative analysis of institutional approaches in Australia and India', *Society and Natural Resources*, 14, 2: 145–60.

Rasmussen, D. (1990) *Reading Habermas*, Cambridge: Blackwell.

Rättilä, T. (2000) 'Deliberation as public use of reason – or, what public? whose reason?', in M. Saward (ed.) *Democratic Innovation – Deliberation, Representation and Association*, London: Routledge.

Raulet, G. (1983) 'Structuralism and post-structuralism: an interview with Michel Foucault', *Telos*: 55.

Ravetz, J. (1999) 'Citizen participation for integrated assessment: new pathways in complex systems', *International Journal of Environment and Pollution*, 11, 3: 331–50.

Rawls, J. (1971) *A Theory of Justice*, Cambridge: Harvard University Press.

Rechichi, V. (1998) 'Residents fight for forest and jobs', *The West Australian*, 30 May: 43.

Rechichi, V. (1999) '5 arrests as war restarts in forests', *The West Australian*, 12 January: 10.

Rees, T. (1999) 'Greenies and Greedies take off the gloves', *The West Australian*, 12 January: 14.

Reich, R. (1988) *The Power of Public Ideas*, Massachusetts: Ballinger.

Rein, M. (1989) 'Frame-reflective policy discourse', in H. Stretton (ed.) *Markets, Morals and Public Policy*, Sydney: Federation Press.

Reissman, L. (1975) *The Visionary: Planner for Urban Utopia*, London: Hutchinson and Ross.

Rhodes, R, and Marsh, D. (1992) 'Policy networks in British politics', in D. Marsh, and R. Rhodes (eds) *Policy Networks in British Government*, Oxford: Clarendon Press.

Richardson, J. and Jordan, A. (1979) *Governing Under Pressure*, Cambridge: Martin Robertson.

Richters, A. (1988) 'Modernity – postmodernity controversies: Habermas & Foucault', *Theory, Culture and Society*, 5: 611–43.

Ritzer, G. and Gindoff, P. (1994) 'Agency–structure, micro–macro, individualism–holism –relationism: a methatheoretical explanation of theoretical convergence between the United States and Europe', in P. Sztompka (ed.) *Agency and Structure*, Amsterdam: Gordon and Breach.

Roderick, R. (1986) *Habermas and the Foundations of Critical Theory*, New York: St Martin's Press.

Rooksby, P. (1998) 'Smoothing the kinks?' unpublished Hons thesis, Department of Urban and Regional Planning, Curtin University, Perth.

Rorty, R. (1989) *Contingency, Irony and Solidarity*, Cambridge: Cambridge University Press.

Rose, D. B. (1999) 'Indigenous eulogies and an ethic of connection', in N. Low (ed.) *Global Ethics and Environment*, London: Routledge.

Rose, R. (1998) 'Hilliger pledge too late', *The West Australian*, 25 July: 34.

Rose, R. (1999) 'Margetts count dumped', *The West Australian*, 19 August: 10.

Rose-Ackerman, S. (1999) *Corruption and Government: Causes, Consequences and Reform*, Cambridge: Cambridge University Press.

Routledge, P. (1997) 'The imagineering of resistance: Pollock Free State and the practice of postmodern politics', *Transactions of the Institute of British Geographers NS*, 22: 359–76.

Roßteutscher, S. (2000) 'Associative democracy – fashionable slogan or constructive innovation?', in M. Saward (ed.) *Democratic Innovation – Deliberation, Representation and Association*, London: Routledge.

Rubin, J. (1991) 'Some wise and mistaken assumptions about conflict and negotiation', in W. Breslin and J. Rubin (eds) *Negotiation Theory and Practice*, Cambridge: Harvard Law School, Program on Negotiation.

Rundell, J. (1991) 'Jürgen Habermas' in P. Beilharz (ed.) *Social Theory*, Sydney: Allen and Unwin.

Ryan, P. (1999) 'Discourse, democracy (and socialism?): a reading of Habermas' *Between Facts and Norms*', in *Studies in Political Economy*, 60: 121–39.

Sabatier, P. (1987) 'Knowledge, policy-oriented learning and policy change', *Knowledge*, 8, 4: 649–87.

Sabatier, P. (1993) 'Policy change over a decade or more', in P. Sabatier and H. Jenkins-Smith (eds) *Policy Change and Learning: an Advocacy Coalition Approach*, Boulder: Westview.

Sabatier, P. (ed.) (1999) *Theories of the Policy Process*, Boulder: Westview.

Sabatier, P. and Jenkins-Smith, H. (1999) 'The Advocacy Coalition Framework: an assessment', in P. Sabatier (ed.) *Theories of the Policy Process*, Boulder: Westview.

Sadler, B. (1995) 'Canadian experience with environmental assessment: recent changes in process and practice', *Australian Journal of Environmental Management*, 2: 112–30.

Sager, T. (1994) *Communicative Planning Theory*, Aldershot: Avebury.

Sager, T. (1998) 'Loyalty and the impossibility of Paretian advocacy planning', *Journal of Planning Education and Research*, 18: 103–12.

Sager, T. (2001) 'Manipulative features of planning styles', *Environment and Planning A*, 33: 765–81.

Salvation Army (2001) *Stepping into the Breach*, Melbourne: Salvation Army.

Sampson, E. (1993) 'Identity politics: challenges to psychology's understanding', *American Psychologist*, 48: 1219–30.

Sandercock, L. (1998) *Towards Cosmopolis*, New York: Wiley.

Sassi, S. (2001) 'The transformation of the public sphere?' in B. Axford and R. Huggins (eds) *New Media and Politics*, London: Sage.

Saward, M. (ed.) (2000) *Democratic Innovation: Deliberation, Representation and Association*, London: Routledge.

Schattschneider, E. (1960) *The Semi-Sovereign People*, New York: Holt, Rinehart and Winston.

Scheuerman, W. (1999) 'Between radicalism and resignation: democratic theory in Habermas' *Between Facts and Norms*', in P. Dews (ed.) *Habermas: A Critical Reader*, Oxford: Blackwell.

Schlozman, K., Verba, S. and Brady, H. (1999) 'Civic participation and the equality prob-
    lem', in T. Skocpol and M. Fiorina (eds) *Civic Engagement in American
    Democracy*, Washington, DC: Brookings Institute.

Schmitter, P. (1995) 'The irony of modern democracy and the viability of efforts to reform
    its practice', in E. Wright (ed.) *Associations and Democracy*, London: Verso.

Schon, D. and Rein, M. (1994) *Frame Reflection*, New York: Basic Books.

Schwartz, D. (1997) *Culture and Power*, Chicago: University of Chicago Press.

Scott, A. (1990) *Ideology and the New Social Movements*, London: Unwin Hyman.

Scott, J. (1990) *Domination and the Arts of Resistance*, New Haven: Yale University
    Press.

Scott, J. (1998) *Seeing Like a State*, New Haven: Yale University Press.

Shapiro, M. (1989) 'A political approach to language purism', in B. Jernudd and
    M. Shapiro (eds) *The Politics of Language*, New York: Mouton de Gruyter.

Sheridan, A. (1980) *Michel Foucault: The Will to Truth*, London: Tavistock.

Shields, R. (1997) 'Spatial stress and resistance: social meanings of spatialisation, in
    G. Benko and U. Strohmayer (eds) *Space and Social Theory*, Oxford: Blackwell.

Shire of Swan (1996) Advertising folder, Midland: Shire of Swan.

Shotter, J. (1993) *Conversational Realities*, London: Sage.

Sibley, D. (1998) 'Problematising exclusion: reflections on space, difference and knowl-
    edge', *International Planning Studies*, 3, 1: 93–100.

Simon, H. (1982) *The Sciences of the Artificial* (2nd edition), Cambridge: MIT Press.

Skarlicki, D. and Folger, R. (1997) 'Retaliation in the workplace', *Journal of Applied
    Psychology*, 82: 434–43.

Skelcher, C., McCabe, A., Lowndes, V. and Nanton, P. (1996) *Community Networks in
    Urban Regeneration*, Bristol: Polity Press.

Skocpol, T. and Fiorina, M. (1999) 'Making sense of the civic engagement debate', in
    T. Skocpol and M. Fiorina (eds) *Civic Engagement in American Democracy*,
    Washington, DC: Brookings Institute.

Smith, G. (2000) 'Toward deliberative institutions', in M. Saward (ed.) *Democratic
    Innovation – Deliberation, Representation and Association*, London: Routledge.

Smith, L. G., Nell, C. and Prystupa, M. (1997) 'The converging dynamics of interest rep-
    resentation in resources management', *Environmental Management*, 21, 2:
    139–46.

Smith, T. (1991) *The Role of Ethics in Social Theory*, Albany: State University of New
    York Press.

Sparks, L. (2001) 'The Chair and Chief Officer: a many sided relationship', *Planning
    Theory and Practice*, 2, 1: 86–90.

Spriggins, D. (1999) 'Foresters don't deserve hatred', *The West Australian*, 14 January: 14.

Stack, C. (1975) *All Our Kin: Strategies for Survival in a Black Community*, New York:
    Harper and Row.

Stavrakakis, Y. (1999) *Lacan and the Political*, New York: Routledge.

Stengel, U. (1997) 'Beware the manipulators', *Fremantle Herald*, 1 February: 28.

Stiftel, B. and Harkness, C. (1998) 'Overcoming agency ratification obstacles in environmental negotiation: lessons from labour management practice', unpublished paper presented at ACSP conference, Pasadena.

Strohmeyer, U. (1997) 'Belonging: spaces of meandering desire', in Benko, G. and Strohmeyer, U. (eds) *Space and Social Theory*, Oxford: Blackwell.

Sustainable Economic Growth in Regional Australia (SEGRA) (2001) *Lobbying for Regions: Strategies and Steps*, Brisbane: Conference brochure, Management Solutions (Qld) Pty Ltd.

Sutton, P. (1997) 'Residents rage at rash development', *Property Age*, 15 October: 2–3.

Syme, G., Macpherson, D. and Seligman, C. (1991) 'Factors motivating community participation in regional water allocation planning', *Environment and Planning A*, 23: 1779–95.

Sztompka, P. (1990) 'Agency and progress: the idea of progress and changing theories of change', in J. Alexander and P. Sztompka (eds) *Rethinking Progress*, London: Unwin Hyman.

Sztompka, P. (1991) *Society in Action: The Theory of Social Becoming*, Cambridge: Polity Press.

Sztompka, P. (1993) *The Sociology of Social Change*, Oxford: Blackwell.

Tannen, D. (2001) 'Rites of demolition', *The Australian*, 12 April: 41.

Tannen, D. (ed.) (1993) *Framing in Discourse*, Oxford: Oxford University Press.

Tarrow, S. (1989) *Struggle, Politics and Reform: Collective Action, Social Movements and Cycles of Protest*, Ithaca: Cornell Studies in International Affairs, Western Societies Papers, 2.

Tarrow, S. (1992) 'Mentalities, political cultures, and collective action frames: constructing meanings through action', in A. Morris and C. Mueller (eds) *Frontiers in Social Movement Theory*, New Haven: Yale University Press.

Tarrow, S. (1994) *Power in Movement*, Cambridge: Cambridge University Press.

Taylor, C. (1986) 'Foucault on freedom and truth', in D. Hoy (ed.) *Foucault: A Critical Reader*, Oxford: Blackwell.

Taylor, C. (1993) 'To follow a rule', in C. Calhoun, E. Lipuma and M. Postione (eds) *Bourdieu, Critical Perspectives*, Cambridge: Polity Press.

Taylor, C. (1999) 'To follow a rule …', in R. Shusterman (ed.) *Bourdieu: A Critical Reader*, Oxford: Blackwell.

Teck, F. C. (1997) *Reminiscenses of an Ancient Strategist: The Mind of Sun Tzu*, Singapore: Horizon.

Tewdwr-Jones, M. (2002) 'Personal dynamics, distinctive frames and communicative planning', in P. Allmendinger and M. Tewdwr-Jones (eds) *Planning Futures: New*

Directions for Planning Theory, London: Routledge.

Tewdwr-Jones, M. and Allmendinger, P. (1998) 'Deconstructing communicative rationality: a critique of Habermasian collaborative planning', *Environment and Planning A*, 30: 1975–89.

Thatcher, M. (1987) 'Interview', *Woman's Own*, October: 8–10.

Thibout, J. and Walker, L. (1975) *Procedural Justice: a Psychological Analysis*, New York: Erlbaum.

Thomas, J. (1993) *Doing Critical Ethnography*, Newbury Park: Sage.

Thompson, D. (1987) *Political Ethics and Public Office*, Cambridge: Harvard University Press.

Thompson, P. (1986) *Myles Dunphy – Selected Writings*, Sydney: Ballagirin.

Thompson, W. (2001) 'Policy making through thick and thin: thick description as a methodology for communications and democracy', *Policy Sciences*, 34: 63–77.

Thomson, S. (1999) 'The agony and the ecstacy: Foucault and Habermas and the problem of recognition', in S. Ashenden and D. Owen (eds) *Foucault and Habermas*, London: Sage.

Thrift, N. (1996a) *Spatial Formations*, London: Sage.

Thrift, N. (1996b) 'New urban eras and old technological fears: reconfiguring the goodwill of electronic things', *Urban Studies*, 33, 8: 1463–93.

Throgmorton, J. (1990) 'Passion, reason and power: the rhetorics of electric power planning in Chicago', *Journal of Architectural and Planning Research*, 7, 4: 330–50.

Throgmorton, J. (1996) '"Impeaching" research: planning as persuasive and constitutive discourse', in S. Mandelbaum, L. Mazza and R. Burchell (eds) *Explorations in Planning Theory*, New Brunswick: Rutgers.

Throgmorton, J. (2000) 'On the virtues of skillful meandering: acting as a skilled-voice-in-the-flow of persuasive argumentation', *Journal of Planning Education and Research*, 66, 4: 367–80.

Throgmorton, J. (2001) *Small World*, unpublished manuscript.

Tilly, C. (1975) 'Revolutions and collective violence', in F. Greenstein and N. Polsby (eds) *Handbook of Political Science*, Vol. 3, Reading, MA: Addison-Wesley.

Tilly, C. (1978) *From Mobilisation to Revolution*, Reading: Addison-Wesley.

Tilly, C. (1986) *The Contentious French*, Cambridge: Harvard University Press.

Tilly, C. (1995) *Popular Contention in Great Britain 1758–1834*, Cambridge: Harvard University Press.

Torfing, J. (1999) *New Theories of Discourse: Laclau, Mouffe and Zizek*, Oxford: Blackwell.

Touraine, A. (1981) *The Voice and The Eye*, Cambridge: Cambridge University Press.

Touraine, A. (1985) 'An introduction to the study of New Social Movements', *Social Research*, 52: 749–87.

Touraine, A. (1994) 'Democracy', *Thesis Eleven*, 38: 1–15.

Touraine, A. (2000) *Can We Live Together?*, Cambridge: Polity Press.

Trigger, D. (1997) 'Mining, landscape and the culture of development ideology in Australia', *Ecumene*, 4, 2: 161–80.

Truman, D. (1951) *The Governmental Process*, New York: Knopf.

Tuckey, W. (1999) 'A workable forest policy is the aim', *The West Australian*, 9 January: 14.

Tuckey, W. and Edwardes, C. (1999) *Media Statement*, 4 May, Perth: CALM.

Tully, J. (1995) *Strange Multiplicity*, Cambridge: Cambridge University Press.

Tully, J. (1999) 'To think and act differently: Foucault's four reciprocal objections to Habemas' theory', in S. Ashenden and D. Owen (eds) *Foucault and Habermas*, London: Sage.

Turner, B., Ferguson, I. and Fitzpatrick, N. (1999) *Report by the Expert Panel on the Calculation of a Sustainable Sawlog Yield for the Jarrah and Karri Forests of WA, Perth*: CALM.

Turner, S. (1994) *The Social Theory of Practices*, Cambridge: Polity Press.

Tyler, T. and Blader, S. (2000) *Co-operation in Groups*, Philadelphia: Psychology Press.

Tyler, T., Boeckmann, R., Smith, H. and Huo, Y. (1997) *Social Justice in a Diverse Society*, Boulder: Westview Press.

Tyler, T., Lind, E. and Huo, Y. (2000) 'Cultural values and authority relations', *Psychology, Public Policy and Law*, 6, 4: 1138–63.

van Erp, H. (2000) *Practical Reason and Interest*, Aldershot: Ashgate.

van Waarden, F. (1992) 'Dimensions and types of policy networks', *European Journal of Political Research*, 21, 1–2: 29–52.

Vigar, G., Healey, P., Hull, A. and Davoudi, S. (2000) *Planning, Governance and Spatial Strategy in Britain*, Basingstoke: Macmillan.

Villa, D. (1996) *Arendt and Heidegger*, Princeton: Princeton University Press.

Villa, D. (1999) *Politics, Philosophy, Terror*, Princeton: Princeton University Press.

Wacquant, L. (1992) 'Toward a social praxeology: the structure and logic of Bourdieu's sociology', in P. Bourdieu and L. Wacquant (eds) *An Invitation to Reflexive Sociology*, Cambridge: Polity Press.

Wainwright, H. (1994) *Arguments for a New Left*, Oxford: Blackwell.

Walzer, M. (1981) 'Philosophy and democracy', *Political Theory*, 9, 3: 379–99.

Walzer, M. (1986) 'The politics of Michel Foucault', in D. Hoy (ed.) *Foucault: A Critical Reader*, Oxford: Blackwell.

Walzer, M. (1995) 'The civil society argument', in R. Beiner (ed.) *Theorising Citizenship*, Albany: State University of New York Press.

Walzer, M. (1999) 'Deliberation, and what else?' in S. Macedo (ed.) *Deliberative Politics*, Oxford: Oxford University Press.

Warren, M. (2001) *Democracy and Association*, Princeton: Princeton University Press.

Watson, I. (1990) *Fighting Over the Forests*, Sydney: Allen and Unwin.

Way, B. (1995) *Living Intuitively*, Melbourne: Lothian.

Webb, J., Schirato, T. and Danaher, G. (2002) *Understanding Bourdieu*, Sydney: Allen and Unwin.

Weber, M. (1978) *Economy and Society* (trans. G. Roth and C. Wittich) Berkeley: University of California Press.

Weir, L. (1993) 'Limitations of New Social Movement Analysis', *Studies in Political Economy*, 40: 73–102.

Wekerle, G. and Peake, L. (1996) 'New Social Movements and women's urban activism', in J. Caulfield and L. Peake (eds) *City Lives and City Forms*, Toronto: University of Toronto Press.

West Australian Forest Alliance (WAFA) (1998) *The West Australian Forest Alliance Proposal for a Comprehensive, Adequate and Representative Forest Conservation Reserve System and Sustainable Timber Production in WA*, Perth: WAFA.

West Australian Forest Alliance (WAFA) (1998b) 15 Major Failings in the RFA 'Public Consultation paper', Perth: WAFA.

West Australian Forest Alliance (WAFA) (1999) Update on RFA outcomes, website, http:\\wafa.org.au

Whatmore, S. and Boucher, S. (1993) 'Bargaining with nature: the discourse and practice of environmental planning gain', *Transactions of the Institute of British Geographers NS*, 18: 166–78.

White, S. (1988) *The Recent Work of Jurgen Habermas*, Cambridge: Cambridge University Press.

White, S. (1991) *Political Theory and Postmodernism*, Cambridge: Cambridge University Press.

White, S. (ed.) (1995) *The Cambridge Companion to Habermas*, Cambridge: Cambridge University Press.

Wildavsky, A. (1979) *Speaking Truth to Power*, Boston: Little, Brown and Co.

Williams, C. and Windebank, J. (2000) 'Rebuilding social capital in deprived urban neighbourhoods', *Town and Country Planning*, December: 351–53.

Williams, R. (2001) 'Reconciling: a place for the heart?', *Geography Research Forum*, 21: 77–98

Willmott, P. (1986) *Social Networks, Informal Care and Public Policy*, London: Policy Studies Institute.

Wilson, G. (1990) *Interest Groups*, Oxford: Blackwell.

Wittgenstein, L. (1958) *Philosophical Investigations*, Oxford: Blackwell.

Wolf, N. (1993) *Fire with Fire*, London: Chatto and Windus.

Wolin, S. (1996) 'Fugitive democracy', in S. Benhabib (ed.) *Democracy and Difference*, Princeton: Princeton University Press.

Wright, E. (1995) 'Introduction', in E. Wright (ed.) *Associations and Democracy*, London: Verso.

Wright, E. and Wright, E. (eds) (1999) *The Zizek Reader*, Oxford: Blackwell.

Wuthnow, R. (1999) 'The culture of discontent: democratic liberalism and the challenge of diversity in late twentieth century America', in N. Smelser and J. Alexander (eds) *Diversity and its Discontents*, Princeton: Princeton University Press.

Wuthnow, R., Hunter, J., Bergesen, A. and Kurzweil, E. (1984) *Cultural Analysis*, London: RKP

Yearley, S. (1993) 'Standing in for nature', in K. Milton (ed.) *Environmentalism*, London: Routledge.

Yiftachel, O. (1998) 'Planning and social control: exploring the dark side', *Journal of Planning Literature*, 12: 395–406.

Yiftachel, O. (2001) 'Can theory be liberated from professional constraints? On rationality and explanatory power in Flyvbjerg's *Rationality and Power*', *International Planning Studies*, 6, 3: 251–56.

Yiftachel, O. and Huxley, M. (2000) 'Debating dominance and relevance: notes on the "communicative turn" in planning theory', *International Journal of Urban and Regional Research*, 24, 4: 907–13.

Young, I. M. (1990) *Justice and the Politics of Difference*, Princeton: Princeton University Press.

Young, I. M. (1993) 'Communication and the Other: beyond deliberative democracy', unpublished mimeograph.

Young, I. M. (1995) 'Social groups in associative democracy', in E. Wright (ed.), *Associations and Democracy*, London: Verso.

Young, I. M. (1997a) 'Asymmetrical reciprocity: on moral respect, wonder and enlarged thought', *Constellations*, 3, 3: 340–63.

Young, I. M. (1997b) *Dilemmas of Gender, Political Philosophy and Policy*, Princeton: Princeton University Press.

Young, I. M. (2000) *Inclusionary Democracy*, Oxford: Oxford University Press.

Young, I. M. (2001) 'Activist challenges to deliberative democracy', *Political Theory*, 29, 5: 670–90.

Young, M, and Willmott, P. (1957) *Family and Kinship in East London*, London: RKP.

Zekulich, M. (1998) 'New life for timber town', *The West Australian*, 27 August, Travel: 4–5.

Zizek, S. (1989) *The Sublime Object of Ideology*, London: Verso.

Zizek, S. (1990) 'Beyond discourse analysis', in E. Laclau (ed.) *New Reflections on the Revolution of our Time*, London: Verso.

Zizek, S. (1991) *For They Know Not What They Do*, London: Verso.

Zizek, S. (1996) 'Fantasy as a political category: a Lacanian approach', *Journal for the Psychoanalysis of Culture and Society*, 1, 2: 77–85.

Zizek, S. (1997) *The Abyss of Fear*, Ann Arbour: University of Michigan Press.

Zizek, S. (1999) *The Ticklish Subject*, Lonson: Verso.

Zizek, S. (2001) 'Welcome to the Desert of the Real', online: [http://www.mii.kurume-u.ac.jp/~leuers/zizek-welcome_to_the_desert_of_the_real. html]

Zolo, D. (1992) *Democracy and Complexity*, Cambridge: Polity Press.

END NOTES

PREFACE

1   The Thing, to Lacan, is the intrusion of some excessive, monstrous Real; a grimace from the Real which questions our constructions of reality by way of a lawlessness, or kind of Truth, which unveils the symbolic Other.

2   On a 2002 visit to Argentina, bin Laden T-shirts seemed to be one of the most popular images after those of Diego Maradona and Che Guevara.

PART 1

1   I take as my working definition of Prudence, 'a range of active steps to secure oneself against future misfortune' (adapted from Rose, 1999: 158) noting that 'caution, skepticism, and political capacity are intertwined' (Mandelbaum, 1996: 432).

2   I only list here what I regard as the key texts in the authors' development of collaborative/communicative planning theory.

3   For a summary of the main concepts of the 'new institutionalism' and links to planning practice see Vigar *et al.* (2000, chapter 2).

4   I have insufficient space here to engage with the plethora of theories of language and linguistics and their relationship to analysis of space. For overviews see Mumby (1993), Lemke (1995), Crang and Thrift (2000) and Lee and Poynton (2000).

5   It should be remembered that there are important differences between trying to integrate macro and micro theories and attempting to develop theory which can deal with the relationships between macro and micro levels of social analysis (Ritzer and Gindoff, 1994).

PART 2

1   Readers wishing to follow the development of influences on Habermas' thoughts in more detail are referred to the wide range of material now available, including, in chronological order, Wuthnow *et al.* (1984); Roderick (1986); Pusey (1987); Rasmussen (1990); Braaten (1991); Calhoun (1992); Kelly (1994); Outhwaite (1994); Chambers (1996) and Dews (1999).

2   Habermas here follows Fraser's (1992) distinction between weak and strong publics in which weak publics are not burdened by the task of formal decision-making and strong publics (elected legislatures) take the decisions.

3   'can war provide an analytical tool to account for power relations?'

4   'civil order is fundamentally battle order'.

5   '(the speaking subject) is engaged in a battle, it has opponents, it fights for victory.'

6   'truth which functions like a weapon'.

7   See Tully (1999) for detailed discussion of Foucault's objections to Habermas' theory.

8   'more and more brittle, more and more worthless, more and more bound to illusion,
     to fantasy, a hoax.'
9   The Habermasian Systematic Distortion of Communication, explained in Chapter 2.
10   See Tully (1999) for detail of Habermas' principal objections to Foucault.
11   We must remember to distinguish between voice and argument (Forester, 1995:
     388).
12   See Elster (1983) on 'sour grapes' and Hillier (1996) for discussion of systematic
     distortion of communication.
13   Formal rules and group procedures tend to be codified; informal actions include
     personal experiences with authorities. Tyler and Blader (2000: 127) give the
     example of a police officer interacting with citizens and suggest that over the
     course of a day one would see variation in the manner in which the officer inter-
     prets formal rules, depending on the person with whom they are dealing and the
     issue involved.
14   See Baird's (2001) demonstration that in Germany people regard legalistic proce-
     dures as more than just political procedures and that people are therefore more
     forgiving of displeasing legal decisions even if the decisions have been made in a
     political manner.

PART 3

1   'To translate is also to express in one's own language what others say and want'
     (Callon, 1986: 223).
2   Utilisation or manipulation of information to persuade others to a certain viewpoint
     provides linkages to the Habermasian concept of the systematic distortion of com-
     munication (Habermas, 1970). The common tactic of delegitimisation of other
     actors' claims or silencing them by denial that proposed impacts/effects may
     occur is a further act of SDC for reasons of persuasion. Non-toxicity, for example,
     is as much a social construct as toxicity. See Beck's (1992; 1995) discussion of
     organised irresponsibility in what he terms the 'dance of the veiling of hazards'
     (1992: 101). 'Official institutions use all the instruments at their disposal (the judg-
     ments of experts, maximum safe levels) in order to claim that hazards are harmless,
     and hide them in state monopolies over definitions' (Beck, 1995: 98).
3   It is impossible to conceptualise a diagram of actor-networks over time. I offer the
     metaphor of an infinitely expanding Rubik cube, wherein each small segment rep-
     resents an actor, interacting with the others it touches. Through time, the cube may
     be turned partially or entirely. The faces of some segments will remain touching in
     their previous 'networks', whilst others will form new networks. New patterns and
     relationships of networks are formed with every twist of the cube, while the traces
     of some old patterns (or their influence) may still be retained.
4   See Hunter and Staggenborg (1988: 259) for discussion of differences in out-
     sider tactics between wealthier and poorer communities. In wealthier communities,
     financial capital is available to purchase necessary services, such as an expert con-
     sultant, legal representation, copying and printing, etc. whilst poorer communities
     tend to rely more on their own human capital and effort.

5 I use the term 'lobbying' as a collective noun to incorporate a wide spectrum of tactics and activities which Butcher *et al.* (1980) list as ranging from campaigning to civil disobedience and coercion, and which include presentation of survey evidence, petitions, lobbying, letter-writing, deputations, demonstrations and sit-ins, rallies and marches, use of media, etc. The key aspect of lobbying remains, however, access to individuals with decision-making power over the respective issue.

6 As Schattschneider (1960: 35) put it, 'the flaw in the pluralist heaven is that the heavenly chorus sings with a strong upper-class accent'. In Australia forums on 'effective lobbying' provide training on lobbying processes and tactics for agencies of local governance (SEGRA, 2001). Jordan and Maloney (1997) similarly demonstrate that members of environmental lobby groups in the USA and the UK are predominantly middle class, professional, educated women aged 45–64 who belong to more than one organisation.

7 More detailed contextual information can be found in Hillier (1994) and Healey and Hillier (1996).

8 Interviews with developers did not furnish sufficient usable information for this analysis.

9 More detail can be found in Hillier (1998c; 2000b and 2000c); Hillier and van Looij (1998) and Hillier (2001).

10 Jarrah = *Eucalyptus marginata*; marri = *Eucalyptus calophylla*; karri = *Eucalyptus diversicolor.*

11 I have adapted Norton's (1996: 129) idea of a correlation of human concerns and natural system dynamics at different temporal scales to two temporal horizons (short- versus long-term). I agree with Norton that economic frames tend to dominate shorter term values and preferences, whilst ecological dynamics and the interaction of species (including human and non-human nature) become more important on an intergenerational timescale. My frame differs from that of Killingsworth and Palmer (1992: 14) who distinguish between nature as resource and nature as object, with the latter being the perspective of traditional experimental science.

12 Such consumers may include Simcoa Operations Pty Ltd who use jarrah charcoal for silicon production. Simcoa has 'security of supply' of up to 150,000 tonnes of jarrah annually 'guaranteed under the Silicon (Kemerton) Agreement Act 1987 of the West Australian Parliament'.

13 Latour (1987: 60) suggests that approximately 90 per cent of people will give up and not read such scientific discourse; 9 per cent will go along with the text, and only 1 per cent will work through the text in a systematic manner, attempting to challenge it wherever possible.

14 Fraser (1992: 134) defined a weak public as a public whose deliberative practice consists exclusively in opinion formation and does not encompass decision-making.

PART 4

1 See Aberbach *et al.* (1981); Majone (1991).

2 Material on *habitus* which follows is largely derived from the Introduction written by Hillier from Hillier and Rooksby (2002). I acknowledge Emma Rooksby's critical comment on the Introduction.

3   Foucault (1994a) also employs the analogy of a game in discussing games of truth
     and games of strategy (i.e. power). He understands power relations as 'strategic
     games between liberties' (1994a: 299).
4   Putnam's (1993) well-known account of social capital formation in Italy develops
     Bourdieu's notion of social capital and has subsequently spawned what might be
     termed a 'social capital industry' with government initiatives internationally aimed at
     provision of incentives for creation of social capital, regarded virtually universally as
     a 'good thing'. See for example, Gittell and Vidal (1998); Williams and Windebank
     (2000).
5   Bourdieu's discussion of linguistic capital is not unlike Habermasian communicative
     ethics. In describing political conversation as communicative action, for instance,
     Kim *et al.* (1999) actually borrow Bourdieu's (1984) term of 'political talk *habitus*'.
6   See Bourdieu (1972, 1989).
7   'Phronesis' is variously translated as practical wisdom or prudence. It goes beyond
     both analytical and technical knowledges and involves an instinctive knowledge of
     how to behave in particular circumstances. See Bernstein (1983), Flyvbjerg
     (1993, 2001), Forester (2001), Hillier (1995b) and Nussbaum (1990).
8   See Bourdieu and Wacquant (1992: 128) for explanation of how opinion 'falls
     right' without knowing how or why and actors do what they 'have to do' without
     conscious calculation.
9   Scott also invokes a game analysis, in this instance, of soccer, in explanation of the
     'tricks of the trade' of *mètis*.
10   See Gyford (1985) and Campbell and Marshall (2000: 304–5) for discussion of
     increasing assertiveness of British local government councillors over planning offi-
     cers and the collision of political and professional objectives.
11   I also acknowledge Judith Innes' recent work with Judith Gruber (1999) in which
     they demonstrate how a collaborative style of decision-making conflicts with a
     'political influence' style to pull interests in different directions.
12   Although I depict the process as fundamentally linear for simplicity of representa-
     tion, I appreciate that it is often extremely messy and non-linear in practice.
13   For a beginning consideration of other gaps see Dewar (1999) for an example of
     the gap between full council and Ministerial ratification ('the judges said that the
     Secretary of State was not bound by his own guidance. ...This means that even
     after a council goes through all the correct procedures it is still up to the Secretary
     of State what he wants to do' (Dewar, 1999: 3)), and Rooksby (1998) for exam-
     ples of the gap between decision and implementation where landscape architects
     and engineers seemingly altered details of public, planner and elected representa-
     tive consensus decisions to suit themselves. Stiftel and Harkness (1998) would
     regard this latter as an example of a 'multiple-table problem' and offer some useful
     insights into why gaps occur here.
14   I use the term mayor to denote the elected representative leader of the council or
     shire president.
15   Given the nature of the information sought I only approached elected representa-
     tives whom I knew and who felt they could trust me with some ethically

controversial material. This resulted in my interviewing only more 'honest' politicians, although I believe their stories of experience of others' dealings have been valuable. I also appreciate that in my position as 'half-learned', that I may not fully realise that those I interviewed 'both know and resist the truth they claim to reveal' and the extent to which they engage in 'games of self-deception which make it possible to perpetuate an illusion for oneself and to safeguard a bearable form of "subjective truth" in the face of calls to reality and to realism' (both quotes Bourdieu, 2000: 190).

16 See Hillier (2000a).

17 The WA Criminal Code, S83, defines an act of corruption as 'any public officer who, without lawful authority or a reasonable excuse a) acts upon any knowledge or information obtained by reason of his office or employment ... so as to gain a benefit, whether pecuniary or otherwise, for any person, or so as to cause a detriment, whether pecuniary or otherwise' (cited in Department of Local Government, 1999). For other definitions see Alatas (1990), Heidenheimer *et al.* (1989), Heywood (1997), Perry (1997) and Rose-Ackerman (1999).

18 Ignatius (2000) presents a long list of countries in which 'crony capitalism' is widespread, not solely in developing nations, but including the Elf scandal in France and Citibank in the USA.

19 See Komter (1996) for detailed analysis of gifts, gift-giving and gift-receiving.

20 See also the *Planning Theory and Practice* (2001) *Interface* on the topic of planners and politicians by Campbell, Sparks, Johnson and Krumholz respectively.

21 Those seeking to engage with this debate are referred to Arato and Rosenfeld (1998) and respective essays by Habermas, Bernstein and Michelman. These issues relate to deeper philosophical questions of the right versus the good, which I have not space to enter in this volume.

22 See also Hoch (1994).

23 See also Campbell and Marshall (2002: 102–3) who demonstrate in detail how a performance criteria-based approach can take on a 'life of its own', in which 'satisfying the performance criteria becomes everything and the underlying purpose of the activity can become lost'.

24 There is an element of overlap here with deceptive strategies below.

25 See Hoch (1994) and Krumholz and Forester (1990) for examples.

26 That these are ancient well-honed skills of strategy, see the similarities with Sun Tzu's *The Art of War* which is now some 2,500 years old (Teck, 1997).

27 Shugarman (1990, 2000) lists the six main reasons for getting 'dirty hands' as:

(i)   the cruel reasons for acting are the protection and/or promotion of public good;

(ii) when it comes to considering as well as judging a public act, the criterion is the consequence/s;

(iii) 'wicked means' of deception can be employed for beneficial ends;

(iv) when normally reprehensible means are used for 'good' purposes, their use is morally defensible;

(v)   public life is carried on in an atmosphere akin to warfare;

(vi)   public life requires heroic leadership.

Readers are left to judge for themselves the relevance of this list to planning practice.

28   See also Dovey (2002) for an excellent discussion of the complicitous silence of architecture.

29   See detailed discussions in Rynard and Shugarman (2000) and Cliffe, Ramsay and Bartlett (2000).

30   See Albrechts (1997, 1999) for a detailed example of a planner involved in acts of 'making friends', lobbying, bargaining and so on.

31   Dobel's (1999) chapter on 'Political Prudence' goes into far more detail than I can here of the need for public officials to engage with political prudence and the role of prudence in completing the Triangle of Judgement.

32   See Beiner (1999).

33   See Innes and Gruber (1999).

34   See Baum (1999) for a good example of how *habitus* as memories, etc. of the past may hinder planning as management of change.

PART 5

1   See also Dalby and Mackenzie (1997).

2   I am not concerned here with the public/civil society dualism debate. My own vote is cast with those who regard the public as penetrating all aspects of civil society and blurring edges between the spheres.

3   There are now many such empirical examples, such as the redevelopment of Battersea Power Station in London (Banks, 1998).

4   See the volume by McAdam, McCarthy and Zald (1996) which contains several chapters exploring aspects of political opportunity structures. Most authors seem to list the following as dimensions of political opportunity:

•   the relative openness or closure of the institutionalised political system;

•   the stability or instability of that broad set of alignments which typically underpin a polity (e.g. tradition, mass media access, etc.);

•   the presence or absence of elite allies;

•   the state's capacity and propensity for repression (McAdam, 1996: 27).

One major and obvious difference in political opportunity structure, for example, would be between the more fragmented political structure of the USA which would offer opportunities for communicative consensus-building, and the strong state structures in the UK and Australia which tend to encourage more strategic, adversarial rationality.

5   There are considerable similarities between coalitions of actors in land use planning networks and those which Grabher (2001) describes as projects–networks. Projects are described as 'temporary systems' or processes of 'negotiating meaning' in which actors co-operate in communities of practice 'at the same time shaped by past experience and affected by the shadow of future (potential) collaboration' (Grabher, 2001: 1330).

6   See Allmendinger (2001: 127–37) for detailed critique of the possibility of attaining Habermasian consensus and the importance of politics and power in consensus prevention.

7   See J. Bryson and B. Crosby (1992) on forums, arenas and courts for possibilities of operationalising such ideas.

8   Healey (1997: 227–30) describes clientelism as involving an interactive relationship between politicians and government officials through the social networks which politicians and officials substitute for governance structures of resource allocation. Such social networks are not open to democratic scrutiny.

9   Melucci (1996: 116–7) points out that political organisation is designed for the pursuit of long-term goals through progressive accumulation of results and resources. It must also mediate between short- and long-term goals. However, the rise of a plurality of partial, dynamic and complex networks of interest threatens to destabilise the organisation's traditional structures if they cannot be adjusted to accommodate new demands for flexibility and immediacy. Although writing about political organisation, I believe Melucci's comments are valid with regard to organisations of planning.

10 This appears similar to the rise of Christian fundamentalism and the Patriots and their political influence in the USA (Castells, 1997).

11 See Warren (2001) for detailed discussion of democracy and association.

12 Secondary associations include neighbourhood associations, environmental groups, women's associations, etc. They are characterised by their organisational autonomy from the state and their role in politically representing and shaping the interests of individuals.

13 Promotion of the organised representation of presently excluded interests, however, risks invoking similar reactions to those described above with regard to more successful, more visible NSMs.

14 However, the groups 'will not have had the benefit of exposure to deliberative diversity and discussion' (Phillips, 1995: 155) and may not agree with the arguments of their representative. Deliberation may thus be lengthily protracted.

15 An alternative strategy, of mandating representatives to vote in accordance with agreed group desires, severely limits any ability for representatives to negotiate effectively.

16 Wilson (1990) identifies a variety of techniques which can be used by governance to foster more unified interest group systems, including forcing actors by legal compulsion to join groups.

17 See Driscoll et al. (1998) Lynn and Wathern (1991) Sadler, 1995 and Boer et al., (1991) and Economou, (1993) respectively.

18 Young (1997) suggests a way forward in terms of moral rather than political respect, with the idea of asymmetrical reciprocity. Communicating parties mutually recognise one another, even if only to recognise irreducible or asymmetrical points of view.

19 Their work has generated much debate, e.g. Macedo (1999) and the special issue of Social Philosophy and Policy (2000) devoted to the subject.

20 See also the example of Gusty Spence from the Ulster Volunteer Foundation (UVF) negotiating areas of agreement with the Irish Republican Army (IRA) in the Maze prison in Northern Ireland (Garland, 2001).

21   For a detailed examination of Habermas' consideration of compromise see van Erp
      (2000: 129–35).

22   *jouissance* in Lacanian thought represents unfulfillable desire. Desire is unlike
      'needs' or 'demands' which can be satisfied by particular objects, as the only
      object of desire is a lost object, Lacan's *objet petit a.*

23   *L'objet petit a* is the cause of Lacanian desire. The notion of consensus can be
      equated to the Lacanian Real. If this Real becomes visible 'as such', reality disinte-
      grates. Therefore, in order to maintain the consistent edifice of reality, one of the
      elements of reality has to stand in for the Real. This element is the Lacanian *objet
      petit a.*

24   I recognise that chameleon planning officers would probably argue that they are
      politically neutral and lobby in the nebulous 'public interest' as a whole, in contrast
      to the self-interested lobbying and activities of others. While it may be that plan-
      ners do take a wider range of issues into consideration than do other actors, I
      would contest any suggestion that planning is a politically neutral activity and that
      planners can make politically neutral recommendations. I would also argue that
      planners may overlook the interests of some actors or underestimate the impact of
      a policy on them. It would appear that judgements of fairness of practice may well
      come down to the issue of the outcome achieved. But what would be a 'best' out-
      come? In whose opinion? How would it be 'measured' as being best?

PART 6

1   See Susskind *et al.* (1999) and especially the chapter by Carlson, for good dis-
     cussion of scoping situations to ascertain their potential for consensus.

2   The term 'smuggler' has connotations of illegality and underhandedness, unfortu-
     nately. Perhaps a more appropriate term might be the literal translation of *passeur*
     as 'ferryman' (*sic*) or a 'translator'.

3   See Alcoff (1991) and Young (2000) for detailed discussion of this issue.

4   See the *Debates* section in the *International Journal of Urban and Regional
     Research* (2000), volume 24, number 4.

INDEX